# THE COMPLETE
# ENCYCLOPEDIA OF
# FLIGHT
## 1939–1945

# THE COMPLETE
# ENCYCLOPEDIA OF
# FLIGHT
## 1939–1945

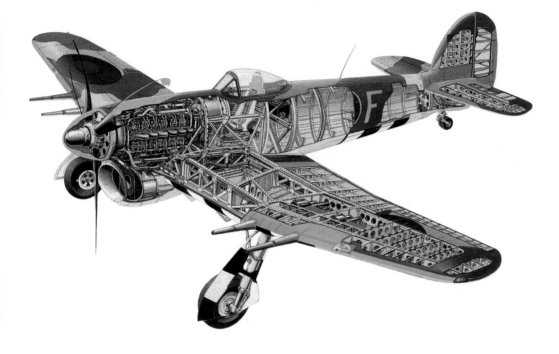

JOHN BATCHELOR & MALCOLM V. LOWE

CHARTWELL
BOOKS, INC.

Published by Rebo International b.v., Lisse, The Netherlands in association with Publishing Solutions (www) Ltd., Great Britain

Text: Malcolm V. Lowe
Illustrations: John Batchelor
Production, layout and typesetting: The Minster Press, Dorset, Great Britain
Cover design: The Minster Press, Dorset, Great Britain

Proofreading: Emily Sands, Jeffrey Rubinoff, Eva Munk

This edition published in 2005 by
CHARTWELL BOOKS, INC.
A division of BOOK SALES, INC.
114 Northfield Avenue
Edison, New Jersey 08837
USA

Printed in Slovenia.

ISBN-13: 978 90 366 1706 2
ISBN-10: 90 366 1706 5

# Contents

# Introduction

**1939–1945**

The Second World War began in September 1939 and ended in September 1945, almost exactly six years later. It was the largest, most widespread conflict that has ever taken place on earth, touching the lives directly or indirectly of almost every living person. It not only involved combatants on the battlefield, but whole civilian populations in their own homes. Lastly, it was the first and greatest conflict in which aircraft played a decisive role.

This book deals with the era of the Second World War, and covers many of the important warplanes of that incredible period in aviation and world history. It charts the significant progress that was made in the development of aviation and aeronautics of the era, including the huge advances in the manner of propulsion of military aircraft and the weapons that they carried. Many other important aspects are covered or touched upon, illustrated throughout by the world-famous artwork of John Batchelor. Although it is possible to include information regarding many significant aircraft and personalities, any work of this size inevitably pays more attention to some well-known characters and less to others, no doubt to the exclusion of some people's favorites. There were so many different military aircraft, from so many manufacturers, that to include every one from the period would be impossible without resorting to an almost infinite amount of writing, and so we have concentrated on a representative selection of the great and the lesser-known. The final Volume of this Encyclopaedia will cover the decades after World War Two, and bring the story of aviation up to the present.

**Historical Background**

From its limited and faltering beginnings in the nineteenth century and at the start of the twentieth century, aviation gradually took hold, following the successes of the Wright brothers in the United States in December 1903. The Wright brothers were the first men ever to successfully fly a man-carrying powered aircraft in controlled flight. This most significant step forward in the history of aviation marked the start of manned heavier-than-air flight. Those early days in the development of aircraft are described in Volume 1 of *The Complete Encyclopedia of Flight*. As aviation gradually developed in the years after 1903, it was not long before aircraft began to be used for belligerent purposes. The first deployment of aircraft in war-related activities most likely took place in 1911 when Italy attacked rebel forces in North Africa.

World War One began in August 1914. At that time, a number of countries were developing military aviation organizations, or already had such structures in place. However, military aviation was in its infancy at the start of the war, and military aircraft were mostly low-performance, unarmed types more suited to simple visual reconnaissance than to full combat activities. This changed very quickly. It was not long before aircraft were armed and took on an important role in the war. By the end of the war, the potential of military aircraft had been explored and developed to such a point that military aircraft were performing roles that are familiar to us today. Design, construction and manufacturing techniques developed in leaps and bounds, and by the end of the war in November 1918, mass-pro-

*Bristol Beaufort.*

duction of aircraft, aerial weapons and aero engines was the norm.

Just as importantly, the First World War not only showed how influential aircraft could be in warfare, but also the importance of the establishment of military organizations to properly manage and operate military aircraft. The process had commenced prior to the war, with most of the major countries attaching their fledgling air forces to newly-formed branches of often long-established army organizations. In some cases naval aviation grew as an off-shoot of established naval structures. The enormous growth of military aviation led to the need to formalise these structures, and in some cases an independent air force was the result. In Britain, a separate naval air arm, the Royal Naval Air Service, was created in July 1914. The Royal Flying Corps, an offshoot of the army, had existed since May 1912. On 1 April 1918, these came together to form the Royal Air Force, an early example of the importance of autonomous military aviation services within a leading country's military structures. In France, the Aéronautique

Militaire (sometimes abbreviated to Aviation Militaire) was founded in 1910, with the Armée de l'Air being created in 1933/1934. In the United States, an aviation branch of the Signal Corps was founded as early as 1907 and gave way to the U.S. Army Air Service in May 1918 and the U.S. Army Air Corps in July 1926. This service became the U.S. Army Air Force (technically called the U.S. Army Air Forces) just prior to the American entry into World War Two in 1941, while an independent air force did not arise in the United States until 1947. The Luftwaffe of Nazi Germany was built up rapidly following the accession to power of Hitler's National Socialists in 1933, although its existence was only officially revealed in 1935.

**The Road to War**
The growing employment of aircraft in warfare changed the face of war forever. From the small beginnings of military aviation prior to the First World War to the huge build-up of military air arms during World War One, aircraft were developed into fighter, bomber, reconnaissance, transport, training and a host of other military tasks that would have surprised and probably shocked early aviation pioneers. Continuing development in the decades after World War One, today referred to as the inter-war years, witnessed ever-growing performance capabilities. These came about partly due to refinements in aircraft design and materials, and partly as a result of the growing performance capabilities of aero engines. These developments, however, came about against the backdrop of extremely low defence budgets in many countries in the 1920's and early 1930's. Mass production on the scale that had arisen in World War One was quickly forgotten, resulting in

manufacturers struggling to gain meaningful military orders. The situation was exacerbated by the economic climate in the inter-war period, the Wall Street Crash and Great Depression causing markets to shrink even more. After the rise to power of Adolf Hitler's National Socialists in Germany, a growing uneasiness helped lead to rearmament in order to meet the menace posed by the Fascist countries of Germany, Italy and Japan. Unfortunately this rearmament took place too slowly to save some countries from disaster in World War Two.

Great advances during the inter-war period took place in aeronautical design and construction, although the foundations for this had been put in place much earlier. One of the most important developments was the widespread adoption of metal in aircraft construction, for the structure and, in notable cases, for the aircraft's skin as well. There were several pioneers in this sphere, including Junkers and Dornier in Germany. While many of aviation's significant inventions and advances have received great fanfare at their birth, others have met with much less publicity. One of the latter was the birth of the all-metal airplane, which nevertheless transformed aviation. Virtually every type of aircraft up to the middle of World War One was made of wood of various types, with fabric covering. Metal was primarily used for rigging wires, or as a part of the structure. Thanks to pioneering work by Junkers, Dornier and others, all-metal aircraft came into being long before the beautifully-streamlined, all-metal, stressed-skin fighters of the Second World War. Eventually, this type of construction was enthusiastically taken up by many of the great designers and manufacturers.

Advances in materials alone could not guarantee success, however. The development of stressed-skin all-metal fighters in the period leading up to World War Two went hand-in-hand with advances in aircraft design, streamlining, and the birth of increasingly powerful engines. Continuing developments in related fields, such as the creation of variable-pitch propellers, the invention of powered gun turrets for the defence of bomber aircraft and, of course, the key to many designers' dreams, the retractable undercarriage, were also a big help. The power available from engines also led to huge increases in the performance of civil and military aircraft as the 1930's wore on. The 1,030 hp available from the early production Rolls-Royce Merlin inline piston engines that powered initial models of the superlative Supermarine Spitfire and Hawker Hurricane fighters of World War Two makes an interesting comparison to the power available to the Sopwith Camel, one of the greatest fighter aircraft of World War One. A number of engine types were used in the production run of the Camel, but fairly typical were the Clerget rotary engines of 130 hp.

In fact, the adoption of the monoplane layout for front-line military aircraft (and indeed for civil commercial aircraft) was not as straightforward as it might have seemed. The biplane fighter in particular evolved into an efficient and powerful military aircraft that continued to have its adherents well into the 1930's. Fortunately there were more far-sighted designers such as the legendary R.J. Mitchell who, with his Supermarine design team was responsible for the Spitfire. Mitchell saw the potential of the low-wing retractable undercarriage monoplane layout for future fighter design, and developed it into the superlative Spitfire. Some of the biplane adherents nevertheless tried to wring the remaining capability from their chosen layout by fitting retractable undercarriages themselves. They continued to point out the capabilities of the biplane layout, such as exceptional manoeuvrability. Although the monoplane camp eventually won the day, some countries adopted the retractable undercarriage monoplane fighter and bomber too late and were overwhelmed by better-equipped forces when World War Two commenced.

The inter-war period, in fact, included several wars in which aircraft played an important part. In the Far East, Japanese expansion resulted in brutal conflict with the Chinese. In Spain, the legitimately-elected government was challenged in 1936 by rebels whose cause was enthusiastically taken up by the Fascist powers of Germany and Italy. In both these conflicts and in a number of colonial skirmishes and other wars, aircraft came to play an important part. In both the Spanish Civil War and the Far East, aircraft were used on a number of significant occasions by the so-called 'Axis' powers (Japan, Italy and Germany) against civilian targets. This was a disturbing precursor of what was to come.

The Second World War was the most extensive and costly armed conflict in history, eventually embroiling most of the countries of the world. It was fought simultaneously in several major theaters of war, and cost approximately 55 million lives – exact figures will never be known. In its simplest terms, the war was fought between two groups of powers. The first of these was the eventually victorious alliance of Britain and the British Commonwealth (formerly the British Empire), together with (eventually) the United States, the Soviet Union (which started out on the opposing side), various Chinese groupings, and countries such as Czechoslovakia, France, Poland and other European nations which were occupied before or early in the war by Germany. Collectively they were known as the Allies. Opposing them were the Axis powers, due to the Axis alliance signed prior to the war between Germany under Adolf Hitler, Italy under Benito Mussolini, and later extended to include Japan under an Imperial dynasty led by Emperor Hirohito. This grouping also had the support of other smaller nations. Nationals of various other countries also fought for the Axis, including militants in countries overrun by the Germans, who perceived an opportunity to free their homelands from previous oppressors. Most of the fighting took place in and around Europe, North Africa, where

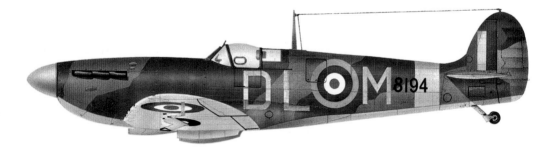

*Supermarine Spitfire Mk.IIA showing off the classic lines of this early production version.*

several European powers had colonies, and in the Pacific theater across the vast distances of the Pacific Ocean and in eastern Asia.

## Total War

The war commenced with the German invasion of Poland on 1 September 1939. This unprovoked attack marked the final death of a hopeless policy known as 'Appeasement' which had been pursued principally by Britain in the 1930's, in the face of ever-growing demands for territory by Nazi Germany. 'Appeasement' aimed to give Hitler what he wanted in order to avoid war at any cost, even though many knew that this policy would never work. Others realized that the static, trench warfare that had characterized much of World War One was a thing of the past by the late 1930's. Technological advances in weaponry, particularly the development of tanks (which had brought a swift end to World War One) and aircraft for tactical warfare – exemplified by the fast-moving and initially invincible 'Blitzkrieg' of German forces – were to bring a totally different face to modern warfare.

The Second World War was significant for many reasons. One of the most important is that it was the first war in which air power was an important – indeed, ultimately decisive – factor. The first combat operations of World War Two were German bombing attacks against Polish targets during which the first air combats took place, and the first air-to-air victories were scored. The war was unique in causing more civilian casualties than had been created by any war in history. This was partly due to its unprecedented scale, but was directly caused by the first extensive use of aerial bombing against civilian populations – a policy initiat-ed by the German Luftwaffe, first against Poland and later France and Britain. The same general strategy was later used more extensively against German cities by the RAF, and against Japanese cities by the U.S. Army Air Force. Civilians had been deliberately targeted before the war, most famously during the Spanish Civil War (1936 to 1939), but World War Two saw civilians targeted as never before and this aspect remains to this day one of the most controversial aspects of the conflict.

After several years of territorial expansion without threat of retaliation due to the 'Appeasement' practised by the Allies, Hitler laid claim to parts of Poland in 1939 and concluded a non-aggression agreement with the Soviet Union – a diplomatic move that caused great surprise. This was in effect a response to a defensive alliance concluded between Poland, France and Britain earlier in 1939. The German invasion of Poland on 1 September 1939 was followed by Britain and France declaring war on Germany on 3 September 1939 – and promptly doing absolutely nothing to give any military aid to the Poles! On 17 September, the Soviet armed forces joined the invasion of Poland from the east, and shortly after the Polish government fled the country for Romania. Hostilities ended with France and Britain giving no assistance to the Poles. The period from the conclusion of the invasion of Poland in October 1939 until the German invasion of the Low Countries and France in May 1940 became known as the Phoney War (or 'Drole de Guerre' in French). Following the defeat of Poland, Soviet Russia turned its attention to the Baltic countries (Estonia, Latvia, and Lithuania) and to Finland, where the Winter War (from late 1939 to 1940) showed that a small but determined country like Finland could achieve military successes against its larger neighbor. Although the Finns were eventually defeated, they made good use of aircraft in the Continuation War against Russia from 1941. After crushing Poland, the Germans turned their attention to Denmark and Norway, both of whom fell to German forces, although the fighting for Norway hung in the balance for a number of days. In response to this increased German aggression, France mobilized and manned its heavily fortified border (the Maginot Line) along part of its perimeter with Germany. Similarly, Britain sent a large expeditionary force to France which included air elements to bolster the still feeble French air force. Apart from a brief attack by the French across the Rhine, there were few hostilities at that time as both sides built up their forces.

The hammer blow to the West came on 10 May 1940. German forces attacked the Low Countries (The Netherlands, Belgium and Luxembourg), and simultaneously swept into France. The Low Countries were occupied quickly and overwhelmed, their air forces putting up stubborn but limited resistance in response to the huge numerical and technical superiority of the German Luftwaffe. The Germans' 'Blitzkrieg' tactics succeeded in defeating the French and British armies in France in rapid succession, sending shock waves around the world. The British Expeditionary Force (B.E.F.) evacuated Dunkirk in 'Operation Dynamo,' leaving much of its heavy equipment behind, and the French government was forced to make peace with the Germans. This effectively left the Germans in control of northern France, with a pro-German but French-controlled government at Vichy in charge

of much of southern France. The French armistice came into effect on 25 June 1940.

After a brief respite, German air operations commenced in earnest over Britain in the summer of 1940, with a view to defeating the Royal Air Force and gaining air superiority as a prelude to a major invasion across the English Channel. This led to the most famous air campaign of all time, the Battle of Britain. British pilots, bolstered by flyers from many other countries now occupied by the Germans, succeeded in defeating the Luftwaffe in one of the turning points of history – the first one in which aircraft played an absolutely central role. Despite heavy aerial fighting and attacks on the RAF's airfields and infrastructure, the Luftwaffe was unable to defeat the Royal Air Force and gain the air superiority needed to invade Britain. In addition to the excellent aircraft – the Hawker Hurricane and Supermarine Spitfire – that armed most of the RAF's fighter squadrons, the British also had ground-based early-warning radar, which allowed the British defences to respond in an organized and competent way to German air raids. This, coupled with the determination of the RAF pilots, represented the first time that the Luftwaffe had met really effective air opposition, and it paid off for the British. In particular, the much-vaunted Junkers Ju 87 'Stuka' dive-bomber and twin-engined Messerschmitt Bf 110 heavy fighters, which had previously enjoyed much success, were utterly defeated – and henceforth obliged to operate in less dangerous theaters, or to find new roles. German tactics switched to a strategic bombing campaign carried out largely at night, which the British called the Blitz, and an attempt to blockade Britain in what became known as the Battle of the Atlantic. Britain failed to succumb. Indeed, the night Blitz led to the creation of new defences, the miniaturization of radar allowing aircraft to fly with radar equipment on board to take on the night-time raiders. This started the trend towards a completely new type of aircraft, the night fighter, and revealed the need for aircraft able to operate at night and in bad weather – an absolute necessity for just about all front-line combat aircraft today. The production of aircraft in Britain was considerably bolstered by supplies from the United States, which began even before America's entry into World War Two in late 1941. Under Lend-Lease agreements, Britain (and also the Soviet Union) received large numbers of combat aircraft from the increasingly productive American aircraft industry (direct purchases having been made by Britain prior to that time), and aided Britain's overall war effort immensely. Under the resolute leadership of Winston Churchill, who came to power as Prime Minister in May 1940, Britain fought on against Nazi Germany and held the line in Europe successfully until the offensive

could be taken inside German borders by the end of the war.

In 1922, Benito Mussolini and his Fascist supporters had risen to power - in Italy. Mussolini's Italian Fascists shared some ideological common ground with Hitler's Nazis in Germany and, although Mussolini distrusted Hitler, the two countries formed an agreement in 1936 that became known as the 'Rome-Berlin Axis.' Hostilities began in North Africa in 1940. Italy had entered World War Two by declaring war on France on 10 June 1940, when it appeared that France was soon to be defeated by Germany. Fighting commenced in North Africa when the comparatively limited British forces in Egypt repulsed an advance by the Italian colony in Libya. The British and Commonwealth units then advanced, but were halted in 1941 by German forces under the famed General Erwin Rommel, which landed in North Africa to bolster the failing Italian line. In June 1941, Australian and other Allied forces invaded Vichy French Syria, capturing Damascus and eventually bringing Syria and Lebanon under Free French (anti-German) control. Rommel's Afrika Korps

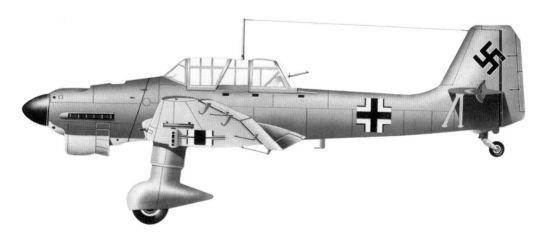

*The workman-like lines of the Junkers Ju 87 'Stuka.' Early production aircraft had prominent 'trouser' fairings over their main undercarriage, but the fixed, spatted arrangement shown here was included on the Ju 87B and all subsequent production models.*

advanced rapidly eastward, laying siege to the strategically important seaport of Tobruk. The Australian and British troops in the city resisted, but a renewed Axis offensive captured the city and drove the British Eighth Army back to a line at El Alamein in Egypt. German forces advanced to the last defensible point before Alexandria and the Suez Canal. Fortunately they out-ran their own supply lines, and British and Commonwealth action stopped their advance. The subsequent famous Battle of El Alamein between late October and early November 1942 was fought under the command of the renowned General Bernard Montgomery. Commonwealth forces were victorious, subsequently taking the offensive and driving back the Africa Korps. Rommel's forces retreaed, and this time did not stop falling back until Tunisia. To complement this victory,

on 8 November 1942, American and British forces landed in Morocco and Algeria in 'Operation Torch.' The local forces of Vichy France put up limited resistance before joining the Allied cause. Ultimately, German and Italian forces were caught in the pincers of a twin Allied advance. Moving forward from both the east and west, the Allies completely pushed the Germans out of Africa. In May 1943, the survivors of the Axis forces in North Africa sur-rendered. Some 250,000 prisoners were taken, mirroring the losses in Germany's defeat to Russian forces at Stalingrad. Later in 1943, the Allies launched invasions of Sicily and then mainland Italy.

In June 1941, Germany attacked the Soviet Union, with whom it had previously signed a non-aggression pact, in 'Operation Barbarossa.' So began

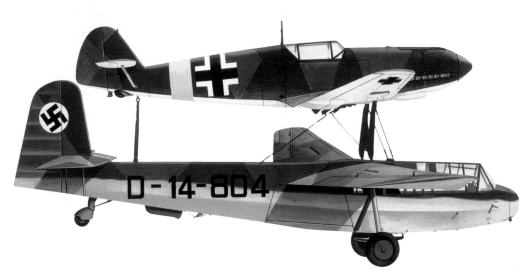

*A completely different approach to the problem of delivering a glider to its destination (instead of conventional towing behind a transport aircraft or converted bomber) was tried out in Germany using a variety of aircraft types mounted above the glider to give it power. The glider type used in these experiments was the DFS 230 as shown here, but a variety of aircraft were test-ed. The idea was for the combination to take off together, power being provided by the aircraft, until the glider was near to its destination. The aircraft would then release itself and fly away, allowing the glider to continue on to its destination. The combination drawn here, with a Messer-schmitt Bf 109E as the aircraft part of the combination, was most successful, but the idea did not reach operational status. Instead, the 'Mistel' composite aircraft program, using the same basic principles but with an armed bomber as the lower component, was further developed in Germany and went into operational service.*

what is known in Russia to this day as the Great Patriotic War. The Russians were caught largely by surprise, and the Wehrmacht (the German army) initially conquered vast areas of territory and captured hundreds of thousands of troops. The Soviet air force suffered massive losses, and it was a surprise to many that it was able to fight back so effectively later in the war despite the mauling that it received in 1941. The Soviets were initially obliged to withdraw, and managed to move most of their heavy industry and aircraft plants away from the front line and re-establish them in more remote areas. Stubborn and tenacious defence by Russian soldiers and civilians prevented the Germans from capturing Moscow before the 1941 winter set in. The Germans had expected the campaign in Russia to be over in a few months, and were ill-equipped to operate in the bitter Russian winter.

Despite this, five days after the Soviets launched their first major counterattack on German forces, on 11 December 1941, Germany declared war on the United States following the Japanese attack on Pearl Harbor. This move almost guaranteed Germany's final defeat at a single stroke, unleashing the slumbering giant of America's industrial and military strength. Nevertheless, in the spring of 1942 the German army made renewed attacks on the Soviet Union, splitting resources between further attacks in the direction of Moscow and the oilfields in the southern expanse of the Soviet Union. Moscow was again spared, and at the end of 1942 the Soviets succeeded in smashing the Axis' front lines in the south, and eventually surrounded the German 6th Army in and around the strategically vital city of Stalingrad. Despite a fran-

tic airlift, the survivors of the 300,000-strong German forces surrendered in February 1943. In the spring of 1943, the Wehrmacht was able to temporarily restore the front line, with air assets constantly playing a vital role in support of German ground forces, but the German offensive at the massive Battle of Kursk (July 1943) was so unsuccessful that the Soviet army was able to counterattack and regain the ground previously lost. Kursk was the greatest tank battle ever fought, and was also a major action for ground attack and anti-tank aircraft, both sides using large numbers of warplanes. The Soviet Union then had the initiative in the East, and with their increasingly well-equipped air forces, the Russians were able to make sweeping gains. By early 1944, Soviet forces had successfully relieved the beleaguered strategic city of Leningrad, which had undergone arguably the longest and most costly siege of the war. The German disaster at Stalingrad was soon followed by the defeat of similar importance in North Africa, representing huge setbacks for the German armed forces and for the German war effort. Thereafter the Allies were able to invade Sicily in July 1943, and mainland Italy during September 1943. Winston Churchill had described Italy as 'the soft underbelly of Europe,' but the fighting in Italy was harder than anticipated. Although Mussolini was effectively deposed, and Italian forces under Badoglio surrendered to the Allies, German forces quickly moved to disarm the Italians and set about fighting for what was left of Italy themselves. They established a series of tough defensive lines in mountainous country, ideally suited to defense and progress by the Allies was slow despite their air supremacy. The Germans were aided by pro-Fascist Italians, while other Italians fought on the Allied side against them.

The Allies invaded Normandy in northern France ('Operation Overlord') on 6 June 1944. Similar landings were made in southern France in August 1944. After many hard land battles, in which ground attack aircraft in particular played a key role, Allied forces liberated most of France and a part of the Low Countries by the end of the year. Late in June 1944, the Soviets began a significant offensive comprised of large numbers of men and tanks which attacked along a major central front. Eventually they completely destroyed the German army forces and took more 150,000 prisoners. By this time, the Soviet air force was well-equipped, partly with its own indigenous aircraft and partly with aircraft supplied by the United States under Lend-Lease, and was a major factor in the Russians' mounting successes against the increasingly beleaguered German forces. The Germans withdrew from the Balkans and managed to hold their position in Hungary until the early months of 1945. After a desperate but failed counter-offensive by the German army in the Ardennes during the Battle of the Bulge in December 1944, the Allies entered Germany in 1945. In a major airborne operation known as the Rhine Crossing, Allied forces gained a significant foothold on German soil. By then the Soviets were reaching the eastern fringes of the German Reich itself, and the fate of the German armed forces was sealed. Depleted by the Allied aerial bombing offensive, which was destroying Germany's infrastructure and communications, as well as its oil industry, the German army and Luftwaffe were in no shape to fight the overwhelming numbers of Allied ground forces and aerial power by the end of the war. The Soviet army captured the Austrian capital Vienna in mid-April, and the final assault on

Berlin began shortly after. As the Russians surrounded Berlin, Hitler and his staff moved into a bunker underneath the Chancellery. There, on 30 April 1945, Adolf Hitler committed suicide as Russian shells exploded in the Chancellery garden above. It was twelve years and two months since he had become the dictator of Germany. He appointed Admiral Karl Dönitz as his immediate successor, but one week later the German armed forces surrendered unconditionally.

The war in the Pacific raged simultaneously. In the First World War, Japan was on the side of the Allied powers, but played only a minor role in fighting German colonial forces in eastern Asia. In 1924, the American Congress passed the Exclusion Act prohibiting further immigration from Japan, and a number of other problems during the inter-war period eventually drove Japan towards the Fascist powers of Germany and Italy, and away from Britain and America. In 1933, Japan withdrew from the League of Nations (precursor to today's United Nations) having been heavily criticized for her actions in China. In 1940, Japan occupied French Indochina (modern-day Vietnam) upon agreement with the then-new French Vichy government, and joined the Axis powers of Germany and Italy. These actions intensified Japan's arguments with the United States and Britain, triggering an oil boycott. The Japanese had already invaded China in 1937, before World War Two started in Europe. American President Roosevelt signed an executive order in 1940 allowing U.S. military personnel to resign from American military service so that they could participate in covert operations in China against the Japanese. This led to the creation of the American Volunteer Group, more commonly known as Chennault's Flying Tigers. With the United States and other countries cutting exports to Japan, Japan attacked American territory on 7 December 1941 without warning or declaration of war. Severe damage was done to the American Pacific Fleet at Pearl Harbor in Hawaii, although its aircraft carriers fortunately escaped because they were at sea at the time. Japanese forces rapidly invaded the British possessions of Malaya and Borneo and the American-occupied Philippines with the intention of seizing the oilfields of the Dutch East Indies. The British island fortress of Singapore was easily captured in what Churchill considered one of the most humiliating British defeats of all time.

In May 1942, the Japanese commenced attacks on Port Moresby in New Guinea. Had these operations been successful, they would have put Japanese forces within range of a possible occupation of Australia. In one of the turning points of the war, the Japanese were held back by the Allies in the Battle of the Coral Sea, the first successful opposition to Japanese plans and the first naval battle fought only between aircraft carriers.

Although aircraft carriers had by then already figured significantly in several important engagements elsewhere in the world, their vital role was established during the Coral Sea battle and they have been a significant force in naval aviation ever since. A month later, the U.S. Navy prevented the invasion of Midway Island, this time destroying several Japanese aircraft carriers in the first real major defeat for the Japanese in the Pacific war. Japanese industry could not replace these significant losses. However, in July the Japanese Army attempted an overland attack on Port Moresby, along the rugged Kokoda trail. Australian reservists fought a stubborn defensive action, until they were relieved by Australian regular troops.

Japanese aggression in the Pacific and America's entry into World War Two as a combatant could have resulted in a plan to defeat Japan prior to any major action in Europe against Germany, but Allied leaders agreed that priority should be given to the defeat of Germany. Even so, U.S. and Australian forces under General Douglas MacArthur began to attack and re-take previously captured territories. Amongst the first such actions was the

*The Hawker Typhoon was an important ground attack aircraft and, after problems with fuselage failure ahead of the tail were rectified, proved to be rugged and dependable.*

bitter fight for the island of Guadalcanal. In early August 1942, the island was assaulted by United States Marines. In late August and early September, while the battle raged on Guadalcanal, Australian forces fought off a Japanese amphibious attack on the eastern tip of New Guinea at Milne Bay, the first conclusive defeat suffered by Japanese land forces. The Americans triumphed on Guadalcanal in the early part of 1943.

Australian and US forces then began the slow and difficult process of retaking the occupied parts of New Guinea and the Dutch East Indies, experiencing some of the toughest Japanese resistance of the Pacific war. Most of the Solomon Islands were retaken in 1943, New Britain and New Ireland in 1944. The Philippines were attacked in late 1944 following the Battle of Leyte Gulf, one of the major sea battles of World War Two, which underlined the importance of aircraft carrier-based aviation. American and Allied submarines and aircraft also relentlessly attacked Japanese merchant shipping, with North American B-25 Mitchell medium bombers proving particularly effective as commerce raiders. This important work deprived Japanese industry of many of the raw materials that Japan had initially gone to war to obtain. The effectiveness of this stranglehold increased as U.S. forces captured islands closer to the Japanese mainland. Nationalist Kuomintang army forces under Chiang Kai-shek and the Communist Chinese army under Mao Tse-tung both opposed the Japanese occupation of China, but never truly united against the Japanese. Nevertheless, as Chinese forces began the slow and costly process of driving back the Japanese on mainland China, Japanese resources were stretched thin as British and Commonwealth forces strove to do the same in Burma. Capture by the Allies of islands such as Iwo Jima and Okinawa brought the Japanese home islands within range of naval and air attacks. Initially the Boeing B-29 Superfortress heavy bomber was employed by the U.S. Army Air Force to attack industrial and military targets with precision. However, a lack of sufficiently sophisticated navigational and bombing aids – and often simply poor weather – rendered many of these attacks ineffective. This fuelled a considerable debate within the Army Air Force as to whether the B-29 should be used for precision attacks from high altitude, or from lower altitudes in mass incendiary raids against Japanese cities. Eventually this dispute was resolved with the latter camp holding sway, and there followed a series of terrible fire raids on Japanese cities which killed thousands. Tokyo and other major cities were firebombed during the course of 1945 to deadly effect.

The fear of the cost of a direct invasion of the Japanese mainland continued to haunt American planners who bore in mind the stiff resistance that the Japanese had put up as American forces pushed across the Pacific and retook island after island. The Americans in fact held a trump card that was to transform the whole face of warfare, and lay the foundations for confrontation in the post-war years. For some time American scientists had been working on nuclear fission, with a view to creating a powerful bomb that would benefit not from standard and established high explosives, but from the splitting of the atom. They were aided in their work by scientists who had fled persecution in Nazi Germany, and eventually the world's first atomic weapons were created under the 'Manhattan Project.'

The only bomber capable of carrying the resulting very large and very heavy bomb was the B-29 Superfortress, and it was this aircraft that was to end the Second World War at a stroke. The first-ever atomic bomb to be used in war, nicknamed 'Little Boy,' was dropped from the B-29 'Enola Gay' on 6 August 1945. It destroyed much of the port city of Hiroshima. On 8 August 1945 the Soviet Union declared war on Japan, attacking her possessions in Manchuria. A day later, over Nagasaki, another atomic bomb, 'Fat Man' was dropped by the B-29 'Bockscar.' The use of these two hugely destructive weapons has been mired in controversy virtually ever since, but at the time it had an immediate effect on the minds of the Japanese leadership. The Japanese committed themselves to a ceasefire on 15 August 1945, and signed, amid great publicity, the actual surrender documents on 2 September 1945 aboard the battleship U.S.S. Missouri in Tokyo Bay.

So came to an end the most famous war in history. Aerial bombardment had achieved what has since been called an 'airpower victory,' and the face and tactics of warfare were rewritten completely during the war. Unfortunately, hopes that the post-war world would be a better place were soon compromised. Much of Europe was in ruins; the results of aerial

*During World War Two, the United States became the 'Arsenal of Democracy,' and its factories produced vast quantities of war material instrumental in the Allies winning the war. This excellent production line photograph shows a part of the Consolidated Factory in San Diego, California. B-24D bombers for the U.S. Army are in the final stages of construction, although the third aircraft in the line nearest to the camera has tail markings indicating that it was destined for the U.S. Navy as a PB4Y-1 (Photo: Consolidated).*

bombing and massively destructive ground warfare as well as the use of tactical ground attack aircraft. The war also saw a complete political and geographical re-drawing of the pre-war world map. In particular, the United States finally came out of its so-called 'isolationism' to become a dominant world power both politically and militarily. The defeat of Germany and Japan saw these two powers shake off their totalitarian and absolutist rule, and eventually rebuild themselves into major industrial powers. With massive financial assistance from the United States under the famed Marshall Plan, Western Europe was re-built and many of the formally defeated powers emerged as important constituent members of the North Atlantic Treaty Organization (NATO) during the 1950's. Colonial powers such as Britain lost much of the influence that they had enjoyed prior to the war. The many defeats that Britain had suffered prior to the final victory caused a massive reduction in Britain's post-war prestige and influence. The successful development

of the atomic bomb, and the emergence of the United States and the Soviet Union as global superpowers with atomic and nuclear and chemical arsenals, as well as large military infrastructures, were hugely important developments that shaped the following decades. The so-called Cold War that developed quickly in the post-war years saw the United States and its Allies ranged against a new grouping in Central and Eastern Europe dominated by the Soviet Union. This influenced many military trends in the coming decades. The Second World War also directly led to the creation of the international body known as the United Nations, which was founded by the victorious Allies partly to prevent such a large, disastrous and destructive conflict from ever breaking out again – something that, thankfully, it has so far managed to achieve. Nevertheless, smaller but no less deadly conflicts have broken out in many parts of the world following the end of World War Two, and in these wars aviation has played a major part on many occasions.

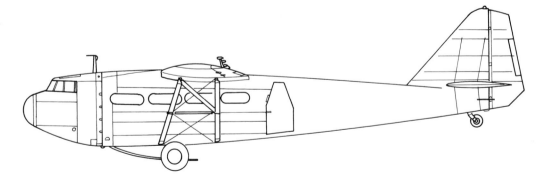

*A number of glider designs were also developed by the Japanese. There were strong German influences in some of these gliders, although their combat use was limited. Illustrated is the Kokusai Ku-8-II (Army Type 4) assault glider, believed to be the only Japanese glider used in action. Similar to the German DFS 230 but with more capacity, the Ku-8 was derived from the Kokusai Ki-59 twin-engined light transport aircraft, utilising the fuselage design and general layout of this aircraft. The Ku-8-II was known to the Allies for identification purposes as 'Gander,' and is believed to have seated up to 20 troops or a small field gun or a light vehicle. The Japanese armed forces also developed an airborne organization, similar to the Germans and the Allies, and used its paratroopers in limited but effective actions in the Dutch East Indies in 1942.*

The fascinating aeronautical story of aviation after the Second World War, during the Cold War era and up to the present day, is the subject of the third and final volume of this encyclopaedia. In any historical narrative, authors and artists are indebted to historians and colleagues for their assistance and practical help. It is always pleasant to acknowledge friends and experts whose assistance and advice have been invaluable when piecing together much of the information and photographic content of this second Volume of *The Complete Encyclopedia of Flight*. Particular recognition must go to Derek Foley, Martin Hale, Jack Harris, my father Victor Lowe, Lucy Maynard, Jim Smith, Derek Spurgeon, Gordon Stevens and Paul Tuckey, for their assistance with information and illustrations, former Royal Air Force flight crew Reg Black and Frank Etherington, many overseas colleagues including Philippe Jalabert, Miroslav Khol, Hans Meier, Michal Ovcacik and Peter Walter. Particular thanks also to Martin Hale and David Willis for their assistance with information and text summaries, especially for some of the British-operated aircraft. Special recognition must additionally go to Chris Slocock of Publishing Solutions (www) Ltd. All have been essential contributors to a comprenensive and accurate history of aviation during World Two.

*Side elevation of a Consolidated PBY-5A Catalina amphibian, or one of its direct equivalents used extensively by the Allies.*

## Author's Note

*The Complete Encyclopedia of Flight sets out to give the most accurate figures available for specifications, based on manufacturer's or service data. However, there remain a number of aircraft types where more information is needed – or might eventually be unearthed – regarding specifications, or where contemporary sources seriously disagree. The same is true where metric dimensions have been translated over the years into imperial specifications, and vice versa, with the attendant loss of specificity that such calculations often create. In similar fashion, there exist serious differences of opinion regarding facts such as first flight dates and production totals. Again, those quoted here are those which have withstood the test of time or which draw from Second World War era sources.*

*Two special adaptations of the Avro Lancaster. The upper drawing shows a Lancaster specially modified without the standard dorsal turret and with a cut-out beneath the fuselage, to take the 22,000 lb 'Grand Slam' bomb – the largest conventional bomb carried by any bomber during World War Two. The lower drawing illustrates a 'Dambuster' Lancaster, with the special equipment beneath the modified fuselage to spin and release the cylindrical bomb used to destroy two dams in Germany in May 1943.*

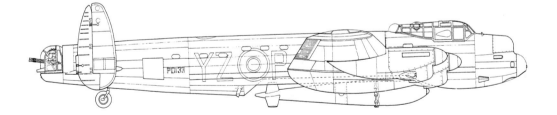

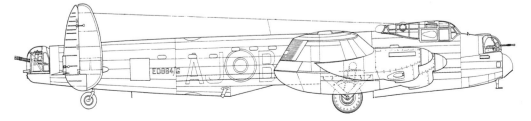

# Vickers-Supermarine Walrus

From the same company that created the superlative Supermarine Spitfire came the utilitarian but effective Walrus amphibian. The Walrus was one of the select band of aircraft types that served throughout World War Two, and although old-fashioned in appearance, it was useful and successful in its varied operational roles. The Walrus traced its ancestry back to the Supermarine Seagull V biplane amphibian which first flew in 1933. This aircraft, the last in a line of Seagull amphibians, was ordered by Australia. Eventual evaluation by Britain's Royal Navy led to the type being ordered by Britain in 1935 as a fleet spotter/reconnaissance aircraft for catapulting from various classes of warships, acting as the 'eyes of the fleet' by spotting for the ships' guns. The type entered full-scale service as the Walrus Mk.I in 1936. One of the Walrus' designers was the legendary R.J. Mitchell, the designer of the Supermarine Spitfire. The Walrus was a biplane amphibian with folding wings (made of wood and metal construction with mainly fabric covering) for ease of storage aboard warships and it featured a somewhat unusual single-engine pusher configuration. Initially the Walrus was intended for the Fleet Air Arm, and the type operated with that service throughout the Second World War. However, the Walrus also later served during the war with Britain's Royal Air Force, primarily for air-sea rescue missions. Many downed Allied (and some enemy) airmen were rescued from the water by the Walrus, which could land on the sea to pick them up. Production of the Walrus was shared by Supermarine, which built the Walrus Mk.I with a metal hull (fuselage), and Saunders-Roe, which manufactured many

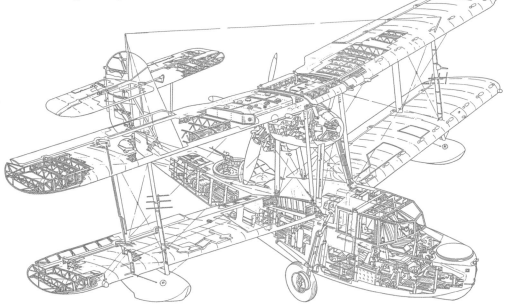

*As a biplane operating in an era of monoplanes, the Walrus was no beauty,*
*but it featured rugged construction and was highly successful as a fleet reconnaissance*
*and air-sea rescue aircraft.*

examples with a wooden hull of its own design. Supermarine appears to have built 287, while Saunders-Roe (according to the company's own records) built 270 Mk.I and 191 Mk.II. The Walrus was slowly superseded from 1944 in Fleet Air Arm units, mainly by another Supermarine biplane, the Sea Otter, which featured a tractor rather than pusher engine layout. The Walrus served with British and Commonwealth forces world-wide, some also operating as communications aircraft while others even acted rarely as bombers, and additional overseas users included Argentina.

*An evocative John Batchelor study of the Walrus in its element – rescuing downed airmen. Countless flyers owed their lives to the Walrus, which could land on the sea to rescue them.*

**Specifications – Supermarine Walrus Mk.II**

| | |
|---|---|
| Wingspan | 45 ft 10 in |
| Length | 37 ft 7 in |
| Maximum speed | 126 mph at sea level |
| Range | approximately 600 miles |
| Service ceiling | 15,900 ft |
| Armament | Up to three (often two) 0.303 in (7.7 mm) machine guns, provision on some aircraft for small bombs or equivalent below the lower wings |
| Engine | One Bristol Pegasus VI radial piston engine, of 750-775 hp |
| Crew | Three or four |

# de Havilland D.H.82 Tiger Moth

One of the most famous training aircraft of all time, the well-known and much-loved Tiger Moth, was the culmination of a successful line of light aircraft that had been developed by Britain's de Havilland company since the 1920's. It was a logical follow-up to the D.H.60 Gipsy Moth (as described in Volume 1 of 'Complete Encyclopaedia of Flight'), and the initial aircraft were more accurately developments of the D.H.60 and direct ancestors of the Tiger Moth itself. Sometimes called Moth Trainers, these were an interim step towards the Tiger Moth line. The first Tiger Moth layout, incorporating various changes from the D.H.60 formula including 'staggered' biplane wings with sweepback, flew in the latter half of 1931. Initially known as the D.H.82 Tiger Moth, a number of additional changes led to the ubiquitous D.H.82A Tiger Moth II – usually simply called the Tiger Moth. This type went on to become world-famous as an *ab initio* trainer. Initial members of the Tiger Moth line originally entered Royal Air Force service between 1932 and 1933, and the type's career with the RAF continued into the 1950's. By the start of World War Two, the Tiger Moth had become a very widespread civil trainer in Britain, often preparing trainee pilots for entry into the RAF. That air force was also increasingly a Tiger Moth user, and the type continued its absolutely vital training role throughout World War Two for British as well as British Commonwealth pilot trainees. It became a significant part of the large Empire Air Training Scheme, but in addition to training duties in several Commonwealth countries, the Tiger Moth sometimes fulfilled other roles including coastal patrol and communications. Production in Britain was shared by de Havilland and later Morris Motors, but significant manufacture also took place overseas. Sweden, Norway and Portugal built and operated the Tiger Moth, and Commonwealth production most notably included Canada. Many Canadian

*Illustrated in classic guise wearing Royal Air Force training colors of World War Two, this D.H.82A Tiger Moth II, N9374, is representative of the hundreds of aircraft that performed such a vital job in training Allied pilots during the war, when thousands of aircrew were needed by the Allied forces.*

examples, known as the D.H.82C were powered by a slightly more powerful Gipsy Major engine, and had provision for enclosed cockpits and skis. A pilotless radio-controlled drone for gunnery practice, called the D.H.82B Queen Bee and often fitted with floats, was built for the RAF and Fleet Air Arm. After the war, innumerable military Tiger Moths were 'demobbed' and flooded onto the civilian market. Many survived the immediate post-war period, and today Tiger Moths are highly prized historic aircraft. A post-war development was the Thruxton Jackaroo, a conversion of existing Tiger Moths with enclosed seating for four people within the fuselage. There is some disagreement over the total number of Tiger Moths built, but most historians agree that the total was well over eight thousand with over half in Britain.

*Photographed air-to-air over Rhinebeck in New York State during August 1974, this is one of the countless Tiger Moths that had survived into more recent times. Today, Tiger Moths are highly prized historic aircraft, and are carefully looked after by their adoring owners.*
*(Photo: John Batchelor).*

### Specifications – de Havilland D.H.82A Tiger Moth II

| | |
|---|---|
| Wingspan | 29 ft 4 in |
| Length | 23 ft 11 in |
| Maximum speed | 109 mph at sea level/1,000 ft |
| Maximum take-off weight | 1,825 lb |
| Range | 302 miles |
| Service ceiling | 13,600 ft |
| Engine | One de Havilland Gipsy Major inline piston engine, of 130 hp |
| Crew | Two |

# Gloster E.28/39

Nowadays almost forgotten, the world's very first viable jet engine was successfully run for the first time on 12 April 1937. Conceived and principally designed by the brilliant British RAF engineer Frank Whittle, and known as the Whittle Unit (WU), the engine was constructed mainly by the British Thomson-Houston company at Rugby in northern England, where the first test was made. Although the successful running of this revolutionary new engine theoretically heralded a new age for aviation, Whittle had to struggle for years against official indifference and disinterest in his forward thinking as to how aircraft could be powered in the future. He patented his jet engine ideas as early as 1930, but even the successful early tests of the WU aroused little official interest until other forward-thinking men in the right places in government and industry saw the value of Whittle's inven-

tion. Further development by his company, Power Jets Ltd., led to an engine capable of being fitted in and powering an aircraft. The British aircraft manufacturer Gloster was given the task of building a proof-of-concept aircraft to flight test the new engine and the great potential that came with it. Built to Specification E.28/39 and known by this designation (although also called by some the Whittle), the little Gloster aircraft was actually advanced in its own right. It featured a tricycle undercarriage, a forward-located cockpit giving excellent pilot view ahead while on the ground, all-metal construction (but with some fabric-covered control surfaces), and it actually had the general layout of most of the early-generation production jet fighters that followed it. The first prototype E.28/39 officially flew on 15 May 1941 with Gloster test pilot 'Gerry' Sayer at the controls, although it might

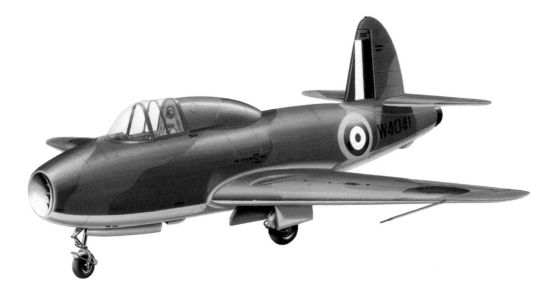

*Britain's first turbojet-powered aircraft, the Gloster E.28/39, was vitally important in the history of aviation. Although designed with the provision to carry armament, it was intended solely as a research and proof-of-concept aircraft. W4041/G, the first prototype, exists to this day and is displayed at the Science Museum in London.*

have made at least one hop a little earlier. The engine employed was the Power Jets W.1, although subsequent test flying (additionally using a short-lived second prototype) was carried out with various other engine types as several power plant companies began to produce equally pioneering jet engines. These British experiments mirrored events in Germany, where Whittle's contemporary, Pabst von Ohain, had worked with the Heinkel company to create an engine and aircraft combination – the Heinkel He 178 and its HeS 3b turbojet engine – that actually flew in August 1939 prior to the Whittle. The He 178 is described in Volume 1 of *The Complete Encyclopedia of Flight*.

*The ground-breaking Whittle engines were of the centrifugal-flow layout and were highly influential in the development of jet propulsion for aircraft.*

**Specifications – Gloster E.28/39 (first prototype)**

| | |
|---|---|
| Wingspan | 29 ft |
| Length | 25 ft 3.75 in (or 25 ft 2 in) |
| Maximum speed | 338 mph (466 mph with W.2B engine) |
| Maximum take-off weight | 3,604 lb (depending on engine fitted) |
| Service ceiling | approximately 42,170 ft (with W.2/500 engine) |
| Engine | One Power Jets W.1 turbojet engine, of 860 lb st (other engine types installed at different times) |
| Crew | One |

# Avro Anson

Like several German and American aircraft of the 1930's, the Avro Anson began life in commercial use but moved on to serve a variety of roles throughout World War Two. Originally designed for Britain's Imperial Airways as a six passenger transport and mail carrier, the first Avro 652 flew on 7 January 1935. Two were delivered to Imperial Airways, but by then interest in the type had arisen as a military coastal reconnaissance and patrol aircraft.

The prototype of the prospective military derivative known as the Avro 652A flew in March 1935, and successfully beat its main competitor, the de Havilland D.H.89M Dragon Rapide biplane (also converted from a civil design). Specification 18/35 covered the production of the Avro 652A as the Anson GR.Mk.I, with the first production/development aircraft flying in late 1935. The type entered RAF service the following year, Ansons duly serving with the RAF's Coastal Command until late 1941/early 1942. With export orders received from countries such as Egypt, Eire, Estonia, Finland and Greece, the Anson entered extensive production. Almost seven thousand Mk.I were built in Britain, but many of these were trainers.

The Anson was recognized even in 1935 as a potential training aircraft for such roles as navigator, observer, wireless (radio) operator, and gunnery training, especially as large numbers of aircrew were increasingly needed for RAF front-line service. The Anson became a part of the vast Empire Air Training Scheme created in late 1939, and Ansons duly served in large numbers as trainers in Canada and other Commonwealth countries. They were also built in Canada, where a major manufacturing program was created involving a number of Canadian companies. Some of these aircraft were powered by American radial engines rather than the Armstrong Siddeley Cheetahs of British-built Ansons. 50 of the Canadian-built Ansons were supplied to the U.S. Army Air Force as the AT-20. Eventually Canadian production led to the indigenous Mk.V, with a completely re-designed fuselage made from plywood rather than the standard Anson fuselage of fabric-covered metal framework with wood fairings. The Mk.V was also powered by American engines. Further develop-

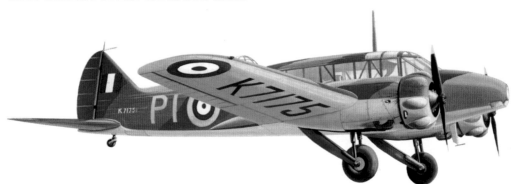

*Known affectionately as 'Faithful Annie,' Avro Ansons fulfilled important roles for the RAF, Royal Navy and Commonwealth countries during World War Two. After the war many ex-military Ansons were used by civil operators.*

ment in Britain led to a string of different versions for training, ambulance and communications roles. Some of these were post-Second World War models, with Anson production continuing until 1952. They included the Anson XIX transport with a modified fuselage design. The final Ansons in RAF service were retired in 1968. Manufacturer's records suggest that 8,138 Ansons were produced in Britain and 2,882 built in Canada.

*Anson gunnery trainers were fitted with a dorsal turret for the training of air gunners – a role that has now all but vanished amongst today's air forces.*

**Specifications – Avro Anson Mk.I (trainer)**

| | |
|---|---|
| Wingspan | 56 ft 6 in |
| Length | 42 ft 3 in |
| Maximum speed | 188 mph at 7,000 ft |
| Maximum take-off weight | 8,000 lb |
| Range | 790 miles |
| Service ceiling | 19,000 ft |
| Armament | One 0.303 in (7.7 mm) fixed forward firing machine gun, one similar gun in dorsal turret when fitted |
| Engine | Two Armstrong Siddeley Cheetah IX radial piston engines, of 350 hp each |
| Crew | Two to three, variable according to role |

# Westland Lysander

The Westland Lysander is proof that a successful warplane does not have to be a high-performance fighter or bomber. Designed as an army liason aircraft, the Lysander eventually flew with great success throughout World War Two. The Lysander was evolved to Specification A.39/34 as a two-seat army liason aircraft for Britain's Royal Air Force, and the first prototype flew on 15 June 1936. An army liason aircraft needed good low-level handling, excellent visibility and the ability to fly from makeshift landing grounds. The Lysander fulfilled all these needs, with its large cockpit windows, and high-lift devices on its high-set monoplane wings that gave it fine low-speed capabilities and the ability to fly from and into comparatively small fields. Light bombs could be carried under the aircraft's removable stub wings that attached to the type's prominent wheel 'spats.'

The first production model was the Bristol Mercury-powered Mk.I, which entered RAF service in mid-1938. It was followed by the Mk.II with a Bristol Perseus radial engine, and the more powerful Mk.III which reverted to the Mercury radial engine, and the Mk.IIIA. Production took place at Westland's Yeovil factories in southern England, and was completed in early 1942. Approximately 1,442 were made. However, construction also took place in Canada, where the National Steel Car Corporation built 75 Mk.II and at least 150 Mk.III.

In RAF colors, the Lysander operated with army liason squadrons early in the war, serving British units and their French allies after the German invasion of France in May 1940. The type was capable of picking up messages using a retractable hook that could be extended when in flight. However, the Lysander served various other roles, including target-towing and air-sea rescue (for the latter, survival containers or inflatable dinghies could be carried under the aircraft's stub wings). The Lysander's most important role was flying from Britain into Occupied France to pick up or drop off agents or leave behind supplies for the French Resistance fighting the occupying German forces in France during the mid-war period. For this task, the Lysanders involved had black-painted undersides, carried a fixed

*V9738 was a Westland Lysander Mk.IIIA, and is shown here in classic 'cloak and dagger' guise as an agent dropper with its external ladder to aid passengers to get in and out of the aircraft, and extra fuel tank below the fuselage. Also Allied airmen who had been shot down and evaded capture were ferried back to Britain from France in this plane.*

A Lysander with RAF markings. Lysanders additionally served with several export customers, including Eire, Finland and Turkey. Commonwealth and Free French forces also used the type, as did the Royal Navy and U.S. Army Air Force.

ladder on their left-hand fuselage sides for passengers to get in or out, and flew into and out of fields in the French countryside at night.

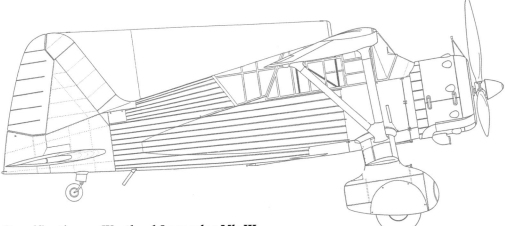

**Specifications – Westland Lysander Mk.III**

| | |
|---|---|
| Wingspan | 50 ft |
| Length | 30 ft 6 in |
| Maximum speed | 211 mph at sea level |
| Maximum take-off weight | 6,330 lb |
| Range | approximately 600 miles |
| Service ceiling | 21,500 ft |
| Armament | Two fixed forward-firing 0.303 in (7.7 mm) machine guns, one (two in some models) 0.303 in (7.7 mm) machine gun on flexible mounting in rear cockpit |
| Engine | One Bristol Mercury XX radial piston engine, of 870 hp |
| Crew | Two |

*The Westland Lysander was of an all-metal structure, with much fabric covering the fuselage and wings.*

# Focke-Wulf Fw 189

In the years following the accession to power in Germany of Hitler's National Socialist (Nazi) party, a major process of rearmament of Germany's Luftwaffe took place. One of the procurement orders issued during the period by Germany's equivalent of Britain's Air Ministry was for a tactical reconnaissance and army liason aircraft. At that time, such aircraft were usually high-wing, single-engine types (such as the Lysander on the previous two pages), but the German requirement for 1937 was addressed by the Focke-Wulf company with an alternative design layout that became the Fw 189. Featuring a twin-engined twin-boom design with

an extensively-glazed central fuselage pod that allowed its crew good visibility, the Fw 189 was of an all-metal stressed-skin construction that proved very durable in combat. The first aircraft flew in July 1938. Manufacture began in 1939–1940 with three pre-production and ten production examples of the Fw 189B series, which had a modified fuselage for crew training. The extensively-glazed reconnaissance models of the Fw 189 were the 'A' series and construction of these commenced in 1940. Deliveries to the Luftwaffe took place late in 1940 and into 1941. The type duly served with distinction on the Eastern Front following Germany's attack on the Soviet

*A Focke-Wulf Fw 189A-2 coded 5D+EH of the Luftwaffe's 1.(H)/31, which was a short-range tactical reconnaissance unit. The Fw 189 gradually replaced the traditionally-configured, high-wing, single-engine Henschel Hs 126 monoplane in the tactical reconnaissance role and served mainly on the Russian Front, but a small number were also used in North Africa.*

*These two photographs show details of the Fw 189A, including the armed transparent tailcone of the fuselage nacelle, and the neat engine installation of the type's comparatively low-powered Argus inline engines (Photos: M.V. Lowe Collection).*

Union in June 1941, some even surviving desperate ramming attacks by Soviet fighters. In addition to Luftwaffe service, both Hungary and Slovakia also used the Fw 189. The initial Fw 189A-1 production series was followed by the more heavily-armed Fw 189A-2, and the A-3 dual-control trainer, plus limited numbers of the more powerful 'F' series. Several other versions were planned but not proceeded with, including a heavily-armed ground attack 'assault' model with a shortened and armored crew nacelle. In addition to the type's intended reconnaissance role (for which a variety of cameras could be installed), late in the war a small number of Fw 189 were fitted out as makeshift night fighters, with altered weapons and an airborne interception radar. Several were also used as staff transports. Production was carried out by Focke-Wulf itself and additionally under Nazi direction in Occupied France, and by the Aero company in the former Czechoslovakia. It is believed that up to 864 examples, including prototype/development aircraft, were built. The names Eule (Owl) and Uhu (Eagle Owl) were sometimes used for the Fw 189.

**Specifications – Focke-Wulf Fw 189A-2**

| | |
|---|---|
| Wingspan | 60 ft 4.5 in |
| Length | 39 ft 5.5 in |
| Maximum speed | 218 mph at 7,874 ft |
| Maximum take-off weight | 9,193 lb |
| Range | 416 miles |
| Service ceiling | 23,950 ft |
| Armament | Six 7.92 mm (0.312 in) machine guns, up to 441 lb of bombs |
| Engine | Two Argus As 410A-1 inline piston engines, of 465–485 hp each |
| Crew | Two or three |

# Junkers Ju 52/3m

The German aircraft designer and pioneer Hugo Junkers was one of the great early advocates of metal construction in aviation. As described in Volume 1 of *The Complete Encyclopedia of Flight*, his Junkers company produced a number of pioneering all-metal aircraft. These included several military aircraft types during World War One that also pioneered corrugated metal skinning, and in the post-First World War period, Junkers produced a series of successful and pioneering all-metal civil airliners. Amongst these was the Junkers F 13, a small single-engine 1920's passenger aircraft. Further development by Junkers led to a larger, single-engine civil transport named the Ju 52, which first flew on 13 October 1930. Later a three-engined derivative was flown, and soon evolved into the famous production aircraft named the Ju 52/3m for its three motors. Only a handful of the original single-engine model were built, and the first examples of the 13–17 passenger Ju 52/3m were delivered to a Bolivian airline in 1932. Originally intended as a transport aircraft, the Ju 52/3m entered service with the German national airline Deutsche Luft Hansa (later Deutsche Lufthansa) in 1932–1933. However, the Ju 52/3m also had potential military applications.

Following the accession to power of Hitler's National Socialists in Germany in 1933, Junkers began to develop the Ju 52/3m as an interim bomber. The resulting major bomber version was the Ju 52/3mg3e, established in Luftwaffe service by March 1934. A makeshift conversion, the type had three small fuselage bomb bays, with the bombs stacked vertically in them. A retractable trashcan-like turret below the fuselage was a part of the type's hastily installed armament. The Ju 52/3m saw service throughout the Spanish Civil War, firstly as a troop transport for General Franco's Nationalist rebels, then as a bomber with the Spanish Nationalist forces and the German Condor Legion. By the start of World War Two the Ju 52/3m bomber had been replaced by newer types such as the Heinkel He 111 in Germany's Luftwaffe, but found its true role during the war as a transport, paratroop carrier, ambulance, anti-sea

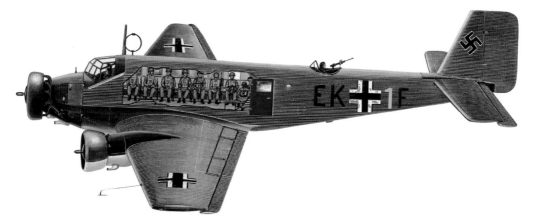

*The Junkers Ju 52/3m was used to carry paratroops during World War Two. Their seating was along the sides within the fuselage, as shown in this cutaway.*

*Hardly an elegant aircraft, the Junkers Ju 52/3m was nevertheless strong and functional. It served the Luftwaffe well throughout World War Two in actions including the invasion of Crete and Russia, although some operations incurred staggering losses.*

mine aircraft (fitted with an external hoop beneath the wings and fuselage), glider-tower. Produced by several plants in Germany, Hungary and Nazi-controlled France, manufacture continued until 1944 when over four thousand eight hundred had been built. Post-war production continued in France (as the AAC.1), and in Spain by CASA, and the type served various airlines world-wide in the immediate post-war period.

*Photographed in the United States during the 1970's, this preserved Ju 52/3m shows the corrugated metal skin of the aircraft (Photo: John Batchelor).*

**Specifications – Junkers Ju 52/3mg3e**

| | |
|---|---|
| Wingspan | 95 ft 11.5 in |
| Length | 62 ft |
| Maximum speed | 171 mph at 2,953 ft |
| Maximum take-off weight | approximately 23,148 lb |
| Range | 808 miles |
| Service ceiling | 19,357 ft |
| Armament | Two 7.92 mm (0.312 in) machine guns, up to 1,102 lb of bombs |
| Engine | Three BMW 132A-3 radial piston engines, of 725 hp each |
| Crew | Four or five, provision for troops, paratroops or stretcher cases when not used as bomber |

# Dornier Do 17 and Do 215

Together with the Heinkel He 111 and Junkers Ju 88, the Dornier Do 17 was one of the three principal medium bombers of Germany's Luftwaffe in the early stages of World War Two. Ironically, the Do 17 was actually designed as a civil aircraft without the intention of having military applications. Created to fulfil the requirement of Germany's national airline Deutsche Luft Hansa for a six-passenger high-speed mailplane, the first prototype flew in 1934. It was a beautifully streamlined aircraft, with all-metal construction and mostly metal skin, and a long thin fuselage that gained the type its nickname 'Flying Pencil.' Three prototype/development aircraft were built, but the aircraft's usefulness as a passenger carrier was negated by the smallness of its two passenger compartments. Later, however, the military potential of the design was recognized, particularly its excellent performance, and development was com-

menced to re-create the Do 17 as a medium bomber. The first production models were the Do 17E bomber and Do 17F reconnaissance aircraft, and Luftwaffe units began receiving these types in the first half of 1937. They differed from the original civil aircraft in the installation of a bomb bay, twin-tailed tailplane and the addition of much military equipment and armament. A specially-configured Do 17 performed well at a famous aviation meeting at Zürich, Switzerland in 1937, showing the bomber to be faster than many contemporary fighters – and led to a major export order together with production under license from Yugoslavia. Further development created the more powerful Do 17M bomber and Do 17P reconnaissance series and the redesigned Do 17U pathfinder. A completely re-designed and larger nose compartment with a lower rearwards-firing gun position was introduced on the Do 17Z. Over 500 of this important bomber model are believed to have

*The Dornier Do 215 was an inline-engined development of the Do 17Z configuration, and principally served with Luftwaffe reconnaissance units, including this 'T5'-coded example. A small number flew with Hungarian forces.*

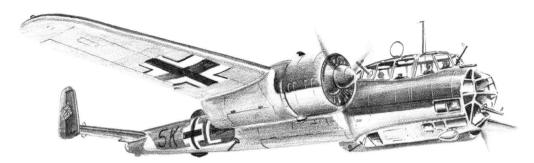

*The Dornier Do 17Z was an important bomber in the Luftwaffe's inventory early in World War Two. This '5K'-coded Do 17Z flew with bomber wing KG (Kampfgeschwader) 3 'Blitz.'*

been made, and a small number were converted as makeshift night fighters. Continuing development led to the Daimler Benz DB 601 inline-engined Do 215, originally created for export but used instead by the Luftwaffe principally as a reconnaissance aircraft and makeshift night fighter. Following Nazi intervention in the Spanish Civil War on behalf of the rebel Nationalists, the Do 17 was a major component of the Luftwaffe's bomber forces. The type subsequently served over Poland, Norway, the Low Countries and France, in the Battle of Britain, the Yugoslav invasion and over Russia. Some later served as glider-towers. Do 17Z bombers flew with Croatian forces and were supplied to Finland for combat against the Russians. The Do 17/Do 215 series was superseded by the larger Dornier Do 217 (see pages 142 to 143).

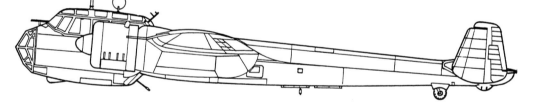

*The Do 17Z introduced a more substantial nose section for its crew which broke up the hitherto pencil-like fuselage profile of previous Do 17 models.*

**Specifications – Dornier Do 17Z-2**

| | |
|---|---|
| Wingspan | 59 ft 0.66 in |
| Length | 51 ft 10 in (or slightly less) |
| Maximum speed | 255 mph at 4,000 ft |
| Maximum take-off weight | 18,937.5 lb |
| Range | approximately 721 miles |
| Service ceiling | 22,966 ft |
| Armament | Six 7.92 mm (0.312 in) machine guns, up to 2,205 lb of bombs |
| Engine | Two Bramo Fafnir 323P radial piston engines, of 1,000 hp each |
| Crew | Four |

# Dewoitine D.520

The best French fighter of World War Two was the Dewoitine D.520. Potentially an excellent aircraft, the D.520 went through a long period of development partly due to the unsatisfactory way that French military procurement was carried out in the 1930's. The once great French aircraft industry of the First World War and 1920's was nationalised in the mid to late 1930's, which also did not help the situation. Dewoitine had previously created the advanced D.500/D.501/D.510 series of monoplane fighters in the early 1930's (described in Volume 1 of this 'Complete Encyclopaedia of Flight'), but these were obsolete by the start of World War Two. Nonetheless Dewoitine continued his forward thinking, and the D.520 prototype was built as a private venture – the prototype first flew on 2 October 1938. Eventually the French military realized the worth of this advanced fighter and ordered it in large numbers, having at last recognized the threat posed by Nazi Germany.

The D.520 entered service with the French air force in early 1940, but only one Groupe de Chasse was fully equipped with the type when the German attack against France was launched on 10 May 1940. By the capitulation of France in late June 1940, five Groupes had become operational and had performed well against the German Luftwaffe, but they were too few and too late to affect the outcome of the conflict. The D.520 was later flown by the pro-German Vichy French air force, and production of the D.520 was resumed in 1941 under German authorisation. The precise number of D.520s that were built is hard to determine due to fragmented production under French and then German auspices, but it was at least 905. Vichy French-operated D.520s flew against the Allies in Syria and during the Operation 'Torch' landings in North Africa. The D.520 also served with the Luftwaffe primarily as a fighter trainer, and additionally flew with the Bulgarians, Romanians, and Italians.

*The D.520 was a capable fighter that was rushed into production and served in too few numbers during the Battle of France in May/June 1940 to pose serious problems to the Germans. Shown is a D.520 of Groupe de Chasse II/6 or its partial successor GC I/4 during 1943, on the Allied side flying with Free French forces.*

*A D.520 serving possibly in late 1940 with 1AC, a Vichy French naval air arm unit (note the white distinguishing flash along the fuselage side, denoting a Vichy French-operated machine).*

After the Allied Invasion of France in June 1944, some D.520s formerly used by the Germans were taken over by the Allies and subsequently flown by Free French pilots on the Allied side, mainly in ground attack missions against German forces remaining in France. After World War Two, a two-seat version, the D.520DC, was converted from some exis-ting D.520 fighters for training purposes, approximately 14 of these conversions being made.

*The D.520's cockpit layout was utilitarian and fairly typical of its era. The device at the top of the picture is the OPL RX39 gunsight.*

**Specifications – Dewoitine D.520C.1 (1940 production)**

| | |
|---|---|
| Wingspan | 33 ft 5.5 in |
| Length | 28 ft 8.9 in |
| Maximum speed | 332 mph at 17,717 ft |
| Maximum take-off weight | 5,842 lb |
| Range | 466 miles |
| Service Ceiling | 33,465 ft |
| Armament | One 20 mm cannon engine-mounted, four wing-mounted 7.5 mm (0.30 in) machine guns |
| Engine | One Hispano-Suiza 12Y45 inline piston engine, of 920–930 hp |
| Crew | One |

# Heinkel He 111

A truly classic German aircraft of World War Two, the Heinkel He 111 was employed on all fronts where the Luftwaffe was operational, and served as a bomber and a transport. The original order for the development of the type came in 1932, before Hitler's National Socialists gained power in Germany. It was designed as a high-speed transport, and as a bomber for the pre-Hitler era German military. Heinkel drew on the design of the graceful and efficient single-engine He 70 for important aspects of the new aircraft's layout. The first proto type/development aircraft, the He 111a (V1), flew for the first time on 17 November 1934. The second example flew in May 1935, and was a transport version with a revised wing. Flown by Deutsche Lufthansa

and named 'Rostock,' it was later used for clandestine reconnaissance missions. The initial pre-production/production model was the He 111A, powered by two 750 hp BMW VI engines. This was not a success, being overweight and underpowered, and only a handful were built, six later going to China. The He 111B followed, powered by two 910 hp Daimler-Benz DB 600C inline engines. The first production model for the Luftwaffe was the He 111B-1 and initial deliveries were made in late 1936. Some He 111B-1 were delegated to the Condor Legion in Spain where they proved very successful, their speed enabling them to evade Republican-operated fighters. Some 413 He 111Bs were followed by the production of the He 111E bomber with Junkers Jumo 211-series inline engines and approximately 210

*The Heinkel He 111 went through a number of design changes, particularly with its wing planform. Later models were of all-metal construction, but some early aircraft had some fabric covering. Note the vertical stowage of the bombs within the fuselage, necessitated by the arrangement of the aircraft's structure.*

were built by several manufacturers in Germany. Some of these also served in the Spanish Civil War. The He 111G was another transport version, some serving with Turkish forces. However, the principal bomber versions of the He 111 were the He 111P and He 111H. The He 111P was powered by two 1,015 hp Daimler-Benz DB 601A inline engines and significantly incorporated a fully-glazed asymmetric nose, instead of the conventional stepped cockpits of the earlier variants. 834 He 111Ps were built before production fully switched to the main production model, the He 111H. Powered by two Junkers Jumo 211 engines of various versions, there were several sub-variants of the He 111H series. These versatile aircraft formed the backbone of the Luftwaffe's bomber force between 1940 and 1943. About 6,000 were built before production ended in September 1944. Ten production He 111Z 'Zwilling' (Twin) two-fuselage, five engine He 111 derivatives were also built, the first flying in August 1942. These were intended to tow the largest gliders, such as the Messerschmitt Me 321. Conventional He 111s were also used to air-launch V1 flying bombs (see pages 302 to 303). Hungary and Romania, two of Germany's allies, also operated the He 111. After the war, production continued in Spain by CASA. Some of the Spanish-built aircraft were powered by British Rolls-Royce Merlin engines and remained in service through the 1970's.

*The five-man crew of the He 111 can be seen in this view. The 'G1' fuselage code is for the Luftwaffe bomber wing KG (Kampfgeschwader) 55.*

## Specifications – Heinkel He 111H-16

| | |
|---|---|
| Wingspan | 73 ft 9.75 in |
| Length | 53 ft 9.5 in |
| Maximum speed | 251.7 mph at 19,685 ft |
| Maximum take-off weight | 30,864 lb |
| Range | 1,280 miles |
| Service ceiling | 21,980 ft |
| Armament | One 20 mm cannon in nose, one 13 mm (0.51 in) machine gun in dorsal position, several 7.92 mm (0.312 in) machine guns in various other flexible mounts, up to 4,409 lb of bombs internally and/or externally |
| Engine | Two Junkers Jumo 211F inline piston engines, of 1,350 hp each |
| Crew | Five |

# P.Z.L. P.37

The first shots of what quickly grew into World War Two were fired in the early morning of 1 September 1939, when substantial German forces started their invasion of Poland. Included in the German attack were large numbers of Luftwaffe aircraft, including bombers and their fighter cover. Opposing them, and attempting to stem the overwhelming tide of the German advances, was the Polish air force. The Polish order of battle comprised a mix of various fighters, bombers and reconnaissance aircraft, some of which were not particularly modern. The best fighters available were P.Z.L. P.11 parasol-wing monoplanes – little match for the Germans' Messerschmitt Bf 109 – together with the P.Z.L. P.37 Los (Elk) medium bomber. One of the better medium bomber designs of its era, the P.Z.L. P.37 was always hampered by a lack of appreciation on the part of the Polish authorities controlling aircraft procurement. The prototype P.37/I flew in late June 1936 with two 873 hp Bristol Pegasus XII radial engines. This prototype, and nine of the first ten similarly powered initial Los A production aircraft, had a single vertical tail. The P.37/II second prototype, and all other production Los bombers, had a twin-

tail assembly. The P.37/II, which flew in April 1937, was the development aircraft for the Los B version, differing principally in its more powerful Pegasus XX engines and twin-wheel main undercarriage legs. Delivery of production Los Bs began in the autumn of 1938, when existing Los As were mainly relegated to training duties. Unfortunately, catastrophic blundering amongst Polish military leaders resulted in Poland's air force being relegated to little more than army support, with consequent cut-backs in the procurement of aircraft that could have posed a serious threat to the Germans. Showing the promise of the Los design despite this, P.Z.L. had received potential export orders from Bulgaria, Romania, Turkey and Yugoslavia, with possibilities of other orders and licenced production elsewhere before the war started. However, no export aircraft were delivered, and the Polish armed forces only had some ninety Los bombers on order when Germany's attack began. Lack of any form of co-ordinated resistance to the German invasion, the overwhelming air superiority of the Luftwaffe, and swift German advances, rendered the Los bomber force completely ineffective

*The P.Z.L. P.37 was one of the better medium bombers of the immediate pre-World War Two period, but was hampered by official indifference and lack of vision on the part of Poland's military leaders.*

*Four of the initial production P.Z.L. P.37A Los A medium bombers, showing the single vertical tail of these initially-manufactured aircraft. Early Los were powered by licence-built Bristol Pegasus XIIB radial engines (Photo: via Hans Meier).*

despite the undoubted qualities of the aircraft. In the second week of fighting, nine more were acquired, but twenty-six of the forty-five operational machines were lost during the sixteen or so days before the Soviet Union invaded Poland from the east. Most of the surviving aircraft were subsequently withdrawn to Romania, in whose colors they later fought alongside the Germans against Soviet forces.

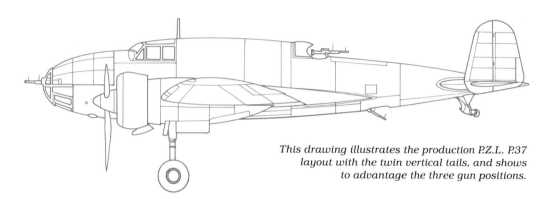

*This drawing illustrates the production P.Z.L. P.37 layout with the twin vertical tails, and shows to advantage the three gun positions.*

### Specifications – P.Z.L. P.37B Los B

| | |
|---|---|
| Wingspan | 58 ft 8.75 in (possibly slightly more) |
| Length | 42 ft 4.75 in |
| Maximum speed | 276.5 mph at 11,155 ft |
| Maximum take-off weight | 19,621 lb |
| Range | 932 miles |
| Service ceiling | approximately 19,685 ft |
| Armament | Three 0.303 in (7.7 mm) machine guns flexible-mounted in nose, dorsal and ventral positions, up to 5,688 lb of bombs |
| Engine | Two P.Z.L.-built Bristol Pegasus XX radial piston engines, of 925 hp each |
| Crew | Four |

# Hawker Hurricane

The Hawker Hurricane was one of Britain's principal fighters during World War Two, although it has always been overshadowed by the Spitfire. It was initially built around Specification F.36/34, and was powered from the start by the superlative Rolls-Royce Merlin engine. The prototype first flew in November 1935, and the type's early history is covered in Volume 1 of *The Complete Encyclopedia of Flight*. The initial production version was the Hurricane Mk.I. Hurricanes operated with RAF squadrons based in France from early in World War Two, and outnumbered the Spitfire by about two to one during the Battle of Britain in the summer and autumn of 1940, when these two

types were Britain's main means of defence against the Luftwaffe. During the second half of 1940, Hurricane Mk.Is, with a distinctive sand filter beneath the nose began operating in the Middle East, following the entry of Italy into the war. In 1942, Hurricanes made their operational appearance in the Far East, as fighters and fighter-bombers. In June 1940, the prototype Hurricane Mk.II was flown, with a 1,185 hp supercharged Merlin XX engine. Early production Mk.IIs retained the standard 8-gun armament of the Mk.IA, as the Mk.IIA. With twelve machine-guns the designation was Mk.IIB, and the Mk.IIC had a wing armament of four 20mm cannons. The Hurricane was used increasingly as a fighter-bomber due to the appearance of better Axis fighters. Some Hurricane IIs were equipped to carry underwing rocket

The Hawker Hurricane was a highly significant aircraft to the RAF, and fought alongside the much better-known Supermarine Spitfire during the Battle of Britain. Several famous pilots flew the Hurricane – this Mk.I belongs to Robert Stanford Tuck of No.257 Squadron, who scored many victories while flying Hurricanes.

*Hawker Hurricanes of No.501 Squadron, RAF, breaking away for the attack. The nearest aircraft was flown by another Hurricane personality, Peter Townsend, later a night fighter pilot.*

projectiles, and the Mk.IID was a special anti-tank version with two larger-caliber under-wing cannons. The only other British production model was the Mk IV, also a ground attack type, with a variety of possible weapon arrangements. The foregoing were all land-based Hurricanes for the RAF and Commonwealth forces but the other major operational form of the aircraft was the Sea Hurricane, equipped for catapult take-offs and (except for initial examples) an arrester hook. The derivative first appeared in 1941 as an interim means of protecting convoys from German U-Boats and Focke-Wulf Fw 200 maritime patrol bombers. Initially Sea Hurricanes were carried on catapult-armed merchant (C.A.M.) ships. Once launched, they had to 'ditch' in the sea after whatever combat they had engaged in so that the pilot could be picked up by any available ship. Later they operated from aircraft carriers. The total number of Sea Hurricanes built or converted was approximately eight hundred. Some 14,531 Hurricanes of all kinds were manufactured, including production in Canada. The Soviet Union received almost three thousand, and other export users included Finland, Belgium and Yugoslavia (all these flying the type in combat), Portugal, Persia, Turkey, and others. One RAF Battle of Britain Hurricane pilot, James Nicholson, was awarded the Victoria Cross.

**Specifications – Hawker Hurricane Mk.IIC**

| | |
|---|---|
| Wingspan | 40 ft |
| Length | 32 ft 2.25 (alternatives often quoted) |
| Maximum speed | 329 mph at 18,000 ft |
| Maximum take-off weight | 8,100 lb |
| Range | 460 miles |
| Service ceiling | 35,600 ft |
| Armament | Four fixed wing-mounted forward-firing 20 mm cannons, up to 1,000 lb of bombs beneath the wings |
| Engine | One Rolls-Royce Merlin XX inline piston engine, of 1,280–1,300 hp |
| Crew | One |

# Curtiss P-40 Warhawk Series

Immortalised by the exploits of the famous 'Flying Tigers' volunteer group in China, and by the huge 'shark mouth' decorations painted on their big noses by the R.A.F., the Curtiss P-40 line has a particular place in the history of the Second World War. Despite this, the P-40 series were not spectacular performers, particularly at high-level, but they did manage to hold the line for the Allies in the Far East and North Africa until better Allied fighters came along later in the Second World War. The P-40 family had its roots in the Curtiss P-36 Hawk series of the 1930's, which are described in Volume 1 of *The Complete Encyclopedia of Flight*. The P-36 was a radial-engined fighter and one of the U.S. Army Air Corps' first 'modern' fighter types' of the 1930's, although eventually outclassed by contemporary designs such as the Supermarine Spitfire. Further development by Curtiss entailed the installation of an Allison inline engine in place of the P-36's radial, and in this form the XP-40 prototype first flew

on 14 October 1938. This design came at the time of increasing rearmament for the Army Air Corps, and large orders soon followed during 1939 when the type won an Army Air Corps fighter competition. These included export orders for France, which were not fulfilled before France's defeat in 1940. Some of these aircraft were diverted to Britain, which later became one of the principal users of the P-40 line, the initial versions supplied being called Tomahawk. The famed American Volunteer Group ('Flying Tigers') in China used the type effectively against the Japanese in 1941–1942. Deliveries to the Army Air Corps of the initial P-40 (Model 81) production version began during 1940, early models of the P-40 having a neat air intake beneath the nose. A re-design, altered armament and the addition of a more powerful Allison V-1710 inline engine

The Curtiss P-40 series, with all-metal construction and mostly powered by the Allison V-1710 inline engine shown, was best used at low level, especially as a fighter-bomber. This U.S.-operated P-40N, 'Lope's Hope,' was flown by Don Lopez, who in recent years was a leading member of the National Air and Space Museum in the U.S.A.

mark, resulted amongst other alterations in a bigger chin radiator intake, first seen in quantity on the P-40E. Equivalents of these later Warhawks for the RAF and Commonwealth forces were known as Kittyhawks. British or Commonwealth units used them particularly in the Middle East, Mediterranean and Far East. Indeed, progressive development had led by 1944 to a whole family of P-40 versions, some with re-designed rear fuselage or cockpit features. There were additionally several two-seat trainers. In response to the type's poor high altitude performance, the P-40F version was powered by the Rolls-Royce Merlin inline engine (albeit a low-altitude model). Total production, which ended in late 1944, ran to some 13,738, with many of the later examples being relegated to transition trainers for trainee fighter pilots in the United States. Other users included the Soviet Union, Turkey and Free French forces.

*Illustrative of the good use that Allied pilots put the P-40 to despite its performance and aerodynamic shortcomings, this P-40C from the American Volunteer Group ('Flying Tigers') belongs to 'Tex' Hill, one of several pilots who scored well on the P-40.*

**Specifications – Curtiss P-40C Warhawk (Tomahawk Mk.IIB)**

| | |
|---|---|
| Wingspan | 37 ft 3.5 in |
| Length | 31 ft 8.5 in |
| Maximum speed | 345 mph at 15,000 ft |
| Maximum take-off weight | approximately 7,500 lb |
| Range | 730 miles |
| Service ceiling | 29,500 ft |
| Armament | Two 0.5 in (12.7 mm) machine guns in upper forward fuselage, four wing-mounted 0.3 in (7.62 mm) machine guns, all fixed forward-firing (some examples with different caliber guns) |
| Engine | One Allison V-1710-33 inline piston engine, of 1,040 hp |
| Crew | One |

# Junkers Ju 87 'Stuka'

A legendary and arguably notorious aircraft that fought all the way through World War Two, the infamous Ju 87 'Stuka,' was conceived by people who believed in the concept of dive-bombing to deliver a bomb onto a specific target with greater accuracy than was possible with conventional 'level' bombing. Nicknamed 'Stuka' (a contraction of 'Sturzkampfflugzeug,' a German term for ALL dive-bombers), the Ju 87 became a chief instrument of the 'Blitzkrieg' or 'Lightning War' that the Germans used to great success in the early stages of World War Two.

Hitler's National Socialists came to power in Germany during 1933 and at once began developing weapons for offensive (rather than defensive) warfare, of which the Ju 87 was the most dramatic early example. It arose from the second stage of the Nazi plan to create a dive-bomber force for Germany's Luftwaffe, the first part of this plan being centered on the biplane Henschel Hs 123 (as described in Volume 1 of *The Complete Encyclopedia of Flight*). In comparison to the Hs 123, the Ju 87 was a very modern warplane of all-metal monoplane layout and construction. The original, twin-tailed prototype first flew in 1935, powered by a British Rolls-Royce Kestrel inline engine. Refinement of the basic design led to the Ju 87A, the first production model, with a conventional tailplane and German Junkers Jumo 210 inline engine. Deliveries of the Ju 87A with its distinctive 'trousered' main undercarriage to the Luftwaffe began in spring 1937 and were followed by the improved Ju 87B model in 1938 and later the related Ju 87R. The 'Stuka' was successfully combat-tested by the Germans during the Spanish Civil War on the side of the Spanish Nationalist rebels. The type was subsequently highly successful in Germany's opening campaigns of World War Two, where the aircraft's sinister undercarriage-mounted siren caused terror in addition to the destructive capacity of its bombload. However, when faced by modern, well-equipped

*The Ju 87 (seen here is a Ju 87B series aircraft) had the ability to carry an underfuselage bomb on a crutch that swung the bomb on release away from the diving aircraft to prevent the weapon from hitting the aircraft's propeller.*

fighter opposition during the Battle of Britain, the 'Stuka' was easy to defeat in air combat. Nevertheless, the Ju 87 subsequently saw considerable combat, particularly over North Africa and the Soviet Union. Later models were the refined and more powerful Ju 87D and the Ju 87G, the latter carrying a large pod beneath each wing mounting a single 37 mm cannon for anti-tank attack work. A navalised Ju 87C model was also developed, for Germany's only aircraft carrier, which was never finished. Production of the Ju 87 continued well into 1944, and eventually over 5,700 were built. In addition to German service, the Ju 87 was used by Hungary, Romania, Croatia, Slovakia, Bulgaria, and particularly Italy – Regia Aeronautica Ju 87s seeing much combat in the Mediterranean area.

*An interior view of the pilot's instrument panel and controls in a Ju 87.*

**Specifications – Junkers Ju 87B-1**

| | |
|---|---|
| Wingspan | 45 ft 3.25 in |
| Length | 36 ft 5 in |
| Maximum speed | 238 mph at 13,410 ft |
| Maximum take-off weight | 9,370 lb |
| Range | approximately 342 miles |
| Service ceiling | 26,247 ft |
| Armament | Three 7.92 mm (0.312 in) machine guns, one 1,102 lb bomb beneath the fuselage; or one 551 lb bomb beneath the fuselage and four 110 lb bombs beneath the wings |
| Engine | One Junkers Jumo 211 series inline piston engine, of 1,100–1,200 hp |
| Crew | Two |

# Fairey Swordfish

Although antiquated in appearance, the Fairey Swordfish biplane fought with gallantry and often success virtually throughout the Second World War. Developed from the private venture T.S.R.I biplane, the prototype Swordfish, initially known as the T.S.R. II, first flew on 17 April 1934. Following extensive testing in both its land plane and seaplane forms, the Swordfish was eventually ordered into production under specification S.38/34. A contract for 86 machines followed, to be powered by a 690 hp Bristol Pegasus IIIM engine, driving a Fairey three blade metal propeller. The Swordfish was constructed of a conventional fabric-covered welded steel tube fuselage, which provided accommodation for the crew of three: pilot, observer and telegraphist/air gunner. The two bay wings were of metal structure, covered with fabric and could be folded backwards about the rear spar to lay alongside the fuselage. The main landing gear com-

prised individual oleo units, which could be exchanged for floats. Offensive armament could consist of a single 18 caliber torpedo carried beneath the fuselage, or up to 1,500 lb of bombs, mines, depth charges, together with flares and smoke floats beneath the wings and fuselage. Later marks were powered by the more powerful Pegasus XXX engine and were also equipped to carry four rocket projectiles under each wing. Radar was also introduced to the Swordfish and this culminated in the Mk III, which featured a large radome for its ASV Mk.10 between the undercarriage legs. Entering service with No.825 Squadron of Britain's Fleet Air Arm in July 1936, the Swordfish rapidly

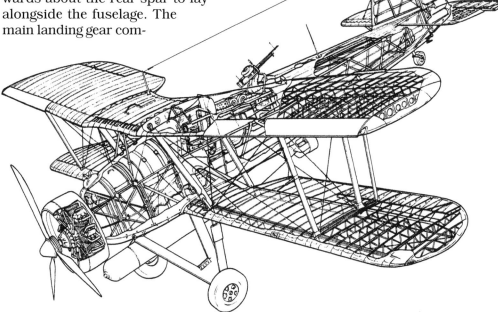

*Despite its almost 1920's appearance, the Swordfish was a rugged and dependable warplane even in the context of World War Two combat. Its wings could be folded to allow for ease of stowage within the confines of an aircraft carrier's lower deck.*

replaced the Fairey Seals, Blackburn Baffins and Sharks in the Torpedo Spotter Reconnaissance squadrons of the Royal Navy. Rearmament and the outbreak of World War Two led to increased production orders for the Swordfish, and to meet these commitments Fairey transferred production to Blackburn Aircraft of Brough, Yorkshire, with a total of 2,391 examples being produced by both firms. Best known for the highly successful raid on the Italian fleet at Taranto in November 1940, the Swordfish also distinguished itself in the Norwegian campaign of 1940, operations in the Western Desert, and in convoy operations in the North Atlantic while operating from aircraft carriers. A torpedo strike from a Swordfish disabled the German battleship Bismarck, leading to its sinking in May 1941 by British warships. A Fleet Air Arm Swordfish pilot, Eugene Esmonde, was posthumously awarded Britain's highest military gallantry award, the Victoria Cross, for his actions in attacking German battleships in the English Channel during February 1942.

*P4216 was a Swordfish Mk.I, shown here in the markings of No.821 Squadron, Fleet Air Arm. Note the torpedo beneath the aircraft's fuselage.*

**Specifications – Fairey Swordfish Mk.II**

| | |
|---|---|
| Wingspan | 45 ft 6 in |
| Length | 35 ft 8 in |
| Maximum speed | 138 mph at 5,000 ft |
| Maximum take-off weight | 7,510 lb |
| Range | approximately 570 miles |
| Service ceiling | 17,000 ft |
| Armament | one fixed and one flexible 0.303 in (7.7 mm) machine gun, one 18 in (457 mm) torpedo, or up to 1,500 lb of bombs, mines, depth charges, or (later) rocket projectiles. |
| Engine | One Bristol Pegasus IIIM radial piston engine, of 690 hp; or one Bristol Pegasus XXX radial, of 750 hp |
| Crew | Three |

# Vickers Wellington

One of Britain's three principal medium bombers at the start of World War Two (the other two being the Armstrong Whitworth Whitley and Handley Page Hampden), and arguably the most successful, the Vickers Wellington was designed like the Hampden to Specification B.9/32. Similar to its predecessor, the Vickers Wellesley, the aircraft featured geodetic construction. The prototype, designated Type 271, flew on 15 June 1936. This aircraft was destroyed in April 1937, causing the production prototype Wellington Mk.I, and all subsequent aircraft, to be fitted with revised tail surfaces adapted from Vickers' parallel project, the Vickers B.l/35, (later named Warwick). Considerable modification was also made to the fuselage design. The first Mk.I, ordered to Specification 29/36, flew on 23 December 1937, powered by two Bristol Pegasus XX radial engines. Deliveries began to Bomber Command in late 1938. Wellingtons in RAF service in September 1939 were the Pegasus-engined Mks.I and IA, the latter having slightly increased overall dimensions. The most numerous early model was the Mk.IC, which had Pegasus XVIII engines. Differing little from the Mk.IA, the fuselage of the Wellington Mk.IC was slightly revised and reshaped behind the nose turret to allow the turret greater traverse. The type also had beam gun positions to replace the earlier drag-producing ventral gun turret, and self-sealing fuel tanks. 2,685 Wellington Mk.IC were built. Wellingtons were in action right from the start of the war, at first in daylight until losses to German fighters caused the general move by the RAF to night bomber operations. The Wellington entered combat in the Middle East in 1940, and in the Far East early in 1942. By then, the principal version in service with Bomber Command was the Mk.III (1,519 built), with two 1,500 hp Bristol Hercules XI radial engines replacing the much less reliable Pegasus. The Mk.IV was powered by twin American Pratt & Whitney Wasp radial engines. Coastal Command also made good use of the versatile Wellington, employing several GR (General Reconnaissance) versions, some of which

*This Vickers Wellington Mk.III, serial number Z1572, wears the 'VR' codes of Canadian-manned No.419 Squadron, R.C.A.F. Bomber Command Wellingtons had black undersides like this during their night operations, and were crewed by airmen from many nationalities, particularly from Britain and Commonwealth countries.*

had ASV Mk.II radar and carried torpedoes. Their service included operations in the Mediterranean, where Maltese-based Wellingtons flew against Axis shipping sailing between Europe and North Africa. Some Wellingtons had a powerful Leigh Light searchlight to find surfaced U-Boats or enemy ships at night. The last bomber version of the Wellington was the Mk.X, and there were several other marks, including the GR.XII and GR.XIV anti-submarine aircraft; a special conversion for clearing mines at sea; and two pressurized high-altitude versions which did not see service. Total Wellington manufacture ran to 11,461, and some operated in the Mediterranean and elsewhere well into 1945. One Wellington crew member was awarded the Victoria Cross for gallantry. The Wellington served as a trainer after the war in Britain, and some also flew in France and Greece.

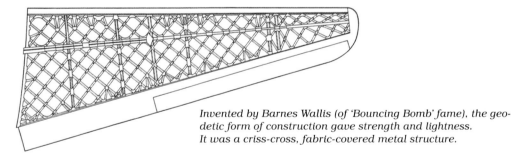

Invented by Barnes Wallis (of 'Bouncing Bomb' fame), the geodetic form of construction gave strength and lightness. It was a criss-cross, fabric-covered metal structure.

## Specifications – Vickers Wellington Mk.IC

| | |
|---|---|
| Wingspan | 86 ft 2 in |
| Length | 64 ft 7 in |
| Maximum speed | 235 mph at 15,500 ft |
| Maximum take-off weight | 28,500 lb |
| Range | 2,550 miles |
| Service ceiling | 18,000 ft |
| Armament | Two 0.303 in (7.7 mm) machine guns in nose turret, two similar in tail turret and beam positions, up to 4,500 lb of bombs |
| Engine | Two Bristol Pegasus XVIII radial piston engines, of 965 hp each |
| Crew | Six |

# Supermarine Spitfire Mk.I to Mk.VIII

Undoubtedly one of the most famous aircraft ever built, and a contender for the title of best fighter of all time, the excellent Supermarine Spitfire was the product of a fine aircraft company, Supermarine, its brilliant Chief Designer – Reginald J. Mitchell, and an equally accomplished aero engine company, Rolls-Royce. The Spitfire essentially began life as a private venture, and was helped along by Air Ministry Specification F.5/34 which required an eight-gun fighter for the Royal Air Force. Its early history is described in Volume 1 of *The Complete Encyclopedia of Flight*. The prototype, serial number K5054, powered by a 990 hp Rolls-Royce Merlin C engine, first flew on 5 March 1936, at Eastleigh airfield near Southampton in southern England. The pilot for this historic flight was Joseph 'Mutt' Summers, the Chief Test Pilot of Vickers Ltd, which took over Supermarine in 1928. Originally known as the Type 300 but eventually adopting the name Spitfire, the new aircraft was undoubtedly the most advanced fighter in the world at that time. Initial orders for production of Spitfires were for 310 aircraft, paralleling the Expansion Scheme of rearmament then developing within the RAF. The first deliveries of Spitfire Mk.I aircraft to an RAF front-line unit

reached No.19 Squadron at Duxford in August/September 1938. By the start of World War Two in September 1939, there were nine Spitfire-equipped RAF squadrons. Although RAF Spitfires saw some combat in the early months of the war, it was the Hawker Hurricane (see pages 46 to 47) which bore the brunt of the air fighting for the RAF during the Battle of France in May and June 1940. However, some Spitfires were in action during the famous evacuation of Allied forces from Dunkerque (Dunkirk). This kept much of the growing RAF Spitfire force in Britain for the air defence of Britain itself. It was just as well. The Luftwaffe's aerial assault on Britain began soon after the German victory over France in late June 1940. The ensuing aerial battle over Britain became known as the Battle of Britain, and it is the most celebrated aerial conflict in history. If ever aircraft have had a direct bearing on the course of history, then the ultimate example was the Battle of Britain, when the whole course of World War Two was changed by the success of RAF-operated Spitfires and Hurricanes against the Luftwaffe's bombing offensive. This offensive that was a prelude to the planned Nazi invasion of Britain – an invasion that never came, due to the success of

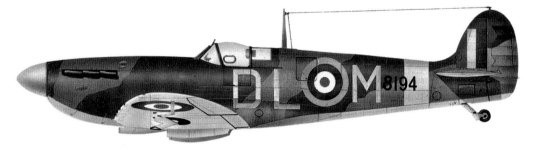

*Wearing the 'DL' coding of No.91 Squadron, RAF, this Spitfire Mk.IIA shows the classic lines of this early production Spitfire version. It has the eight-gun wing.*

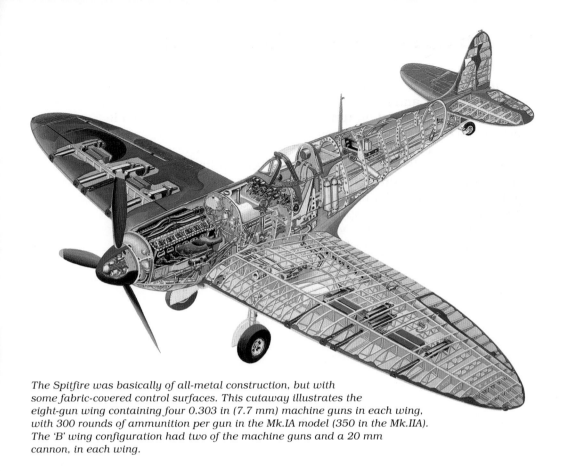

*The Spitfire was basically of all-metal construction, but with some fabric-covered control surfaces. This cutaway illustrates the eight-gun wing containing four 0.303 in (7.7 mm) machine guns in each wing, with 300 rounds of ammunition per gun in the Mk.IA model (350 in the Mk.IIA). The 'B' wing configuration had two of the machine guns and a 20 mm cannon, in each wing.*

the gallant Allied fighter pilots who flew in that great aerial conflict. The principal version of the Spitfire during that desperate time was the Mk.I, the classic Mk.IA with an eight machine gun armament (four in each wing), which was the most formidable opposition that the Luftwaffe had met up to that time. Over fifteen hundred Spitfire Mk.I (powered by the 1,030 hp Merlin II or III engine) were built, a number that would

have been unthinkable in the peaceful 1930's. They were the start of a production run that eventually extended throughout the war, and included many versions for both the RAF and the Fleet Air Arm (navalised Spitfires were called Seafires and could be operated from aircraft carriers.) There

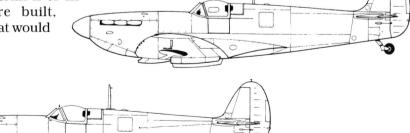

# Supermarine Spitfire Mk.I to Mk.VIII *continued*

were far too many versions to name here, but suffice to say that Spitfires eventually served on all war fronts world-wide. Everywhere they operated, they were a formidable opponent for German, Italian or Japanese aircraft.

It was realized early on in its development that the Spitfire could fulfil roles in addition to aerial fighting, and one of the earliest additional uses for the Spitfire was photo reconnaissance. The type's height and speed abilities were exploited to the full for this role, and a separate line of photo reconnaissance Spitfires was developed to provide vital intelligence of targets for bombing missions, post-strike analysis, and created much important information about occupied Europe and its defences. Indeed, Spitfires were eventually used in a variety of roles from fighter-bomber work to air-sea rescue coverage. They were used by a wide selection of

overseas operators in addition to British forces, notably the U.S. Army Air Force.

In the Far East, Spitfires were flown to great effect by the Royal Australian Air Force.

The Mk.II (920 built) was delivered from mid-1940 onwards, and continuing development led to an interim

*The interior of the Spitfire's cockpit was functional and typical of its time. It came before the era of side consoles that tidied up much of the equipment that was attached later. In the Spitfire's case, they were attached directly to the side walls and structure of the fuselage interior.*

MONTSERRAT

SPITFIRE MK.1a OF FLT. LT. FRANK HOWELL. 1940          $5

*N3029 was a Spitfire Mk.IA, seen here wearing the codes 'DW' of No.610 Squadron. This was one of the RAF squadrons that was in the thick of the action during the Battle of Britain, operating for a time from Biggin Hill airfield in Kent.*

*The Spitfire Mk.IA of Flight Lieutenant Frank Howell, of No.609 Squadron, RAF, is shown here during the Battle of Britain period bringing down a Luftwaffe Junkers Ju 87 'Stuka.'*

model that grew into one of the classic Spitfire marks, the Mk.V. This model entered widespread service in 1941, and 6,464 are believed to have been built. Many had 'clipped' wings with squared-off wing-tips, reflecting the variety of wing variations that eventually became available. Continuing development led to the Mk.VIII, which many pilots believed to be the finest Spitfire model, and thence to the superlative Mk.IX. That and further Spitfire marks are described on pages 238 to 239.

**Specifications – Supermarine Spitfire Mk.IIA**

| | |
|---|---|
| Wingspan | 36 ft 10 in |
| Length | 29 ft 11 in |
| Maximum speed | 370 mph at 18,500 ft |
| Maximum take-off weight | 6,275 lb |
| Range | approximately 395 miles |
| Service Ceiling | 32,800 ft |
| Armament | Eight fixed forward-firing 0.303 in (7.7 mm) machine guns |
| Engine | One Rolls-Royce Merlin XII inline piston engine, of 1,175 hp |
| Crew | One |

# Armstrong Whitworth Whitley

Ordered from the drawing board as part of the RAF's rearmament expansion, the Whitley was designed to Specification B.3/34 and was one of three principal medium bombers in service with Britain's RAF at the start of World War Two (the others being the Wellington and Hampden). The Whitley featured a distinctive thick wing whose angle of incidence gave the aircraft a slightly nose-down attitude in flight. The prototype Whitley first flew from Whitley Abbey on 17 March 1936. The Armstrong Siddeley Tiger radial engine in its Mk.IX and Mk.VIII (845 hp) versions powered the Whitley Marks I and II respectively. Offensive armament for the Whitley Mk.I consisted of a maximum of 4,220 lb of bombs split between the fuselage bomb bay and both inner and outer wing cells. Defensive armament consisted of a single 0.303 caliber machine gun in manually-operated turrets in the nose and tail. Later aircraft featured the addition of a power-operated nose turret, and a ventral turret containing two 0.303 machine guns. Due to its detrimental effect on performance the latter was deleted after the Mk.III production run and was often removed in service. The requirement for extra power led to the introduction of the Rolls-Royce Merlin from the Mk.IV on-wards and this engine, in its Mk.IV form (1,030 hp) enabled extra fuel to be carried and allowed the bomb load to rise to a maximum of 7,000 lb. Merlin X engines of 1,145 hp were introduced in the Whitley Mk.V and a power-operated tail turret containing four 0.303 machine guns was fitted to Whitleys from the Mk.IV onwards. The final variant of the Whitley was the Mk.VII and this model, built for the RAF's Coastal Command, featured extra fuel capacity and ASV Mk.II radar.

The Whitley entered service with No.10 Squadron at RAF. Dishforth in March 1937, and on the night of 3 September 1939 carried out leaflet raids over the Ruhr. Following Italy's entry into the war, Whitleys performed raids on Genoa and Turin on 11/12 June 1940. On 25 August 1940, the type dropped its first bombs over Berlin. The Whitley was retired from front-line service with Bomber Command in April 1942 but some examples were recalled from Operational Training Units to take part in the 1,000 bomber raid over Cologne in May 1942. One of the first successes for the Whitley Mk.VII came on 30 November 1941, when an aircraft of No.502 Squadron sank a U-Boat in the Bay of Biscay. The Whitley's latter years were spent in

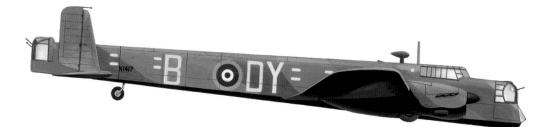

*Armstrong Whitworth Whitley Mk.V, N1417, is shown here in classic night bomber camouflage of the early war period, and wearing the 'DY' codes of No.102 Squadron, RAF.*

parachute training and operations, glider-towing and special duties operations. Fifteen unarmed aircraft were also operated by B.O.A.C. on the West Africa, Gibraltar and Malta communications/freight services. One of the last Whitleys in service was an example serving with No.734 Squadron Fleet Air Arm (an engine-handling unit) in 1946. 1,814 Whitleys were built.

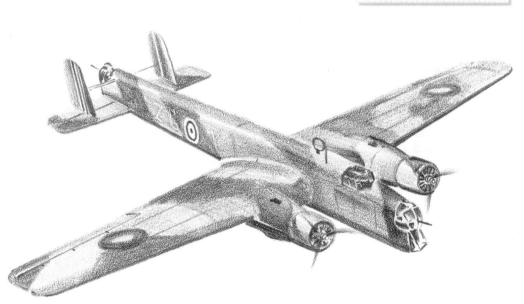

*The Whitley was an advanced aircraft when it first entered service, but was eventually replaced with newer and higher performance types. It had all-metal construction with fabric-covered control surfaces.*

### Specifications – Armstrong Whitworth Whitley Mk.V

| | |
|---|---|
| Wingspan | 84 ft |
| Length | 70 ft 6 in |
| Maximum speed | 230 mph at 16,400 ft |
| Maximum take-off weight | 33,500 lb |
| Range | 1,630 miles |
| Service ceiling | 26,000 ft |
| Armament | Five 0.303 in (7.7 mm) machine guns (four in power-operated rear turret), up to 7,000 lb of bombs |
| Engine | Two Rolls-Royce Merlin X inline piston engines, of 1,075–1,145 hp each |
| Crew | Five |

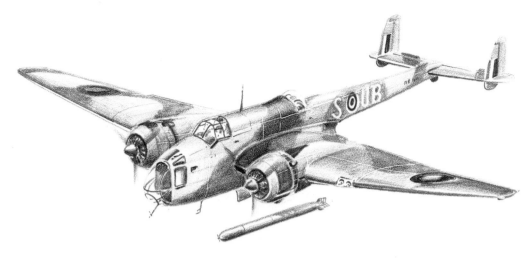

*Flight-Lieutenant Bob Linderman flies Hampden Mk.I 'S for Sugar' of No. 455 Squadron, Royal Australian Air Force, on torpedo dropping trials. This squadron was seconded to Coastal Command for these trials and many of its aircraft were eventually painted in Coastal Command gray colors.*

tually abandoned. Hampdens also served on anti-ship mine-laying operations and for meteorological reconnaissance. Two examples were re-engined with American Wright Cyclone radial engines as the Mk.II, but no production of this type resulted. However, a re-engined derivative named the H.P.53 Hereford with curious and unreliable 'H'-layout Napier Dagger inline engines was produced (150 examples), but saw little operational use and some examples were converted into Hampden configuration. Two Hampden crew members were awarded the Victoria Cross for gallentry.

**Specifications – Handley Page Hampden B.Mk.I**

| | |
|---|---|
| Wingspan | 69 ft 2 in |
| Length | 53 ft 7 in |
| Maximum speed | 265 mph at 15,500 ft |
| Maximum take-off weight | 18,756 lb |
| Range | 1,885 miles |
| Service ceiling | 22,700 ft |
| Armament | Three (later six) 0.303 in (7.7 mm) machine guns, up to 4,000 lb of bombs |
| Engine | Two Bristol Pegasus XVIII radial piston engines, of 980–1,000 hp each |
| Crew | Four |

# Messerschmitt Bf 109E and Bf 109F

One of the most famous, and arguably one of the greatest, combat aircraft of all time, the Messerschmitt Bf 109 was one of Germany's principal fighter aircraft during World War Two. The early development of this significant aircraft is described in Volume 1 of the 'Complete Encyclopaedia of Flight'. The first prototype flew in September 1935, several months before the Supermarine Spitfire (see pages 56 to 59) that became one of its main opponents in subsequent years. The Bf 109 successfully competed against three other designs in a competition for a new standard Luftwaffe fighter, gaining a development contract and going on to become very widely produced. Initial Bf 109B-1 production aircraft were delivered in February 1937. Some of these went to the Luftwaffe's premier fighter wing, JG 132 'Richthofen' (named after the First World War ace).

There was an immediate opportunity for the Bf 109 to be tried out in combat. In the Spanish Civil War the type operated very successfully on the side of the Spanish Nationalist rebels (but flown principally by German pilots), allowing it to be thoroughly combat-tested. Several production models existed before World War Two began, including the Junkers Jumo-powered Bf 109B, Bf 109C, and Bf 109D. Towards the end of the Spanish Civil War, a new and very improved Bf 109 model started to make its appearance in combat. This was the Bf 109E, and it was this mark that was the most important fighter in service with Germany's Luftwaffe in the early World War Two period. The Bf 109E introduced the Daimler Benz DB 601 inline engine of 1,100 hp, and this resulted in a slightly longer fuselage and a vari-

*One of the Luftwaffe fighter wings that was fully involved in the Battle of Britain in 1940 was JG 26 'Schlageter.' One of this unit's Bf 109E fighters is depicted here exactly as it would have looked during the Battle.*

ety of other changes compared to the Junkers Jumo-engined Bf 109D that went immediately before it. The Bf 109E started to reach Luftwaffe units in 1939, the Munich fiasco of 1938 having given the Germans a good breathing space to continue their re-armament. By the start of World War Two, the Bf 109E had almost completely replaced the Bf 109D in front-line Luftwaffe units (although some Bf 109D were still involved in combat over Poland in September 1939 along-side the Bf 109E). In the event, the Bf 109E was produced by a variety of manufacturers at various locations in Germany, in several distinct fighter and fighter-bomber models.

The Bf 109E was involved in all the Luftwaffe's early World War Two campaigns, including service in North Africa where specially-configured 'tropicalised' models were in combat. They were far superior to much of the fighter opposition that they faced in the early war years, with the notable and very important exceptions of the British Hawker Hurricane and especially the Supermarine Spitfire. The Bf 109E was the main German fighter type during the Battle of Britain, but an Achilles heel of the Bf 109 in all its various marks was a lack of range, and this was an important factor in the Luftwaffe's eventual defeat in the Battle of Britain. Nevertheless, the Bf109E was well-liked by its pilots (despite it being small and cramped, and often ground-looping due to its narrow-track main undercarriage), and many fighter pilots achieved fame and (for some) a considerable string of victories while at its controls. They included such legendary flyers as Adolf Galland, Johannes Steinhoff, and Josef Priller. Some of these pilots were amongst the top-scoring fighter 'aces' of all time. A considerable advantage for the Bf 109 over the Spitfire was the inclusion of fuel-injection for its Daimler Benz engine, allowing it the luxury of inverted flight for longer than the Spitfire with its carburettor-fed Rolls-Royce Merlin engine.

Export customers for the Bf 109E included such countries as Yugoslavia, Yugoslav-operated Bf 109s potentially flying in combat against German-operated examples during the German invasion of Yugoslavia in 1941.

*One of the famous Bf 109Es of the Battle of Britain was this Bf 109E-4 from JG 3 'Udet,' flown by Franz von Werra. It crash-landed in Kent on 5 September 1940 during the Battle, and von Werra was taken prisoner. Famously, he escaped from captivity in Canada and returned to Germany to fly once more with the Luftwaffe later in World War Two – the only German to achieve this.*

# Messerschmitt Bf 109E and Bf 109F continued

*This pristine Bf 109E is preserved in the RAF Museum at Hendon in North London*
*(Photo: John Batchelor).*

*A beautiful painting showing the lethal elegance of the Messerschmitt Bf 109E. This is the aircraft of Franz von Werra also depicted on page 65. Von Werra was immortalised by his famous escape from Allied captivity, and by the movie, 'The One That Got Away,' which dramatized his exploits.*

Partly in an effort to keep the Bf 109 competitive with developments introduced to the Supermarine Spitfire, a major improvement of the Bf 109 was attempted with the Bf 109F model. This version included a redesigned wing of different span and configuration, in addition to various other changes. Deliveries to the Luftwaffe started in 1941, and amongst the various production models there was a dedicated reconnaissance version with cameras installed. Further development led on to the Bf 109G and later types, described on Pages 236 to 237.

*Now on display at the Imperial War Museum's collection at Duxford airfield, north of London, is this Battle of Britain-vintage Bf 109E. Crash-landed in Kent during September 1940 by its JG 26 pilot Horst Perez, it languished unrestored in storage for many years at Bournemouth before the Imperial War Museum obtained it, restored it and put it on display in an excellent diorama depicting its belly-landing during the Battle of Britain.*

**Specifications – Messerschmitt Bf 109E-3**

| | |
|---|---|
| Wingspan | 32 ft 4.5 in |
| Length | 28 ft 4.5 in |
| Maximum speed | 354 mph at 12,303 ft |
| Maximum take-off weight | 5,875 lb |
| Range | approximately 413 miles |
| Service Ceiling | 36,090 ft |
| Armament | Two fixed forward-firing 7.92 mm (0.312 in) machine guns, two wing-mounted 20 mm cannons |
| Engine | One Daimler Benz DB 601A inline piston engine, of 1,100 hp |
| Crew | One |

# Fokker D.XXI

One of the great personalities in the history of early aviation in the twentieth century was Dutchman Anthony Fokker. As described in Volume 1 of *The Complete Encyclopedia of Flight*, Fokker achieved much pioneering work before World War One, and his Fokker company created several important military as well as civil aircraft. These included a famous line of fighters during the First World War for German military service, and several well-known and commercially successful airliners in the post-war period. Fokker established an American connection in the 1920's, but nevertheless continued to design and construct aircraft in Holland as well. On 27 March 1936, the first flight was made by the prototype of a neat, radial-engined monoplane fighter known as the Fokker D.XXI. This aircraft was developed by Fokker to satisfy a request for a modern fighter to serve in the Dutch East Indies. Unfortunately, changing and confused official perceptions of future fighter requirements led to the D.XXI not immediately receiving a production order. Instead it attracted an order from Finland. Seven Bristol Mercury radial-engined D.XXI were bought by the Finns plus a license agreement to build the fighter, and 93 were later built there, including 50 with American-built Pratt & Whitney radial engines, and five with the Bristol Pegasus radial. The Finnish export success renewed interest in the D.XXI in Holland and eventually 36 were ordered for the Dutch air arm for aerial defence of the Netherlands. The first of these flew in July 1938, and the last was delivered just days after World War Two began. In addition, two examples were ordered by Denmark, as well as another ten built under license by the Danes. A plan to license the building of 50 D.XXI in Spain for the air arm of the Spanish government during the Spanish Civil War ended

*A Dutch-operated Fokker D.XXI bearing the 'Three White Mice' engine cowling emblem of the 1st Ja. V. A. (fighter group) based near to Den Helder north of Alkmaar. Aircraft of this unit fought a brave battle against overwhelming odds during the German invasion of Holland in May 1940, but D.XXI No.237 (shown here) was destroyed on the ground on the first day of the German invasion.*

with the seizure of the factory by Spanish Nationalist rebels. The D.XXI in Danish and Dutch service saw brief action during the German invasions between April and May 1940 respectively. Dutch D.XXIs achieved a number of air combat victories, but were unable to stem the tide of the German invasion of the Netherlands. However, the D.XXI flew with great success in Finnish service against the Russians, especially during the Continuation War from 1941 onwards. The type remained active in Finnish service until 1949 and one model was fitted with a retractable undercarriage.

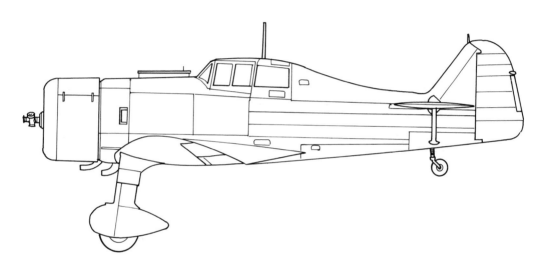

*The Fokker D.XXI was a mixture of old and new fighter technology, with predominantly wooden wings, metal fuselage partly fabric-covered, and a fixed spatted undercarriage. It was some 75 mph slower than its main opponent, the German Messerschmitt Bf 109E.*

**Specifications – Fokker D.XXI**

| | |
|---|---|
| Wingspan | 36 ft 1 in |
| Length | 26 ft 11 in |
| Maximum speed | 286 mph at 16,732 ft |
| Maximum take-off weight | 4,519 lb |
| Range | 590.5 miles |
| Service ceiling | 36,090 ft |
| Armament | Four 7.92 mm (0.312 in) machine guns |
| Engine | One Bristol Mercury VIII radial piston engine, of 760 hp |
| Crew | One |

# Fokker G.I

Among the more advanced fighters in service at the start of World War Two was the Fokker G.IA. The Dutch Fokker company was well-known during the 1920's and 1930's for its successful aircraft designs. In 1934 work began at Fokker on creating a new, advanced fighter design for Dutch military service. The design evolved as a heavy fighter, featuring the novel and somewhat revolutionary concept of a twin-boom configuration with a central fuselage nacelle. This layout was later used successfully during the Second World War by two very different aircraft types, the German Focke-Wulf Fw 189 and the American Lockheed P-38 Lightning. Also advanced in the design of the new Dutch fighter was the idea of making the planned aircraft a multi-role combat aircraft, combining the roles of fighter, fighter-bomber and reconnaissance – again unusual in the mid-1930's. The prototype G.I (sometimes written G-1)

was demonstrated at the Paris aviation exhibition in November 1936 where it caused much interest. It first flew on 16 March 1937. Originally powered by two Hispano-Suiza radial engines, the type had to be re-engined to suit Dutch military service with two British Bristol Mercury radials, so as to be powered by the same engines as contemporary Dutch military types. In fact, the G.IA (G-1A) production model, 36 of which were ordered for Dutch military service in November 1937, was somewhat different to the prototype; it was larger and heavier and with a standardized armament of eight nose-mounted machine guns – a formidable combination for its day. The first production aircraft flew on 11 April 1939, and initial deliveries to the Dutch armed forces were made in July 1939. Of mixed metal and wood construction, with fabric-covered rudders, the G.IA was of traditional manufacture. It caused much interest abroad, with Estonia, Finland, Sweden and Spain intending to order the type, and Denmark hoping for a production licence. In any event, none of

*The Fokker G.I was an elegant fighter with an excellent forward-firing armament. No. 346 was part of the batch of G.IB intended for Finland that were embargoed and reserved instead for Dutch service.*

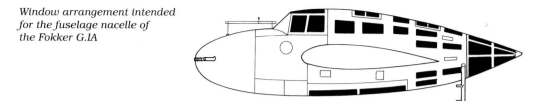

*Window arrangement intended for the fuselage nacelle of the Fokker G.IA*

these foreign sales were filled. Finland's 26 aircraft were to be of a slightly smaller G.IB (G-1B) type, but none were delivered. Completed aircraft were instead hastily taken over for Dutch service as the international situation worsened. On 10 May 1940, when the Netherlands was invaded by German forces, 23 G.IA were available for Dutch military service. In addition, three of the Finnish G.IB were quickly rushed into Dutch service. In combat against German aircraft, the type operated effectively, but there were too few to stem the inexorable tide of the German advance through the Netherlands. All but one had been destroyed or put out of action by the end of the Dutch resistance several days after the invasion. The Germans duly took over the remaining aircraft, and probably used them as trainers. Total manufacture is usually seen as 62 examples from the two production orders.

*Fokker G.I No.348 was a G.IB intended originally for Finland, but later taken over for Dutch service. It was subsequently captured by the Germans and given German markings.*

**Specifications – Fokker G.IA**

| | |
|---|---|
| Wingspan | 56 ft 3.25 in |
| Length | 37 ft 8.75 in |
| Maximum speed | 295 mph at 9,022 ft |
| Maximum take-off weight | 10,582 lb |
| Range | 876 miles |
| Service ceiling | 30,512 ft |
| Armament | Eight 7.92 mm (0.312 in) machine guns fixed forward-firing in nacelle nose, one of this caliber flexible-mounted in rear of crew nacelle, up to 661 lb of bombs |
| Engine | Two Bristol Mercury VIII radial piston engines, of 830 hp each |
| Crew | Two or three |

# Junkers Ju 88

Originally designed according to a 1935 request for a fast medium bomber for Germany's Luftwaffe, the Junkers Ju 88 became one of the most versatile and effective combat aircraft of World War Two, and was of great importance to the Luftwaffe throughout the war. The type served as a bomber, dive-bomber, close support aircraft, long-range heavy fighter, night fighter, reconnaissance aircraft and torpedo-bomber. The prototype Ju 88 flew for the first time on 21 December 1936, powered by two 1,000 hp Daimler Benz DB 600A inline engines. Although all Ju 88s had round engine cowlings, many were powered by inline engines with annular radiators which had a round appearance – although some later versions did have a radial engine, the ubiquitous BMW 801. The initial production Ju 88A-ls were just entering service as World War Two was commencing. The first operational mission – an attack on British warships – was in late September 1939.

The Ju 88A was built in various different variants up to the Ju 88A-17, with progressively uprated engines, differing defensive armament and other upgrades. The most widely used sub-type was the Ju 88A-4, which served in both northern Europe and North Africa. Indeed, Ju 88s flew on all fronts where the Luftwaffe operated, including the Balkans and the Mediterranean, attacking convoys of supplies bound for northern Russia, and on the Russian Front. Later bomber models included the Ju 88P attack/anti-tank version, plus the fast Ju 88S, which used specially-boosted engines. The Ju 88 showed its versa-

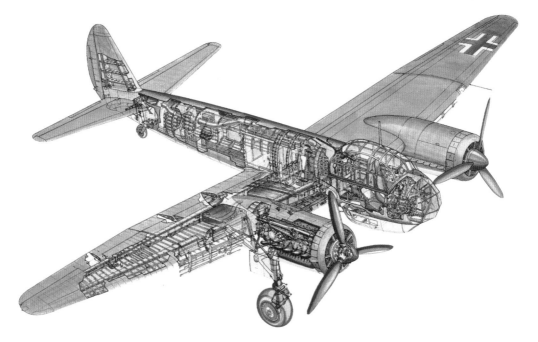

*The Junkers Ju 88 design layout had much growth potential, and a large variety of production versions and roles grew from the basic Ju 88A illustrated here. The Ju 88 was of all-metal construction and featured inline engines even though its cowlings were round.*

*There were several successful Ju 88 night fighter versions. Most had cumbersome (and drag-producing) external radar arrays such as that shown here. A number of different types of night fighter radar were fitted to Ju 88s.*

tility and considerable growth potential with the development of the Ju 88C heavy fighter. Some of the C-series were night fighters with radar, others were night intruders. Further development led to the highly-successful Ju 88G. This version featured the 'squared off' vertical tail of the Ju 188, was equipped with Lichtenstein interception radar, and was a highly effective night fighter against RAF night raids over Occupied Europe and Germany. Later fighter developments included the Ju 88R. Reconnaissance versions were the Ju 88D, Ju 88H,

and Ju 88T. The Ju 88 was additionally a major part of the 'Mistel' composite aircraft program (see pages 304 to 305).

A number of other countries operated the Ju 88, including Romania, Hungary, Italy and Finland. The Free French used captured Ju 88s against German forces in 1944. Total production of the Junkers Ju 88 is reputed to be 14,676 aircraft, built by several different companies. Continuing development through the Ju 88B led to the Ju 188 – see pages 212 to 213.

## Specifications – Junkers Ju 88A-4

| | |
|---|---|
| Wingspan | 65 ft 7.5 in |
| Length | 47 ft 3 in |
| Maximum speed | 292 mph at 17,390 ft |
| Maximum take-off weight | 30,864 lb |
| Range | 1,112 miles |
| Service ceiling | 26,902 ft |
| Armament | Seven 7.92 mm (0.312 in) machine guns in various fixed and flexible mountings, up to 4,409 lb of bombs internally and below the wings |
| Engine | Two Junkers Jumo 211J inline piston engines, of 1,350 hp each |
| Crew | Four |

# Boeing Stearman

One of the classic American light aircraft of all time, the Stearman gained immortality by being the aircraft with which many fledgling Allied pilots performed their pilot training – pilots who later flew Allied front-line combat aircraft in World War Two.

The naming of this aircraft is a story in its own right. Almost always called a Stearman, the company that actually built the majority of these aircraft was in reality a part of the Boeing aviation empire, but the name Kaydet was also applied to the type, apparently for the first time in Canada. Originally designed by the Stearman Aircraft Co., the initial biplane trainer that led to the Stearman line was the two-seat X70 design of 1933–1934. This was first adopted by the U.S. Navy, which engined its initial NS-1 production model of 1935 with the 220–225 hp Wright Whirlwind radial engine. Orders from the U.S. Army Air Corps soon followed, leading to a line of PT-13 (PT = Primary Trainer) trainers, powered by a Lycoming R-680 radial. The Model numbers 73 and 75 covered many of these aircraft. In

1938–1939, the Stearman company came under the Boeing umbrella as its Wichita subsidiary, and the considerable line of production models of the Stearman now appeared as Boeing aircraft. Manufacture for the U.S. Navy continued under the N2S-1 to –5 designations: Continental R-670 or Lycoming R-680 powered models. The U.S. Army series were the PT-13, PT-17 (Continental-powered), PT-18 and PT-27. The latter was developed for Lend-Lease deliveries to Canada, some featuring cockpit canopies and cockpit heating – most other Stearman models were open-cockpit trainers. Standardization between the U.S. Navy and the U.S. Army models came with the basically similar N2S-5 and PT-13D versions respectively. All these aircraft duly gave sterling service as primary trainers for American aircrew in the United States, while some trained British and Commonwealth aircrew in North America under the Empire Air Training Scheme. The exact number built is open to considerable debate amongst historians, but the total is certainly above 9000. In ad-

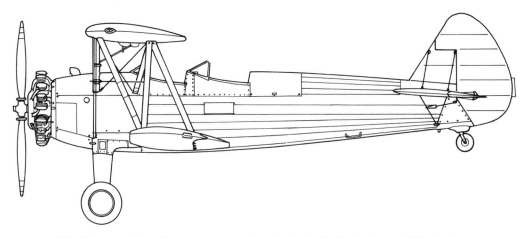

*The Stearman line of trainers was used extensively for the training of Allied pilots and included several distinct versions, although most models looked basically the same.*

dition, small numbers went to civil operators, while others (including some armed examples) were exported to such diverse countries as the Philippines, Argentina, Brazil and Venezuela. Post-war, many Stearmans were sold onto the civil market, some even acting as crop-sprayers, and a significant number survive in private hands to this day.

*The 'business' end of a preserved Stearman (Photo: John Batchelor).*

*A beautiful painting of a Stearman in its element.*
*With fabric-covered wings constructed mainly of wood and a metal fuselage structure the Stearman was a rugged aircraft with excellent handling qualities.*

**Specifications – Boeing-Stearman PT-13D Kaydet**

| | |
|---|---|
| Wingspan | 32 ft 2 in |
| Length | 25 ft 0.25 in |
| Maximum speed | 124 mph at sea level |
| Maximum take-off weight | 2,717 lb |
| Range | 505 miles |
| Service ceiling | 11,400 ft |
| Engine | One Lycoming R-680-17 radial piston engine, of 220 hp |
| Crew | Two |

# Short Sunderland

With an endurance of over 13 hours and a heavy armament, the Short S.25 Sunderland flying-boat was the ultimate maritime patrol aircraft of World War Two, and was a vital weapon in the fight against German U-Boats (submarines) to keep the sea lanes open for Allied shipping. Designed according to Specification R.2/33 for a general purpose and reconnaissance flying-boat, the Sunderland represented a huge step forward over the biplanes that fulfilled these roles for Britain's Royal Air Force in the 1920's and 1930's. The Sunderland's design drew heavily on the ground-breaking Short 'C' Class passenger flying-boats, which successfully opened up long-distance commercial air routes in the 1930's. The prototype Sunderland first flew in October 1937, and 90 Mk.I initial production examples were built by Short Brothers and Blackburn Aircraft. They entered RAF service in 1938–1939. Further development led to the more powerful Mk.II with improved armament options, 43 of this model being built from 1941. Most numerous was the Mk.III, which introduced such improvements as air-to-surface vessel (ASV) radar for surface ship and surface U-Boat hunting. Some 456 Mk.III were built, by Short and Blackburn. The final production version, the Mk.V, was introduced in 1944–1945. It was powered by four American Pratt & Whitney R-1830 series Twin Wasp radial engines of 1,200 hp each (rather than the British radials of preceding Sunderlands), and included a more advanced ASV radar whose aerials were neatly faired into underwing housings rather than the prominent external aerials of most of the Mk.III series (some Mk.III also had this equipment, as Mk.IIIA). 150 or 155 Mk.V were built by Short and Blackburn. The Sunderland Mk.IV was a developmental dead-end – created

*The Sunderland was a big aircraft, an all-metal construction with some fabric-covering of control surfaces. The large flat-topped structures in the right-hand wing are fuel tanks. This aircraft has the radar configuration of the Sunderland Mk.III, and the markings of No.10 Squadron, Royal Australian Air Force.*

for the Pacific area, it was redesignated S.45 Seaford but led mainly to the Solent civil transport flying-boat. RAF Coastal Command's Sunderlands successfully hunted submarines during World War Two, sinking approximately 31 U-Boats directly and sharing in the destruction of some fifteen others. The type also performed transport/evacuation work, air-sea rescue, and many related tasks. Some flew passengers for Britain's B.O.A.C. airline on transport duties.

Sunderlands remained in service after the war, and operated in the Berlin Airlift of 1948–1949, the Korean War of 1950 to 1953 and 1950's anti-Communist operations in Malaya. The final

RAF Sunderland was retired in May 1959, but the type continued to serve in New Zealand and France after this. Civil conversions of existing Sunderlands and further development resulted in the Sandringham civil transport flying-boat.

*The Sunderland's underwing bomb and stores racks could be retracted into the fuselage when not in use. Note the prominent ASV radar aerials on this aircraft.*

### Specifications – Short Sunderland Mk.III

| | |
|---|---|
| Wingspan | 112 ft 9.5 in |
| Length | 85 ft 4 in |
| Maximum speed | 212 mph at 10,000 ft |
| Maximum take-off weight | 58,000 lb |
| Range | approximately 3,000 miles |
| Service ceiling | 20,500 ft |
| Armament | Eight or more 0.303 in (7.7 mm) machine guns (some aircraft also had additional forward-firing armament), up to 4,960 lb of bombs, depth charges or mines |
| Engine | Four Bristol Pegasus XVIII radial piston engines, of 1, 050–1,065 hp each |
| Crew | Seven to ten |

# Miles Master

The introduction of high-performance monoplane front-line aircraft such as the Spitfire and Hurricane into service with Britain's Royal Air Force in the later 1930's created the need for a new generation of training aircraft to prepare pupil pilots to fly these modern fast combat aircraft. The Miles aircraft company recognized this growing requirement sooner than Britain's Air Ministry, and designed an advanced trainer named the Kestrel, whose top speed was only a little less than that of the Hurricane fighter.

An advanced low-wing monoplane powered by the Rolls-Royce Kestrel inline engine, the Kestrel first flew in June 1937. A year later, a slightly revised successor with various alterations was at last ordered into production under the name Master.

The initial production model, the Master Mk.I, differed from the Kestrel in several ways, including the installation of a de-rated 'training' 715 hp Kestrel engine that reduced the type's top speed but nonetheless left it with a very creditable performance for a training aircraft. 900 Master Mk.I were constructed, the first flying in March 1939. To increase the field of vision of the instructor was seated in the rear cockpit. In many Masters, his seat could be raised slightly to give a better forward view. Some were fitted with a revised windscreen and related glazing as the Mk.IA.

Of mainly wood construction, the Master Mk.I became the RAF's main advanced trainer for pupil pilots who had already learned to fly on such types as the Tiger Moth and were moving up through the pilot training syllabus towards final graduation and the eventual opportunity to fly a front-line operational type. The growing unavailability of the Kestrel engine, and the need to introduce a radial engine layout to mimic the growing number of radial-engined front-line aircraft in the RAF's inventory, led to the Bristol Mercury-engined Master Mk.II. It was followed by another radial-engined model, the Mk.III, powered by an American Pratt & Whitney Twin Wasp Junior engine of 825 hp. Total production of the Master amounted to something over 3,200 examples, including a small batch converted to fully-armed emergency fighters with a

*N7408 was a Miles Master Mk.I, and in this view it shows off the clean streamlined appearance of this advanced trainer. The Master's construction was mainly of wood.*

*There were two distinct versions of the Master which were fitted with a radial engine, the Mk.II with a Bristol Mercury, and the Mk.III with the American Pratt & Whitney Twin Wasp Junior.*

wing-mounted armament which were deployed during the dark days of the Battle of Britain. Some Masters also served as glider tug trainers, and a batch was despatched to South Africa, but their wooden airframes suffered badly en route. Further development led to a dedicated target-towing derivative, the Martinet.

**Specifications – Miles Master Mk.II**

| | |
|---|---|
| Wingspan | 39 ft<br>(some later with reduced span wings due to wing-tip squaring off) |
| Length | 29 ft 6 in |
| Maximum speed | 242 mph at 6,000 ft |
| Maximum take-off weight | 5,573 lb |
| Endurance | approximately 2 hours |
| Service ceiling | 28,000 ft |
| Armament | One fixed forward-firing machine gun on some aircraft, also provision for small bombs if required |
| Engine | One Bristol Mercury XX radial piston engine, of 870 hp |
| Crew | Two |

# Boulton Paul Defiant

During the early 1930's, the development of gun-turrets for military aircraft moved forward, particularly in France and Britain. Manned turrets were eventually adopted for many bomber aircraft of the Second World War period, but one of the first applications was made by Britain's Boulton & Paul company in the Overstrand bomber.

A lumbering biplane, the twin-engine Overstrand was nevertheless revolutionary in having a large, power-operated turret in its nose. Further work by the re-named Boulton Paul company led to the use of a turret in a modern, sleek single-engine monoplane that entered production as the Defiant. Designed to Air Ministry Specification F.9/35, the Defiant concentrated all its firepower into its turret, thus establishing a new tactical concept in which the aircraft's pilot positioned the fighter so that its gunner could get the best shot at enemy bombers.

The turret had a good field of fire especially above, the idea being to shoot at enemy bombers from below. Unfortunately no other armament was fitted, leaving the type vulnerable to fighter attack from the front. The first prototype flew on 11 August 1937, but development problems delayed operational entry with Britain's Royal Air Force until late 1939/early 1940. At first Defiants were successfully deployed as day fighters, especially over Dunkirk, but Luftwaffe pilots soon became wise to the Defiant's operational and armament limitations. After some success, accompanied by devastating losses, the Defiant found a new role as a night fighter. At first used ad hoc in this task, eventually some Defiants were fitted with early Airborne Interception (AI) radar and were operated quite successfully against German night bombers. The Defiant Mk.I was joined in production by the less numerous, slightly refined and more powerful Mk.II. The Defiant's fighter career ended in 1942,

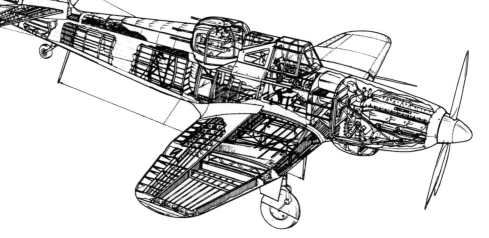

*The Boulton Paul Defiant was a sleek low-wing monoplane of modern design and construction, comprising an all-metal stressed-skin construction, with some of its control surfaces fabric-covered. Unfortunately it did not feature a forward-firing armament, instead relying solely on its turret-mounted armament. This concept proved to be operationally ineffective.*

as more capable night fighters became operational, but the type also served as an air-sea rescue aircraft carrying two air-droppable dinghies, as a target-tower, and two operated in early trials as ejection-seat development aircraft. A specialist target-towing model, the TT.Mk.III was built without the turret fitted (140 examples), and many other existing Defiants were converted to target-towing standard for gunnery training; the type served with both the RAF and the Royal Navy. Approximately 1,060 Defiants of all models (some historians quote very different figures) were built.

*Perhaps the best-known operator of the Boulton Paul Defiant for day fighter operations was the RAF's No. 264 Squadron, to which Defiant Mk.I N1535 PS-A (as illustrated here) was attached. Often flown by No. 264's commanding officer, Squadron Leader Philip Hunter, with his gunner Sergeant Fred King, this aircraft scored several successes, but was shot down into the English Channel 24 August 1940 with Hunter and his gunner aboard.*

**Specifications – Boulton Paul Defiant F.Mk.I**

| | |
|---|---|
| Wingspan | 39 ft 4 in |
| Length | 35 ft 4 in |
| Maximum speed | 304 mph at 17,000 ft |
| Maximum take-off weight | 8,350 lb |
| Range | 465 miles |
| Service ceiling | 30,350 ft |
| Armament | Four 0.303 in (7.7 mm) machine guns in power-operated dorsal turret |
| Engine | One Rolls-Royce Merlin III inline piston engine, of 1,030 hp |
| Crew | Two |

# Fairey Battle

Initially designed as a light day bomber to Specification P.27/32, the Fairey Battle was eventually built to the revised Specification P.23/35. Ordered, as were many new aircraft types of this period, from the drawing board as part of the RAF's Expansion Scheme, the Battle was a low-wing cantilever monoplane of all-metal stressed-skin construction. Provision was made for three crew consisting of a pilot, observer/navigator and wireless operator/air gunner. Power was supplied by a single Rolls Royce Merlin Mk.I engine, developing 1,030 hp. The Mark number of the Battle depended upon which mark of Merlin engine was fitted to the aircraft; the Mk.I Battle had the Mk.I Merlin fitted, the Mk.II Battle had the Mk II Merlin, and so on.

First flying on 10 March 1936, the Battle was able to carry a load of four 250 lb bombs in individual cells in the wings. A defensive armament was fitted, with one 0.303 caliber machine gun in the right-hand wing and one 0.303 caliber machine gun on a Fairey High Speed Mounting in the rear cockpit. The actual number of Battles produced is open to debate, but based on individual aircraft histories we arrive at a total of 2,202 production examples, including 1,029 built by Austin Motors of Longbridge and 18 manufactured under licence by Avions Fairey in Belgium. Approximately 360 Battles were assembled in Australia from sets of parts supplied from Britain.

Early experience with the Battle had shown that it was too slow, lacked maneuverability and was too lightly armed. This was to be painfully underlined in early operations with the type. Following the outbreak of war, Battle squadrons formed a large part of the RAF's Advanced Air Striking Force in France – and suffered heavy casualties following the German invasion of France and the Low Countries in May 1940. Despite heavy losses and often operating unescorted, Battles continued to harry the advancing enemy. On 12 May 1940, two posthumous Victo-

*The RAF's Fairey Battles fought a gallant but hopeless campaign against overwhelming German forces after the 10 May 1940 German invasion of France and the Low Countries. This Battle wears the 'HA' code letters of No.218 Squadron, RAF, during that period.*

ria Crosses were won by Flying Officer D.E. Garland and Sergeant T. Gray while leading an attack on bridges over the Albert Canal in Belgium by Battles of No.12 Squadron RAF. Other notable attacks were carried out against specific, well-defended targets in attempts to stem the German advance.

Following the fall of France the Battle was rapidly withdrawn, from front-line service. Surviving Battles served out the remainder of the war as target-towers, crew trainers, and engine test beds both in Britain and Canada, South Africa and Australia. Many Battles were converted or completed as dual-control trainers with distinctive separate cockpits.

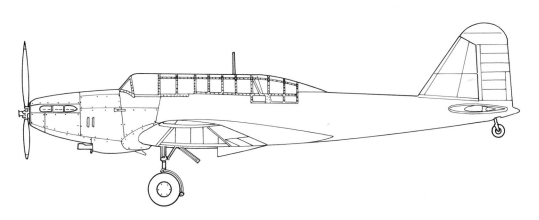

*The Battle was of all-metal construction, but with fabric-covered control surfaces. A small batch was built in Belgium in addition to British production – the Belgian-operated Battles also fought a gallant, but short-lived war against overwhelming German air superiority in May 1940.*

**Specifications – Fairey Battle Mk.I**

| | |
|---|---|
| Wingspan | 54 ft |
| Length | 42 ft 1.75 in (or slightly more) |
| Maximum speed | 257 mph at 15,000 ft |
| Maximum take-off weight | 10,792 lb |
| Range | approximately 1,000 miles |
| Service ceiling | 25,000 ft |
| Armament | One 0.303 in (7.7 mm) machine gun forward-firing wing-mounted, one similar caliber machine gun rearwards-firing flexible-mounted, up to four 250 lb bombs in wing cells |
| Engine | One Rolls-Royce Merlin I inline piston engine, of 1,030 hp |
| Crew | Three |

# Fairey Fulmar

Designed to Specification O.8/38 for a fleet fighter for service with Britain's Royal Navy, the Fulmar derived from the earlier P.4/34 light bomber project that eventually spawned the Fairey Battle (see the previous two pages). The thinking behind the Fulmar in fact represented something of a confusion of role and capability. In the later 1930's, the concept of the two-seat fighter still existed in the minds of some military planners, even though the future by then for front-line fighters lay very much with streamlined and agile single-seaters such as the Messerschmitt Bf 109 and Supermarine Spitfire. Following Fairey's confirmation to the Admiralty that their design could indeed meet the Specification's requirements, 127 examples were ordered off the drawing board. This order was increased to 250 examples with the onset of the 1938 Munich Crisis.

The Fulmar, which first flew from Ringway airfield on 4 January 1940, was of all-metal construction with folding wings, and initial production examples were powered by the Rolls-Royce Merlin VIII engine of 1,080 hp. Armament comprised an impressive array of eight wing-mounted forward-firing 0.303 caliber machine guns, four in each wing. Provision was made for a crew of two: the pilot and an observer/navigator or telegraphist/air gunner. In practice, the rear seat crew member often carried hand-held weapons such as Tommy guns, and even on occasion toilet rolls, these being released into the slipstream in order to distract a pursuing pilot from his aim! The lack of proper rearward-firing armament was a constant problem throughout the Fulmar's operational career.

*Like many aircraft that live aboard aircraft carriers, the Fairey Fulmar was a big, impressive machine. The type gave useful service to Britain's Fleet Air Arm from 1940 onwards, until the advent of such aircraft as the Fairey Firefly later in the Second World War.*

The initial order for 250 Fulmars was followed up by further orders for some 352 aircraft. These later machines were of the updated Mk II version which featured the Merlin 30 engine of 1,300 hp.

Although hampered by a relatively low top speed for a fighter, the Fulmar distinguished itself in operations escorting Malta convoys and in reconnaissance work during the hunt for the German battleship Bismarck. Along with converted Hurricanes, Fulmars operated from the converted seaplane carrier H.M.S. Pegasus, and were partly responsible for the introduction of the Catapult Armed Merchantman (CAM Ship) concept, prior to the appearance of escort carriers for convoys.

Following the commencement of night attacks by Italian aircraft in 1941, efforts were made to adapt the Fulmar to the night fighter role and, equipped with the AI (Airborne Interception) Mk.IV radar, about 100 Fulmars were converted to this role. Night fighter Fulmars were most active protecting convoys to Archangel and Murmansk in northern Russia and were the last Fulmars remaining in front line service, as late as March 1945.

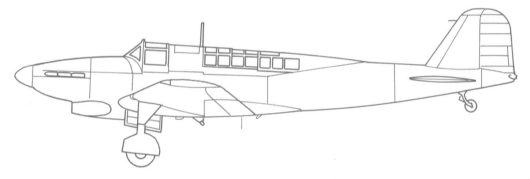

*The Fairey Fulmar was produced in two distinct versions, the Mk.I and the rather more powerful Mk.II. The design was characterized by the long fuselage accommodation for the aircraft's two crew members, although the rear seat occupant was somewhat unnecessary when the Fulmar was used purely as a day fighter.*

## Specifications – Fairey Fulmar Mk.II

| | |
|---|---|
| Wingspan | 46 ft 4.5 in |
| Length | 40 ft 2 in |
| Maximum speed | 272 mph at 7,250 ft |
| Maximum take-off weight | 9,672 lb |
| Range | approximately 780 miles |
| Service ceiling | 27,200 ft |
| Armament | Eight 0.303 in (7.7 mm) machine guns, provision in some aircraft for a similar additional rearwards-firing machine gun in the rear cockpit |
| Engine | One Rolls-Royce Merlin 30 inline piston engine, of 1,300 hp |
| Crew | Two |

# Blackburn Skua and Roc

Britain's first naval aircraft to feature all-metal construction and a retractable undercarriage, the Blackburn Skua was designed to meet Specification O.27/34 for a naval fighter/dive-bomber and was ordered into production straight from the drawing board. The prototype made its first flight on 9 February 1937. The Skua was of all-metal, stressed-skin construction and featured the then novel concept of built-in floatation compartments. Its wings had upturned tips to improve lateral stability. The wings folded backwards when required near the rear spar to lie alongside the fuselage. Rather under-powered for its fighter role, the Skua's large flaps, however, gave it great stability in a dive, making the type an excellent platform as a dive-bomber. Armament for the Skua comprised four forward-firing 0.303 calibre machine guns in the wings and a similar caliber gun for the observer on a flexible mount in the rear cockpit. One 500 lb bomb could be carried in a recess under the fuselage. Operationally, the Skua first entered service with Nos.800 and 803 Squadrons aboard H.M.S. Ark Royal in 1938 and went on to serve with distinction during the Norwegian campaign of April 1940. These two squadrons achieved one of the Skua's finest moments when operating from Hatston in the Orkneys. They sank the German light cruiser Königsberg, which was lying at Bergen. Just days later, these same squadrons were decimated during an attack on German shipping at Narvik. Skuas also provided fighter cover for the Dunkirk evacuation. They additionally took part in early operations in the Mediterranean, helping to navigate RAF Spitfires from H.M.S. Furious to Malta.

Following their withdrawal from front-line service, most surviving Skuas served as target-towers. 190 production Skuas were built. A related but different aircraft, the Blackburn Roc was designed as a fleet turret fighter and was similar in concept to the RAF's Defiant (see pages 80 to 81). The Roc first flew on 23 December 1938 and resembled the Skua in construction, but differed in having a widened fuselage to accommodate its Boulton Paul power-operated turret. The increase in side area provided by

*The Blackburn Skua has a major claim to fame: in September 1939 the first German aircraft to be shot down by British aviation elements in World War Two was a Dornier Do 18 flying-boat brought down by a Skua of No. 803 Squadron, Fleet Air Arm.*

the turret obviated the need for the up-turned wing tips of the Skua. Armament consisted of four 0.303 caliber machine guns in the power-operated turret and up to eight 30 lb bombs beneath the wings. Powered by the same engine as the Skua, the Roc struggled to attain 200 mph and was unable to catch most of its intended targets. Following a predictably brief operational career during which only one enemy aircraft, a Heinkel He 59, is recorded as being damaged, the Roc was relegated to second-line duties as a target-tower and fleet requirements aircraft. A floatplane version was studied, but did not enter production. 136 Rocs were built.

*Something of a failure, the Blackburn Roc was conceived along the same lines as the Boulton Paul Defiant. Dimensionally it was similar to the Skua, but manufacturer's data shows that it was 2 in shorter in wingspan and had inferior performance.*

## Specifications – Blackburn Skua

| | |
|---|---|
| Wingspan | 46 ft 2 in |
| Length | 35 ft 7 in |
| Maximum speed | 225 mph at 6,500 ft |
| Maximum take-off weight | 8,228 lb |
| Range | 760 miles |
| Service ceiling | 19,100 ft |
| Armament | Four fixed forward-firing 0.303 in (7.7 mm) machine guns, one similar caliber weapon in the rear cockpit, one 500 lb bomb beneath the fuselage and up to eight 30 lb bombs beneath the wings |
| Engine | One Bristol Perseus XII radial piston engine, of 890 hp |
| Crew | Two |

# Arado Ar 196

The incredible scope and extent of German rearmament following the accession to power in Germany early in 1933 of Hitler's National Socialists had seen a huge expansion not only of Germany's military aviation elements, but of other armed services as well. The German navy, eventually titled the Kriegsmarine, had also massively expanded. An important feature of Germany's new capital ships was their ability to deploy float-equipped aircraft for observation and other duties – such aircraft could be catapult-launched from suitable platforms on the otherwise cramped decks of these ships. Germany was not alone in the use of catapult seaplanes like this, but Germany's Luftwaffe became an important operator of this type of aircraft. In 1936 the German air ministry issued a specification for a new generation of catapult seaplane to replace existing Heinkel He 60 biplanes then in service. The German companies

Focke-Wulf and Arado responded to this request; the former with a biplane design and the latter with a neat monoplane called the Ar 196. It resembled the earlier biplane Ar 95 already being developed by Arado. Eventually two Ar 196 prototypes were evaluated during the summer of 1937 not long after their first flights, in a competitive examination against the rival Focke-Wulf design. The Arado aircraft were the clear winners. Early prototype Ar 196's were in fact either of the twin-float design, or had a single underfuselage float together with underwing outrigger floats. The former layout entered production as the Ar 196A. Of basically all-metal construction and with some metal and some fabric covering, the Ar 196A was the last-ever production German floatplane.

The initial batch of Ar 196A-1 went into service in 1939 as catapult-seaplanes aboard several major German warships. The Ar 196A-2 model that fol-

*The '7R' code carried by this Arado Ar 196A identifies it as belonging to SAGr. 125(the designation standing for Seeaufklärungsgruppe or maritime reconnaissance group)or its immediate predecessor Aufkl.Gr.(See) 125. This unit operated the Ar 196 as well as the Blohm und Voss Bv 138 flying-boat for over-water patrol missions.*

lowed it was for coastal patrol, and was more heavily-armed for attacks against shipping and to harass Royal Air Force Coastal Command aircraft particularly over the Bay of Biscay. This version entered service in early 1940, and was followed into service in the spring of 1941 by the major production model, the Ar 196A-3. This version was a strengthened and better equipped model, and was followed by the catapult-capable Ar 196A-4. The final production version was the more heavily-armed Ar 196A-5, and production ceased in 1944 after over five hundred of all types had been built (although some historians argue that the total was less than five hundred). In addition to the manufacture by Ara-

*An Ar 196A in its element, on the catapult aboard a German warship*
*(Photo: via Hans Meier).*

do, a French factory also constructed some examples, as did Fokker in Holland. The Ar 196 was also operated by Romania and Bulgaria.

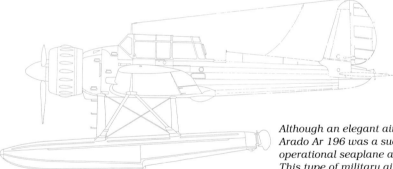

*Although an elegant aircraft, the Arado Ar 196 was a successful operational seaplane as well. This type of military aircraft has completely died out since that time.*

### Specifications – Arado Ar 196A-3

| | |
|---|---|
| Wingspan§ | 40 ft 9.75 in |
| Length | 35 ft 11.5 in |
| Maximum speed | 199 mph at 2,953 ft |
| Maximum take-off weight | 7,282 lb |
| Range | 497 miles |
| Service ceiling | 22,966 ft |
| Armament | Two 20 mm cannon fixed forward-firing in wings, one 7.92 mm (0.312 in) machine gun forward-firing in fuselage, one similar caliber machine gun flexible-mounted in rear cockpit, two 110 lb bombs beneath wings |
| Engine | One BMW 132K radial piston engine, of 960–970 hp |
| Crew | Two |

# Bloch M.B.151 and M.B.152

At the start of World War Two, several fighter designs were being either developed or actively delivered to the French air force (the Armée de l'Air). These included the Morane-Saulnier M.S.406 (Volume 1 of *The Complete Encyclopedia of Flight*), and the very capable Dewoitine D.520 (see pages 40 to 41). However, French rearmament had started too late to match the growing threat from Nazi Germany, and several of the French fighter and bomber designs that were hastily coming into service were a less than adequate match for the increasing excellence of Germany's Luftwaffe. One such fighter was the Bloch M.B.151/152 series.

Development of this type started from a 1934 French Air Ministry specification for a modern fighter that was subsequently much revised. Although a modern design with all-metal construction, the prototype M.B.150 failed to get airborne for its first flight in July 1936. Re-designed and revised, it first flew on 29 September 1937 – showing a considerable loss of time from the original specification of 1934. Further re-design and development improved the type so that it was ordered into production, but additional revision was needed to prepare it for series manufacture. This led to the first production model, the M.B.151, not flying until 18 August 1938. Powered by a 920 hp Gnome-Rhone 14N35 radial engine, the type saw limited production but was eventually outnumbered by a more powerful derivative, the M.B.152. This new model first flew in December 1938. Unfortunately, deliveries to the French air force subsequently encountered many problems, with a lack of propellers and gunsights being but two problems, and few of the initial production aircraft were combat ready. Continued engine cooling problems had already led to some re-design of the engine cowling, and this difficulty

*The Bloch M.B.151 and M.B.152 were not particularly successful in their one major period of combat, the Battle of France in May/June 1940. However, after the war, their creator, Marcel Bloch, changed his name to Marcel Dassault. Today the Dassault company is one of the world's leading combat aircraft manufacturers.*

continued during series manufacture. The production aircraft were built by various factories within France's nationalized aircraft industry, and a sufficient number were in service in May 1940 for the type to be at the forefront of the aerial fighting against the German invasion of France. In combat the M.B.152 did not perform particularly well, even though it was maneuvrable with a reasonable gun platform. Too few were in service.

Following the defeat of France, the M.B.152 continued to fly with Vichy French forces, but few survived to the end of the war. Further development and design revision, however, led to the improved M.B.155. This aircraft was just entering service in the summer of 1940, and a number later flew with the Vichy French. A further improved design, the M.B.157, flew during the Vichy French era and showed an excellent top speed of some 441 mph, but was not placed in production.

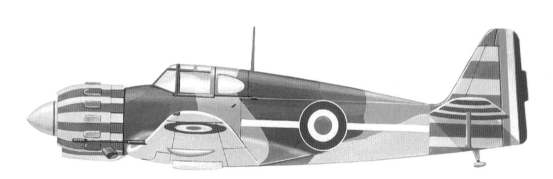

*A Bloch M.B.152 showing the distinctive yellow and red striping, and the white fuselage line, characteristic of Vichy French-operated aircraft. A small number of M.B.151 are believed to have been supplied to Greece, and M.B.152 production was probably just less than five hundred.*

**Specifications – Bloch M.B.152C.1**

| | |
|---|---|
| Wingspan | 34 ft 7 in |
| Length | 29 ft 10.5 in |
| Maximum speed | 316 mph at 13,125 ft |
| Maximum take-off weight | 6,058 lb |
| Range | 336 miles |
| Service ceiling | 32,808 ft |
| Armament | Four 7.5 mm (0.295 in) machine guns wing-mounted, or two 7.5 mm (0.295 in) machine guns and two 20 mm cannons wing-mounted |
| Engine | One Gnome-Rhone 14N49 radial piston engine, of 1,060 hp |
| Crew | One |

# Nakajima B5N

One of the most famous and fateful dates of World War Two was 7 December 1941. On that infamous Sunday morning, the American naval base and facilities at Pearl Harbor in Hawaii were attacked by aircraft carrier-based warplanes of the Japanese naval air arm. The Japanese attacks were highly successful, and the resulting response from the United States was to enter World War Two on the Allied side – an act that ultimately led to the total defeat of the Axis powers including Japan.

One of the Japanese aircraft types involved in the Pearl Harbor strike was the Nakajima B5N, a carrier-based torpedo and level tactical bomber that was originally conceived in the mid-1930's. Designed in response to a Japanese naval requirement for a carrier-based attack aircraft, the Nakajima design was a very neat streamlined attack aircraft whose layout seems to

have been influenced by a Northrop design from the United States. The prototype first flew in January 1937, with production go-ahead later that year. Some of the initial production B5N1 aircraft saw combat service with Japanese forces in the war against China prior to the outbreak of World War Two. The original B5N2, which was followed in production by the improved and more powerful B5N2, which entered service in 1940. Many of the former were then relegated for use as trainers, like the B5N1-K. The B5N2 could be used as a torpedo bomber or for level bombing, and just over one hundred and forty B5N participated in the two waves of the Pearl Harbor attack in December 1941. The type continued to serve in the early years of Japan's war against the United States in the Pacific, although it was increasingly vulnerable as more advanced American fighters began to gain the upper hand in the air war. Their final front-line operational use was in 1944, although the

*The Nakajima B5N 'Kate' could be used as a level bomber or as a torpedo-carrier, and featured folding wings so that it could fit in the confined space aboard aircraft carriers.*

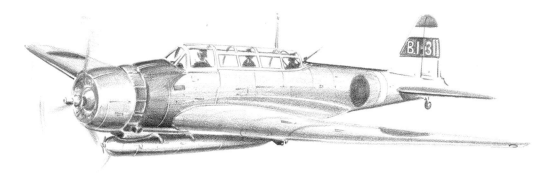

*During the Japanese strike against Pearl Harbor in December 1941, 'BI' coded Nakajima B5N torpe-do-bombers operated from the aircraft carrier 'Soryu' in the first of two waves during the attack.*

type continued to be employed for maritime patrol duties – some examples were reputedly fitted with an early form of air-to-surface radar. Total production is believed to have been 1,149 examples from three manufacturers. The B5N series was known to the Allies for identification purposes as 'Kate.'

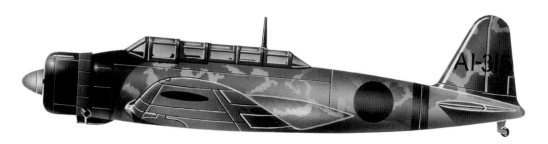

*The Nakajima B5N was a sleek and rather elegant aircraft for its time, and was a useful attack aircraft in the early phases of the war in the Pacific during World War Two.*

**Specifications – Nakajima B5N2**

| | |
|---|---|
| Wingspan | 50 ft 11 in |
| Length | 33 ft 9.5 in |
| Maximum speed | 235 mph at 11,811 ft |
| Maximum take-off weight | 9,039 lb |
| Range | 1,237 miles |
| Service ceiling | 27,100 ft |
| Armament | Up to four (in later production examples) 0.303 in (7.7 mm) machine guns, one 1,764 lb torpedo or equivalent bomb load |
| Engine | One Nakajima Sakae 11 radial piston engine, of 970–1,000 hp |
| Crew | Two or three |

# Fiat C.R.42 Falco

Although most principal aircraft-producing countries had advanced to the design and manufacture of monoplane fighter and bomber aircraft by the start of World War Two, one country in particular persisted with the biplane fighter concept longer than most. This was Italy, and the Italian air force continued to employ biplanes of indigenous manufacture well into World War Two. During the 1930's the famous Fiat company produced an important biplane fighter design called the C.R.32. Although it proved effective in the skies over Spain during the Spanish Civil War, the C.R.32 was outclassed though still widely-used as a front-line type by the start of Italy's involvement in the Second World War in June 1940. By that time Fiat was producing a successor to the type called the C.R.42. Developed to requirements of the Italian air ministry, Fiat's designers refined their earlier successful biplane concepts and added a Fiat A.74 radial engine – the C.R.32 had been inline engined.

Deliveries of the C.R.42 to Italy's Regia Aeronautica began in 1939, comparatively soon after the first flight. The C.R.42 was of all-metal construction with some metal and much fabric covering. Its neatly enclosed undercarriage was fixed, and it had the familiar open cockpit favored by Italian pilots. Italian-operated C.R.42s were in action early in Italy's involvement in World War Two with attacks on southern France in June 1940, and against Britain from bases in Belgium later in 1940. The type also participated in the war against Greece in 1941, but saw most action in North Africa. Successful against some Allied fighter types, the C.R.42 was outclassed by more modern Allied fighters that it later met such as the monoplane Hawker Hurricane. The C.R.42 was duly

*Highly maneuverable and well-liked by its pilots, the Fiat C.R.42 was one of the world's last biplane fighters. It was often called Falco (Hawk or Falcon).*

relegated to ground attack duties, and some were used for night attack and as makeshift night fighters with rather optimistic searchlights fitted beneath their wings. Special models included the C.R.42 AS, with a sand filter for operations in the desert. Some were converted into two-seat trainers, and several survived the war in Italy to serve as trainers post-war.

The C.R.42 won early export success in Belgium, and at least 34 were supplied. However, these played little part in the rapid Belgian defeat after the German invasion of May 1940. Other export users were Hungary, which operated the type in action on the Eastern Front alongside German forces against the Russians. Sweden also flew the C.R.42 (as the J 11), receiving 72 examples, some remained in service until 1945 after which several were used as target-towers. Most historians agree that 1,781 C.R.42 were built. Contemporary with the C.R.42 was the Fiat G.50 monoplane fighter (see pages 120 to 121).

*The Fiat C.R.42 featured the Warren truss-like wing strut arrangement characteristic also of the preceding C.R.32. Italian-operated C.R.42 day fighters were rarely fitted with a radio.*

**Specifications – Fiat J 11 (C.R.42)**

| | |
|---|---|
| Wingspan | 31 ft 10 in |
| Length | 27 ft 1 in (or possibly longer) |
| Maximum speed | 267 mph at 17,487 ft |
| Maximum take-off weight | 5,060 lb |
| Range | 482 miles |
| Service ceiling | 33,465 ft |
| Armament | Two 12.7 mm (0.5 in) machine guns fixed forward-firing in upper forward fuselage |
| Engine | One Fiat A.74 R1C.38 radial piston engine, of 840 hp |
| Crew | One |

# North American T-6 Texan/Harvard

Equally as famous as some front-line combat aircraft, the North American Aviation Texan (Harvard to the British and Commonwealth) was a high-performance trainer that provided the advanced training required by future Allied warplane pilots of the Second World War. Despite its eventual fame and widespread production, the type actually had humble beginnings as an unpretentious open cockpit fixed undercarriage trainer. This was the North American NA-16, developed in response to a U.S. Army Air Corps requirement for a basic trainer. It first flew on 1 April 1935. Some re-design led to the Wright Whirlwind radial engined BT-9 series for the U.S. Army (BT = Basic Trainer), and the differently-powered NJ series for the U.S. Navy. This type had a fixed undercarriage, and some of the early models had fabric covering on their fuselages. Export successes included orders from France for the related NA-57/NA-64. Further development with the NA-26, which had a retractable undercarriage and Pratt & Whitney R-1340 radial engine, met a U.S. Army requirement for a basic combat trainer, leading to the BC-1 (BC = Basic Combat) series. There were several different combinations of rounded rudders, rounded wingtips and other airframe alterations on these early machines – before the distinctive triangular fin/rudder shape and squared-off wingtips that so characterized the majority of the Texan/Harvard line were finally adopted. The definitive shape appeared on the BC-1A. Thereafter, versions for the U.S. Army were re-designated as AT-6 (AT = Advanced Trainer), with equivalent

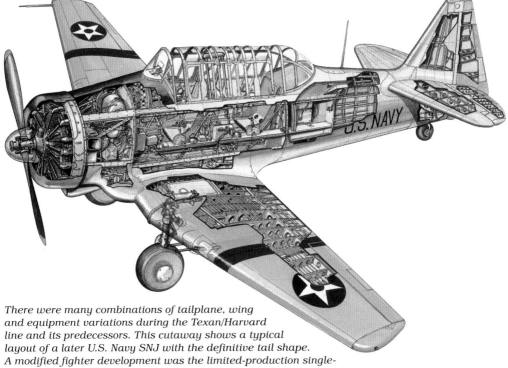

There were many combinations of tailplane, wing and equipment variations during the Texan/Harvard line and its predecessors. This cutaway shows a typical layout of a later U.S. Navy SNJ with the definitive tail shape. A modified fighter development was the limited-production single-seat P-64, and also related was the Commonwealth Wirraway line in Australia (see pages 290 to 291).

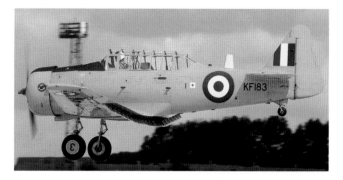

*Three Harvards remained in service in Britain well after most of their fellow Harvards had been withdrawn from use, one of them being shown here (Photo: John Batchelor).*

models for the U.S. Navy, called SNJ. The Navy's SNJ-5 and the Army Air Force's AT-6D, for example, were direct equivalents, but some of the early SNJ examples were comparable to the BC-1 line. There was provision for armament training in addition to pilot training, and some armed examples actually served in the Pacific with the U.S. Marine Corps. The AT-6 was known as Texan to some of its American users, but a parallel line of Harvard trainers was produced for Britain and the Commonwealth. Many of these served in the large Empire Air Training Scheme. The AT-6 (T-6 after 1948) line eventually served world-wide for training purposes, particularly post-war when many were exported, and after the war production continued in Canada. Texans or Harvards flew in combat as light attack aircraft in many places after the war, users included France (in Alge-

ria), Spain, the U.S. Air Force (in Korea), Britain (in Kenya), Portugal (in Angola). Approximately 17,096 of all Texan/Harvard versions, including their direct predecessors, were produced.

*This gleaming late-model AT-6 or SNJ illustrates the all-metal construction and fuselage skin of later Texans.*

**Specifications – North American SNJ-5**

| | |
|---|---|
| Wingspan | 42 ft 0.25 in |
| Length | 29 ft 6 in |
| Maximum speed | 205 mph at 5,000 ft |
| Maximum take-off weight | 5,300 lb |
| Range | 750 miles |
| Service ceiling | 21,500 ft |
| Armament | One 0.3 in (7.62 mm) machine gun fixed forward-firing in upper forward fuselage, one similar flexible-mounted in rear cockpit (some aircraft unarmed, some with wing guns) |
| Engine | One Pratt & Whitney R-1340-AN-1 Wasp radial piston engine, of 550 hp |
| Crew | Two |

# Handley Page Halifax

The Handley Page Halifax was one of the three four-engined heavy bombers that Britain's Royal Air Force operated to such devastating effect during World War Two. The other two, the Avro Lancaster and Short Stirling, are also worthy of note. The prototype H.P.57 Halifax first flew on 25 October 1939.

Often overshadowed by the exploits of the Lancaster, the Halifax (like the Lancaster) was developed from an unsuccessful twin-engined design. That was the Rolls-Royce Vulture-engined H.P. 56, designed to Specification P.13/36. The first RAF squadron to use the Halifax was Bomber Command's No.35 Squadron, the type going into action in March 1941. There was a variety of Halifax production versions, early models were identified by a system unique to Handley Page. Early production aircraft were Rolls-Royce Merlin-engined Halifax Mk.Is, including the Mk.I Series I, which was followed by the Mk.I Series II with a higher maximum take-off weight, and the Series III, with increased fuel tankage. The first major modification appeared in the Mk.II Series I, which had a two-gun dorsal turret and uprated Merlin XX engines. The Mk.II Series I (Special) had a fairing in place of the nose turret, plus revised engine exhausts. The Mk.II Series IA was the first variant to introduce a neat and streamlined drag-reducing molded Perspex nose (this became a feature on all subsequent Halifaxes), a four-gun dorsal turret, and Merlin 22 engines. The Mk.II Series IA also introduced rectangular vertical tail surfaces, because control problems had been experienced with the original 'triangular' tail shape. To further satisfy the statisticians, versions of the Mk.II Series I (Special) and Series IA, with modified undercarriages, were designated Mk.V Series I (Special) and Mk.V Series IA. The Halifax Mk.III, powered by four 1,615 hp Bristol Hercules XVI radial engines, was arguably the most important Halifax version. There were also the Hercules-powered Mks.VI and VII, which were the ultimate bomber versions, which were produced in relatively small numbers. Some Halifax IIIs, Vs and VIIs were specially-configured for paratroop dropping and glider-towing – the Halifax was the only British aircraft capable of towing the Hamilcar vehicle-carrying glider (see pages 204 to 209). The Halifax Mk.VIII, developed late in the war, was a transport version with faired-over gun positions and a detachable freight pan-

*A Handley Page Halifax Mk.III wearing the markings of No.78 Squadron, RAF. The RAF's wartime Bomber Command contained many nationalities (as indeed did Fighter Command), including a complete Group (No.6 Group) of Canadian squadrons that flew the Halifax.*

nier under the fuselage. The final Halifax version was another transport, the Mk.IX, but this only served post-war. A number of Halifaxes also operated with RAF. Coastal Command as long-range shore-based maritime patrol aircraft, alongside Liberators and Flying Fortresses. The total Halifax production figure of 6,176 examples plus two prototypes includes just over two thousand Mk. IIIs. During World War Two, Halifaxes dropped approximately 227,610 tons of bombs. A post-war civil derivative/conversion was the Halton transport.

*The cockpit of the Halifax was fairly typical of its period.*
*Note in particular the engine controls for the four engines in the center.*

### Specifications – Handley Page Halifax B.Mk.III

| | |
|---|---|
| Wingspan | 104 ft 2 in (early aircraft had slightly less) |
| Length | 71 ft 7 in |
| Maximum speed | 282 mph at 13,500 ft |
| Maximum take-off weight | 65,000 lb |
| Range | 1,985 miles |
| Service ceiling | 24,000 ft |
| Armament | Nine 0.303 in (7.7 mm) machine guns (including two four-gun turrets), up to 13,000 lb of bombs |
| Engine | Four Bristol Hercules XVI radial piston engines, of 1,615 hp each |
| Crew | Seven |

# Fairey Albacore

Although chiefly remembered as the aircraft that was out-lived by the Fairey Swordfish (see pages 52 to 53), the design that it was intended to replace, the Albacore nevertheless achieved considerable distinction during its operational career. Designed to Specification S.41/36 for a three-seat Torpedo Spotter Reconnaissance aircraft for Britain's Royal Navy as a replacement for the Swordfish, the Albacore was ordered from the drawing board as a part of Britain's hastily-conceived rearmament plans prior to World War Two. The first prototype flew on 12 December 1938 at Fairey's Great West Aerodrome (now a part of London's Heathrow Airport). The Albacore's fuselage was basically an all-metal monocoque, with fabric-covered metal wings

which hinged about the rear spar to fold alongside the fuselage. Power was supplied by a Bristol Taurus II sleeve valve radial engine of 1,065 hp (later a Taurus XII of 1,130 hp was substituted). Accommodation was provided for a crew of three – pilot, observer and telegraphist/air gunner. Defensive armament comprised of one 0.303 in (7.7 mm) machine gun in the right-hand wing and twin 0.303 in (7.7 mm) machine guns on a flexible mounting in the rear cockpit. Offensive armament consisted of a torpedo carried under the fuselage, or up to 2,000 lb of bombs or depth charges, carried beneath the wings.

Operationally the Albacore is best remembered for its torpedo attacks on the Italian battleship Vittorio Veneto at

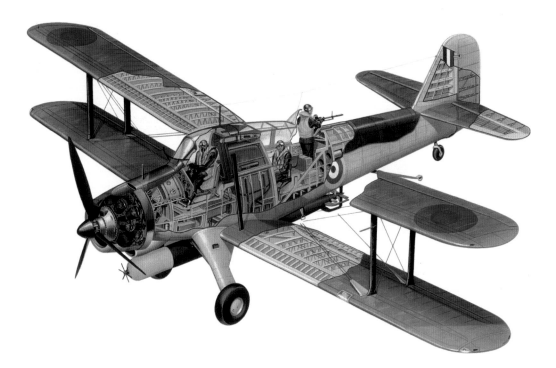

*The three-man Albacore featured folding wings to allow it to be stored below deck within the confines of its aircraft carrier when not in use. The type operated from 1940 onwards.*

the Battle of Cape Matapan, and for its anti-shipping operations from Malta against Axis supply convoys crossing the Mediterranean to North Africa. Unusually for a naval aircraft, the Albacore really came into its own in land-based night bombing and flare-dropping operations in support of the Eighth Army in the Western Desert, where the quietness of its sleeve valve engine often gave it the vital element of surprise. The first that the enemy sometimes knew of the attacks was when the bombs and flares began to fall. Albacores were also active during Operation 'Torch,' the Allied invasion of North Africa in late 1942, when a number of aircraft were badly mauled by Vichy French-operated Dewoitine D.520s. The final operational role for the Albacore was with No.415 Squadron, Royal Canadian Air Force, carrying out night-time anti-shipping strikes in support of the Normandy landings of 6 June 1944. Approximately eight hundred Albacores were built.

*The Fairey Albacore has always been overshadowed by the much more famous Fairey Swordfish, the biplane which it was theoretically supposed to replace in Britain's Fleet Air Arm.*

**Specifications – Fairey Albacore Mk.I**

| | |
|---|---|
| Wingspan | 50 ft |
| Length | 39 ft 10 in |
| Maximum speed | 161 mph at 4,000 ft |
| Maximum take-off weight | 10,460 lb |
| Range | 930 miles |
| Service ceiling | 20,700 ft |
| Armament | One fixed forward-firing and two flexible rearward-firing 0.303 in (7.7 mm) machine guns, one 1,610 lb torpedo beneath the fuselage or up to 2,000 lb of bombs or depth charges beneath the lower wings |
| Engine | One Bristol Taurus II radial piston engine, of 1,065 hp |
| Crew | Three |

# Short Stirling

The Short Stirling was designed to Specification B.12/36, itself a development of specification P.13/36 for a bomber transport. It was one of the three four-engined heavy bombers that the RAF used during the war, alongside the Avro Lancaster and Handley Page Halifax. The wingspan of the Stirling was under 100 ft to keep the aircraft's weight under control, and to assist in hangar storage. This resulted in a higher angle of attack for the wing and gave the Stirling its characteristic tall undercarriage. This 'short' wing span led to a lack of maneuverability, other than at low level, and restricted the type's operational ceiling.

Prior to the first flight of the prototype Stirling, Short constructed a half-scale flying model of the aircraft known as the S.31. This was powered by four small Pobjoy Niagara engines and, following its first flight on 19 September 1938, was used to test the type's potential flight characteristics. The first full-size prototype Stirling (Short S.29) first flew on 14 May 1939, and was powered by four 1,375 hp Bristol Hercules II engines. The Mk.I Stirling had the 1,595 hp Hercules XI engine, and the 1,650 hp Hercules XVI was fitted in the Mk.III Stirling. This engine type continued to be used in subsequent Stirling variants. The Stirling had a large bomb-carrying capacity of some 14,000 lb in the fuselage and inner wing cells. Alternatively 2,000 lb mines could be carried in the fuselage bomb bay. This bomb bay did not, however, allow carriage of any bomb larger than 2,000 lb. Towards the end of the type's operational service, a number of Stirlings were fitted

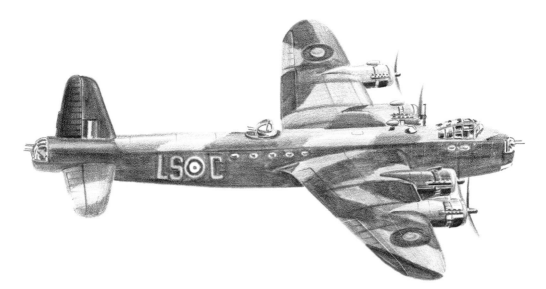

*Illustrated here by an aircraft of No.XV (15) Squadron, RAF, the Short Stirling was a big bomber that never won the publicity accorded to its contemporary, the Avro Lancaster.*

with H2S radar for the pathfinder role – this radar, and other bombing aids that became operational as the war progressed, was also available for use with other Allied heavy bombers.

The Stirling first entered service with No.7 Squadron, RAF in August 1940 and flew its initial operational mission in February 1941. Notable targets attacked by Stirlings included Berlin, Emden, Hamburg, Milan and Turin. Owing to the restrictions on its performance and load-carrying capacity, the Stirling began to be phased out of Bomber Command service from late 1943, flying its final operational mission in September 1944. Two Stirling crew members were posthumously awarded the Victoria Cross for gallantry. Although the Stirling's days as a bomber drew to a close, the Mk.IV was used as a glider tug and featured prominently in the D-Day landings, the Arnhem assault, and the crossing of the Rhine. The Mk.V Stirling was built as a dedicated transport aircraft able to carry forty troops or twelve stretchers. Twelve of these Mk.Vs were converted to civil use and exported, post-war, to Belgium. Including the two prototypes, production of the Stirling totalled 2,383 examples.

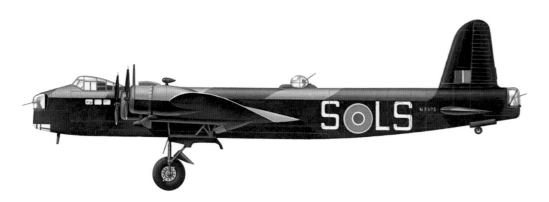

*Serial number N3675 was a Short Stirling Mk.I, and is shown here wearing the 'LS' code letters of No.XV (15) Squadron, RAF. The Stirling's tall, gawky undercarriage is evident in this drawing.*

## Specifications – Short Stirling B.Mk.III

| | |
|---|---|
| Wingspan | 99 ft 1 in |
| Length | 87 ft 3 in |
| Maximum speed | 270 mph at 14,500 ft |
| Maximum take-off weight | 70,000 lb |
| Range | 2,010 miles |
| Service ceiling | 17,000 ft |
| Armament | Eight 0.303 in (7.7 mm) machine guns, two in nose and dorsal turrets, four in tail turret, up to 14,000 lb of bombs |
| Engine | Four Bristol Hercules XVI radial piston engines, of 1,650 hp each |
| Crew | Eight |

# Supermarine Stranraer

Something of an anachronism by the early phases of World War Two, the Stranraer was nevertheless representative of the large flying-boats and amphibians that graced the skies in the service of various military air arms in the late 1930's and early 1940's. Developed by the same company that produced the famous Spitfire fighter, the Stranraer also shared the same designer – R.J. Mitchell. There the similarity ended. The Stranraer was a big, heavily-braced biplane that was the most developed form of the series of biplane flying-boats that were designed and built for Britain's RAF by Supermarine. This line started with the impressive, twin-engined Southampton of the 1920's, which was a successor to the Felixstowe flying-boats of World War One. The Supermarine line thence progressed to the Scapa of the early 1930's, before further development led to the Stranraer. Named after a coastal town in western Scotland and developed to Specification R.24/31,

the Stranraer was larger than the Scapa and featured a sturdy metal fuselage (hull), but retained the heavily strut and wire-braced biplane configuration of its predecessors. Originally named Southampton V, the Stranraer was intended for coastal patrol and general service duties in British skies and overseas around some of Britain's far-flung territories, with an endurance of some nine hours. The prototype flew in July 1934, and initial deliveries were made to the RAF for operational use in 1937. A total of 17 were built in addition to the prototype, and 15 were still active at the start of World War Two. They continued in service on anti-submarine and general patrol duties during the early war period, but in October 1942, all surviving RAF biplane flying-boats were grounded and relegated for scrapping. However, by then the Stranraer already had a second career in operation in Canada, where 40 examples were built following an order for a coastal patrol flying-

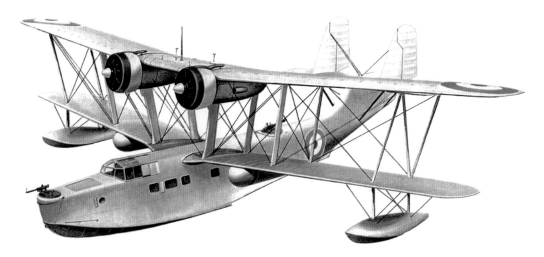

*The Supermarine Stranraer was the final biplane flying-boat built for the RAF, and was the culmination of the biplane maritime patrol aircraft concept that stretched back to the Felixstowe flying-boats of the First World War.*

boat in late 1936. These aircraft were built by Canadian Vickers at Montréal. The first was delivered in late 1938, with full service entry during 1939, and the type operated with the Royal Canadian Air Force until late 1945/early 1946. Post-war, some of the Canadian Stranraers took on a new career for civil companies and fourteen were allocated Canadian civil registrations. They flew passengers and equipment particularly up and down the western coast of Canada with such operators as Queen Charlotte Airlines.

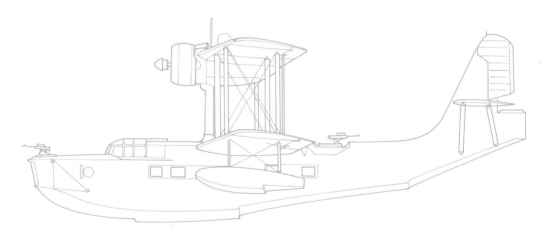

*The Stranraer was a large, heavily strut and wire-braced biplane with a shapely metal fuselage (hull) that gave valuable if unspectacular service to the RAF, and for a longer period in Canadian skies. Canadian pilots preferred its sturdy hull construction, and better take-off performance, compared to more modern types such as the Canso described on pages 232 to 233.*

**Specifications – Supermarine Stranraer**

| | |
|---|---|
| Wingspan | 85 ft |
| Length | 54 ft 10 in |
| Maximum speed | 165 mph at 6,000 ft |
| Maximum take-off weight | 19,000 lb plus |
| Endurance | over nine hours |
| Range | 1,025 miles plus |
| Service ceiling | 18,500 ft (5,639 m) |
| Armament | Three 0.303 in (7.7 mm) machine guns, various loads beneath lower wings including depth charges and bombs |
| Engine | Two Bristol Pegasus X radial piston engines, of 875–920 hp each |
| Crew | Five or six (five to seven in Canadian-operated wartime service) |

# de Havilland D.H.98 Mosquito

Nicknamed the 'Wooden Wonder' due to its predominantly wood construction – unusual in an era where all-metal stressed-skin manufacture had come to dominate – the de Havilland Mosquito was a unique and highly successful fast bomber, fighter bomber, night fighter and reconnaissance aircraft. The innovative de Havilland company had gained considerable experience in the creation of fast, wood construction twin-engined aircraft with the design of the famous D.H. Comet racing aircraft of the early 1930's, which won the England to Australia air race of 1934 – and is described in Volume 1 of *The Complete Encyclopedia of Flight*. The company had also created the beautifully-streamlined pre-war Albatross airliner. Design of the Mosquito drew on these experiences, and commenced in 1938 as a private venture warplane. Although de

Havilland's thinking in that direction had been prompted by the British Air Ministry's Specification P.13/36 for a new medium bomber, the company wanted to go further than this requirement and at first looked at bomber adaptations of existing designs such as the Albatross. Eventually, however, a new design for a twin-engined wood-construction bomber was decided upon. It would be aerodynamically clean, powered by the superb Rolls-Royce Merlin engine, and it was hoped it would be fast enough to out-run enemy fighters – and therefore would not need defensive armament such as gun turrets or their gunners. This was a complete contradiction of contemporary established design philosophy. The Mosquito project was thus totally radical from the start, and it received much opposition from the

*The de Havilland Mosquito was a legendary aircraft at the time of its famous World War Two exploits. The Mosquito design was very versatile, and developed into distinct families of fighters and bombers, with related reconnaissance and naval torpedo-carrying models as well.*

old, backward-thinkers in Britain's Air Ministry. Nonetheless, with help from some friends in high places, a prototype was eventually ordered and the aircraft first flew on 25 November 1940. It gave a breathtaking performance, and became yet another bomber design from an era famous for its high performance fighters (even the Spitfire would have had trouble in keeping up with a Mosquito at full throttle). Initial orders were received by de Havilland for reconnaissance and fighter models. Bomber derivatives were ordered later, once the final opposition to the design had been overcome.

The Mosquito was first flown operationally by the RAF as a reconnaissance aircraft from autumn 1941, its long range giving it great potential in this role. The first bomber model, the superb Mk.IV, began operations in the spring of 1942. The Mosquito excelled in fast low-

*Sporting D-Day stripes for operations at the time of the Allied Invasion of France in June 1944, this Mosquito fighter bomber shows the full eight-gun nose and forward fuselage armament carried by some models of this well-armed aircraft.*

level bombing and had a slight speed advantage even over the Luftwaffe's excellent Focke-Wulf Fw 190 fighter (see pages 274 to 277). Mosquito bombers particularly excelled in precision and well-pub-

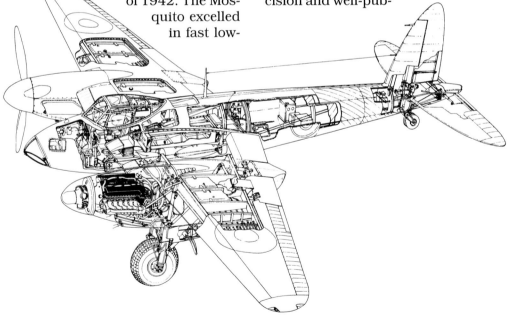

*The Mosquito's basic structure was wood, with much use of plywood and a soft wood called balsa wood – the latter is very familiar to model aircraft builders. Its crew of pilot and navigator/bombardier sat side-by-side in a comparatively roomy cockpit – the smallest crew in a British bomber. Gun turrets for defence and their associated gunners were not needed by the speedy Mosquito since their weight and drag were contrary to the Mosquito's design philosophy. The Mosquito was comparatively easy to manufacture, and dispersed manufacturing during the war brought in a lot of civil wood-working, furniture manufacturing and carpentry organizations to help with Mosquito production.*

# de Havilland D.H.98 Mosquito *continued*

licized pin-point raids on specific targets in Occupied Europe – a famous example being the December 1942 raid on the Philips factories at Eindhoven in Holland. Mosquito bombers of several different marks eventually ranged over most of Occupied Europe, bombing targets with precision from low or high altitude, acting as pathfinders and target markers for the RAF's heavy bombers such as the Avro Lancaster, and dropping anti-shipping mines. Technological advances eventually aided the Mosquito in its work, a navigation aid code-named 'Oboe' being particularly useful for the Mosquito's precision targeting. The largest bomb load carried by Mosquito bombers was 4,000 lb, for which a fuselage modification was needed to deepen the bomb bay. Later versions featured two-stage Merlin engines which considerably improved high-altitude performance.

Separate but related were the fighter Mosquito models. Early fighters carried a formidable array of forward-firing armament of four nose-mounted 0.303 in (7.7 mm) machine guns and four 20 mm cannons in the lower forward fuselage. They had a different windscreen to the bomber Mosquitos, and a different means of enterance. Almost at once, the Mosquito was seen as a possible contender in the then developing art of night fighting, and with the installation of AI (Airborne Interception) radar, the aircraft became one of the principal night fighters of the Second World War. A series of specific versions were created, all carrying AI radar – some of the later models featuring American rather than British radar equipment.

*Two Mosquito bombers in their element. The first RAF Mosquito B.MK.IV operations started in 1942, and the type served with great distinction in the RAF's Bomber Command, having the lowest loss rate amongst all the RAF's main Second World War bombers. Some later models were pressurized for specialist high-altitude work.*

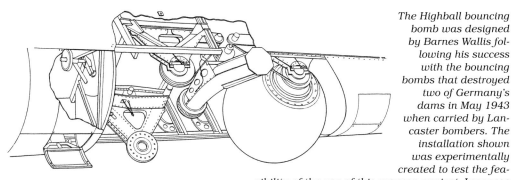

*The Highball bouncing bomb was designed by Barnes Wallis following his success with the bouncing bombs that destroyed two of Germany's dams in May 1943 when carried by Lancaster bombers. The installation shown was experimentally created to test the feasibility of the use of this weapon against Japanese shipping in the Far East. Earlier, at least one Mosquito had been used in the testing of the famous 'Dambuster' bomb that was used in May 1943.*

A number of famous and (at the time) highly celebrated night fighter pilots flew the Mosquito night fighter, including John 'Cat's Eyes' Cunningham. The Mosquito also excelled at fighter bomber and maritime strike missions, and a complete strike force, the legendary Banff Strike Wing in Scotland, proved highly successful in attacking German shipping in and around the Norwegian coasts.

In addition to RAF use, Mosquitos served with Commonwealth air forces, and were widely exported particularly after World War Two. The U.S. Army Air Force also made use of the Mosquito (as the F-8) for reconnaissance, weather reconnaissance and special duties, and a number of Mosquitos were used by Britain's civil airline B.O.A.C. for clandestine missions in and out of neutral Sweden during the war. A navalized Sea Mosquito was used by Britain's Royal Navy, some versions of which had folding wings. Production was performed in Canada and Australia by de Havilland's associated companies in those countries in addition to manufacture in Britain. In total, some 7,781 Mosquitos were built, the final aircraft being completed in late 1950. There were 43 separate versions, and the final RAF.-operated Mosquitos were stood down in late 1955.

**Specifications – de Havilland D.H. Mosquito B.Mk.IV**

| | |
|---|---|
| Wingspan | 54 ft 2 in |
| Length | 40 ft 9.5 in |
| Maximum speed | 385 mph at 21,000 ft |
| Maximum take-off weight | 22,380 lb |
| Range | 1,220 miles |
| Service ceiling | 31,000 ft |
| Armament | up to 2,000 lb of bombs, or 4,000 lb with fuselage modification for deeper bomb bay |
| Engine | Two Rolls-Royce Merlin 21 inline piston engines, of 1,230 hp each |
| Crew | Two |

# Avro Lancaster

Ranking with the Supermarine Spitfire, P-51 Mustang and Focke-Wulf Fw 190 amongst the truly great aircraft of World War Two, the Avro Lancaster was immortalized by its exploits including such world-famous air attacks as the Dams Raid of May 1943. It is by far the most well-known of the trio of heavy bombers employed by the Royal Air Force's Bomber Command in World War Two (the other two being the Halifax and Stirling). The Lancaster revolutionized the concept of night bombing, and was one of the significant tools that led to the defeat of Nazi Germany in 1945. The origins of the Lancaster actually lie with the failed Avro Manchester, a new-generation bomber built to Specification P.13/36 for a twin-engined bomber of greater capacity and capability than contemporary RAF bombers. The prototype first flew on 25 July 1939, and the first operations were made by Manchesters in February 1941. The Manchester never fulfilled its promise. Its un-reliable and under-developed Rolls-Royce Vulture engines were a major problem, resulting in the Manchester seeing only limited service with the RAF – the type was finally withdrawn from operations in mid-1942, after just over two hundred had been made. However, continuing development by Avro's design team under Roy Chadwick (partly to save Avro from having to build the products of other companies) led to the re-design of the Manchester and the adoption of four of the excellent Rolls-Royce Merlin inline engine. With an increased wingspan and a host of other changes, the first aircraft with Lancaster configuration flew on 9 January 1941. It was an immediate success, and was eventually ordered into widespread production. Abandoning the Manchester's triple fin/rudder configuration for the distinctive Lancaster lay-

*The Avro Lancaster was a classic of its time and its construction reflected the norms that had become established by the early 1940's for most (though admittedly not all) modern warplanes. These included all-metal construction, although with fabric covering for some control surfaces. The Lancaster design was also successful because it had growth potential – it could be adapted as newer and larger weapons came along.*

*A fine illustration showing a Lancaster in its element – on a night raid against targets deep inside Germany. Lancasters of the RAF's Bomber Command kept up this type of night raid during most of the latter part of World War Two, in concert with American bombers operating by day.*

out of the twin tails, the first production Lancaster flew in October 1941. The first RAF squadron to re-equip with the type, No.44 Squadron, began to receive its first Lancasters in late 1941. This unit began operations in March 1942. From then to the end of the war, Lancasters became the chief tool of the RAF's Bomber Command in many night bombing raids across Occupied Europe. Eventually this bombing offensive was carried out in conjunction with the U.S. Army Air Force and its B-17 Flying Fortress and B-24 Liberator heavy bombers, which bombed specific industrial targets by day. This was maximum effort, all-out sustained warfare of a type unprecedented in history, and Lancasters were at the center of it. No less than ten Victoria Cross awards were made to Lancaster crew members or those associated with the aircraft. Controversially, the RAF's bombing offensive, directed by 'Bomber' Harris, led to the destruction of many civilian areas in German cities, on a larger scale but in the same way that Germany's Luftwaffe had bombed civilian areas across Europe earlier in the war. Many different targets were attacked during the Lancaster's wartime

offensive, including a major campaign against oil targets to starve the German armed forces of gas. Lancasters were also used for tactical bombing in conjunction with smaller bombers and fighter-bombers against targets in Occupied France prior to and during the D-Day landings in June 1944, and against V-weapon sites (see pages 302 to 303). The Lancaster's bomb-carrying capacity was considerable and grew during the war to include the largest conventional weapons available to the Allies, in addition to the 'Bouncing Bomb' special weapon of Barnes Wallis for use against the German dams in May 1943.

The first major Lancaster production version was the Merlin-powered Mk.I. A feared shortage of Merlin engines led to the Mk.II, which was powered by Bristol Hercules radial engines but was not widely built. The Mk.III introduced American Packard-built Merlin engines, and there was sometimes a cross-over between the British and American-built engines on individual aircraft – the Lancaster design itself staying basically the same throughout production. The final production model was the Mk.VII with revised

# Lancaster *continued*

armament. Lancasters were built by Avro and several sub-contractors in Britain, while construction also took place in Canada by Victory Aircraft. As usual, historians disagree on the exact production numbers, but the final total of Lancasters built, including prototype/development aircraft, was some 7,377, including 430 in Canada. At least 59 squadrons of Bomber Command flew the Lancaster, and Lancasters are credited with flying 156,192 sorties, while dropping 608,612 tons of bombs – representing more tons dropped per aircraft lost than either the Halifax or Stirling, although wartime operational losses were well over three thousand aircraft. At the end of the war, Lancasters dropped food to starving civilians in Europe and repatriated former prisoners of war. Further development led to the Avro Lincoln that was operated post-war by the RAF and Argentina, although the Lancaster itself continued to serve after the war in several

*The so-called 'Bouncing Bomb' of Barnes Wallis was carried beneath the Lancaster's converted fuselage on a special mounting that contained a drive to rotate the bomb prior to release. It was a simple but ingenious and effective device. It was used for the famous Dams Raid of May 1943 by No.617 Squadron, RAF.*

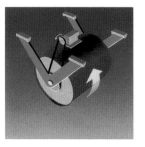

*Illustrating the fact that the majority of Lancasters were not just used on night raids deep into Germany, Lancaster VR-O is shown here being piloted by Flight Lieutenant George Marjoram (an Englishman) of No.419 Squadron, RCAF, in the early hours of D-Day in a tactical mission over the Merville Battery in France.*

The Lancaster is shown here in its classic night bomber form. The code letters 'VR' indicate No.419 Squadron, Royal Canadian Air Force. Canadian squadrons formed an important part of the RAF's Bomber Command during World War Two, exemplifying the fact the RAF's wartime operations contained airmen of many different nationalities.

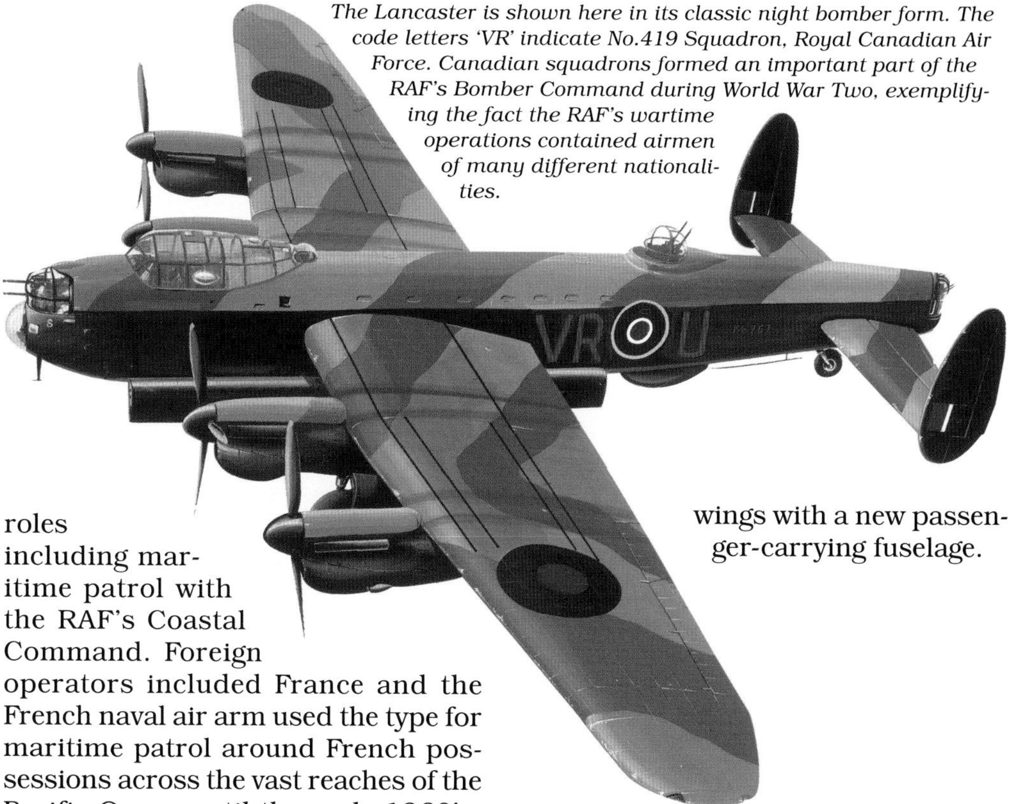

roles including maritime patrol with the RAF's Coastal Command. Foreign operators included France and the French naval air arm used the type for maritime patrol around French possessions across the vast reaches of the Pacific Ocean until the early 1960's. Some Lancasters were also used in post-war Britain as engine test-beds including jet engine development work. A civil derivative was the Lancastrian transport, and the Avro York grew out of the Lancaster by using its wings with a new passenger-carrying fuselage.

**Specifications – Avro Lancaster Mk.I**

| | |
|---|---|
| Wingspan | 102 ft |
| Length | 69 ft 6 in (or 69 ft 4 in) |
| Maximum speed | 287 mph at 11,500 ft |
| Maximum take-off weight | 70,000 lb |
| Range | 2,530 miles |
| Service ceiling | 24,500 ft |
| Armament | Eight 0.303 in (7.7 mm) machine guns (two in nose and dorsal turrets, four in rear [tail] turret), up to 14,000 lb of bombs (some aircraft could carry more) |
| Engine | Four Rolls-Royce Merlin XX, 22 or 24 inline piston engines, of 1,280 hp or (later) 1,640 hp each |
| Crew | Seven |

# Brewster Buffalo

In the field of naval aviation, the United States was somewhat unprepared for battle when the Second World War commenced in September 1939. The 1930's had been a colorful period for the U.S. Navy, with biplane fighters as the standard equipment, and although some modernisation was taking place, American naval aircraft design in 1939 was undoubtedly behind many other major nations. Nevertheless, in the mid-1930's the Navy's bureau of aeronautics had issued requests for new fighter designs. Three companies, including Grumman and Brewster, submitted competing proposals. Grumman was already well established as a supplier of naval aircraft designs, but Brewster was new to the field. The Brewster proposal was nevertheless the winner and a prototype of the Model B-139 was ordered in June 1936. Luckily, the Grumman proposal, which began life as a biplane but grew into the very capable F4F Wildcat monoplane (see pages 182 to 183), was also encouraged to proceed. The prototype Brewster, called the

XF2A-1, flew in late 1937 or early 1938. 54 of the initial F2A-1 production models were ordered. Some were allocated to the U.S. Navy fighter squadron VF-2, which became the first Navy squadron to fly a modern monoplane fighter.

The Buffalo represented a huge leap forward in performance compared to the biplanes which preceded it in the U.S. Navy, but it was inferior in many ways to many other contemporary monoplane fighters. Most of the F2A-1 batch, however, plus an additional aircraft, were supplied to Finland, and flew with distinction and considerable success against Russian forces in the Continuation War between these two countries up to 1944. The F2A-2 (43 ordered), and the slightly refined and improved F2A-3 (108 built) followed the F2A-1. Some of the latter flew with the U.S. Marine Corps fighter squadron VMF-221 at the Battle of Midway, where they were slaughtered by Japanese fighters. Britain received 170 export Buffalo, in addition to around 28 or 29 from an unfulfilled

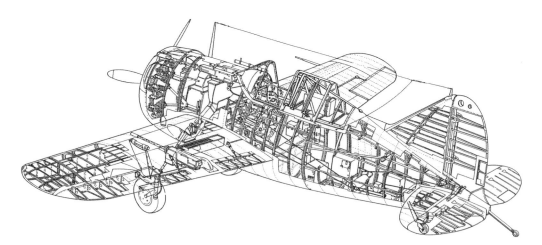

*The portly and ungainly Buffalo was not a particularly pleasant aircraft to fly, and was found to be inferior to its Japanese fighter opposition. Of all-metal construction with some fabric-covered control surfaces, it was the first monoplane fighter ordered for the U.S. Navy.*

*AS412 was from the batch of Buffalo intended for Belgium which were taken over by Britain, and is seen here wearing British markings (Photo: M.V. Lowe Collection).*

order for Belgium. Many of these were wiped out in the futile British and Commonwealth fight against the Japanese invasion of Malaya and Singapore. Dutch East Indies aviation elements also obtained the Buffalo, receiving approximately 72 examples. Some were flown by the Dutch in the heroic but failed defence of the Dutch East Indies against invading Japanese forces in early 1942.

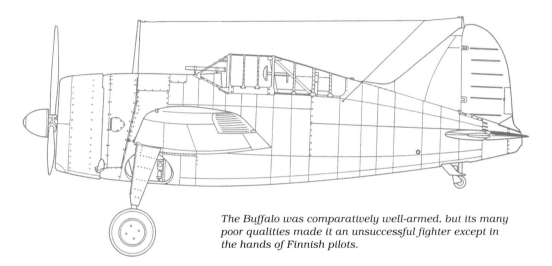

*The Buffalo was comparatively well-armed, but its many poor qualities made it an unsuccessful fighter except in the hands of Finnish pilots.*

## Specifications – Brewster F2A-3 Buffalo

| | |
|---|---|
| Wingspan | 35 ft |
| Length | 26 ft 4 in |
| Maximum speed | 321 mph at 16,500 ft |
| Maximum take-off weight | 7,159 lb |
| Range | approximately 900 miles |
| Service ceiling | 33,200 ft |
| Armament | Four 0.5 in (12.7 mm) machine guns, provision for light bombs beneath the wings |
| Engine | One Wright R-1820-40 Cyclone radial piston engine, of 1,200 hp |
| Crew | One |

# Dornier Do 26

One of the most beautifully stream-lined flying-boats ever built, the Dornier Do 26 was the culmination of a series of successful all-metal water-borne aircraft designed and built by Germany's Dornier company. These included the Wal of the 1920's, and the Do 18 and Do 24 of the 1930's. The latter two types served during World War Two, although the design of the Do 18 (described in Volume 1 of *The Complete Encyclopedia of Flight*) actually dated back to the mid-1930's. The Do 26 was evolved to fill a request from the German national airline Deutsche Lufthansa for a mail carrier with transatlantic range, able to carry some 1,102 lb of mail and four crew members from Lisbon to New York. The Do 26 was a highly streamlined design with all-metal construction and cantilever gull wings, unlike the parasol wing arrangement of its Dornier predecessors. Its four Junkers Jumo 205 diesel engines were mounted in tandem pairs and the drive shafts to and the propellers of the rear two engines were capable of elevation by 10 degrees to raise the propeller blades clear of water spray. Retractable sta-bilising floats at roughly mid-span under each wing also added to the type's clean lines when in flight. The first prototype flew on 21 May 1938 against a 1937 order for three Do 26 from Deutsche Lufthansa. The first two aircraft served with Lufthansa before World War Two commenced, making some 18 crossings of the South Atlan-tic, but never traversed the North Atlantic. The third aircraft served as a prototype for a passenger-carrying version, and three further Do 26s were ordered as pas-senger transports. How-ever, the outbreak of World War Two led to all six of

*The streamlined design layout of the Do 26 can be seen in this illustration, together with the neat engine installation of the four Junkers Jumo 205D diesel engines.*

*The very clean, streamlined lines of the Do 26 are readily apparent in this view of one of the six aircraft in flight (Photo: Hans Meier Collection).*

the Do 26s being taken over by Germany's Luftwaffe, and no further manufacturing took place. The six aircraft served mainly as coastal patrol and reconnaissance with the Luftwaffe, and some if not all received defensive armament. The designation Do 26D was given to at least some of these aircraft, and they also served as troop transports – notably during the Norwegian fighting in 1940, when two were shot down. Finally a lack of spares grounded the remaining Do 26s later in the war.

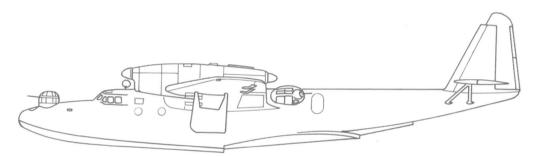

*The Do 26 received armament while in German Luftwaffe service, the front gun turret in particular breaking up the otherwise clean lines of the type.*

## Specifications – Dornier Do 26D

| | |
|---|---|
| Wingspan | 98 ft 5.1 in |
| Length | 80 ft 8.5 in |
| Maximum speed | 201 mph at 8,530 ft |
| Maximum take-off weight | 46,220 lb |
| Range | 2,979.5 miles |
| Service ceiling | 14,764 ft |
| Armament | Three 7.92 mm (0.312 in) machine guns, one 20 mm cannon |
| Engine | Four Junkers Jumo 205D diesel engines, of 880 hp each |
| Crew | Four |

# C.R.D.A. Cant Z.506

A number of aircraft that fought on the front line in World War Two were designed as civil aircraft, or with intended civil as well as military applications, during the pre-war period. One of these was the Italian C.R.D.A. (Cantieri Riuniti dell'Adriatico) Cant Z.506. A big, attractive wooden floatplane with metal floats, the Z.506 served throughout the war and in a limited capacity for some time afterwards.

The prototype Z.506 first flew on 19 August 1935. It was derived from the Z.505 tri-motor mail-carrying seaplane, and was developed as a passenger aircraft primarily for the enchanting seaplane civil air routes in the Mediterranean that existed in the 1930's. Accommodation was normally for 12 to 14 passengers, and the first production aircraft were allocated to the Italian airline Ala Littoria. A further Z.506C civil model was also explored by Cant. The military potential of this big and comparatively powerful aircraft was clear, especially after a number of world records had been set by the Z.506 for its class of aircraft in distance, altitude and speed. A revised design, the Z.506B, was therefore developed in 1936–1937 for military service as a level bomber and torpedo-bomber. It featured a redesigned and raised flight crew compartment, dorsal gun turret, and lower fuselage fairing for a bombardier, bomb bay, and lower rear gunner. The type was ordered into quantity production, with the first being built in 1937–1938. Newly entered into Italian military service, several were flown in Spain during the later stages of the Spanish Civil War for the Spanish Nationalist forces, mainly for reconnaissance and air-sea rescue duties. A number of specific production series ensued, including an export order from Poland (most of which were taken over by the Italians due to the defeat of Poland, but of which one might have been delivered). The Z.506B served with Italian forces in various campaigns during World War Two, but were mainly used for second-line duties at the time of the fall of Mussolini in 1943. Examples subsequently flew with both the pro-German and pro-Allied Italian

*A big, elegant seaplane, the Cant Z.506 was built in both military and civil models.*
*It belongs to a different age – there is nothing like this type of aircraft in service today.*

forces, and during the post-war period some aircraft continued to serve in Italy on air-sea rescue duties until the later 1950's. The total production of the Z.506B was approximately 324, in addition to the civil examples, some of which had themselves flown with the Italian military during World War Two.

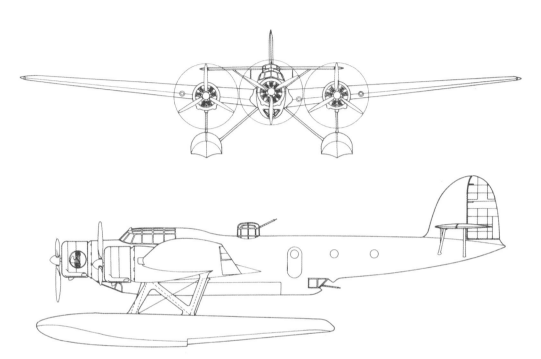

*The name Airone (Heron) is usually associated with the Z.506. A rescue version, the Z.506S, was developed in addition to the Z.506B bomber and the civil models, while a larger derivative, the Z.509, was built in small numbers.*

**Specifications – C.R.D.A. Cant Z.506B Airone (late production)**

| | |
|---|---|
| Wingspan | 86 ft 11.25 in |
| Length | 63 ft 1.75 in |
| Maximum speed | 218 mph at 13,125 ft |
| Maximum take-off weight | 28,009 lb |
| Range | approximately 1,242.8 miles |
| Service ceiling | 24,000 ft |
| Armament | Two or three 7.7 mm (0.303 in) and one 12.7 mm (0.5 in) machine guns, up to 2,645 lb of bombs or a 1,764 lb torpedo |
| Engine | Three Alfa Romeo 126 RC.34 radial piston engines, of 750 hp each |
| Crew | Four or five |

# Fiat G.50 Freccia

An aircraft type closely associated with Italy's war effort during the Second World War is the diminutive Fiat G.50 fighter. Often called the Freccia (Arrow), the G.50 was originally conceived in 1935, reflecting Fiat's intention to create a modern, all-metal monoplane fighter. The G.50 design, alongside the Macchi C.200, was one of several proposals chosen to meet a 1936 Italian Air Ministry fighter requirement, and the first prototype flew in February 1937. Early production G.50s reached the Italian military later in 1938, and some were duly deployed to Spain. These early G.50s had the full 'glass-house' cockpit, tall tail, short fuselage and spatted tailwheel layout that characterized early production aircraft. They arrived too late to fully participate in the Spanish Civil War, and

some were later passed to the newly re-formed Spanish air force after hostilities in Spain ceased.

The first major, fully operational G.50 Regia Aeronautica (Italian air force) unit was the 51st Stormo in the winter of 1939/1940. Italian G.50s subsequently flew over southern France and Corsica after 10 June 1940 when Italy entered the Second World War; from Belgium in mainly abortive operations against Britain later in 1940; over Greece and the Balkans where the type gained somewhat more success; and principally over North Africa. G.50s were deployed in numbers to Libya in early 1941 and served with some distinction in the desert war, particularly in ground attack missions. In combat with Allied fighters, the Fiats proved

*A Fiat G.50 bis of the Regia Aeronautica's 376th Squadriglia, 154th Gruppo, probably in early to mid-1941. The open-cockpit layout of many of the G.50 aircraft was much favored by Italian pilots.*

lacking in overall performance and firepower.

Following the defeat of Italian and German forces in North Africa and the Allied invasion of Sicily in 1943, comparatively few G.50s remained in front line service. However, both the Croats and the Finns also operated the G.50, the latter with considerable success, in air-to-air combat against Russian forces from early 1940 onwards. The exact total number of G.50s of all types that were built has been open to some debate, but the best figure now available is 791 – including 244 basic G.50 models, 439 G.50 bis, and 108 two-seat G.50B trainers. Best of all were the G.50 bis, which had several detail improvements including a slightly lengthened fuselage end, a revised rudder with a straight lower edge and various equipment changes. Some, like the G.50 bis/AS especially used in North Africa, had a sand filter below the cowling. The first G.50 bis flew in September 1940, and production of the final VII Series G.50 bis was completed in August 1942. Several projects and experimental models were also tried out but did not reach production. They included the G.50V, powered by a German Daimler Benz DB 601 engine, a navalized single-seat G.50 with an arrester hook and catapult-launching equipment installed for possible use aboard the planned Italian aircraft carrier Aquila and the dedicated and enlarged ground-attack G.50 bis A (Assalto) with provision for increased armament.

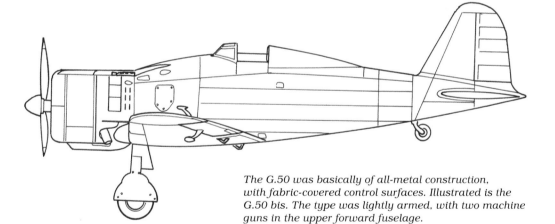

The G.50 was basically of all-metal construction, with fabric-covered control surfaces. Illustrated is the G.50 bis. The type was lightly armed, with two machine guns in the upper forward fuselage.

**Specifications – Fiat G.50 bis (VII Series)**

| | |
|---|---|
| Wingspan | 36 ft 0.5 in |
| Length | 27 ft 2.5 in |
| Maximum speed | 292 mph at 16,405 ft |
| Maximum take-off weight | 5,560 lb |
| Range | 276.5 miles plus |
| Service ceiling | 35,105 ft |
| Armament | Two 12.7 mm (0.5 in) machine guns |
| Engine | One Fiat A.74 RC.38 radial piston engine, of 840–870 hp |
| Crew | One |

# Focke-Wulf Fw 200

With a potential endurance of some 14 hours, the Focke-Wulf Fw 200 Condor was one of the ultimate maritime patrol and anti-shipping aircraft of World War Two. It was also one of very few four-engined long-range aircraft to serve in great numbers with Germany's Luftwaffe during the war. The Fw 200 was in fact originally designed as a civil aircraft. Focke-Wulf proposed a four-engined airliner design to Deutsche Lufthansa in 1936. DLH duly awarded Focke-Wulf a development contract and the first aircraft flew on 27 July 1937. Several pre-production/production airliner models were rapidly built and delivered to DLH and airlines in Denmark and Brazil. Capacity was four crew and 26 passengers. A specially-appointed example was used by Adolf Hitler as a personal transport. One of the early development aircraft flew non-stop from Berlin to New York in August 1938, showing the range and endurance potential of the Fw 200. The Japanese also took an interest in a military long-range maritime reconnaissance aircraft derived from the Fw 200. This order was never fulfilled but a development aircraft, the Fw 200V10, was used to pioneer a stop-gap military version for maritime patrol and ulti-

mately anti-shipping work for the Luftwaffe until the delayed Heinkel He 177 (see pages 240 to 241) was ready. The first front-line derivative of the Fw 200 was the 'C'-series, with a pre-production batch ordered in September 1939. Ironically, the first Condors to see action were transport models, including some former DLH aircraft, which served during the Norwegian campaign in April 1940. The initial anti-shipping configured aircraft started to enter service at about that time. The first production dedicated anti-shipping model was the Fw 200C-1, built later in 1940. Subsequently a number of versions were produced, with many detail changes and sub-variants relating to armament fits and equipment alterations. From the C-3 model onwards there was also structural strengthening – the comparatively lightly-built Condor's civil heritage leading to structural failures, especially broken backs caused the hardships of operational flying.

Condors were spectacularly successful in their early operations, and the C-3 and C-4 versions – later equipped with advanced sea-search radar – posed a real threat to Allied shipping in the Atlantic on the way to northern Russia, especially when cooperating

*The Focke-Wulf Fw 200 was a big, powerful and impressive aircraft.*
*Armed with bombs or anti-ship missiles, it was a real threat to Allied shipping.*

*A Focke-Wulf Fw 200C in its element. Note the under-wing bomb-carriers outboard of the outer engines.*

with U-Boats. However, eventually they fell within the range of Allied fighters, especially from escort aircraft carriers, and they were increasingly less effective. Later the Fw 200C-6 and C-8 models were equipped with underwing Henschel Hs 293 guided anti-ship missiles. Some Condors were removed from their anti-shipping duties to help in the attempted air relief of surrounded German forces at Stalingrad. Approximately 280 Condors were built.

*Unfortunately the censor has removed the upper gun position behind the flight deck on this Fw 200 photograph, but many other details show, including the complicated main undercarriage units (Photo: Hans Meier Collection).*

### Specifications – Focke-Wulf Fw 200C-3/U4 Condor

| | |
|---|---|
| Wingspan | 107 ft 9.5 in |
| Length | 76 ft 11.5 in |
| Maximum speed | 223.75 mph at 15,748 ft |
| Maximum take-off weight | 50,045 lb |
| Range | approximately 2,759 miles |
| Service ceiling | 19,029 ft |
| Armament | Three 13 mm (0.51 in) machine guns flexible-mounted, one 20 mm (0.787 in) cannon flexible-mounted, one 7.92 mm (0.312 in) machine gun flexible-mounted and one similar turret-mounted, up to some 4,630 lb of bombs |
| Engine | Four Bramo Fafnir 323R radial piston engines, of 1,200 hp each |
| Crew | Seven |

# Bristol Beaufort

Designed as a joint response to British Air Ministry Specifications M.15/35 and G.24/35, the Bristol Beaufort was eventually built to Specification 10/36 and first flew on 15 October 1938 as the Bristol Type 152. Powered by two Bristol Taurus VI engines of 1,130 hp, the Beaufort was designed as a land-based torpedo-bomber with some commonality with the Bristol Blenheim (see pages 128 to 129). Provision was made for a crew of four – pilot, navigator, wireless operator and air gunner.

Production of the Beaufort commenced with an order for 78 Mk.I aircraft, and early in the type's career the decision was taken to construct the Beaufort under license in Australia – in addition to production in Britain. The first flight of an Australian-manufactured Beaufort took place in May 1941. Australian-operated Beauforts were virtually identical to their RAF counterparts. However, early experience with the Taurus VI engine had shown that it was prone to overheating. Accordingly these were replaced in some Australian-built aircraft with licence-manufactured American Pratt & Whitney Twin Wasp radials of 1,200 hp each. These engines also necessi-

tated a slightly increased fin area in order to cope with their increased power output. In total, 700 examples of the Beaufort in several versions were built in Australia. The overheating problems with the early Taurus engines also led the Air Ministry to order the fitting of Twin Wasp engines in the British-made Beauforts – although supply problems eventually led to the re-introduction of the Taurus in its Mk XII form on the British production lines. Including licence-built versions, at least 2,080 Beauforts were finally produced (possibly 2,129).

The Beaufort entered service with No.22 Squadron of the RAF's Coastal Command in January 1940, and undertook its first operations in April 1940. Beaufort squadrons were heavily involved in anti-shipping operations in European waters, and specifically in raids like those against the major German warships the *Scharnhorst*, *Gneisenau* and *Prinz Eugen* both during their time in Brest and in the subsequent famous Channel Dash in February 1942. RAF Beauforts also distinguished themselves in operations in the Middle East and in anti-shipping strikes from Malta. Australian-operated Beauforts were active

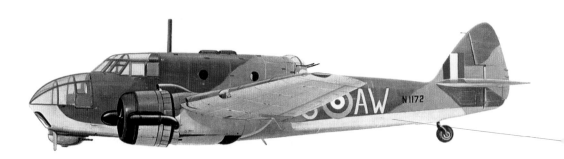

*N1172 was a Bristol Beaufort Mk.I of No.42 Squadron, RAF, with the code letters S-AW ('AW' being the identification for this squadron).*

in the South-West Pacific theater of war, particularly over the Timor Sea, New Guinea and the Soloman Islands.

*Below: The Bristol Beaufort was designed as a torpedo-bomber, and it fulfilled this role efficiently but with little publicity. The painting shows Beauforts of No.86 Squadron, RAF, in action. A pilot of No.22 Squadron, Flying Officer Kenneth Campbell, was posthumously awarded the Victoria Cross for his torpedo attack on the Gneisenau in Brest harbor in April 1941.*

### Specifications – Bristol Beaufort Mk.I

| | |
|---|---|
| Wingspan | 57 ft 10 in |
| Length | 44 ft 2 in (or slightly longer) |
| Maximum speed | 260 mph at 6,000 ft |
| Maximum take-off weight | 21,230 lb |
| Range | 1,035 miles |
| Service ceiling | 16,500 ft |
| Armament | Two 0.303 in (7.7 mm) machine guns in dorsal turret and various combinations of similar fuselage or wing-mounted machine guns. One 1,605 lb torpedo or 1,500 lb plus of bombs or mines |
| Engine | Two Bristol Taurus VI radial piston engines, of 1,130 hp each |
| Crew | Four |

# Lavochkin Fighters

When the Germans invaded the Soviet Union on 22 June 1941, a new and violent phase of World War Two began which was to stretch Germany's resources to the limit – and eventually lead to catastrophic defeat in the East. Even so, there was massive success at the start of the German invasion, and the Luftwaffe gained almost total ascendancy over the Soviet air force. Early in the German offensive, the Soviets had a mixture of mainly poor fighters which were no match for the German Messerschmitt Bf 109. One of these Russian aircraft was the LaGG-3, but although not itself particularly noteworthy, it led to a successful series of Lavochkin fighters that played a major part in the Russian victories

in later years. LaGG stood for Lavochkin, Gorbunov and Gudkov, the three Russians principally responsible for the LaGG-3's creation within Russia's cumbersome centralized aircraft industry. Its predecessor, the LaGG-1, first flew as the I-301 in March 1940. A new specification requiring increased range led to re-design which meant that no LaGG-1s were built as such, but the re-designed layout entered production as the LaGG-3.

Of all-wood construction – highly unusual by 1940 – but with metal-framed fabric-covered control surfaces, the first production LaGG-3 flew in December 1940. The type was entering service as the German attack intensified the following year, and

*The Lavochkin La-5FN was an excellent if totally straightforward and simple fighter, which served the Soviet air force well and was a match for the best of the German fighters pitted against it. This aircraft, No.14, is reputed to be one of those flown by Ivan Kozhedub, the highest scoring ace fighter pilot on the Allied side in World War Two with 62 victories.*

LaGG-3s bore the brunt of much of the early fighting. Many production aircraft were found to be unsatisfactory – Russia's archaic manufacturing process involved aircraft plants building aircraft types designed elsewhere in the Soviet Union, and some were not up to the task of high-quality aviation-standard manufacture.

The LaGG partnership was later broken up, leaving Lavochkin to concentrate on upgrading the LaGG-3 layout. He substituted the type's Klimov M-105 inline engine with a big, powerful Shvetsov M-82 radial. With other refinements, the famous La-5 series was born. It proved to be one of Russia's war-winners, an aircraft that was the equal of Germany's fighters. The first operational-quality La-5 (initially called LaG-5) was completed in mid-1942, and continuing development led to the better La-5FN with a more powerful M-82FN radial, and thence to the excellent (if still rather rustic) La-7.

Initial production La-7s was completed in summer 1944, and the type was in widespread use during late 1944, in time to support the increasingly victorious Soviet army. A number of sub-types were produced, including two-seat trainers, and continuing development led to the La-9 and La-11, which were of more importance during the post-war period and were contemporaries of the Grumman F8F Bearcat. Many high-scoring Russian pilots flew the Lavochkin fighters, and production was considerable – 5,753 La-7 alone were built before the end of the war.

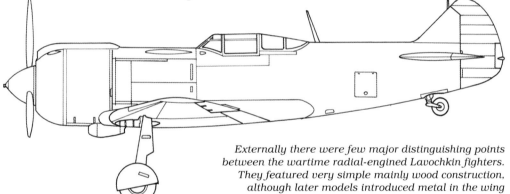

*Externally there were few major distinguishing points between the wartime radial-engined Lavochkin fighters. They featured very simple mainly wood construction, although later models introduced metal in the wing structure, and a cut-down rear fuselage to improve visibility.*

**Specifications – Lavochkin La-5FN**

| | |
|---|---|
| Wingspan | 32 ft 2 in |
| Length | 28 ft 5.25 in |
| Maximum speed | 385 mph at 20,177 ft |
| Maximum take-off weight | 7,324 lb |
| Range | 360 miles plus |
| Service ceiling | 35,105 ft |
| Armament | Two 20 mm cannons fixed forward-firing in the upper forward fuselage |
| Engine | One Shvetsov M-82FN (ASh-82FN) radial piston engine, of 1,470 hp (1,850 hp for take-off) |
| Crew | One |

# Bristol Blenheim

An important day bomber of the early to mid-World War Two period, the Bristol Blenheim represented a huge step-up in capability for the Royal Air Force when it entered service in 1937. Before then, Britain's light to medium bomber capability had principally comprised biplanes such as the Hawker Hart and Hind. A streamlined all-metal structure monoplane, the first Blenheim flew on 25 June 1936, and initial deliveries of the production-standard Blenheim Mk.I began in March 1937. The first unit to receive the type was the RAF's No.114 Squadron. Great interest was shown in the Blenheim by various countries, and eventually Finland, Yugoslavia, and Turkey received the Blenheim Mk.I, with Finland and Yugoslavia also building the type under license. In RAF service the Mk.I was used as a day bomber or a fighter (Mk.IF) – for the latter role a gun pack of four 0.303 in (7.7 mm) machine guns was fitted under the fuselage. British, Finnish and Yugoslav Blenheim I aircraft were fully involved in combat during the early stages of World War Two, but the type was generally too lightly armed and armored. Some British fighter Blenheims were used as early night fighters with radar installed. Further development led to the improved and longer-range Blenheim Mk.IV. This featured a redesigned, longer nose with additional fuel tanks in the wings (except in early Mk.IVs). What was in effect the prototype, a converted Mk.I, flew on 24 September 1937, and was initially called Blenheim Mk.II. Several changes were made and the name Bolingbroke was tried out before the title Blenheim Mk.IV was confirmed. The name Bolingbroke was retained for Canadian-built examples manufactured by Fairchild of Canada. RA. Blenheims were in action right from the start of World War Two, serving widely in Britain, the Middle East and

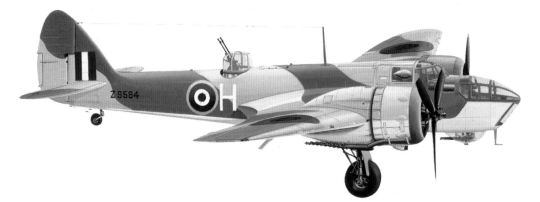

*The Bristol Type 149 Blenheim Mk.IV was a more purposeful and logical development of the Blenheim Mk.I, the early history of which is covered in Volume 1 of*
The Complete Encyclopedia of Flight.

Far East. Fitted with a lower fuselage gun pack like that of the Mk.I, the Mk.IVF was a fighter version. Greece, Finland (including licence-manufacture), Free French and other Commonwealth forces also flew the Mk.IV. Total Mk.IV production is believed to have reached over three thousand eight hundred examples. Continuing development led to the Blenheim Mk.V, a slightly more powerful 'solid' nose but heavier derivative originally named Bisley. The first aircraft flew on 24 February 1941, and 942 production examples were eventually built. The type unfortunately proved slow and vulnerable to fighter attack, and one Blenheim V pilot was posthumously awarded the Victoria Cross. A related line of development from the basic Blenheim layout led to the Bristol Beaufort (see pages 124 to 125).

*Two views of the engine installation of preserved Blenheim Mk.IVs. The trusty Bristol Mercury radial engine was used in several other British aircraft types as well as the Blenheim, and was generally a very reliable engine even if lacking in power compared to later radial engine developments (Photos: John Batchelor).*

## Specifications – Bristol Blenheim Mk.IV

| | |
|---|---|
| Wingspan | 56 ft 4 in |
| Length | 42 ft 9 in |
| Maximum speed | 266 mph at 11,800 ft |
| Maximum take-off weight | 14,400 lb |
| Range | approximately 1,950 miles |
| Service Ceiling | 27,000 ft |
| Armament | One fixed forward-firing 0.303 in (7.7 mm), two turret-mounted 0.303 in (7.7 mm) machine guns, and two similar rearward-firing machine guns in fairing beneath nose, up to 1,000 lb of bombs internally and 320 lb externally |
| Engine | Two Bristol Mercury XV radial piston engines, of 920 hp each |
| Crew | Three |

# Douglas Boston and Havoc

One of the most widely-used and well-known tactical bombers and attack aircraft of World War Two, the Boston originally appeared in 1936 as a Douglas design concept called 7A. Revised in 1937 and re-named 7B, it was entered in a U.S. Army Air Corps design competition that called for a light bomber and attack aircraft. This was a very successful competition – not only was the victorious 7B entered into production for foreign users, but the competition also led to the Martin Maryland (and later the Martin Baltimore), and the North American B-25 Mitchell. The prototype Model 7B first flew on 26 October 1938. At that time several European countries including Britain and France were rapidly re-arming in the face of the growing threat from Nazi Germany. Although no orders were immediately forthcoming from the U.S. Army, the French ordered 100 Model 7B aircraft from Douglas in February 1939 – the first of several such orders. The original 7B prototype crashed in January 1939, and a complete re-design led to the famous DB-7 series. The first DB-7 type aircraft flew on 17 August 1939,

and production started later in 1939. In June 1939 the U.S. Army ordered an attack derivative called the A-20 Havoc, and Britain ordered a model similar to an initial A-20 layout in February 1940 under the name Boston. The first DB-7 reached French forces in North Africa in January 1940, but too few were in service to make any difference after the German invasion of France in May 1940. After the fall of France, many of the DB-7 and DB-7A ordered by France were diverted to Britain (and called Boston Mk.I and Mk.II) respectively. Britain later received its own model, the DB-7B (Boston Mk.III). This Boston, and the related Boston Mk.IIIA, served Britain's RAF well for short-range intruder and tactical bombing missions over Occupied Europe in day and night operations. In addition, some of the early aircraft were converted into night fighters called Havoc, with Airborne Interception (AI) radar installed. Some had a huge 'Turbinlight' searchlight installed in the nose. The U.S. Army Air Force (so named after mid-1941) ordered a variety of increasingly more capable models with different equip-

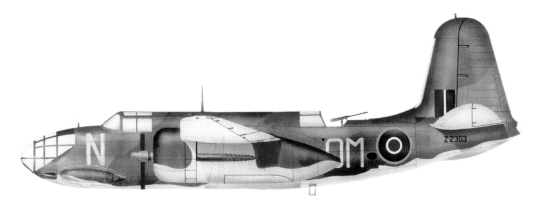

*Z2303 was a Douglas Boston Mk.I, operated by the RAF's No.107 Squadron ('OM' code letters).*
*It is typical of the Bostons operated by the RAF on daylight tactical bombing operations*
*over Occupied Europe.*

ment and armament, starting with the A-20A and culminating in the A-20K. Some of these later models also served with the RAF. An American makeshift night fighter version of the A-20 was the P-70, which saw combat in the Pacific against Japanese forces until purpose-built night-fighters took over. Indeed, the Boston/Havoc series operated world-wide during the war, with American, British, and Commonwealth forces. Many were supplied to Russia. Production ceased in 1944. Researchers disagree on the total number built, although one Douglas historian claims 7,479.

*The A-20 Havoc was much used by the U.S. Army Air Force. This example, serial number 43-21745, carries black and white D-Day 'Invasion Stripes' and is an A-20J-15-DO (built by Douglas at Santa Monica, California). It has the black and white rudder markings of the 410th Bomb Group, U.S. Ninth Army Air Force, and the '8U' code of the 646th Bomb Squadron. It carried the names 'Irene' and 'The Real McCoy' and was based at Gosfield, England.*

## Specifications – Douglas Boston Mk.IIIA

| | |
|---|---|
| Wingspan | 61 ft 4 in |
| Length | 47 ft 3 in |
| Maximum speed | 342 mph at 13,000 ft |
| Maximum take-off weight | 24,500 lb |
| Range | 1,050 miles |
| Service ceiling | 24,250 ft |
| Armament | Two or four forward-firing 0.303 in (7.7 mm) machine guns in the nose, two similar machine guns in dorsal position, sometimes one similar in ventral position, plus up to 2,000 lb of bombs |
| Engine | Two Wright R-2600-23 or similar Cyclone radial piston engines, of 1,600 hp each |
| Crew | Three (usually) |

# Lockheed Hudson

The Hudson was Lockheed's first major combat aircraft, and was derived from the Lockheed Model 14 civil transport. Faced with the need for rapid rearmament, Britain looked to the United States in the late 1930's as a potential supplier, and an early result of this was an order during 1938 for 200 Model B14L (later Model 214) Hudson Mk.Is followed by an order for 250 more later. The type was seen as a potential replacement for the Avro Anson general reconnaissance aircraft within RAF Coastal Command. 2,584 Hudsons of all models would be built, and the first would fly on 10 December 1938. A total of 351 Hudson Mk.Is were followed by 20 Mk.IIs (Model 314), 428 Short Range (SR) and Long Range (LR) Mk.IIIs (Model 414) and 409 LR and SR Mk.Vs ordered for the RAF. Soon after the RAF ordered the Hudson, the Royal Australian Air Force did the same, confusingly ordering Model 414s as Hudson Mk.Is

and Mk.II. These later became Hudson Mk.IVs to avoid misunderstanding with the early RAF versions, that air arm ordering 30 further examples for its own use. With the introduction of the Lend-Lease Act in the U.S., 800 Hudson Mk.IIIAs were produced as A-29 and A-29As, the latter with convertible interiors for use as troop transports. The U.S. Army repossessed around 170 with 20 being diverted to the U.S. Navy as PBO-1s, while many Mk.IIIAs (and other marks) were supplied to Commonwealth countries. The other Lend-Lease versions were the A-28A, of which 450 were supplied as Hudson Mk.VIs and the A-28, 52 of which went to the R.A.A.F. as Mk.VIAs. The U.S. Army Air Force converted 24 for photo-

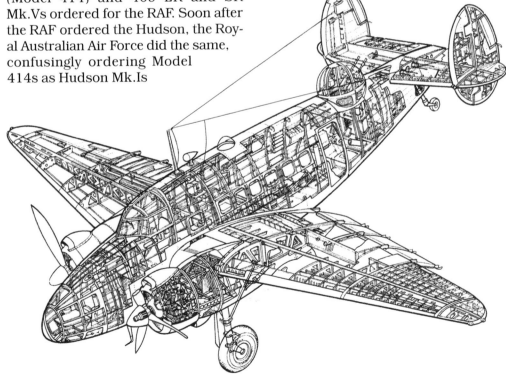

*The Lockheed Hudson was an advanced all-metal warplane for its day. Its civil airliner ancestry is revealed by the passenger-type windows along the fuselage sides.*

graphic reconnaissance as A-29Bs, while it also acquired 217 AT-18s and 83 AT-18As for use as gunnery and navigation trainers. The Hudson first entered operational service with No.224 (GR) Squadron, RAF, in the first half of 1939. One shot down the first German aircraft claimed by an RAF aircraft operating from Britain in World War Two on 8 October 1939. RAF-operated Hudsons provided vital coverage of the seas around Britain during the early part of the war, some being equipped with ASV Mk.I search radars from early 1940, but by mid-1942 they had been largely replaced by longer-range aircraft. Many found secondary roles as transports, or in air-sea rescue and meteorological reconnaissance roles. After the war, the Hudson quickly disappeared from military service, although the Lockheed PV Ventura and Harpoon, developed from the Lockheed Model 18 Lodestar (itself a development of the original Lockheed 14) served well into the post-war period.

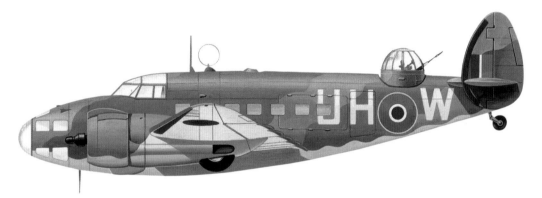

*The principal front-line user of the Lockheed Hudson in several different versions was the RAF and Commonwealth forces, but the type was also employed by the U.S. military in a number of distinct models.*

## Specifications – Lockheed Hudson Mk.VI

| | |
|---|---|
| Wingspan | 65 ft 6 in |
| Length | 44 ft 4 in |
| Maximum speed | 261 mph at 6,500 ft |
| Maximum take-off weight | 18,500 lb |
| Range | 2,160 miles |
| Service ceiling | 27,000 ft |
| Armament | Two 0.303 in (7.7 mm) machine guns in forward fuselage and in dorsal turret, and (some aircraft) one 0.303 in (7.7 mm) machine gun in ventral position (option for two similar caliber machine guns in beam positions), plus up to 1,000 lb of bombs or depth charges |
| Engine | Two Pratt & Whitney R-1830-S3C4G (or –67) Twin Wasp radial piston engines, of 1,200 hp each |
| Crew | Five |

# Martin Maryland

The U.S. Army Air Corps' design competition that led to the creation of the Douglas Boston and Havoc series (see pages 130 to 131) also gave rise to the Martin aircraft that became the Maryland, and thence to the Martin Baltimore. The Glenn L. Martin Company of Baltimore, Maryland, entered the U.S. Army's competition with its Model 167 proposal. This was not accepted by the U.S. Army, but at that time Britain and France in particular were looking to buy suitable foreign aircraft as a part of their rearmament efforts. The French ordered 115 examples of the Martin Model 167 in January 1939, before the first aircraft had even flown. The prototype, known as the XA-22 (A = Attack) first flew on 14 March 1939. Production aircraft for France were designated Model 167F (the French often called them Martin 167 A-3, or simply 'Glenns'). They were powered by 950-1,100 hp Wright R-1820 Cyclone radial engines. A further 100 were later ordered, and some 140 were eventually delivered to France. They served in the fighting after the invasion of France by Germany in May 1940. Some of the survivors duly operated with Vichy French forces in various campaigns such as Dakar, Syria, and North Africa against the Allied

invasion in November 1942. The balance of the French order (approximately 75 aircraft) was diverted to Britain due to the defeat of France in June 1940. Called Maryland Mk.I, most if not all were refitted with Pratt & Whitney Twin Wasp radial engines. Some former French-operated aircraft were also used by the RAF, and a further batch of 150 was ordered by Britain as Maryland Mk.II with slightly more powerful Twin Wasps – giving them a creditable top speed of 316 mph. The Marylands duly served with the RAF, Fleet Air Arm and South African Air Force, mainly in North Africa and East Africa. With excellent performance, they were employed for fast light tactical bombing and attack, long-range reconnaissance, and some on Malta even acted as improvised local defence night fighters. On numerous occasions Marylands were also employed as makeshift day fighters, and scored some air-to-air victories, including several Junkers Ju 52/3m transports over the Mediterranean and North Africa. A Royal Navy-operated reconnaissance Maryland of No.771 Squadron discovered the departure of the German capital ship, the Bismarck, from its base in Norway, leading to its hunting down and sinking in

*The Martin Maryland was a slender, sleek and fast reconnaissance aircraft and light bomber with a narrow fighter-like cockpit for its pilot.*

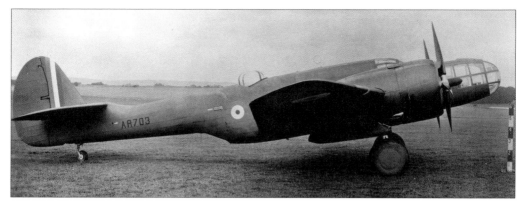

*Serial number AR703 was one of a batch of 50 Maryland Mk.I which are sometimes forgotten by historians, no fewer than 275 Marylands actually being allocated British serial numbers in addition to a handful of ex-French operated examples (Photo: Peter Redhead Collection).*

May 1941. Eventually Marylands were replaced by Baltimores (see pages 218 to 219) and other types in British service later in the war. Some served with Free French forces on the Allied side against the Germans, even into 1944.

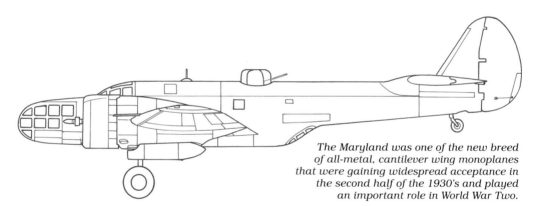

*The Maryland was one of the new breed of all-metal, cantilever wing monoplanes that were gaining widespread acceptance in the second half of the 1930's and played an important role in World War Two.*

### Specifications – Martin Maryland Mk.I

| | |
|---|---|
| Wingspan | 61 ft 4 in |
| Length | 46 ft 8 in |
| Maximum speed | 304 mph at 13,000 ft |
| Maximum take-off weight | 15,297 lb |
| Range | 1,300 miles |
| Service ceiling | 29,500 ft |
| Armament | Four fixed forward-firing wing-mounted machine guns, one machine gun in dorsal and ventral positions (calibers varied depending on original source of aircraft), 1,250 lb of bombs (possibility for more) |
| Engine | Two Pratt & Whitney R-1830-SC3G type Twin Wasp radial piston engines, of 1,050 hp each |
| Crew | Three or four |

# Bell P-39 Airacobra

Although the Bell P-39 Airacobra appeared almost completely conventional when in flight, it was in fact of a radical design layout. Designed around the concept of a flying cannon-armed fighter, the P-39 mounted a potentially formidable 37 mm cannon firing through its propeller spinner. To achieve the installation of this weapon within the aircraft, the engine was moved backward from its usual position in the nose to amidships behind the cockpit, from where it drove the propeller with an extended drive shaft. A tricycle undercarriage layout was also used, the first on a major production American fighter. The P-39's manufacturer, the Bell Aircraft Corporation, was a relative newcomer to fighter aircraft design in similar fashion to Brewster (see pages 114 to 115). Unlike Brewster, however, Bell produced a fighter in the P-39 that was

comparatively successful – albeit at low levels, even though it had been intended as a high altitude fighter. The curious decision to delete the turbo (exhaust-driven) supercharger from the Airacobra's Allison engine reduced its effectiveness at high altitudes, but it performed reasonably well at lower levels.

Bell's original design concepts for the Airacobra gained an order in 1937 from the U.S. Army Air Corps for a prototype, the XP-39, and this first flew in April 1939. The first real production model was the P-39C, which entered Army Air Corps service in early 1941. Several major production models followed, all with the same basic layout. Most had the 37 mm cannon, but some examples mounted a 20 mm cannon in its place. A number of other armament changes also took place with the type's wing-mounted

*Illustrated is a P-39J Airacobra, serial number 41-7073, in typical early war colors and markings worn by U.S. Army Air Force aircraft.*

136

armament. The last major production model, the P-39Q, could be fitted with underwing gun pods, and did away with the internally-mounted wing guns of earlier models.

The P-39 served the Army Air Force comparatively well in low level air combat and ground attack, particularly in North Africa and significantly in the Pacific, where it helped to hold the line against the advancing Japanese alongside the Curtiss P-40 (see pages 48 to 49) until newer and better fighters entered service.

675 Airacobras were ordered by Britain but saw little British service, most serving Russian or American units instead, where they were known as the P-400. Several other users included France, pro-Allied Italian forces, and Australia. A navalised derivative, the XFL-1 Airabonita, was tested in prototype form but did not enter production. Further development of the P-39 led to the improved Bell P-63 Kingcobra. Historians disagree as to how many Airacobras were built, the total being somewhere around 9,558.

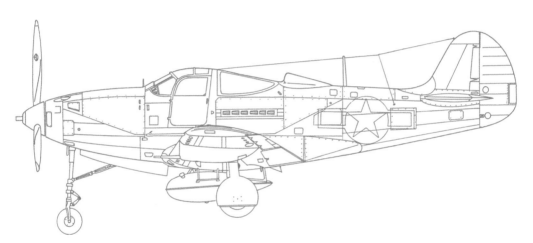

*The P-39Q Airacobra as shown here introduced underwing gun pods for a single 0.50 caliber machine gun beneath each wing. 4,905 of this model were built, many were supplied to the Soviet Union. Several Russian pilots scored well in air combat while flying the Airacobra.*

## Specifications – Bell P-39Q Airacobra

| | |
|---|---|
| Wingspan | 34 ft |
| Length | 30 ft 2 in |
| Maximum speed | 376 mph at 15,000 ft |
| Maximum take-off weight | 8,350 lb |
| Range | approximately 650 miles plus |
| Service ceiling | 35,000 ft |
| Armament | One 37 mm cannon, four 0.5 in (12.7 mm) machine guns (two in optional pods beneath the wings) |
| Engine | One Allison V-1710-85 inline piston engine, of 1,200 hp |
| Crew | One |

# Blohm und Voss Bv 138

The giant Blohm und Voss shipbuilding company of Hamburg became involved in aircraft design and manufacture in the early 1930's. Following the accession to power in Germany of Hitler's National Socialists in 1933, Blohm und Voss set up the Hamburger Flugzeugbau as an aircraft-producing subsidiary. Several aircraft designs were developed before an official requirement in late 1933/early 1934 for an ocean-going reconnaissance and patrol flying-boat led to Hamburger's first successful design. This was the Ha 138, and it was originally designed in several distinct layouts. The design that was initially intended to be built in prototype form was a twin-engined layout, but this was soon altered to an unusual three-engined configuration. The prototype first flew on 15 July 1937. Considerable re-design was found to be needed, and the altered aircraft was thenceforward known by the Blohm und Voss designation Bv 138A (some-

times BV 138A). In particular, the hull (fuselage), tail and rear booms were revised.

The first Bv 138A flew in February 1939. A number of A-series development aircraft were followed by 25 production Bv 138A-1 examples, which began test-flying in April 1940 (delayed due to ice on the nearby River Elbe), and entered Luftwaffe service straight away due to operational commitments in Norway. Further revision and strengthening, and altered armament, resulted in the Bv 138B series, of which 19 or 21 were built. These modest numbers were followed by the more widely-produced Bv 138C model of 1941 onwards. 227 of these strengthened and refined flying-boats were eventually built, production ending in 1943. Some examples of this production

*The Blohm und Voss Bv 138's unusual tri-motor power plant arrangement is well illustrated in this drawing. The type was sometimes nicknamed the 'Flying Clog' due to its hull shape. Although manufactured in comparatively modest numbers, the Bv 138 was a useful long-range maritime patrol aircraft for Germany's Luftwaffe that could put up a good fight if challenged by Allied aircraft.*

model were specially equipped for catapult-launch from ships at sea, and the type could also be fitted with take-off assistance rockets. A small number of Bv 138 were specially modified for mine-sweeping operations with a prominent anti-mine hoop attached to the upper hull as the Bv 138MS – in similar fashion to the anti-mine Junkers Ju 52/3m model (see pages xx to xx). Despite the Bv 138's slow start to operational service the later production Bv 138 aircraft were highly successful in their long-range maritime reconnaissance missions. They were well enough armed to put up a good fight against any Allied aircraft that they encountered, as well as being able to perform limited attack missions of their own. Bv 138s eventually operated over the Bay of Biscay, the Baltic Sea, the North Atlantic and Arctic Ocean areas. Some flew from Romania over the Black Sea, and the type could be refuelled at sea after landing by surfaced U-Boats. Some Bv 138s were still operational in 1945 near the end of the war.

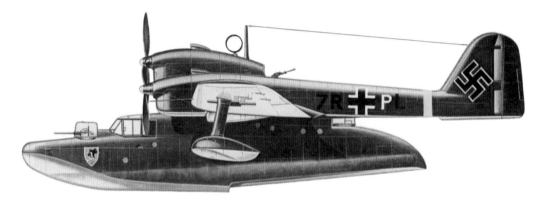

*The '7R' code carried by this Bv 138 identifies it as belonging to SAGr. 125 (the designation standing for Seeaufklärungsgruppe or maritime reconnaissance group) or its immediate predecessor Aufkl.Gr.(See) 125. This was one of several such wartime units that operated the Bv 138 in addition to other types for over-water patrol missions.*

## Specifications – Blohm und Voss Bv 138C-1

| | |
|---|---|
| Wingspan | 88 ft 7 in |
| Length | 65 ft 3.5 in (or slightly less) |
| Maximum speed | 177 mph at sea level |
| Maximum take-off weight | 32, 408 lb |
| Endurance | normally 6.5 hours, maximum 18 hours |
| Service ceiling | 16,405 ft |
| Armament | Two 20 mm cannons, one mounted in bow (front) turret, one 13 mm (0.51 in) machine gun, three 110 lb bombs (or four 331 lb depth charges in Bv 138 C-1/U1 model) |
| Engine | Three Junkers Jumo 205D diesel engines, of 880 hp each |
| Crew | Five or six |

# Messerschmitt Bf 110

One of the icons of Germany's Luft-waffe during World War Two, the Mes-serschmitt Bf 110, was designed as a twin-engined fighter, with high speed and long endurance for the pursuit of enemy aircraft – the classic Zerstörer (destroyer, or strategic fighter and bomber escort) role. Design work began in 1934/1935, and the first Bf 110V1 flew on 12 May 1936 pow-ered by two Daimler Benz DB 600 inline engines. Faster than the Bf 109B-2, but far less maneuverable, it was ordered into production as the Bf 110B powered by the inline Junkers Jumo 210Ga. This was a stopgap until the preferred Daimler Benz DB 601 inline engine became available in quan-tity, and in the event only around 45 B-series Bf 110s were built. The Bf 110C series had DB 601A inline engines and this restored performance capabilities. The type was issued to units manned with the cream of the Luftwaffe's fighter pilots in time for the start of World War Two. Initial victories in September 1939 over outdated Polish fighters led to the conclusion that the Bf 110 could be effective against sin-gle-engined fighters, a premise that was to be proven wrong in the subse-quent fighting over France and during the Battle of Britain in 1940.

The Bf 110D series was a long-range fighter and anti-shipping convoy escort aircraft, while members of the 'E' and 'F' series were heavy fighter-bombers. Some of these early models were mod-ified as austere night fighters. It was in fact in this role that the Bf 110 was to find its niche in later years, arguably because it had better performance and was cheaper to produce than rival Ju 88G and Do 217 night fighter variants. The Bf 110F-4, powered by the DB 601F, became one of the first dedicat-ed night fighter versions, equipped with night-compatible instrumentation The F-4a featured FuG 202 Lichten-stein BC interception radar. Armament options were revised for the night fight-er role, with some examples fitted with the upward-firing 'Schräge

*As a comparatively long-range heavy day fighter, the Messerschmitt Bf 110 had its best successes early in World War Two. This is a Bf 110C-series aircraft, showing the type's all-metal construction.*

Musik' 30 mm cannons that proved potentially devastating to RAF night bombers. Heavy-fighter development intended to counter U.S. day bombers continued with the DB 605B-1 powered G-series, while versions of the Bf 110G-4 model carried various radars and armaments specifically for night fighting. In the hands of *experten* (aces) such as Heinz-Wolfgang Schnaufer (121 nocturnal kills), the Bf 110G-4 night fighter was a deadly weapon. Increasingly, however, the Allies developed countermeasures to the Luftwaffe's radars and the appearance of British Mosquitos turned the hunter into the hunted. The Germans' failure to produce more advanced night fighters in sufficient numbers and the unsuccessful Messerschmitt Me 210 program kept the Bf 110 in production much longer than anticipated. Approximately 6,050 were built in many different sub-types. Some of Germany's allies, notably Italy and Hungary, also flew the type.

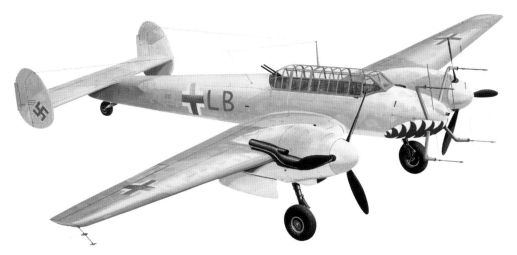

*The Messerschmitt Bf 110G-series was one of the classic night fighters of the Second World War, fitted with Lichtenstein interception radar and working with the extensive ground-based radar system developed by the Germans.*

**Specifications – Messerschmitt Bf 110C-1**

| | |
|---|---|
| Wingspan | 53 ft 3.75 in |
| Length | 39 ft 7.25 in (or slightly more) |
| Maximum speed | 336 mph at 19,685 ft |
| Maximum take-off weight | 14,881 lb |
| Range | 680 miles plus |
| Service ceiling | 32,808 ft |
| Armament | Two 20 mm cannons and four 7.92 mm (0.312 in) machine guns in the nose fixed forward-firing, one 7.92 mm (0.312 in) machine gun flexible-mounted in the rear cockpit |
| Engine | Two Daimler Benz DB 601A inline piston engines, of 1,050–1,100 hp each |
| Crew | Two or three |

# Dornier Do 217

The successful Dornier Do 17 series of medium bombers (see pages 38 to 39) was a mainstay in the early days of the development of the Luftwaffe as a major air force, and operated in the Spanish Civil War and the early days of World War Two. In 1937, the German Air Ministry developed a requirement for a longer-range and higher specification bomber with additional dive-bomber capabilities (the latter need was eventually dropped). Dornier's response was to scale up and give more capability to the Do 17 layout. This proposal gained official acceptance and led to the well-known and successful Do 217 series of bombers, night fighters and reconnaissance aircraft.

Although bearing a close resemblance to the Do 17Z which preceded it, the Do 217 series were essentially new, larger aircraft. The initial example, the Do 217V1, first flew in August 1938 powered by Daimler Benz DB 601A inline engines. Later prototypes flew with Junkers Jumo 211A inlines, which led to a range of different power plants being installed on production models, eventually including the BMW 801 radial engine. Unfortunately, early test flying revealed that unlike the Do 17, the Do 217 did not enjoy particularly good flying qualities (the Do 217V1 eventually crashed), and some modifications were needed. The first main mass-produced version was the Do 217E bomber, produced in a variety of major sub-types, and preceded by a small number of Do 217A-0 reconnaissance aircraft. The Do 217E entered service in the spring of 1941 with bomber wing KG 40. Attacks were made against British towns in the famous 'Baedeker' raids. Further development led to the Do 217K and M-series bombers, with a completely re-designed and more rounded-nosed forward fuselage. The increasing need for night fighters to counter RAF night bomber raids over Germany led to the improvised use of the Do 217 as a night fighter in its Do 217J and more refined Do 217N versions. Most were radar-equipped and had a re-designed nose with forward-firing cannon and machine gun armament. The Do 217N entered service in 1943, although it was not particularly successful or popular compared to the Messerschmitt Bf 110 night fighters. One of the most important tasks of the Do 217 was as a launch aircraft for the new technology of guided missiles. Both the Henschel Hs 293 and the Ruhrstahl 'Fritz-X' anti-ship

*The Dornier Do 217E-5 carried the Henschel Hs 293 guided anti-ship missile, mounted beneath the right-hand wing of the aircraft illustrated, which belonged to bomber wing KG 100.*

weapons were used, initially very successfully, and the first Hs 293 attacks were carried out in August 1943. The Do 217E generally carried the Hs 293, and the long-wingspan Do 217K-2 carried the 'Fritz-X'. Final deliveries of the Do 217 to the Luftwaffe took place in 1944, and up to 1,887 were built.

*Above Right:*
*The long-span Dornier Do 217K-series could carry the 'Fritz-X' guided glide bomb on operations, or the Hs 293 as shown here beneath the wings. The Heinkel He 177 (see pages 240 to 241) also employed the Hs 293 operationally.*

*Right:*
*The cockpit interior of a Dornier Do 217E; the pilot's station is to the left (Photo: Dornier).*

## Specifications – Dornier Do 217E-2

| | |
|---|---|
| Wingspan | 62 ft 4 in |
| Length | 59 ft 8.5 in |
| Maximum speed | 320 mph at 13,125 ft |
| Maximum take-off weight | 36,299 lb |
| Range | 1,429 miles |
| Service ceiling | 29,528 ft |
| Armament | Various combinations of cannons and/or machine guns of varied calibers including 13 mm (0.51 in) in fixed, turret and flexible mountings, up to 6,614 lb (3,000 kg) of bombs |
| Engine | Two BMW 801ML radial piston engines, of 1,580 hp each |
| Crew | Four |

# Bristol Beaufighter

Beginning life as the Bristol Type 156, the Beaufighter was designed as a private venture to produce a two-seat, long-range heavy fighter. The Beaufighter was of similar construction to its stablemate the Beaufort (see pages 124 to 125) and incorporated some Beaufort parts in its construction. The Beaufighter first flew on 17 July 1939, and Britain's Air Ministry was so impressed with the new aircraft's performance that the type was ordered into production under Specification F.17/39, which was written around the new design. The first production Beaufighters were powered by the Bristol Hercules XI radial engine of 1,500 hp and featured the then unheard-of armament of four 20 mm cannon in the fuselage, two 0.303 in (7.7 mm) machine guns in the left-hand wing and four of these in the right-hand wing. A single rearward-firing 0.303 in (7.7 mm) machine gun was also provided on a flexible mount for the observer. From the beginning the Beaufighter was seen as a potential night fight-er. Equipped with AI Mk.IV radar, it was a considerable success in this role for the RAF, and later also served with some American night fighter units. Concerns about possible shortages of Hercules engines led to the development of the Beaufighter Mk.II powered by two Rolls-Royce Merlin XX engines of 1,250 – 1,280 hp. A shift in the center of gravity in this mark necessitated the introduction of slightly extended span tailplanes with 12 degrees of dihedral added. This modification was retained on all subsequent versions of the Beaufighter. In any event, the anticipated shortage in Hercules engines did not materialize and the Mk.II was the only Merlin-powered Beaufighter type. Continued Beaufighter development resulted in the fitting of more powerful models of the Hercules radial engine in the Mk.VI and TF.X versions, the latter being a dedicated anti-ship type. Beaufighter armament continued to be developed throughout the war with provision made for bombs, rockets and, in the TF.X (developed for the RAF's Coastal Command) an 18 in (457 mm) torpedo. Some models featured the

*The Bristol Beaufighter was a big, powerful aircraft that was a success in all its varied roles. This aircraft has radar installed in its specially shaped 'thimble' nose.*

AI Mk.VIII radar housed in a 'thimble' radome in the nose. Operationally, the Beaufighter served in Britain on Home Defence duties, in the Mediterranean and the Western Desert in addition to taking part in anti-shipping strikes. Australian–made Beaufighters served in the Pacific where they were known as 'Whispering Death' because of their quiet sleeve valve engines. Post-war Beaufighter users included Portugal and the Dominican Republic.

*The Beaufighter in its element, making low-level attacks on enemy shipping. Anti-ship Beaufighters were a great success, particularly the squadrons of the RAF's Banff Strike Wing in Scotland, working alongside anti-ship Mosquitos.*

*Anti-ship Beaufighters could carry an 18 in (457 mm) torpedo beneath the fuselage.*

### Specifications – Bristol Beaufighter TF.Mk.X

| | |
|---|---|
| Wingspan | 57 ft 10 in |
| Length | 42 ft 6 in or slightly less |
| Maximum speed | 318 mph at sea level |
| Maximum take-off weight | 25,400 lb |
| Range | 1,500 miles |
| Service ceiling | 15,000 ft |
| Armament | Four 20 mm cannons fixed forward-firing in lower fuselage, one 0.303 in (7.7 mm) machine gun flexible-mounted in rear cockpit, one under fuselage 18 in (457 mm) torpedo, eight 3 in (76.2 mm) rockets beneath the wings, or other combinations |
| Engine | Two Bristol Hercules XVII radial piston engines, of 1,735–1,770 hp each |
| Crew | Two |

# Westland Whirlwind

Fast, maneuverable, and an excellent gun platform, the Westland Whirlwind twin-engined fighter might have attained greater status if it had been more thoroughly developed and fitted with better engines. Designed to Air Ministry Specification F.37/35 for a new-generation fighter, the Whirlwind came from an unlikely source for fighter aircraft. It was designed by the Westland company of Yeovil in southern England, which had already produced a number of radical aircraft concepts to which was being added the successful Lysander multi-purpose aircraft described on pages 32 to 33. Preliminary work on the new fighter began in 1936 and the prototype, flown by Westland test pilot Harald Penrose, first flew on 11 October 1938. Successful flight testing led to a production order in early 1939, but the type's potential was seriously compromised by the choice of power plant. The Rolls-Royce Peregrine inline engine that had been selected failed to live up to expectations, and caused the Whirlwind troubles from the start. Nevertheless the type was probably the most radical fighter to result from the RAF's Expansion Scheme of rearmament in the later 1930's, and was certainly the most heavily-armed, with four 20 mm cannons concentrated in its nose. Unfortunately, delays with flight testing, caused partly by engine problems, and led to production orders being cut. Instead, the increasingly successful and important Hawker Hurricane and Supermarine Spitfire gained priority, and indeed Westland was brought into the production scheme of the Spitfire as a major sub-contractor. In any event, only 114 production Whirlwinds, plus two prototypes were built. Deliveries to No.263 Squadron, the RAF's first operational Whirlwind unit, began in July 1940, but various problems delayed the type's operational debut until late 1940/early 1941. At first employed purely as a fighter, the Whirlwind later found a successful role as a fighter-bomber on fighter 'sweeps' across the English Channel against

*The Westland Whirlwind was a somewhat radical fighter concept, the first such design to serve with the RAF. This example, serial number P7094, HE-T, flew with No.263 Squadron, RAF, the first unit to use the Whirlwind operationally.*

*A Westland Whirlwind shows off its potent four-cannon nose armament*
*(Photo: Library of Congress).*

German military targets in Occupied France. This involved the adaptation of the aircraft to carry bombs beneath the wings outboard of the engines of up to 500 lb under each wing – although this combination tended to impair performance. In the fighter-bomber role Whirlwinds gained a number of successes, but there were too few of them to play a major part in the RAF's offensive activities and only two squadrons used the type operationally. The last major Whirlwind fighter-bomber operations were mounted in October 1943. Further development of the twin-engined fighter design layout by Westland, however, led to the Welkin high-altitude fighter, and to the pioneering work by Normalair on pressurization equipment needed for high-level flight, which had such a great impact on civil and military aviation post-war.

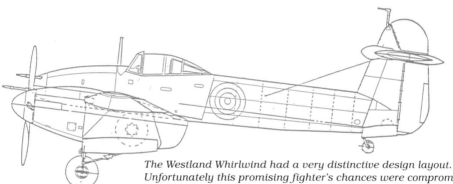

*The Westland Whirlwind had a very distinctive design layout. Unfortunately this promising fighter's chances were compromised by its less than perfect engines – it could and should have been re-engined with Rolls-Royce Merlins.*

**Specifications – Westland Whirlwind Mk.I**

| | |
|---|---|
| Wingspan | 45 ft |
| Length | 32 ft 3 in |
| Maximum speed | 360 mph at 15,000 ft |
| Maximum take-off weight | 10,379 lb |
| Range | 630 miles |
| Service ceiling | 30,300 ft |
| Armament | Four 20 mm (0.787 in) cannons in the nose fixed forward-firing, provision later for bombs below the wings |
| Engine | Two Rolls-Royce Peregrine I inline piston engines, of 880 hp each |
| Crew | One |

# Blohm und Voss Bv 141

The Blohm und Voss Bv 141 was one of the most unorthodox aircraft to fly in World War Two, and it illustrated a completely different design approach to a comparatively straightforward specification. In 1937, the German air ministry issued a requirement for a short-range reconnaissance and observation aircraft with the additional capability to perform light attack duties. Three companies came up with proposals to meet the official requirement. They included Focke-Wulf, whose Fw 189 (see pages 34 to 35) was eventually chosen for operational service – and proved to be highly successful. One of the other companies that attempted to meet the original specification was the Hamburger Flugzeugbau (see pages 138 to 139), the aviation division of the giant Blohm und Voss shipbuilding concern. This company took a completely novel approach to the need for good crew visibility to meet the official requirement for observation duties, by enclosing the aircraft's crew in a cockpit nacelle that was separate to the aircraft's actual fuselage and engine combination. Initially known as the Ha 141, construction of the prototype was initiated as a private venture due to the official preference for the Fw 189. It first flew on 25 February 1938. This aircraft proved to fly very well despite its strange, asymmetrical layout. Although built as a private venture, success with the first aircraft resulted in two further prototype/development examples being officially ordered. These featured a re-designed crew/cockpit compartment, and represented the start of a considerable amount of re-design work that was eventually to help ruin the whole Bv 141 project. Based on this revised layout several A-series development aircraft were built, and these proved successful in various official trials. The whole A-series program was then officially abandoned. Presumably this was due to official misunderstanding of the aircraft and its capabilities, but the excuse was that the Bv 141A was underpowered with its 960 hp BMW 132N radial engine. Blohm und Voss duly re-engined the design with the more powerful BMW 801 radial, which also called for a major re-design of the whole aircraft.

As Bv 141B, the completely revised layout first flew on 9 January 1941,

*The totally unconventional layout of the Blohm und Voss Bv 141B is shown here. Early examples had a completely different tailplane and other important differences and flew quite adequately, but the later Bv 141B design illustrated did not fly particularly well.*

*A Bv 141B, showing the curious design of this type. The type's four small underwing bomb racks can just be seen behind the main undercarriage well cut-outs (Photo: via Peter Walter).*

followed by several B-series development aircraft. The Bv 141B was essentially an entirely new aircraft. It retained the Bv 141's original unconventional layout and its flying characteristics were poor compared to the initial machines. Only one example appears to have reached the Luftwaffe to fly under front-line conditions, and widespread manufacture was never initiated – Blohm und Voss's factories by then were fully engaged on other programs.

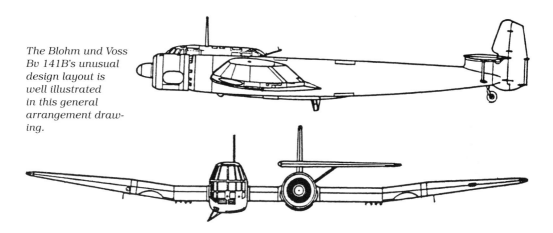

*The Blohm und Voss Bv 141B's unusual design layout is well illustrated in this general arrangement drawing.*

### Specifications – Blohm und Voss Bv 141B

| | |
|---|---|
| Wingspan | 57 ft 3.5 in |
| Length | 45 ft 9.25 in |
| Maximum speed | 272 mph at 16,400 ft |
| Maximum take-off weight | 13, 448 lb |
| Range | 746 miles |
| Service ceiling | 32,808 ft |
| Armament | Two 7.92 mm (0.312 in) machine guns fixed forward-firing, two similar caliber weapons rearwards-firing on flexible mounts, four 110 lb bombs beneath the wings |
| Engine | One BMW 801A radial piston engine, of 1,560 hp |
| Crew | Three |

# Beech Model 18

One of history's most long-running civil and military aircraft, the ubiquitous Beech Model 18 has had a long and varied career, stretching from the 1930's into the current century. The Beech 18 was the second light utility transport designed by the Wichita, Kansas-based Beech Aircraft Co., the first being the Model 17 biplane covered in Volume I of this encyclopedia. The twin-engined Beech 18 first flew on 15 January 1937, and was aimed at both military and civilian customers. The threat of war saw Beech greatly expand its facilities in response to coming large orders from the U.S. military. Alongside the standard utility versions, ordered as U.S. Army C-45 (later UC-45) and U.S. Navy JRB Expeditors, specialized navigation trainers were produced as the AT-7 Navigator. The AT-11 Kansan was used for bombing and gunnery training with a glazed nose and an internal bomb bay. U.S. Navy trainer versions were members of the SNB family. The F-2 Expeditor (sometimes called Discoverer) was a photo survey/reconnaissance version, while in 1944 a handful of UC-45Fs were converted as CQ-3 radio-controlled target directors. Surviving JRB and SNB versions received C-45 designations when the tri-service unified designation system was adopted in 1962. Most C-45 variants in service were used as light transports, but some (including examples employed by U.S. Army aviation in the 1960's) were used to test electronics, were fitted out as V.I.P. transports or were employed as airborne ambulances. A few Navy C-45s survived in service until the early 1970's. During the Second World War, Beech 18 versions were supplied under Lend-Lease to Britain's RAF and Royal Navy as Expeditor Mk.Is, Mk.IIs and Navigator Mk.Is, some 424 British serial numbers being allocated. The

*A Beech Model 18 in one of its many military guises: a U.S. Navy JRB-2 light transport. Beech aircraft from the period are often called Beechcraft, and the Beech name exists to this day.*

Expeditor Mk.3 was a Royal Canadian Air Force version, including several different sub-variants for various post-war roles. Many Beech 18s were also exported overseas after the war, for example to Argentina, Brazil, France, Italy, the Netherlands, Peru, South Vietnam and Turkey. Post-war the Beech 18s were built for business transportation in D18S, E18S, G18S and H18 models, and remained in production until November 1969. Many of the surviving military models were also civilianized as C18S aircraft at the end of their service careers (except for AT 11/SNB-1 examples). In addition, several companies offered conversions of existing Beech 18s (such as Dumod, Hamilton – as the Westwind – and Volpar). Volpar conversions proved to be popular for C.I.A. affiliated activities with Air America, operating in South-East Asia during the 1960's and early 1970's and carrying anything from rice to guns. At the turn of the century at least one Beech 18 (a G18S) remained in military service, with the Tongan Defence Services – Air Wing.

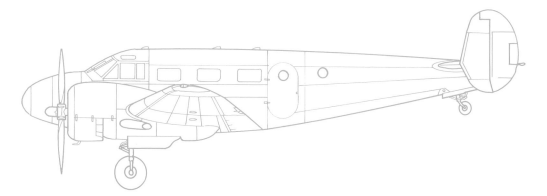

*With an all-metal construction and fabric-covered control surfaces, the Beech Model 18 was a neat and streamlined design that found wide acceptance and served worldwide. Over seven thousand Beech 18 of all types are thought to have been built.*

**Specifications – Beech Expeditor Mk.II (Royal Navy)**

| | |
|---|---|
| Wingspan | 47 ft 8 in |
| Length | 34 ft 3 in |
| Maximum speed | 230 mph at sea level |
| Maximum take-off weight | 7,500 lb |
| Range | 900 miles |
| Service ceiling | 27,000 ft |
| Engine | Two Pratt & Whitney R-985-AN-1 Wasp Junior radial piston engines, of 450 hp each |
| Accommodation | Two crew, approximately six passengers |

# North American B-25 Mitchell

Named after William 'Billy' Mitchell, a great exponent of air power in the 1920's, the North American B-25 Mitchell was a highly capable and successful medium bomber and attack aircraft. Produced by the same company that created the excellent P-51 Mustang fighter (see pages 214 to 217), the Mitchell served with the U.S. Army Air Force and other Allied air arms including Britain's Royal Air Force. The Mitchell was developed to meet the same Army Air Corps design specification for a light bomber and attack aircraft that led to the Douglas DB-7 and Martin Maryland (described elsewhere in this Book). The U.S. Army's requirements, embodied in Circular Proposal 38-385, were for a twin-engined light bomber with attack (close-support) capabilities. The winner

was Douglas' DB-7, but North American's proposals also gained much official interest.

The prototype NA-40, built to meet the original requirement, first flew in January 1939. It was a very different aircraft to the eventual B-25 Mitchell production layout. Amongst other features it was fitted with a shoulder-mounted wing, together with a narrow fuselage (like that of the competing Douglas DB-7 and Martin Maryland). Sadly the prototype soon crashed (as also did the original Douglas prototype). Nevertheless, North American was encouraged to re-design the NA-40 into a fast, modern medium bomber. The resulting new configuration, the NA-62, was ordered into production for the U.S. Army even before it first flew – rearmament by then having become a necessity even for the basically 'isolationist' United States. The

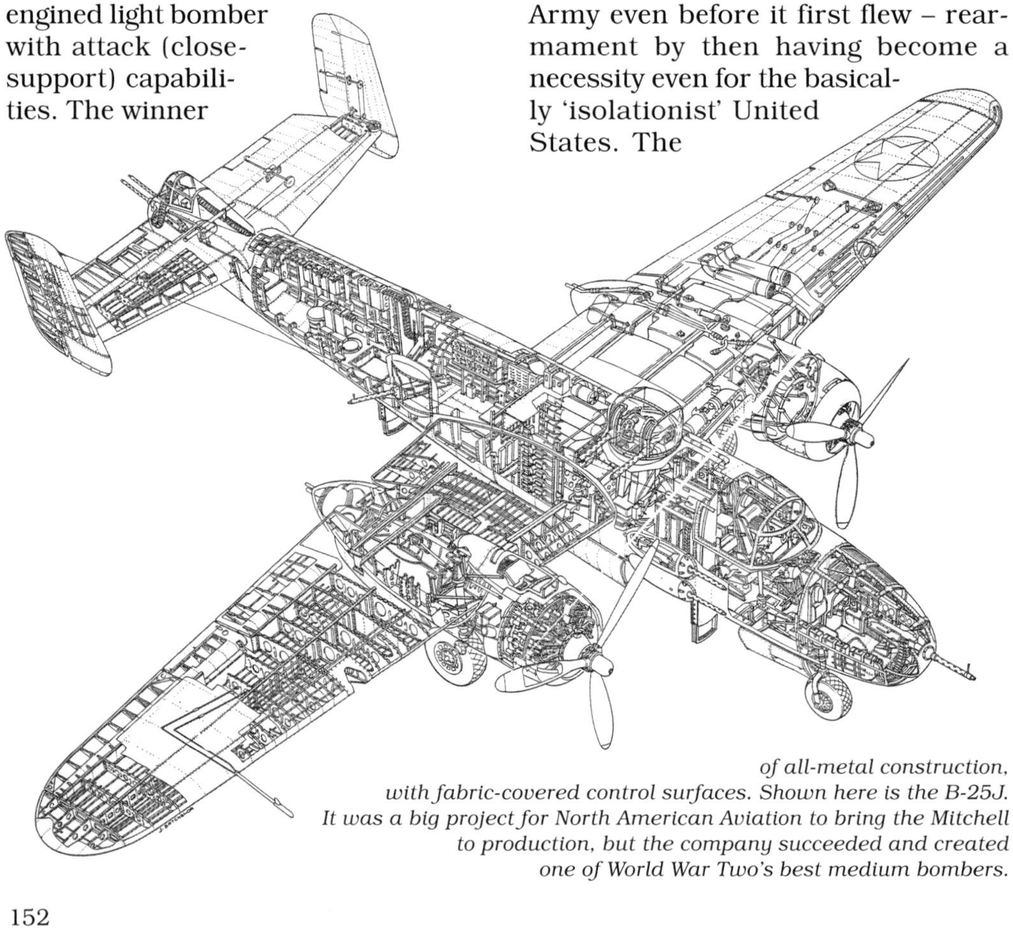

*of all-metal construction, with fabric-covered control surfaces. Shown here is the B-25J. It was a big project for North American Aviation to bring the Mitchell to production, but the company succeeded and created one of World War Two's best medium bombers.*

152

One of the best-known preserved B-25 Mitchells is 'Executive Sweet.' It is seen here in November 2003 at Nellis Air Force Base, Nevada – still going strong some six decades after it was built (Photo: Malcolm V. Lowe).

first aircraft to the new configuration flew on 19 August 1940. Differences incorporated into this new layout included a widened fuselage to allow space for two pilots seated side-by-side on the flight deck, an increased bomb load and more powerful engines as well as relocation of the wing to a virtually mid-fuselage position. Initial production aircraft had a 'straight' wing, but from the tenth production machine onwards, a distinctive, slight 'gull wing' configuration was adopted. Just 24 initial production B-25s were manufactured, but they were the start of a production run that led to some 9,817 Mitchells being built in eight principal production versions. Forty B-25As were subsequently

made, and these started to reach the 17th Bomb Group (Medium) in the latter half of 1941. The Mitchell was thus entering service as the United States was thrown into World War Two by the Japanese attack on Pearl Harbor in December 1941. The B-25A was followed by some 120 B-25Bs. The B-25B design represented a major up-gunning of the Mitchell with the addition of a dorsal fuselage gun turret between the wing and the tail. Next in production was the more powerful B-25C (some 1,625 built, intended for American, British and Dutch service), which had a greater bomb-carrying capacity. Similar to these were 2,290 B-25Ds, built at a second major production facility that had been established in

Serial number 43-4551 was a B-25H-5-NA (Inglewood-built). The B-25H introduced several armament improvements over previous Mitchell versions, and featured a nose-mounted 75 mm cannon – one of the largest aerial weapons yet employed in warfare.

# B. 25 Mitchell *continued*

Kansas City in addition to North America's existing factory at Inglewood in California. By this time the B-25 was proving its worth, particularly in the Pacific theater, not just as a bomber but as a very capable attack aircraft. Its almost fighter-like performance and agility were very useful, and it had excellent growth potential. The B-25G (400 built, plus conversions), featured a formidable 75 mm cannon in a new 'solid' nose together with forward-firing nose-mounted machine guns – although some replaced the big cannon with smaller caliber weapons. The sub-sequent B-25H (1,000 built) also mounted a 75 mm cannon in its nose, together with a number of extra machine guns in fairings on the sides of the nose. The dorsal turret was also relocated to just behind the cockpit, and mid-fuselage waist gun positions were introduced. The definitive B-25J (4,318 delivered) reintroduced the glazed nose of models earlier than the B-25G, but some examples had a 'solid' nose with eight 0.5 in (12.7 mm) machine guns – for a total of 18 of these hard-hitting weapons on some aircraft!

The Mitchell was a great success in combat. It flew with U.S. forces prin-

*The B-25G introduced the 75 mm cannon into the Mitchell's armory. Also added were four 0.5 in (12.7 mm) machine guns in the 'solid' nose arrangement shown here. This made the Mitchell into a dedicated attack aircraft, a role that it had already been fulfilling, although the cannon was replaced with two further machine guns in some B-25G*
*(Photo: U.S. Army Air Force).*

*This is the standard glazed nose, with a position for a bombardier, as used by several versions of the B-25 Mitchell. It is shown here by the preserved B-25 'Executive Sweet' in November 2003 (Photo: John Batchelor).*

cipally in the Pacific and Mediterranean theaters, including combat over North Africa and Italy together with many distant battlegrounds across the huge Pacific war theater. By far the best-known single action carried out by the B-25 took place in April 1942, when 16 specially-prepared and modified early-model Mitchells were employed in a raid on Tokyo and other targets in the Japanese 'Home Islands.' Led by another colorful character associated with the B-25, James H. Doolittle, the Mitchells were launched from the aircraft carrier U.S.S. Hornet. The raid was a huge propaganda success for the Americans as well as a great morale boost for the Allies.

RAF and Commonwealth units also flew the Mitchell in some numbers during the war, including service with the Royal Australian Air Force later in the war, and a significant number were supplied to the Soviet Union. A camera-equipped reconnaissance derivative of the B-25 was the F-10. The U.S. Marine Corps used the Mitchell mainly in the Pacific in several land-based versions designated PBJ. After its successful service in World War Two, the B-25 was exported widely after the war under defence aid arrangements, particularly to South American countries.

*The view from inside the bombardier's position within the nose of the preserved B-25 'Executive Sweet.' It was a 'white-knuckle' ride when Mitchells were flown low and fast like this. Visible in the lower center is the world-famous Norden bombsight, fitted to many U.S. bombers during the war*
*(Photo: John Batchelor).*

### Specifications – North American B-25J Mitchell (glass nose)

| | |
|---|---|
| Wingspan | 67 ft 7 in |
| Length | 52 ft 11 in |
| Maximum speed | 275 mph at 13,000 ft |
| Maximum take-off weight | 35,000 lb |
| Range | approximately 1,500 miles |
| Service ceiling | 24,200 ft |
| Armament | Twelve 0.5 in (12.7 mm) machine guns in various fixed and turret locations, up to 3,000 lb of bombs |
| Engine | Two Wright R-2600-29 Cyclone (sometimes called 'Double Cyclone') radial piston engines, of 1,700 hp each |
| Crew | Five |

# Martin PBM Mariner

The Martin Model 162 PBM Mariner was a twin-engined patrol flying-boat designed as a potential successor to the Consolidated Catalina (see pages 232 to 233). Powered by two Wright R-2600-6 Cyclone radial engines of 1,600 hp, the prototype XPBM-1 first flew on 18 February 1939. The type featured a prominent gull-wing configuration and a roomy hull (fuselage) fitted out with all the spartan amenities for long-range patrol missions. It was of semi-monocoque construction and twin-step configuration. It was armed with up to 4,000 lb of bombs or depth charges, and later this capacity was increased. Alternatively, a pair of torpedoes could be carried on mountings beneath the wings, between the engines and the hull, reflecting the type's capabilities against surface ships as well as submarines.

The first of twenty production PBM-1 aircraft entered U.S. Navy service in late 1940/early 1941. Following a single experimental XPBM-2 that had been stressed for catapult launching, production switched to the important PBM-3 variant. Powered by two Wright R-2600-12 Cyclone engines of 1,700 hp, this series was built in several specific sub-types including radar-equipped models, and some PBM-3B were supplied to the Royal Air Force as Mariner GR.I although they were not widely used. The Royal Australian Air Force also received some Mariners. The PBM-4 was an abortive project that was abandoned in favor of the PBM-5 variant, powered by two 2,100 hp Pratt & Whitney R-2800-34 Wasp radials. It is almost inevitable that historians disagree over the number of Mariners that were built, the total probably being somewhere around 1,400, and the type gave useful if largely unsung service to both the U.S. Navy and the U.S. Coast Guard. However, highlights of the Mariner's career included the sinking of a number of U-Boats. The type also played prominent roles in the invasions of the Philippines, Iwo Jima and Okinawa. Mariners complemented the efforts of such types as the Catalina and the land-based Consolidated PB4Y-1 in the long war against Axis warships and submarines.

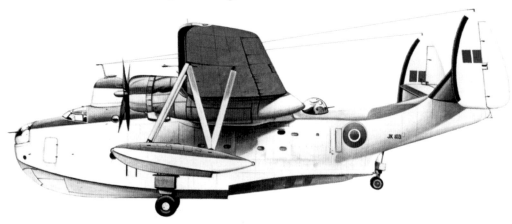

*The Martin Mariner was a big, powerful patrol flying-boat. In addition to operations in World War Two, Mariners gave valuable service to the U.S. Navy during the Korean War of 1950 to 1953. There was also an amphibious version with a retractable undercarriage designated PBM-5A. Illustrated here is a Mariner in British markings.*

*A Martin Mariner spectacularly uses rocket or jet assisted take-off and climbs out at a steep angle. The date of this official U.S. Navy photograph is October 1944 (Photo: U.S. Navy).*

In addition to its patrol mission, the Mariner was also employed in a search and rescue role, and a number of the type were used as transports. The post-war Mariner was additionally operated by the Dutch, Argentine and Uruguayan naval air arms, production only ending in 1949.

**Specifications – Martin PBM-3D Mariner**

| | |
|---|---|
| Wingspan | 118 ft |
| Length | 79 ft 10 in |
| Maximum speed | 211 mph at 16,100 ft |
| Maximum take-off weight | 58,000 lb |
| Range | approximately 2,240 miles |
| Service ceiling | 19,800 ft |
| Armament | Eight 0.5 in (12.7 mm) machine guns in nose, tail, dorsal and waist positions, up to 8,000 lb of bombs, depth charges or torpedo options |
| Engine | Two Wright R-2600-22 Cyclone (sometimes called 'Double Cyclone') radial piston engines, of 1,900 hp each |
| Crew | Seven to ten |

# Grumman JRF Goose

Developed from Grumman's G-21 design of 1936 for a light commercial amphibian, the Goose was manufactured for the U.S. Army as the OA-9, the U.S. Navy as the JRF-1, JRF-2, JRF-4 and JRF-5, and for the U.S. Coast Guard as the JRF-3. The type was basically a six-seat light transport and patrol aircraft with a number of slight variations. Powered by two Pratt & Whitney R-985-AN-6 Wasp Junior radial engines of 450 hp, the Goose first flew during June 1937. Initial production examples, powered by the same engines, were delivered during 1938.

The Goose was a high wing cantilever monoplane, fitted with split flaps and featured a two-step hull (fuselage) of semi-monocoque construction. The crew of two were seated side by side,

with the four-seat passenger cabin immediately aft of the cockpit. In its patrol configuration the Goose was fitted with two underwing racks, each capable of carrying a 250 lb bomb or depth charge. Geese operated by the U.S. Coast Guard were also fitted with an autopilot and anti-ice equipment, in order to allow deployment in northern climates. In addition to the aforementioned roles, the Goose was also employed for photographic survey, navigation training, target-towing, anti-submarine and search and rescue roles. In Britain, the Air Transport Auxiliary (a mainly civilian-manned organization for ferrying and delivering aircraft from factories to the frontline) also used the Goose as a ferry. In addition to the U.S. services, the Goose was operated by the Royal Canadian

*The original caption to this photograph, dated July 1945, claims that the Grumman Goose illustrated is on a rescue mission over Alaska to look for survivors of a crashed aircraft.*
*On locating them, a para-rescue squad will parachute from the Goose to help the survivors*
*(Photo: U.S. Coast Guard).*

Air Force, the French Aéronavale (naval air arm) and Portuguese naval aviation. Although the U.S. Navy discarded its Geese soon after the end of World War Two, the U.S. Coast Guard continued to operate the type for several more years. The final production model was the JRF-6, although some of these may not have been manufactured.

Overall production figures for the Goose are somewhat sketchy, particularly as the picture was clouded due to civil-owned examples being impressed into military service, but it is thought that approximately three hundred military Geese were built in total. It is known, however, that at least 185 of the JRF-5, the most numerous of the military Goose variants, were produced. After the war, the Goose proved popular with civil operators, and a number of upgrades were additionally made including the McKinnon Goose with four engines, and a twin-engined turboprop version. In addition to the Goose, Grumman also manufactured a smaller transport amphibian called the G-44 Widgeon, which similarly saw military use during World War Two.

*The Grumman Goose was a tubby, purposeful amphibian that was built for military as well as civilian use. Many years after the Second World War ended, Geese remained in service with civil operators.*

### Specifications – Grumman JRF-4 Goose

| | |
|---|---|
| Wingspan | 49 ft |
| Length | 38 ft 4 in |
| Maximum speed | 201 mph at 5,000 ft |
| Maximum take-off weight | 7,955 lb |
| Range | 640 miles |
| Service ceiling | 21,000 ft |
| Armament | Two 250 lb bombs or depth charges on underwing racks |
| Engine | Two Pratt & Whitney R-985-AN-6 Wasp Junior radial piston engines, of 450 hp each |
| Accommodation | Two crew, normally four passengers |

# Caproni Ca.313 and Ca.314 Series

An important family of light transport, bomber and torpedo-armed twin-engined aircraft was produced before and during World War Two by the Italian Caproni company. These gave valuable service to the Italian armed forces, and also operated with a number of export customers. The initial member of the family was the Caproni Borea of 1935, an all-wood light transport with a neat trousered main undercarriage. It was developed into the Ca.309, which first flew in October 1936. Named Ghibli (Desert Wind), the Ca.309 was lightly armed and had a fixed, spatted undercarriage. Built in large numbers, the type was used primarily for light transport or as a light bomber, as a 'colonial' aircraft primarily for service in Italy's African colonial possessions. A useful number of these attractive twin-engine aircraft served during World War Two. Virtually concurrent in production was the Ca.310, a developed, modernized and more

powerful radial-engined derivative of the inline-engined Ca.309, equipped with a retractable undercarriage and other refinements. The prototype first flew in the spring of 1937 and, in addition to service with Italy's Regia Aeronautica, the type was succesfully exported. Introduced into the Ca.310bis design was a rounded, extensively glazed nose to replace the conventional windscreen and cockpit cover of the standard Ca.310, and this extensively-glazed nose was characteristic of several subsequent versions. In particular, the Ca.310bis was the basis for the improved and more powerful Piaggio radial-engined Ca.311, which first flew in April 1939. This met an Italian air force requirement for a light reconnaissance-bomber and observation aircraft, and was duly produced for that purpose. However, continuing development saw the line's radial engined-layout replaced by small inline engines in the Ca.313, which continued to use the Ca.311's rounded glazed nose but saw a general improvement in armament options. The prototype flew in December 1939, duly arousing much poten-

*The Caproni Ca.314 was a functional if not particularly elegant maritime patrol, torpedo-bomber and light ground attack type. It featured wooden wings with a metal fuselage structure, partly metal and partly fabric-covered*

tial domestic and export interest. Sweden eventually obtained 84 examples in several sub-types, deliveries commencing in late 1940. Substantial interest was also shown by Britain and France, the latter ordering 200 of the type 'off the drawing board' and receiving a handful of examples prior to Italy's entry into World War Two in June 1940. Britain ordered 300, plus 100 examples of the Ca.311 for training purposes, but again Italy's entry into the war on the Axis side ended that line of interest. Instead some of the aircraft destined for France, plus newly-ordered examples, were used by the Regia Aeronautica, deliveries starting in the spring of 1941. Compara-

tively successful, some were intended for service with Germany's Luftwaffe as liaison and training aircraft. Continuing development led to the Ca.314, the most famous of the family, which reverted to a conventional stepped nose and windscreen arrangement. Versions of the Ca.314 included the Ca.314A maritime patrol and Mediterranean convoy escort aircraft, the Ca.314B torpedo-bomber and the Ca.314C light ground attack aircraft. Production extended to 404 examples plus three prototypes, and the type gave important service to the Regia Aeronautica particularly from 1942 – some soldiering on into the post-war world as light transports.

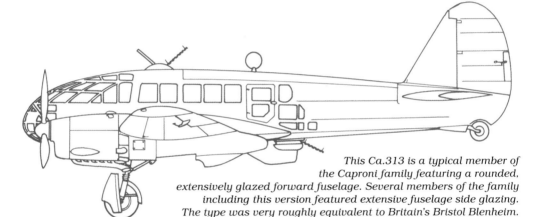

*This Ca.313 is a typical member of the Caproni family featuring a rounded, extensively glazed forward fuselage. Several members of the family including this version featured extensive fuselage side glazing. The type was very roughly equivalent to Britain's Bristol Blenheim.*

**Specifications – Caproni Ca.314A**

| | |
|---|---|
| Wingspan | 54 ft 7.5 in |
| Length | 38 ft 8.5 in |
| Maximum speed | 245 mph at 13,125 ft |
| Maximum take-off weight | 14,594 lb |
| Range | 1,050 miles |
| Service ceiling | 21,000 ft |
| Armament | Two 12.7 mm (0.5 in) machine guns in wing roots forward-firing, one dorsal turret-mounted 7.7 mm (0.303 in) machine gun (or 0.5 in), one similar caliber flexible-mounted in ventral position, up to 1,102 lb of bombs |
| Engine | Two Isotta-Fraschini Delta RC.35 inline piston engines, of 730 hp each |
| Crew | Three or four |

# Reggiane Re.2000 Series

In 1937, a neat single-engine, single-seat monoplane fighter entered U.S. Army Air Corps service. This was the Seversky P-35 and continuing development of this promising design eventually led to the famous Republic P-47 Thunderbolt (see pages 194 to 197). The P-35 also had a considerable effect on a relative newcomer to aircraft design–Reggiane in Italy, a subsidiary of the large Caproni concern. With some aviation connections from World War One, Reggiane was nevertheless a newcomer to modern fighter design, and the P-35 had a great influence on the fighter that Reggiane eventually created for the Italian armed forces. This was the Re.2000, the first of a series of neat and capable fighters produced in comparatively small numbers. The prototype Re.2000 first flew in 1938, and it was very typical for an Italian warplane of that era in being radial-engined. Unfortunately the Fal-co (Hawk or Falcon), as it appears to have been known, lost a competitive evaluation for Italian orders against the Macchi M.C.200. Although more maneuverable, the Re.2000 was judged to be structurally inadequate. This did not stop export orders, however and the Re.2000 was ordered by Sweden and Hungary, with several other countries showing interest (reportedly including Britain). The Italian naval air arm also used the type in limited numbers. Production under license additionally took place in Hungary, and Hungarian-operated examples saw combat alongside the Germans on the Eastern Front against Soviet forces. Breaking with tradition, Reggiane then developed the Re.2000 layout by installing a German inline engine, the Daimler Benz DB 601, into the basic but slightly revised airframe, creating the very capable Re.2001 Falco II. This attracted the interest of the

*The Reggiane Re.2001 Falco II was a nicely-streamlined inline-engined fighter development of the radial-engined Re.2000. A high proportion of the Re.2001 production run were night fighters, although they were not radar-equipped, relying instead on pilot skills to be effective.*

Italian air force, and Regia Aeronautica-operated examples went into action over Malta in 1942, having entered service late the previous year. Powered by an Italian licence-built version of the DB 601 engine, the Alfa Romeo RA.1000, 252 Re.2001 are believed to have been built. Amongst these were some 150 Re.2001 CN basic, radarless night fighters. Continuing development led to the Re.2002 Ariete (Ram) fighter-bomber, powered by a Piaggio P.XIX radial engine in a revised airframe, of which some 50 (possibly many more) were manufactured. The final production model in the series was the further refined Re.2005 Sagittario (Archer) of 1942, an excellent design powered by a Fiat license-built version of the German DB 605 inline engine. 48 are reputed to have been delivered by the time of Italy's capitulation to the Allies in 1943, some later flying with Italian forces that stayed loyal to the Germans. A number of examples of the Re.2000 series also found their way into German hands.

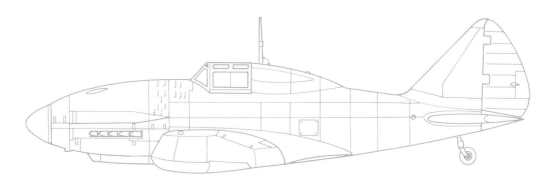

*The Reggiane Re.2001 broke with the tradition of many Italian fighters in being inline engine-powered. The power plant was an Italian license-built version of the excellent German Daimler Benz DB 601 inline engine.*

## Specifications – Reggiane Re.2000 (I Series)

| | |
|---|---|
| Wingspan | 36 ft 1 in |
| Length | 26 ft 2.5 in |
| Maximum speed | 329 mph at 16,405 ft |
| Maximum take-off weight | 6,349 lb |
| Range | 715 miles |
| Service ceiling | 31,168 ft |
| Armament | Two 12.7 mm (0.5 in) machine guns fixed forward-firing in upper forward fuselage |
| Engine | One Piaggio P.XI RC.40 radial piston engine, of 985 hp |
| Crew | One |

# Macchi C.200 Saetta

A contemporary of the Fiat G.50 Freccia (covered on pages 120 to 121), the Macchi C.200 Saetta (Chain-Lightning) was from the pre-Second World War generation of Italian fighters with which Italy commenced World War Two. It embodied, like the G.50, a number of 'modern' features such as a retractable undercarriage and monoplane layout, but also harked back to earlier times with its open cockpit (much favored at that time by Italian pilots) and a big, but not very powerful radial engine.

Although the C.200 began life as a private venture by the Macchi company, it was submitted, along with several other designs, for a 1936 Italian Air Ministry fighter design requirement.

The first prototype flew in the second half of 1937, and the type was duly flown-off successfully against other contenders. A production order followed in 1938 and the first examples were delivered in October 1939. By then the Second World War had already commenced, and the C.200 was not as advanced as front-line fighters of other countries such as the Supermarine Spitfire and Messerschmitt Bf 109. The first operational unit was intended to be the 4th Stormo of the Regia Aeronautica, but re-equipment of the Italian air force under a somewhat ambitious 'program R' was not particularly fast. Nevertheless some 150 C.200 are believed to have been in service when Italy

*Although initial production examples of the Macchi C.200 had an enclosed cockpit, most (like the one illustrated here) were of the open-cockpit variety. The type was built in several series, some by Macchi but others by Breda under licence.*

entered World War Two on 10 June 1940 – although the C.200 did not feature in the brief Italian campaign against southern France. Instead the type entered combat later, as a bomber escort in the initial major Italian air attacks on the island of Malta in 1940. C.200s subsequently served on all fronts where Italian air force elements were operational, including North Africa, the Mediterranean, the Balkans and even on the Eastern Front alongside German units – where the open cockpits of these Macchis must have been most uncomfortable! The type's modest performance and light armament were not conducive to great success in air-to-air combat, but like many Italian fighters it enjoyed excellent maneuvrability. Eventually many C.200s were relegated to light ground attack missions. The total production appears to have been just over one thousand one hundred. Continuing development led to the far better C.202 Folgore.

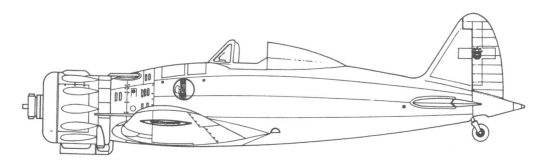

*The Macchi C.200 (sometimes written MC.200 after the initials of its chief designer) was of all-metal construction, with fabric-covered control surfaces. The Italian name Saetta is usually translated as Lightning or Chain-Lightning, but it is also said to refer to the lightning-bolts held by the mythical personality Jupiter, and is occasionally additionally translated as Thunderbolt or even Arrow.*

**Specifications – Macchi C.200 Saetta (mid-Series production)**

| | |
|---|---|
| Wingspan | 34 ft 8.5 in |
| Length | 26 ft 10.66 in |
| Maximum speed | 312 mph at 14,764 ft |
| Maximum take-off weight | 5,710 lb |
| Range | 354 miles |
| Service ceiling | 29,200 ft |
| Armament | Two 12.7 mm (0.5 in) machine guns fixed forward-firing in upper forward fuselage, some aircraft also had two 7.7 mm (0.303 in) machine guns in the wings and provision for light bombs beneath the wings |
| Engine | One Fiat A.74 RC.38 radial piston engine, of 870 hp |
| Crew | One |

# Fairey Firefly

Conceived in response to Specification N.5/40, the Fairey Firefly was designed as a two-seat fleet fighter for Britain's Royal Navy. Powered by a 1,730 hp Rolls-Royce Griffon Mk.IIB engine, the prototype first flew on 22 December 1941. Armament for the Firefly consisted of four 20 mm Hispano cannons, two in each wing. Eight rocket projectiles could be carried, four under each wing, or up to 2,000 lb of bombs. Later production versions of the Firefly introduced the 1,990 hp Griffon Mk.XII.

Like most other naval aircraft, the Firefly featured folding wings for operations aboard the confines of aircraft carriers, the wings pivoting upwards and backwards to lie alongside the fuselage. A fighter reconnaissance version of the Firefly featured an ASH radar housed in a pod under the fuselage.

From an early stage the Firefly was earmarked for the night fighter role and this developed into the NF.II,

a number of which were converted from standard F.Is on the production line. This version featured AI Mk.10 radar, with its associated scanners housed in fairings in the leading edges of the wings. To counteract the weight of this equipment it was necessary to add an 18 in (457 mm) extension forward of the engine firewall in order to maintain the aircraft's center of gravity. It was found later that most of the radar equipment, including the scanner, could be housed in a standard ASH pod. As this did not affect the standard Firefly's center of gravity, production of the NF.II variant was terminated after 37 examples had been constructed. The balance of the contract was covered from Firefly FR.I aircraft converted on the production line. This version was known as the NF.I. The already constructed NF.IIs were converted back to NF.I standard. The best available production figures for

The Fairey Firefly was an effective and successful two-seat fighter, strike and reconnaissance aircraft that was also used as a night fighter. It served up to and beyond the end of World War Two.

these early marks are as follows: 342 FR.I aircraft, 350 FR.I aircraft, 140 NF.I aircraft, and 37 NF.II aircraft, making a total of 869 examples of the type – although some historians disagree with these figures.

Operationally, the Firefly first entered service with No.1770 Squadron, Fleet Air Arm, in October 1943. The type went on to take part in the operations against the German battleship Tirpitz, and other anti-shipping strikes off the Norwegian coast. In the Far East, Fireflies were active in attacks against the Japanese oil facilities in Sumatra, both in the escort and rocket-firing roles. The Firefly went on to have

*A beautifully-preserved Fairey Firefly in the United States, photographed in 2002. It is in fact a Firefly AS.6, a post-World War Two version (Photo: John Batchelor).*

an illustrious post-war career, including service in the Korean War of 1950 to 1953.

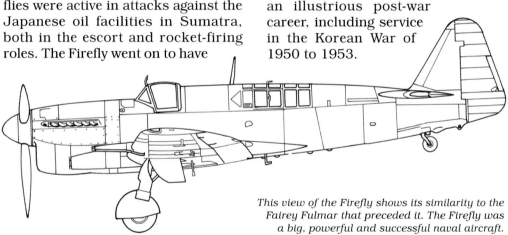

*This view of the Firefly shows its similarity to the Fairey Fulmar that preceded it. The Firefly was a big, powerful and successful naval aircraft.*

### Specifications – Fairey Firefly F.Mk.I

| | |
|---|---|
| Wingspan | 44 ft 6 in |
| Length | 37 ft 7 in |
| Maximum speed | 316 mph at 14,000 ft |
| Maximum take-off weight | 14,020 lb |
| Range | 1,300 miles |
| Service ceiling | 28,000 ft |
| Armament | Four 20 mm cannons fixed forward-firing, two in each wing, up to 2,000 lb of bombs, or eight rockets beneath the wings |
| Engine | One Rolls-Royce Griffon IIB inline piston engine, of 1,730 hp |
| Crew | Two |

# Mikoyan-Gurevich MiG-3

One of the most famous collaborations in the history of aviation is that of Artyom Mikoyan and Mikhail Gurevich. Proof that even an archaic system like that of the Soviet Union can still produce talented aviation designers, these two undoubtedly gifted personalities began their collaboration in 1939 and 1940. The organization that came to bear their names is still in existence today – although in a markedly different form in modern post-communist Russia. It came to symbolize Soviet fighter technology during the Cold War from the 1950's onwards, but the collaboration started in a very quiet way and its first fighter – the MiG-3 – was not an outstanding success. Mikoyan

and Gurevich's collaboration began under the aegis of the famous Russian aviation designer Nikolay Polikarpov, whose design bureau created the well-known I-16 fighter which is covered in Volume 1 of *The Complete Encyclopedia of Flight*. Working initially under Polikarpov until his attentions were turned to other projects, Mikoyan and Gurevich began work on various programs. The most important of these was the I-200 single-engine fighter, powered by the Mikulin AM-35 inline engine. In competition with the work pursued by the Yakovlev design team, Mikoyan and Gurevich's I-200 first flew on 5 April 1940, and entered production as the MiG-1. One hundred

*The Mikoyan-Gurevich MiG-3 was the start of a long line of MiG fighters. In reality, it was not the most auspicious of starts, since the MiG-3 was not one of the better fighters of World War Two. Like the LaGG-3, however, it was a useful stop-gap for the Soviet air force until infinitely better fighters came along from the Russian aircraft industry later in the war. The example pictured here wears 'winter' coloring, the bright wings allowing the aircraft to be spotted easily if brought down in the snow.*

were built before continuing refinement and tinkering led to the MiG-3 production model, which came into widespread service with the Soviet air force when the German invasion began in June 1941. They were simply decimated – the worst hit air division losing 347 of its 409 operational aircraft on the first day. From then onwards the MiG-3's operational career somewhat improved, but the type was generally inferior at lower levels (and not much better elsewhere) against the German Messerschmitt Bf 109. Production ceased after approximately 3,422 MiG-1/MiG-3 had been built, although the type soldiered on in several units into the spring of 1943. As a fighting machine it had many disadvantages, such as collapsing undercarriages, and pilots generally found it better to fly with the cockpit canopy locked open or removed altogether to aid in escape from the aircraft. It also flew poorly and needed an experienced pilot to sort out its flying qualities. Various efforts were made to solve the problems and a string of experimental derivatives were tried including radial-engined versions, but the type was quickly superseded by better fighters from other designers. The MiG partnership however survived to create more successful aircraft in the future – helped by Mikoyan's elder brother, a close ally of Soviet dictator Joseph Stalin.

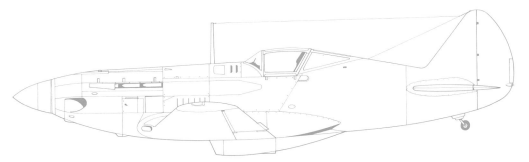

*The Mikoyan-Gurevich MiG-3 was a reasonable performer at high altitude, but was not a particularly accomplished dog-fighter and suffered directional instability and a number of other major problems including limited firepower.*

## Specifications – Mikoyan-Gurevich MiG-3 (1941 production)

| | |
|---|---|
| Wingspan | 33 ft 5.5 in |
| Length | 27 ft 1 in |
| Maximum speed | 398 mph at 25,591 ft |
| Maximum take-off weight | 7,385 lb |
| Range | 509 miles |
| Service ceiling | 39,370 ft |
| Armament | One 12.7 mm (0.5 in) machine gun and two 7.62 mm (0.3 in) machine guns, all fixed forward-firing in the upper forward fuselage |
| Engine | One Mikulin AM-35A inline piston engine, of 1,200–1,350 hp |
| Crew | One |

# Ilyushin Il-2 'Shturmovik'

The Second World War witnessed the mass-production of aircraft on a scale unprecedented since the creation of manned flight at the start of the twentieth century. The aviation industries of several countries produced enormous quantities of aircraft, of various different types, with the United States in particular calling itself the 'arsenal of democracy.' However, the most widely produced aircraft was actually manufactured in factories in the Soviet Union – the Ilyushin Il-2.

A ground attack aircraft with virtually fighter-like performance, the Il-2 grew from design studies for a heavily-armed and armored attack aircraft that were included in the 1937 experimental aircraft construction plan devised for the centralized Soviet aviation industry. The initial prototype, at first called TsKB-55, first flew on 2 October 1939, powered by a Mikulin AM-35 inline engine. After some redesign, a name change to BSh-2 and the installation of a more powerful AM-38 engine, the type entered production as the Il-2 in early 1941 at aircraft factory No.18 in Voronezh. The first production example flew on 10 March 1941.

The Il-2 was, for its time, quite an impressive warplane. In continuing the tradition established in World War One for close-support ground attack aircraft (then sometimes called 'trench fighters'), the Il-2 was heavily-armored, the single pilot, engine and other vital parts protected within metal structure and skinning that was thicker than on conventional aircraft. This gave the Il-2 its almost legendary ruggedness in combat. Nevertheless, at the time of the German invasion of the Soviet Union in June 1941 (Operation 'Barbarossa'), the Soviet air force was only just receiving its initial production examples. The 4th ShAP (attack air regiment) in Voronezh was the first to receive combat-ready examples, and they were soon in action against German forces. From then onwards, the Il-2 increasingly became the principal ground attack and anti-tank warplane defending the Soviet Union during the Great Patriotic War, as World War Two was known there. Continuing development led to a two-seat derivative, starting with the Il-2m3 with a rear-gunner/navigator, although design and production work was sometimes disrupted by the necessary evacuation of

*The Ilyushin Il-2 was a formidable ground attack aircraft for Soviet forces; this example appears to carry additional cannons in underwing fairings, relatively uncommon weapons usually associated with the Il-2-37.*

factories and design offices in the face of German advances. The two-seat Il-2, including some very heavily-armed sub-types, proved highly effective. Eventually some 35,952 (possibly more) were built. The type was also useful as a makeshift fighter against German bombers and transports, leading to the development of the single-seat Il-2I fighter, although this did not enter production. Instead, further development led to the Il-1 spin-off in 1944. This was produced as the Il-10, a more powerful and capable 2,000 hp AM-42 engined two-seater which entered front-line service in February 1945. The type was produced until 1948, with 4,540 Il-10 built. Some saw action against United Nations forces during the Korean War of 1950 to 1953, and also served with Eastern Bloc countries. In Czechoslovakia, the Il-10 was built (approximately 1,200 in total) as the Avia B-33.

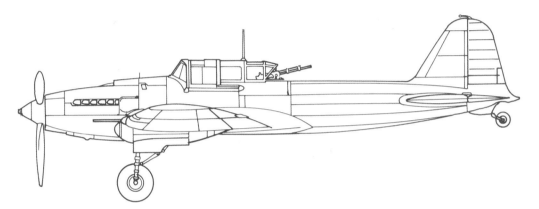

*An Ilyushin Il-2m3 two-seater. The 'Shturmovik' was heavily-armored,*
*the Il-2 series being an important tank-killer for Soviet forces.*
*Some were used by Soviet naval aviation units on anti-ship missions.*

**Specifications – Ilyushin Il-2m3**

| | |
|---|---|
| Wingspan | 47 ft 10.75 in |
| Length | 38 ft 2.75 in |
| Maximum speed | 251 mph at 4,921 ft |
| Maximum take-off weight | 14,021 lb |
| Range | 475 miles |
| Service ceiling | 19,685 ft |
| Armament | Two 23 mm cannons fixed forward-firing in the wings, (some aircraft) two 7.62 mm (0.3 in) machine guns; one 12.7 mm (0.5 in) machine gun flexible-mounted in rear cockpit, 882 lb of bombs internally and other weapons including four unguided rockets beneath each wing |
| Engine | One Mikulin AM-38 or AM-38F inline piston engine, of 1,700–1,770 hp |
| Crew | Two |

# Yakovlev Fighters

One of the great successes of the Soviet Union's aircraft industry during the Second World War, and a symbol of Russian aviation during the Great Patriotic War, the Yakovlev series of single-engine fighters were a part of the Russians' eventual winning line-up. Unlike the MiG-3 (see pages 168 to 169), the initial production model, the Yak-1, was a useful fighter from the start, and the design's considerable development potential led to a string of famous fighters that culminated in the Yak-3 and Yak-9 of the late war period. Initial design work began in 1939, Alexander Yakovlev became one of several talented designers who were brought into rapid prominence as the Russians realized that rearmament was a vital necessity in the face of the growing threat from Nazi Germany. His design office was already well established, but the I-26 that grew into the initial Yak-1 was his first front-line fighter project to gain production status. It was powered by a new and potentially

excellent fighter engine, the Klimov M-105, and this combination was a success from the start. The I-26 first flew on 13 January 1940, and series production of the Yak-1 commenced in the autumn of 1940. The new type was a popular aircraft with its pilots and its mixed construction of fabric and plywood covering was comparatively easy to build.

Early Yak-1 were in action during the early stages of the German invasion of the Soviet Union in June 1941, although production deliveries had been slow with unserviceable aircraft due to poor manufacture. Nevertheless, continuing development led to a significant design improvement with the removal of the original high rear fuselage line behind the cockpit and the addition of a more 'teardrop' shaped cockpit canopy, giving a better all-round view. Some later Yak-1 included this improvement, and it was standard on most subsequent production models, which were off-shoots of the early Yak-1. Continuing production included the Yak-7, and from an

*The Yakovlev fighters were of very straightforward construction and layout. The artist tells us that this is a Yak-3 and it is representative of the series in general, although the Yak-3 was from a different design line to some of the others in the family. All were light and capable fighters that were an important part of the final Russian victory over the Germans. 4,848 of the basic Yak-3 were built.*

*This Yakovlev Yak-3 is preserved in Paris at the Musée de l'Air, and represents the Yak fighters that were flown by French volunteers in Russia (Photo: Musée de l'Air).*

improved design lineage, the Yak-3 and Yak-9. The latter was one of the mainstays of the Soviet fighter force in the later stages of the war and Yak fighters were also flown by French volunteers operating alongside the Russians on the Eastern Front. Transferred to France at the end of the war, these Yak fighters formed an early part of the complement of the newly-reformed French air force. The Yak-3 and Yak-9 continued to be important types for the Russians during the post-war period. Some examples were exported to several of the Soviet Union's allies and saw some action during the Korean War.

**Specifications – Yakovlev Yak-9M**

| | |
|---|---|
| Wingspan | 31 ft 11.5 in |
| Length | 27 ft 10.66 in |
| Maximum speed | 356 mph at 12,303 ft |
| Maximum take-off weight | 6,823 lb |
| Range | 590.5 miles |
| Service ceiling | 31,168 ft |
| Armament | One 20 mm cannon and one 12.7 mm (0.5 in) machine gun fixed forward-firing in the upper forward fuselage |
| Engine | One Klimov VK-105PF inline piston engine, of 1,180 hp |
| Crew | One |

# Mitsubishi A6M Zero

The Mitsubishi A6M Reisen Zero-Sen, or Zero Fighter, known to the Allies for identification purposes as 'Zeke,' is synonymous with Japanese naval air operations during World War Two. Designed to meet a demanding 1937 Imperial Japanese Navy requirement for a carrier-based fighter to supersede the Mitsubishi A5M, the A6M was designed by a team led by Jiro Horikoshi that concentrated on creating a fighter with outstanding maneuverability and an armament of two 20 mm cannons and two 7.7mm (0.303in) machine guns within a light airframe. The prototype first flew on 1 April 1939, with service deliveries of the initial production A6M2 occurring in July 1940 when several examples were sent to China for operational trials. The original Mitsubishi Zuisei 13 powerplant of the A6M1 was replaced in the A6M2 by the more powerful Nakajima NK1C Sakae 12, producing 925–950 hp. Folding

wingtips were introduced on the A6M2 Model 21. The next version, the A6M3, featured clipped wings and a 1,130 hp Sakae 21 engine. Fitted with extra jettisonable fuel tanks the aircraft demonstrated exceptional range, with endurance reaching approximately eight hours. The A6M swept all fighter opposition away prior to the Japanese attack on Pearl Harbor in December 1941, and played a full part in the Pearl Harbor action. It was also extremely successful in the first year of the Pacific war, especially against the mainly obsolete Allied aircraft ranged against it, with the P-39 Airacobra and P-40 Warhawk barely holding the line until better Allied types became available. In addition to the main versions produced, Nakajima built 327 A6M2-N floatplanes, known as 'Rufe' to the Allies. The A6M2-K and A6M5-K were two-seaters designed by the Omura 21st Naval Air Depot as conversion trainers. The tide of the

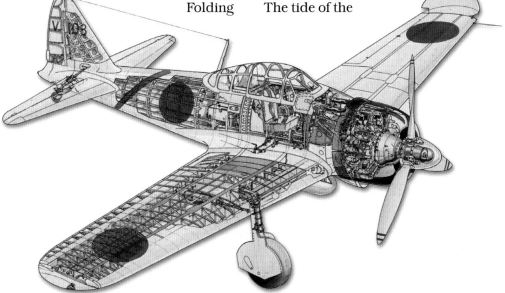

*The Mitsubishi A6M was a thoroughly modern and capable warplane that came as a great surprise to the Allies in the early stages of the Second World War in the Pacific. The A6M2 Model 21 introduced folding wingtips to allow stowage within the hangars of aircraft carriers.*

Pacific war turned against Japan during and after the Battle of Midway and as the U.S. Navy introduced new fighters, Mitsubishi tried to improve the A6M. The A6M5, the main production variant (some six thousand built), introduced individual exhaust stacks giving a little extra thrust for the Sakae 21, but further attempts to wring more power from this engine were not particularly successful. The A6M5 remained in production in 1945, alongside the slightly more powerful A6M7, by which time the comparatively low engine power had relegated the A6M3 and 5s to relatively easy prey for Allied fighters. The lack of armor (especially around the fuel tanks) and the low standard of some Japanese pilots by 1944 meant the days of the Zero were then drawing to a close. Many A6Ms were converted as special attack (Kamikaze) aircraft in an effort to stem the inevitable collapse. Total production of the Zero family is open to debate, but reliable estimates state 10,449, of which some 6,570 were built by Nakajima, plus 327 'Rufe' floatplanes and 515 two-seat trainers.

*The Mitsubishi A6M was the fighter that participated in the December 1941 attack on Pearl Harbor. Altogether 78 Zeros took part together with other types in two waves, plus further examples that provided fighter cover for the Japanese navy aircraft carriers that launched the attack.*

**Specifications – Mitsubishi A6M2 Model 21 Zero-Sen**

| | |
|---|---|
| Wingspan | 39 ft 4.5 in |
| Length | 29 ft 8.75 in |
| Maximum speed | 331 mph at 14,928 ft |
| Maximum take-off weight | 6,164 lb |
| Range | 1,930 miles |
| Service ceiling | 32,808 ft |
| Armament | Two 20 mm wing-mounted cannons and two 7.7 mm (0.303 in) machine guns in upper forward fuselage, two 132 lb bombs |
| Engine | One Nakajima NK1C Sakae 12 radial piston engine, of 950 hp |
| Crew | One |

# Curtiss SO3C Seamew

One of the great aeronautical pioneers in the United States was Glenn Curtiss. Curtiss was a highly successful entrepreneur, and one of his business activities was water-borne aircraft. The Curtiss company subsequently established a long tradition of a wide variety of aircraft types including fighters (see the P-40 entry on pages 48 to 49). Unfortunately, the Second World War era was to see the decline of this once all-conquering company. Even in the domain of water-borne aircraft Curtiss began to founder, and this was most apparent with the rather unsuccessful and unloved SO3C Seamew. In 1934, Curtiss flew the prototype of a biplane two-seat scout/observation aircraft, which became the U.S. Navy's SOC Seagull (SOC = Scout Observation, Curtiss). This aircraft was highly successful, flying from land bases with a conventional wheeled undercarriage, and from the catapults of warships as a seaplane with floats. In 1937, the U.S. Navy invited proposals for a modern replacement of this aircraft, and Curtiss was one of the companies that tendered. Rather surprisingly (in view of what subsequently happened), the Curtiss design won, and was ordered in prototype form as the XSO3C-1.

The first flight was in October 1939, and the new design showed considerable flaws, including instability, from the start. Built of all-metal construction with fabric-covered control surfaces, the Seamew was an ungainly bird, with a thick fuselage, big folding wings, and a heavy float landing gear. Powered by a Ranger inline engine, the Seamew also proved rather underpowered. The addition of large upturned wingtips partly relieved the instability problems, but the main undercarriage legs of the narrow-track wheeled undercarriage layout were fitted well aft, giving the aircraft difficult handling characteristics on the ground.

The initial production version was the SO3C-1, originally called Seagull. The first examples entered service in the summer of 1942. The SO3C-2 second production model featured an

*Ungainly and unloved, the Curtiss SO3C-1 Seamew was not a great success. Just about every-one associated with the aircraft called it a Seagull, which was the name originally bestowed on the type, even though the title Seamew was later officially adopted.*

arrester hook for aircraft carrier operations and provision for a 500 lb bomb. Approximately 100 examples of this version were passed to Britain's Royal Navy as the Seamew Mk.I, where they were not well received, and eventually relegated to training duties in Britain and Canada. Around 30 more were operated as Queen Seamew radio-controlled target drone aircraft. Some 48 other Seamews were passed to the U.S. Coast Guard. Eventually, the aircraft that the Seamew was supposed to replace, the SOC Seagull, persisted in service much longer and ultimately replaced the Seamew in front-line service. The SO3C-3, designed to sort out some of the Seamew's problems, was also unsuccessful and only 39 were built. Total Seamew production is often recorded as being approximately 800, but was probably somewhat less.

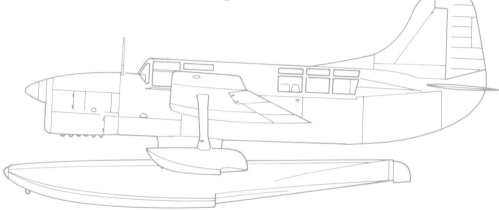

*In its seaplane guise, the Curtiss SO3C-1 Seamew was fitted with a large under fuselage main float, and small outrigger floats beneath the wings. This undercarriage arrangement was interchangeable with the landplane wheeled undercarriage.*

**Specifications – Curtiss Seamew Mk.I (landplane)**

| | |
|---|---|
| Wingspan | 38 ft) |
| Length | 34 ft 2 in |
| Maximum speed | 190 mph at 7,500 ft |
| Maximum take-off weight | 5,588 lb |
| Endurance | approximately four hours |
| Service ceiling | 15,800 ft |
| Armament | One 0.3 in (7.62 mm) machine gun fixed forward-firing, one 0.5 in (12.7 mm) machine gun on flexible mount in rear cockpit |
| Engine | One Ranger V-770-6 (sometimes called SGV-770-6) inline piston engine, of 520 hp (some possibly fitted with more powerful 600 hp version) |
| Crew | Two |

# Aichi D3A

The Aichi D3A, known to the Allies for identification purposes as 'Val,' was a sturdy, fixed undercarriage radial engined dive-bomber with a wing similar in shape to that used by the German Heinkel He 70. Devised to an Imperial Japanese Navy specification to replace the biplane Heinkel He 66-derived Aichi D1A, the prototype of the D3A first flew in January 1938, powered by a Nakajima Hikari 1 radial of 730 hp. That engine was replaced by the 1,000 hp Mitsubishi Kinsei 43 in the production D3A1s (also called the Navy Type 99 Carrier Dive-Bomber Model 11) that were manufactured from December 1939. Later production D3A1s were powered by the 1,080 hp Mitsubishi Kinsei 44. The last of 478 (including prototypes) was rolled out in the summer of 1942. The D3A1 was replaced on the production line by the D3A2 (Type 99 Model 22), powered by the 1,200hp Kinsei 54 radial, increasing performance in most respects except range, which fell by around 70 miles. Production continued until early 1944, with a total of 1,016 (or possibly as few as 816) built.

The D3A1 entered combat in Japan's war against China during 1940. Alongside the Mitsubishi A6M Zero-Sen and Nakajima B5N, the D3A1 dive-bomber was used to attack the American fleet in Pearl Harbor on 7 December 1941 – 129 were committed to this action. In February 1942, D3As successfully attacked Darwin, Australia, and sank the British aircraft carrier H.M.S. Hermes and the heavy cruisers, H.M.S. Cornwall and Dorsetshire, two months later. At the Battle of the Coral Sea, D3A1s helped sink the aircraft carrier U.S.S. Lexington and damage the Yorktown. They continued to fight at Midway, in the Aleutians and at Guadalcanal, but the type was becoming increasingly obsolete and vulnerable to Allied fighters. The improved D3A2 aimed to rectify some of the problems apparent with the D3A1, but still lacked protection for its crews and fuel tanks. By early 1944, most of the experienced D3A pilots had been killed and the effectiveness of the type diminished accordingly. As later types were produced for the dive-bomber role, the D3A found a sec-

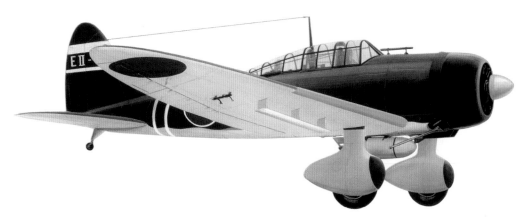

*The Aichi D3A1 was the principal Japanese naval dive-bomber of the Pacific war, and played a leading part in the famous Japanese attack on Pearl Harbor in December 1941 that brought the United States into World War Two. The type featured folding wings, similar to many other carrier-based aircraft.*

ondary role as an advanced trainer. Many were used as special attack (Kamikaze) aircraft.

*Although outdated in appearance, the Aichi D3A1 'Val' was an effective dive-bomber that thrived when Allied air opposition was minimal, as in the early part of the war. (Photo: U.S. Navy).*

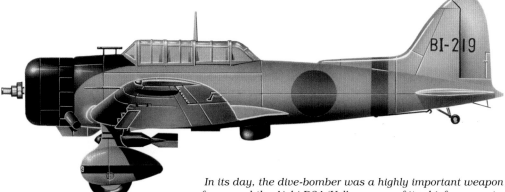

*In its day, the dive-bomber was a highly important weapon of war, and the Aichi D3A 'Val' was one of its chief exponents. It is a type of manned aircraft that no longer exists today.*

**Specifications – Aichi D3A2 Model 22**

| | |
|---|---|
| Wingspan | 47 ft 1.5 in |
| Length | 33 ft 5.4 in |
| Maximum speed | 266 mph at 9,843 ft |
| Maximum take-off weight | 8,377.5 lb |
| Range | 840 miles |
| Service ceiling | 34,449 ft |
| Armament | Two fixed 7.7 mm (0.303 in) machine guns forward-firing in the wings, one flexible-mounted in rear cockpit. One 551 lb bomb beneath fuselage, plus two underwing bombs each of 132 lb |
| Engine | One Mitsubishi Kinsei 54 radial piston engine, of 1,200 hp |
| Crew | Two |

# Macchi C.202 Folgore

The evolution of Italian fighter aircraft immediately before and during World War Two happened in several significant stages. The fighters with which Italy began the war in 1940, such as the radial-engined Macchi C.200 Saetta, and Fiat G.50 Freccia, were in effect a first generation of monoplane fighters, followed by some interim types such as the Macchi C.202 Folgore and Reggiane Re.2001 Falco II. The latter two were part of a second generation, basically re-engined types based on first generation airframes but fitted with excellent German liquid-cooled inline engines. Further development led to several very capable types such as the Macchi C.205 Veltro, again with German inline engines. The Macchi C.202 Folgore (Thunderbolt) was directly derived from the Macchi C.200 Saetta (see pages 164 to 165), which was a robust and maneuverable fighter that nevertheless lacked firepower and had a low-powered radial engine. The engineers at Macchi realized that much better performance could be achieved from the C.200 layout if it was fitted with a good inline engine.

The lack of a high-performance inline engine in Italy is all the more surprising when one remembers that in the famous 1920's Schneider Trophy series of seaplane races, Italian designs powered by high-performance inline engines played a leading part. Afterwards emphasis was placed in Italy on the design of radial engines, and it was not until 1940 that examples of the fine German Daimler Benz DB 601 inline engines were made available to the Italians to start to redress the balance. The re-engining of a C.200 with one of these powerplants resulted in the first flight on 10 August 1940 of what was in effect the prototype for the C.202. This new layout showed dramatic performance increases compared to the C.200, and was at once ordered into production as the C.202. Manufacture subsequently took place alongside the C.200 (rather than replacing the older design), the C.202 being constructed in eleven major series by Macchi and under licence by Breda. Total production reached some fifteen hundred by the time of Italy's capitulation to the Allies in September

*A neat, modern and streamlined warplane, the Macchi C.202 Folgore was one of Italy's main fighters of World War Two. It featured all-metal construction with fabric-covered control surfaces. The inline engine that powered it was an Italian licence-built German DB 601A powerplant.*

1943. The C.202 entered service in the summer of 1941 with the Italian air force's 1st Stormo, which was in combat in North Africa against British forces in late 1941. The type subsequently served in most of the major battles of the Regia Aeronautica including the Mediterranean and North Africa, and in Russia alongside Italy's German allies. By the time of the Italian armistice they were being used to intercept American bomber formations over Italy. Further development by Macchi led to the more capable C.205V Veltro (Greyhound), powered by the German (but Italian-built) DB 605A inline engine. The latter was a contempo-

rary of the Fiat G.55 (see pages 294 to 295) but was too late to play a major part in Italy's war against the Allies prior to September 1943, although some subsequently flew for pro-German Italian forces after the September 1943 armistice. Total C.205V production is believed to have been around 265 examples.

*The Macchi C.202 Folgore was evolved from the radial-engined Macchi C.200 Saetta, and used some C.200 components although the fuselage in particular was re-designed to take the new inline engine, and the cockpit was enclosed rather than open.*

**Specifications – Macchi C.202 Folgore (VIII Series)**

| | |
|---|---|
| Wingspan | 34 ft 8.5 in |
| Length | 29 ft 0.5 in |
| Maximum speed | 373 mph at 18,373 ft |
| Maximum take-off weight | 6,459 lb |
| Range | 475 miles |
| Service ceiling | 37,730 ft |
| Armament | Two 12.7 mm (0.5 in) machine guns fixed forward-firing in upper forward fuselage, some aircraft also had two 7.7 mm (0.303 in) machine guns in the wings |
| Engine | One Alfa Romeo RA.1000 RC.41 (licence-built Daimler Benz DB 601A) inline piston engine, of 1,075 hp |
| Crew | One |

# Grumman F4F Wildcat

The portly Grumman Wildcat monoplane fighter was initially designed in the mid-1930's as a biplane in response to a U.S. Navy requirement. It was modified on the drawing board to become the first monoplane fighter to be built by Grumman, ordered (as an insurance) to compete with the Brewster XF2A-1 Buffalo (see pages 114 to 115). The XF4F-2 made its first flight on 2 September 1937, but its Pratt & Whitney R-1830-66 Twin Wasp proved to be troublesome, and was replaced by a more powerful version of the R-1830 in the prototype, which then became the XF4F-3. In August 1939, the U.S. Navy placed the first production order for an eventual total of 369 F4F-3s with the R-1830–76 and four 0.5 in (12.7 mm) guns in the folding wings. The Wildcat also entered service with the U.S. Marine Corps and it was a VMF-211 F4F-3 that destroyed the first Japanese bomber, at Wake Island, on 9 December 1941. By the start of 1943,

Wildcats equipped every U.S. Navy carrier-based fighter squadron. The F4F-4 had provision for bombs or drop tanks, six 0.5 in (12.7 mm) guns and a 1,200 hp R-1830-86 powerplant. Grumman built 1,169, while 1,060 similar examples were built as FM-1s by the Eastern Aircraft Division of General Motors. Twenty-one similar unarmed photo-reconnaissance versions were built as F4F-7s. The final production version was the FM-2, featuring a taller tail and an R-1820-56 powerplant. 4,127 FM-2s were built. Towards the end of World War Two, the Wildcat was relegated to a fighter-training role with the U.S. Navy and Marines, having been superseded by the F6F Hellcat and F4U Corsair.

Both France and Britain ordered the Wildcat as the G-36A and G-36B respectively. The fall of France saw all the aircraft being diverted to Britain as Martlet Mk.Is and Mk.IIs respectively, although ten Mk.IIs delivered

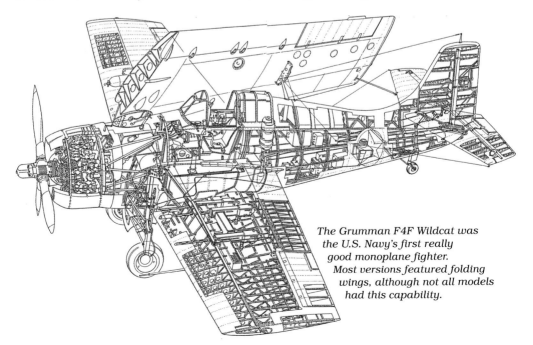

*The Grumman F4F Wildcat was the U.S. Navy's first really good monoplane fighter. Most versions featured folding wings, although not all models had this capability.*

*A line-up of early Wildcats, probably F4F-3 models. Several U.S. Navy pilots scored well while fly-ing the Wildcat, and one was awarded the Medal of Honor for a specific successful combat (Photo: U.S. Navy).*

without folding wings became Mk.IIIs. Other Mk.IIIs delivered were ex F4F-3As (some 95 built) diverted from an order for Greece. The first Martlets were delivered in summer/autumn 1940, at first re-equipping No.804 Squadron at Hatston. Two examples made the type's first kill on Christmas Day 1940, downing a Junkers Ju 88 off Orkney. With the passing of America's Lend-Lease Act, some 220 Martlet Mk.IVs (ex F4F-4), 312 Wildcat Mk.Vs (ex FM-1) and 370 Mk.VIs (ex FM-2) were delivered, the Martlet name being abandoned in January 1944. In Roy-al Navy service, they were used to pro-vide fighter defence from escort carri-ers, but had been largely replaced by the end of the war.

*Early F4F Wildcats wore the colorful pre-war markings much favored by the U.S. Navy. Such flamboyance disappeared completely with America's involvement in World War Two.*

**Specifications – Grumman G-36B Martlet Mk.II**

| | |
|---|---|
| Wingspan | 38 ft |
| Length | 28 ft 9 in |
| Maximum speed | 310 mph at 13,000 ft |
| Maximum take-off weight | 7,512 lb |
| Range | approximately 860 miles |
| Service ceiling | 28,000 ft |
| Armament | Six wing-mounted 0.5in (12.7 mm) machine guns |
| Engine | One Pratt & Whitney R-1830-S3C4G Twin Wasp radial piston engine, of 1,200hp |
| Crew | One |

# Douglas TBD Devastator

The Douglas TBD Devastator was the first cantilever monoplane designed for the U.S. Navy, beating the Great Lakes XTBG-1 biplane for an order for a prototype aircraft carrier-based torpedo bomber on 30 June 1935. At the time it appeared, the design was radically different in layout from the previous generation of aircraft, as it had a thick low set wing, a crew of three and a performance superior to contemporary aircraft. The XTBD-1 prototype made its maiden flight on 15 April 1935, and was followed by production orders for 129 TBD-1s – at that time these were the most advanced carrier-based combat aircraft yet seen. All production aircraft were built by Douglas at Santa Monica, California, and differed from the prototype in having powered folding wings, a taller canopy and other minor improvements. The only other variant was a single example tested on floats as the TBD-

1A, but the U.S. Navy decided not to proceed with a production version of a floatplane Devastator. The Devastator entered service with the U.S. Navy's Torpedo Squadron Three (VT-3), assigned to the aircraft carrier U.S.S. Saratoga in 1937, replacing the biplane designs that preceded it. At the time of the Japanese attack on Pearl Harbor in December 1941 it was the only U.S. torpedo-bomber in operational service with the U.S. Navy. As such it was soon in action, taking part in a number of engagements and (it is claimed) helping to sink a Japanese light aircraft carrier during the Battle of the Coral Sea in May 1942. Even so, combat experience demonstrated that the Devastator was clearly an obsolete design by then, lacking range, overall performance and weapon-carrying ability, and being poorly armed.

The Devastator's swansong was at the Battle of Midway in early June 1942. The torpedo bomber squadrons from the U.S.S. Yorktown (VT-3), Enterprise (VT-6), and Hornet (VT-8) sent 41 TBD-1s against the Japanese fleet. A total of 35 were shot down by ship-

The Douglas TBD Devastator was an advanced aircraft when it first entered service. However, it was completely lacking in performance and the ability to defend itself by the time of its major combat actions against determined Japanese opposition in 1942.

borne anti-aircraft artillery and fighters, while others ran out of fuel before returning to the U.S. carriers. Only three made it back, all from VT-6, but one was so badly damaged it was pushed overboard. No torpedo hits were registered on the Japanese warships. Over thirty per cent of the Devastators produced were lost in this one action and, coupled with previous attrition, the decision was taken to withdraw the type from combat operations. The Devastator was replaced in service by the Grumman Avenger (see pages 198 to 199), which performed far more capably in the following years.

*A Douglas TBD-1 Devastator of the U.S. Navy's torpedo-bomber squadron VT-6. This was one of the units that bravely went into combat during the Battle of Midway against better equipped Japanese forces and suffered heavy losses.*

## Specifications – Douglas TBD-1 Devastator

| | |
|---|---|
| Wingspan | 50 ft |
| Length | 35 ft |
| Maximum speed | 206 mph at 8,000 ft |
| Maximum take-off weight | 10,194 lb |
| Range | approximately 435 miles |
| Service ceiling | 19,700 ft |
| Armament | One 0.3 in (7.62 mm) machine gun fixed in right side of nose, one 0.3 in (7.62 mm) machine gun flexible-mounted in rear cockpit. One 1,000 lb (454 kg) torpedo or bombs/depth charges below fuselage, up to some 1,000 lb of bombs beneath the wings |
| Engine | One Pratt & Whitney R-1830-64 Twin Wasp radial piston engine, of 850 hp |
| Crew | Three |

# Hawker Typhoon

An invaluable weapon in the Allies' inventory during the later stages of World War Two was the Hawker Typhoon and its successor the Hawker Tempest. Almost akin to a piece of flying artillery, the Typhoon was a powerful ground attack aircraft that wreaked havoc amongst German ground forces after D-Day in June 1944 and had the capability of a light bomber in the frame of a big and purposeful fighter. The Typhoon was designed in response to Air Ministry Specification F.18/37 for an aircraft capable of combating heavily armed and armored escort fighters such as the Messerschmitt Bf 110. In response to this requirement Hawker submitted two separate designs, the Type R and Type N. The Type R was powered by a Rolls-Royce Vulture engine. Unfortunately, the underdeveloped Vulture proved to be problematic for all the various British aircraft powered by it. The Vulture-engined Hawker prototype was known as the Tornado and first flew on 6 October 1939, but was dropped when production of the Vulture was eventually abandoned. The Type N, named Typhoon, fared much better – although it too was to suffer years of trouble from its power plant. It was powered by a 2,100 hp Napier Sabre H-configuration inline engine, which was an advanced and powerful engine with more than its fair share of teething troubles. The first of two prototypes flew for the first time on 24 February 1940. The initial production aircraft, however, did not fly until May

*Few paintings could ever better express the low-level importance and effectiveness of the Hawker Typhoon than this depiction of Typhoons flying in support of the Allied armies landing on the Normandy coast of France on 6 June 1944 – D-Day. The picture in particular shows the Typhoon Mk.IB of Flight Lieutenant Jim Kyle from No.197 Squadron, Royal Air Force, just about to cross the beach at 0640 hours on the morning of that momentous day. Note the black and white 'Invasion Stripes' painted on the aircraft for D-Day operations.*

1941. Persistent troubles with the type, especially the engine, resulted in the first Typhoon squadron, No.56, remaining non-operational for some time, although the initial aircraft were delivered to the RAF in September 1941. However, as more of the new fighters were brought into service, initially at the historic Duxford airfield in East Anglia, they became engaged in air defence duties against low-level 'hit and run' German intruders. These were a particular problem over southern and southeast England as the war continued.

The Typhoon Mk.IA was the first main production model. It was armed with 12 0.303 in (7.7 mm) machine guns in the wings, a formidable battery. It was followed by the Mk.IB, which had four wing-mounted 20 mm cannons. These later proved highly effective for ground attack duties. The Mk.IB was powered by the somewhat more reliable Napi-er Sabre II-series engine. Early Mk.I Typhoons suffered from comparatively poor pilot visibility, particularly in the rear, due to their rather curious original frame-type cockpit canopy and car-type access door (an arrangement similar to that used by the Bell P-39 Airacobra, shown on Page 136 of this Book). Like several other Allied fighter types (such as the Spitfire and P-51 Mustang) later production Typhoons were re-designed to fit a clear 'bubble'-type rearwards-sliding canopy. This created a considerable improvement in all-round vision for the pilot, and also added to the aerodynamic cleanness of the design.

Interestingly, the Typhoon continued to have difficulties well into 1943 and its future as a production front-line type hung in the balance on more than one occasion. Eventually many of the engine problems were ironed out, but the type secured a bright future for

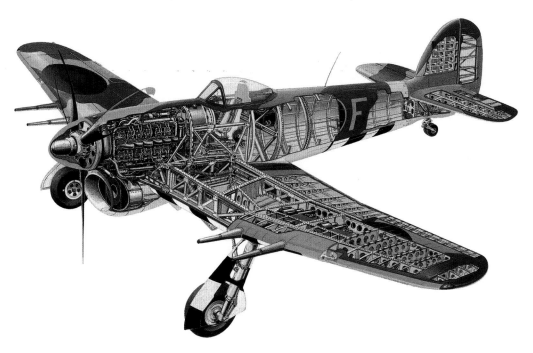

*This cutaway drawing of a Typhoon Mk.IB shows the all-metal structure of the aircraft. Unfortunately, some early Typhoons suffered from fuselage failure just ahead of the horizontal tail. The drawing also shows the big, complex Napier Sabre engine and its enormous oil cooler and intake below the engine.*

# Hawker Typhoon *continued*

The 'PR' code letters identify this Typhoon Mk.IB as belonging to the RAF's No.609 Squadron.
*In this painting, the Typhoon is taking on an old adversary – a Focke-Wulf Fw 190 – and winning.*
*The Typhoon's Belgian pilot forced the German fighter to fly into the ground.*

itself due to its prowess against Luftwaffe low-level intruders. Patrols of Typhoons proved to be effective against the fast, low-flying Luftwaffe Focke-Wulf Fw 190 fighter bombers (see pages 274 to 277) that were engaged on nuisance raids over southern England in 1942 and 1943. From then onwards, the Typhoon excelled, although not in its originally intended role. Operational experience had shown that the Typhoon performed best at low altitudes and this, coupled

with its strength and ability to carry a useful warload, made it into a very capable ground attack type. As the war continued, the RAF increasingly went on the offensive over occupied Europe, with tactical fighter bombers and light bombers attacking many German military targets. Typhoons were eventually allocated to the Allied 2nd Tactical Air Force for this task, and were a highly effective part of this strike force. Typically armed with a pair of underwing 500 lb or 1,000 lb bombs, or eight underwing rocket projectiles in addition to the by-then standardized wing cannon armament, Typhoons proved excellent at attacking German vehicles, communications, shipping, infrastructure and airfields. They were especially active over northern France in the run-up to D-Day in June 1944, and then during the Allied landings and in the subsequent fighting. Their rocket armament in particular was highly effective against German tanks, if a pilot was well versed on how to direct these unguided munitions onto their intended target. Rocket-armed Typhoons became well-known in particular with the effective support of Allied ground forces in the destruction of a German counter-attack at Mortain in southern Normandy and the destruction of the retreating German forces in the infamous 'Falaise Gap.' Typhoons subsequently flew from advanced landing grounds in newly-captured territory so that they could operate close to the front-lines. Attacks were also made against enemy shipping in conjunction with other Allied aircraft.

After all the development problems, 3,330 Typhoons were built nevertheless. Most of these were constructed by Gloster, except for the two prototypes and a batch of fifteen Mk.IAs and Mk.IBs that were manufactured by Hawker. The Mk IB was the major production version, with over 3,000 completed. Approximately two-thirds of these were fitted with the 'bubble'-type canopy rather than the original 'car-door' type. A comparatively small number of Typhoons were fighter-reconnaissance examples with various camera options. Further development of the Typhoon, particularly with regard to improving its high-level performance, was addressed with the Hawker Tempest, covered on pages 284 to 285.

**Specifications – Hawker Typhoon Mk.IB**

| | |
|---|---|
| Wingspan | 41 ft 7 in |
| Length | 31 ft 11.5 in (late production) |
| Maximum speed | 412 mph at 19,000 ft |
| Maximum take-off weight | 13,250 lb |
| Range | 510 miles (fully armed) |
| Service ceiling | 35,200 ft |
| Armament | Four fixed forward-firing wing-mounted 20 mm cannons, various underwing armament options including two 500 lb bombs, eight 60 lb unguided rocket projectiles |
| Engine | One Napier Sabre IIA inline piston engine, of 2,180 hp (other marks of this engine also available) |
| Crew | One |

# Mitsubishi Ki-51

It proved to be a fatal mistake for 'Western' countries to view the Japanese and their technological skills with such disdain during the 1930's. The Japanese aircraft industry had actually proven itself quite capable of designing thoroughly accomplished aircraft, sometimes drawing on the experiences of western aircraft manufacturers and incorporating new advances in design and technology. Famous for designing such well-known types as the A6M fighter (see pages 174 to 175) and other warplanes, the Mitsubishi company created a separate line of single-engine high-performance monoplane combat aircraft during the 1930's, starting with the Ki-15 of 1935/1936. Built in civil and military variants, the Ki-15 became famous for the exploits of its civil prototype, 'Kamikaze' (Divine Wind). This particular aircraft flew from Japan in several stages to London and back in 1936, a considerable achievement. Several more civil machines under the name Karigane were subsequently built, and the Ki-15 military type served with the Japanese Imperial Army air service. Further development by Mitsubishi led to the Ki-30 light bomber. This aircraft had a two-seat, single-engine, fixed-undercarriage configuration like the Ki-15, and served with the Imperial Japanese Army air service in the war against China prior to the outbreak of World War Two as well as in the early stages of the Second World War.

In late 1937, the Imperial Japanese Army formulated a specification for a new ground attack aircraft and to meet this requirement, Mitsubishi drew on the Ki-15 and Ki-30 configuration to

*The Mitsubishi Ki-51 was the continuation of a line of development that had seen the Ki-15 and Ki-30 created earlier in the 1930's.*

create the new Ki-51. The first of two prototypes began service trials during 1939, and they were followed by a batch of service test/pre-production aircraft. The type entered production as the Army Type 99 Assault (Attack) Aircraft, commencing operations during 1940. Initially, the type served during the continuing warfare in China, and was then fully involved in the Japanese war in the Pacific theater following the attack on Pearl Harbor in December 1941. Production is generally accepted as reaching 2,385 examples – 1,472 by Mitsubishi and 913 by an Army air arsenal at Tachikawa. Production appears to have lasted into

1945, and the type was active virtually to the end of the war. In the early stages of the conflict, against meager air opposition the Ki-51 was reasonably successful. However, when the Allies began introducing growing numbers of high-quality fighters into the Pacific conflict, the Ki-51 and other Japanese types suffered significant losses. As with various other Japanese warplanes in the final stages of the war in the Pacific, the Ki-51 was employed on Kamikaze suicide attacks against Allied forces. The Ki-51 was known to the Allies for identification purposes as 'Sonia.'

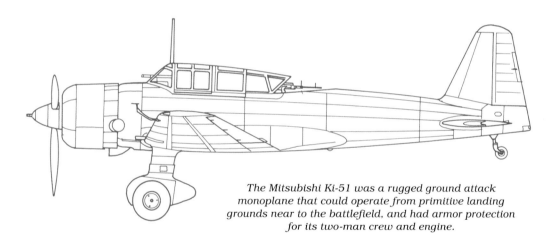

The Mitsubishi Ki-51 was a rugged ground attack monoplane that could operate from primitive landing grounds near to the battlefield, and had armor protection for its two-man crew and engine.

**Specifications – Mitsubishi Ki-51**

| | |
|---|---|
| Wingspan | 39 ft 8.25 in |
| Length | 30 ft 2.25 in |
| Maximum speed | 264 mph at 9,843 ft |
| Maximum take-off weight | 6,437 lb |
| Range | 659 miles |
| Service ceiling | 27,133 ft |
| Armament | Two fixed forward-firing wing-mounted 7.7 mm (0.303 in) machine guns (later replaced by two 12.7 mm (0.5 in) machine guns), one 7.7 mm (0.303 in) machine gun flexible-mounted in rear cockpit, up to 441 lb of bombs |
| Engine | One Mitsubishi Ha-26-II radial piston engine, of 940 hp |
| Crew | Two |

# Lockheed P-38 Lightning

The P-38 Lightning was one of the trio of major American Second World War fighters including the Republic P-47 Thunderbolt and the North American P-51 Mustang, which were introduced late in the war, and were a major part of the Allies' final victory. In fact, the P-38 was usually overshadowed by the other two, but it was a highly capable long-range fighter that gained much success, particularly in the Pacific theater. Its distinctive twin boom appearance was reminiscent of the Fokker G.I fighter (see pages 70 to 71) and it was designed to meet a 1937 U.S. Army Air Corps specification for a high-altitude interceptor. The prototype Allison V-1710-powered Model 22 XP-38 first flew on 27 January 1939. The design showed much promise and was followed by 13 YP-38 pre-production/evaluation aircraft with turbo-supercharged V-1710 engines. The first production version was the basic P-38 of 1941. There was then a succession of slightly upgraded versions, all distinguished by their sharply cut-back lower engine intakes, and small intakes on the sides of the booms. Their Allison V-1710 engines were turbo-supercharged, giving this engine (which was otherwise poor at higher altitudes) a respectable performance. The Lightning first saw combat with the Eleventh Army Air Force, in the little-known Aleutians theater in the northern Pacific, scoring the first victories over Japanese aircraft in August 1941. Britain's Royal Air Force was also interested in the P-38 and took over a planned French order, eventually intending to receive 667s as the Lightning Mk.I and Mk.II. Only three were delivered, however – these were not fitted with the all-important turbo-supercharged engines, and

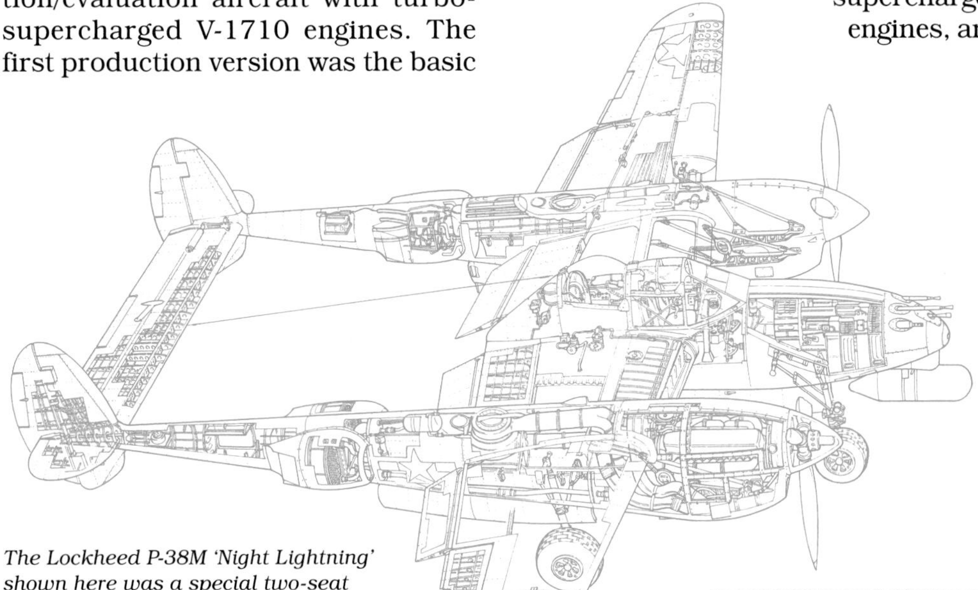

*The Lockheed P-38M 'Night Lightning' shown here was a special two-seat interim night fighter with radar (in the pod below the nose) which did not see combat. It did, however, have the important attributes of all operational P-38s, the turbo-superchargers for its two Allison engines (the circular pipe-fed structures on the upper surfaces of the booms beside the wing trailing edges).*

LE 9

P.38 LIGHTNING U.S.A.F.
(CPT. THOMAS G. LANPHIER)
WHO SHOT DOWN
YAMAMOTO AIRCRAFT

SIERRA LEONE

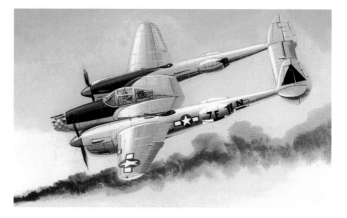

*This P-38J Lightning belongs to the tactical Ninth Army Air Force's 370th Fighter Group, a unit engaged in ground attack missions related to the invasion of France in June 1944. Under-wing jettisonable fuel tanks considerably extended the P-38's range.*

their performance was disappointing enough to end the contract. In 1943 the most important combat model, the P-38J, began to be widely introduced. This featured distinctive chin oil/intercooler intakes beneath the engines, and larger intakes on the boom sides. A small number were fitted with glazed noses for a bombardier and acted as lead aircraft/pathfinders for other bomb-carrying Lightnings. The final major version was the P-38M, a two-seat radar-equipped interim night fighter conversion from the final day fighter model, the P-38L, that was just too late to see combat. Total Lightning production was probably just over ten thousand, of which approximately one thousand were specially-modified or constructed as F-4 or F-5 photo-reconnaissance aircraft. Although based in England as a bomber escort by the Eighth Army Air Force, and used as a tactical fighter by the Ninth Army Air Force in the Mediterranean, the Lightning was far more successful in the Pacific theater, where it excelled as a fighter. The two top American aces of World War Two, Richard Bong (40 victories) and Thomas B. McGuire, Jr. (38 victories) both flew the Lightning in the Pacific (both were additionally awarded the Medal of Honor). Lightnings were also flown at various times by French, Italian and Nationalist Chinese forces.

**Specifications – Lockheed P-38J Lightning**

| | |
|---|---|
| Wingspan | 52 ft |
| Length | 37 ft 10 in |
| Maximum speed | 414 mph at 25,000 ft |
| Maximum take-off weight | 21,600 lb |
| Range | 1,175 miles (1,891 km) plus |
| Service ceiling | approximately 40,000 ft |
| Armament | One 20 mm cannon and four 0.5 in (12.7 mm) machine guns in nose of the fuselage pod fixed forward-firing, potential ombload beneath the wings of 3,200 lb, or unguided rockets |
| Engine | Two Allison V-1710-89 or –91 inline piston engines, of 1,425 hp each |
| Crew | One |

# Republic P-47 Thunderbolt

There are many aircraft types of the Second World War period that can lay claim to being a significant part of the Allied victory in that conflict. One of these is the enormous and highly-successful Republic P-47 Thunderbolt. Sometimes going by the nickname 'Juggernaut' or simply 'Jug' due to its large size, the Thunderbolt was a significant fighter and fighter-bomber that was equally at home at high altitude escorting bombers, or down at lower levels shooting up tactical targets as a very capable fighter-bomber.

Historically, the P-47 was a continuation of a fighter series that had its roots in the mid-1930's. At that time known as the Seversky Aircraft Corporation, the company that eventually created the Thunderbolt started with two neat and attractive single-seat fighters, the P-35 and the P-43 Lancer single-engine monoplanes. Both of these types were bought in comparatively limited numbers by

the U.S. Army Air Corps, but they were related to a variety of Seversky low-wing monoplane designs that included a civilian record-breaker and two-seat combat trainers. These varied aircraft types gave the company a useful pedigree in designing combat aircraft that took into account the latest design innovations and advances. Two Russian immigrants, Alexander de Seversky, a Russian World War One fighter pilot, and designer Alexander Kartveli, were the driving force behind Seversky – and later the Republic company, which the Seversky organization grew into.

The P-47 was originally designed in the late 1930's as a light-weight fighter, but there were lessons to be learned from the fierce air war in Europe in 1940. Both Republic (as the company was then known)

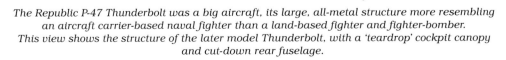

*The Republic P-47 Thunderbolt was a big aircraft, its large, all-metal structure more resembling an aircraft carrier-based naval fighter than a land-based fighter and fighter-bomber. This view shows the structure of the later model Thunderbolt, with a 'teardrop' cockpit canopy and cut-down rear fuselage.*

*A P-47 Thunderbolt in its element, escorting a raid of American heavy bombers. The particular aircraft depicted is a late-model Thunderbolt belonging to the 63rd Fighter Squadron of the famed 56th Fighter Group, which was the first Thunderbolt-equipped Group and was one of the type's greatest exponents. The aircraft shown, nicknamed 'Yorkshire Lass', was flown by Jack Bradshaw (see next page).*

and the U.S. Army looked in detail at the type of air combat that had developed over northern Europe particularly after May 1940. The original XP-47 and XP-47A prototypes were designed to fit an Allison inline engine, but Kartveli felt that this powerplant, with its comparatively poor performance at higher altitudes, would not lead to a useful Army Air Corps fighter. He therefore created a new design around the most powerful engine then available, the new 2,000 hp Pratt & Whitney R-2800 Double Wasp radial. This was a big engine, and the new P-47 layout was for a big aircraft to attach to it. Republic's radical ideas were submitted to the Army Air Corps in June 1940. They were at once successful, orders were subsequently placed 'off the drawing board' for the new XP-47B layout comprising 171 production P-47Bs and 602 P-47Cs.

The two were basically similar, except that the P-47C had a slightly longer fuselage to improve stability. The XP-47B flew for the first time on 6 May 1941. In June 1942, the 56th Fighter Group began to equip with the P-47, and in December 1942-January 1943, it deployed to England. This unit was to become the premier Thunderbolt Group, and it was a significant part of the Eighth Army Air Force's fighter command, which later became so successful in escorting American heavy bombers over occupied Europe and Germany, and in shooting Germany's Luftwaffe from the skies as the war progressed.

The very first Thunderbolt combat missions by units of the Eighth Air Force – initial fighter sweeps over northern France – were made in March and April 1943. By then, huge orders had been placed for the P-47D.

195

# Republic P-47 Thunderbolt *continued*

This version became the most numerous of the Thunderbolt variants, and it was built by three main production centers. There were significant differences between the early and the late model P-47Ds, mainly concerning the fuselage shape. Early P-47D models had the raised fuselage spine behind the cockpit of the P-47B and P-47C, but from the P-47D-25-RE production block onwards the fuselage shape was radically changed. The rear decking of the fuselage was removed, allowing a more streamlined fuselage shape, and giving the pilot much better vision to the rear through a new 'teardrop' cockpit canopy. In total, just over 12,600 P-47Ds were built by Republic, and a further 354 were manufactured by Curtiss-Wright as P-47Gs.

There were good reasons for the Thunderbolt's success as an escort fighter. One of these was the turbo-charging of the P-47's R-2800 engine. America led the world at that time in turbo-supercharging (i.e., the augmentation of a normal engine's power output by the insertion into a part of the engine of its own hot exhaust gases to provide more power – a technology in which the Germans, for all their wartime innovation and know-how, lagged seriously behind). Several top-scoring American pilots flew the Thunderbolt, including Robert S. Johnson, Francis Gabreski, and Neal Kearby. Britain's Royal Air Force was supplied with 240 (possibly more) early-model examples as the Thunderbolt I, while a further 590 later model P-47Ds were received as the Thunderbolt II.

The RAF's Thunderbolts were assigned to squadrons in South-East Asia Command (comprising the India and Burma theaters), where they largely replaced the Hawker Hurricane for ground attack duties. This illustrated the Thunderbolt's versatility. Not only was it an excellent fighter, it could also operate very well at low level, dropping bombs and shooting up any ground targets that presented themselves. The Thunderbolt's eight wing-mounted 0.5 in (12.7 mm) machine guns constituted awesome fire-power in their own right, both for air-to-air combat and for air-to-ground operations. Later in the war, the tactical Ninth Army Air Force flew Thunderbolt fighter-bombers from southern England in the run-up to D-Day (the Allied Invasion in June 1944 of northern France), and afterwards in support of Allied armies advancing through occupied Europe. The Thunderbolt excelled at this role. It was rugged, could take a lot of battle damage and still return to base, and could carry a variety of ordnance including bombs, rockets and napalm tanks. Some Thunderbolts were shipped to the Soviet Union during the war, while others flew with Mexico and Brazil – the latter two countries operating some of their Thunderbolts in combat alongside American units. The next production version of the Thunderbolt was the P-47M, 130 being completed with the 2,800 hp R-2800-57 engine. This was the fastest of all the production Thunderbolts, and was almost like a 'special commission' for the Thunderbolt-loving 56th Fighter Group, which received most of the 130 built. The last production version of the Thunderbolt was the P-47N, a very long-range bomber escort and fighter-bomber, which entered service in the Pacific not long before the end of the war. 1,816 of these were produced. Overall P-47 production, which ended in December 1945, is thought to be 15,683 of all types – the largest ever production run for an American fighter aircraft. A number of 'special' Thunderbolts were built for test or development purposes, including the XP-47H, powered by a large Chrysler inline engine.

Post-war the P-47 did not last long as a front-line type in the U.S. forces (although it soldiered on with reserve units for several years), but surviving Thunderbolts were exported widely, many under mutual defence aid agreements. This included service with several South American countries, while the P-47 was an important early type for the re-born post-war French and Italian air forces.

**Specifications – Republic P-47D Thunderbolt (specifically D-26-RA sub-type)**

| | |
|---|---|
| Wingspan | 40 ft 9.3 in |
| Length | 36 ft 1.75 in |
| Maximum speed | 423 mph (681 km/h) at 30,000 ft |
| Maximum take-off weight | 17,500 lb |
| Range | 1,030 miles (1,658 km) (more if long-range fuel tanks used) |
| Service ceiling | 42,000 ft |
| Armament | Eight (sometimes six) 0.5 in (12.7 mm) machine guns wing-mounted forward-firing, up to 2,500 lb of bombs, rockets or napalm beneath the wings and fuselage |
| Engine | One Pratt & Whitney R-2800-59 Double Wasp radial piston engine, of 2,000–2,300 hp |
| Crew | One |

# Grumman TBF/TBM Avenger

Prior to the outbreak of the war, the U.S. Navy began looking at the possibility of replacing the Douglas TBD-1 Devastator carrier-based torpedo bomber (see pages 184 to 185). Design work by Grumman was rewarded with a contract for two prototypes as the XTBF-1, the first flying in August 1941. Production of 2,291 TBF-1 Avenger sub-variants was followed by 550 TBM-1s and 2,336 TBM-1Cs from the Eastern Aircraft Division of General Motors. All further manufacture came from this second source. The next production model was the TBM-3, entering operational service from the summer of 1944 and differing from the XTBF-1 by provision for jettisonable fuel tanks or rockets beneath the wings. 4,657 were built, either as new or converted to one of the 14 sub-types of this variant. These included versions fitted with various radars (-3D, -3E, -3E2, -3H, -3W), used for photo-reconnaissance (-3P), night attack (-3N), ECM (-3Q), Carrier On-board Delivery (-3R), anti-submarine (-3S) and target-towing (-3U).

The Avenger flew its first operational sorties in June 1942 during the Battle of Midway with U.S. Navy Torpedo Squadron Eight (VT-8), but its early history included heavy losses, mostly because of the inexperience of its three-man crews. It was subsequently present at nearly every naval battle in the Pacific during the war, equipping U.S. Navy torpedo squadrons, plus several night attack squadrons and numerous training and composite squadrons. Others served with the U.S. Marine Corps.

Although designed as a torpedo-bomber, the Avenger was more often used as a level bomber. To its crew the Avenger was known as The Turkey, as it was the 'largest bird in the yard,' and the biggest aircraft to regularly operate from aircraft carriers during the war. A total of 958 Avengers are believed to have been delivered to Britain's Royal Navy during World War Two under Lend-Lease, the name Tarpon at

*Tubby yet purposeful, the Grumman Avenger, made in a variety of versions and sub-types, was well-armed and powerful.*

*One of the roles at which the Grumman Avenger was most adept was torpedobombing, (as demonstrated in this picture), although the type was often used for level bombing as well (Photo: U.S. Navy).*

first being used before Avenger was adopted. The initial deliveries were in 1943 for No.832 Squadron, and the type was widely used by the Fleet Air Arm during the conflict, mostly in the Pacific. New Zealand was the only other country to fly Avengers in World War Two, using them in particular over the Solomon Islands. Total production is believed to have amounted to 9,387 examples. Post-war, Avengers were delivered to Brazil, Canada, France, Japan, the Netherlands and Uruguay. In addition, 100 TBM-3E were allocated to the Royal Navy, entering service in 1953 as Avenger AS.Mk.4s. The French Aéronavale naval air arm was the last military operator, retiring its final examples in the mid-1960's.

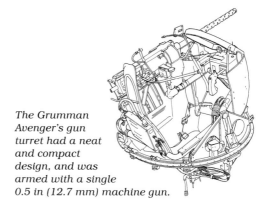

*The Grumman Avenger's gun turret had a neat and compact design, and was armed with a single 0.5 in (12.7 mm) machine gun.*

### Specifications – Grumman (General Motors) TBM-3E Avenger

| | |
|---|---|
| Wingspan | 54 ft 2 in |
| Length | 40 ft |
| Maximum speed | 267 mph at 15,000 ft |
| Maximum take-off weight | 17,895 lb |
| Range | 1,130 miles |
| Service ceiling | 23,400 ft |
| Armament | Two forward-firing 0.5 in (12.7 mm) machine guns in wings, one 0.5 in (12.7 mm) machine gun in dorsal turret and one 0.3 in (7.62 mm) machine gun in ventral position. One 1,921 lb torpedo or up to 2,000 lb of bombs |
| Engine | One Wright R-2600-20 Cyclone 14 radial piston engine, of 1,750 hp |
| Crew | Three |

# Douglas DC-3 and C-47 Series

One of the most famous aircraft types in the history of aviation, the Douglas DC-3/C-47 series of airliners and military transports can also claim to have been in continuous service longer than any other aircraft type. Although designed in the 1930's, when the first production machines entered service, there are still examples operational around the world today – a remarkable record that will probably never be surpassed by any other aircraft. The early history of this outstandingly reliable and successful aircraft was covered in Volume 1 of *The Complete Encyclopedia of Flight*. The Douglas Commercial (DC) line began with the DC-1 of 1933, and developed through the DC-2 (which received military and civil orders) to the DC-3, which first flew (as the Douglas Sleeper Transport) on 17 December 1935. The type was an immediate success, introducing new levels of speed and comfort to civil passenger travel and by the start of World War Two, it had gained considerable commercial success through its DC-3 development.

The type was obviously also suitable as a military transport, and as rearmament started to gear up in the United States, so the DC-3 was ordered as a military aircraft as well. This began during 1940/1941, but Douglas' production capacity was already stretched thin at that time with the manufacture of the successful DB-7 series and its derivatives (see pages 130 to 131). This led to a number of civil-operated examples being pressed (taken over or commandeered) into military service under a variety of designations. Eventually, production of the C-47 – as the DC-3 was known in military guise – got underway in earnest. By the close of of World War Two, over ten thousand

had been built. This was not a massive figure by the standards of the time, but it was a huge total by the norms accepted in the 1930's, when the DC-3 first emerged.

Military C-47s were named Skytrain and were powered by Pratt & Whitney R-1830 radial engines rather than the DC-3's usual Wright Cyclone radials. The initial production model was the C-47, followed by the C-47A and C-47B. These types went on to serve with American forces literally world-wide, as type became the standard U.S. Army Air Force transport from 1942 onwards. Every war front included C-47s carrying freight and passengers (cargo loads even occasionally included Jeep light vehicles), and the type was also the Allies' most important paratroop transport. Many were converted to tow gliders, making them one of the most significant glider-towers for the major Allied operations such as the Invasion of Normandy in June 1944 (D-Day, Operation 'Overlord'), the invasion of southern France, the airborne operations in Holland in September 1944 (the famous Operation 'Market Garden' and the failed assault at Arnhem), and the Rhine Crossing into Germany in March 1945. A closely related derivative, built in comparatively small numbers, was the C-53 Skytrooper, a troop transport which featured just an entrance door in the rear left fuselage rather than the C-

NICARAGUA €3.00

CORREOS '94
DIA "D" 6 DE JUNIO DE 1944 TRANSPORTES C-47
LANZANDO PARACAIDISTAS.

47's combined cargo/passenger door arrangement. The U.S. Navy flew a variety of C-47 versions known as the R4D. In addition to this vitally important usage by American forces, Britain's Royal Air Force was a major C-47 operator; British versions were called Dakota (a name that has also become synonymous with the C-47). Almost 1,900 Dakotas served with the RAF – the Dakota Mk.I corresponding to the C-47, the Dakota Mk.III to the C-47A and the Dakota Mk.IV to the C-47B. An RAF Dakota pilot was posthumously awarded the Victoria Cross, Britain's highest military gallantry award, for actions during the 'Market Garden' operations.

In addition to American production, the C-47 was also built in a modified form in the Soviet Union as the Lisu-

*Photographed in 1978, this preserved DC-3/C-47 was taking part in a re-enactment of D-Day with the Confederate Air Force at Harlingen, Texas (Photo: John Batchelor).*

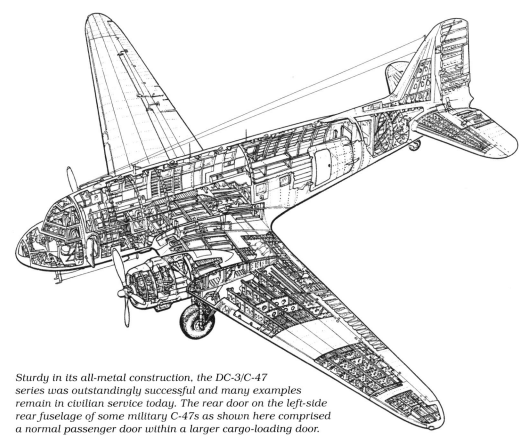

*Sturdy in its all-metal construction, the DC-3/C-47 series was outstandingly successful and many examples remain in civilian service today. The rear door on the left-side rear fuselage of some military C-47s as shown here comprised a normal passenger door within a larger cargo-loading door.*

# Douglas DC-3 and C-47 Series *continued*

*Prominently wearing its black and white D-Day identification stripes, this C-47 is representative of the many examples of its type that took part in the famous D-Day operation in June 1944. They acted as glider-towers as well as carrying paratroops.*

nov Li-2. This development featured different engines and a number of other changes, but some examples also mounted a gun turret in the upper fuselage behind the flight deck. Approximately 2,000 (possibly more) Li-2s were built. In addition, the type was manufactured in Japan, and ironically became a useful transport for Japanese forces fighting the Americans. This followed the supply of civil DC-3 models to Japan in the 1930's, and under Japanese construction the type was built by Showa and Nakajima (485 examples) as the L2D series. The sum total of all DC-3/C-47s and foreign-manufactured spin-offs was just over thirteen thousand.

The end of World War Two did not see the conclusion of the C-47's military career by any means. Large numbers remained in the inventory of the U.S. Army Air Force (from 1947, the U.S. Air Force), and they served in many conflicts and operations in the Cold War period. These included important

involvement in the Berlin Airlift of 1949 to 1950, the Korean War of 1950 to 1953 and the Vietnam War during the 1960's. Service in the latter conflict saw some examples converted into 'gunships,' and these were used to support American and South Vietnamese forces. In addition to this post-Second World War service with the Americans, C-47s were very widely exported. Indeed, it would be easier to list the small number of countries that have not had the C-47 on their inventories at one time or another than the many that have. This type has seen the widest service across the world in war and peace of any aircraft yet produced. Civ-

il operators have flown C-47s in virtually all parts of the world, and a number of attempts have been made to update the type with modifications such as the addition of turboprop engines.

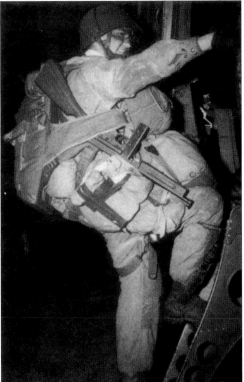

*A heavily-laden U.S. paratroop boards a C-47 for the drop into Normandy early on D-Day, 6 June 1944 (Photo: U.S. Army).*

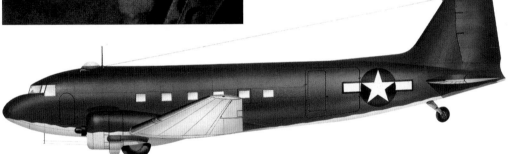

*Although this drawing shows a C-47 in U.S. colors, significant numbers flew with the RAF during World War Two as well, taking part in operations such as D-Day in June 1944 and the 'Market Garden' operation into Holland in September 1944.*

### Specifications – Douglas C-47 Skytrain (Dakota Mk.I)

| | |
|---|---|
| Wingspan | 95 ft |
| Length | 63 ft 9 in (varied due to glider-towing attachment) |
| Maximum speed | 227 mph at 7,500 ft |
| Maximum take-off weight | 26,000 lb |
| Range | 1,600 miles |
| Service ceiling | 24,000 ft |
| Engine | Two Pratt & Whitney R-1830-92 Twin Wasp radial piston engines, of 1,200 hp each |
| Accommodation | Two or three crew, up to 27/28 troops |

# Military Gliders

The employment of military gliders for operational tasks reached its peak during the Second World War. Nowadays there is nothing like the military glider of World War Two in the inventories of any of the major military powers around the world. However, the use of airborne troops (paratroops) – a concept first developed widely in the 1930's – still persists and is significant to this day. Similarly, the use of transport aircraft to deploy men and war material to distant battlefields is a very important concept in modern warfare today, and that concept also developed before World War Two but was widely used for the first time in that conflict. Two of the classic transport aircraft of World War Two that carried troops into battle, the German Junkers Ju 52/3m and the American Douglas C-47, are described here.

It is worth remembering that gliders have a long history – longer in fact than powered aircraft. Readers of the first volume of *The Complete Encyclopedia of Flight* will have seen how gliders – un-powered flying machines – actually pre-dated powered aircraft by a number of years. In the long and sometimes difficult process that eventually led towards the creation of manned, powered flight, aviation pioneers first developed un-powered gliders in the later years of the nineteenth century. These early gliders were used to explore the techniques and aerodynamics needed to create a flying machine, and eventually gliders were sturdy and safe enough to take men aloft. Only then was it possible to move on to the next stage of aviation, the use of an engine in a flying machine to take a man safely into the air with a power source within the aircraft itself. And so gliders have a central place in the history of the development of aviation. Today gliders continue to exist, but the beautiful and graceful sailplanes of our time – usually with seating for only one or two occupants – are far different to those of the pioneers of aviation. By the 1930's, except in Germany, gliders had been largely forgotten by the aviation world. Powered aircraft were everywhere by then, and it was even possible for individuals of modest

*The Gotha Go 242 glider shown was one of several assault gliders envisaged by the Germans for wartime use, being a larger design than the DFS 230 with more capacity. Of mixed wood and metal construction with some fabric covering, the Go 242 could carry up to 21 fully-equipped troops or a small vehicle (loaded into the rear of the fuselage). Service entry was in 1942, and further development led to a powered version with two radial engines, the Go 244.*

finances to buy a powered aircraft, or to fly in a passenger aircraft.

Just who, or which country, actually came up with the idea of developing gliders for warlike purposes – to carry men and war material into battle – is not particularly clear. Several countries started to use aircraft for transporting troops in the 1920's, including the British in trouble spots within the British Empire. The development of reliable mass-produced parachutes in the post-World War One years made the concept of airborne troops (paratroops) possible, and the first country to demonstrate paratroop forces was the Soviet Union in the 1930's. It was not long before these ideas caught on in Nazi Germany. Without doubt the advantages of airborne troops, and the use of transport aircraft to ferry troops, were lessons that were clear to the Germans. At the start of the Spanish Civil War, German transport aircraft aided the rebel Spanish Nationalist forces of General Franco by transporting troops to Spain from North Africa. The concept of using gliders for warlike purposes was also taking root in Germany.

The peace treaties after World War One resulted in Germany losing the right to possess significant forces of high-performance warplanes, or to design and develop this type of machine. In the 1920's, many German aircraft companies and individuals in the German military sought to get around these restrictions. One very obvious way of doing so was to construct gliders, which were not specifically prohibited by the peace treaties. Therefore,

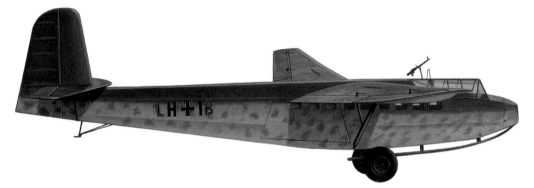

*The ubiquitous German DFS 230 glider really put military gliders 'on the map.' It was the first true production military glider for use in wartime, and it pioneered many of the techniques of the assault glider. Well over one thousand were made and the type came to worldwide notice following storming of the Belgian strongpoint of Fort Eben-Emael in May 1940.*

**Specifications – DFS 230A-1**

| | |
|---|---|
| Wingspan | 72 ft 1.3 in (or slightly less) |
| Length | 36 ft 10.5 in |
| Maximum gliding speed | 180.2 mph |
| Maximum take-off weight | 4,630 lb |
| Armament | One flexible-mounted and two fixed forward-firing 7.92 mm (0.312 in) machine guns (not always fitted) |
| Accommodation | One crew and nine troops, or two crew and eight troops |

# Military Gliders *continued*

glider flying took root very quickly in post-war Germany. A number of well-known glider competitions were held in Germany at that time, especially on the Wasserkuppe. In addition to these developments, as a part of the all-embracing Nazi organizations that were established in Germany following the Nazi accession to power in early 1933, training and air experience organizations were developed to bring military aviation concepts to German youth (and indeed to anyone else who wanted to become involved, or was forced to participate). This included the widespread use of gliders and it was here that the glider started to take on a more warlike potential. The German military was in the process of re-writing the concepts of warfare during those years.

As a part of this, the idea of bringing in troops by air to aid in invasion plans, or to seize point targets of high value, were included and developed. The use of paratroops, troop-carrying transport aircraft, and gliders containing troops and equipment, all came to be a part of the overall picture. The German 'Blitzkrieg,' as used so effectively in the opening stages of World War Two, embraced all these concepts. It was only later that the Allies came to realize the great potential of large gliders to carry men and material into battle. In the end, the tables were turned and the Allies used their own gliders with great effect against the Germans in the Normandy landings in June 1944.

One of the first significant gliders to be used in warfare was the German DFS 230. It was followed by a variety of designs, many of them made from

*Vehicle in the front shows the sheer scale of the Me 321. It was towed either by a single four engined aircraft (Ju 90) or towed by 3 Me Bf 110s!*

### Specifications – Messerschmitt Me 321B-1 Gigant

| | |
|---|---|
| Wingspan | 180 ft 5.3 in |
| Length | 92 ft 4.25 in |
| Maximum gliding speed | approximately 87 mph |
| Maximum take-off weight | 86,860 lb |
| Armament | Two 7.92 mm (0.312 in) machine guns flexible-mounted in the nose, plus whatever weapons could be fired from fuselage openings by troops aboard |
| Accommodation | Two or more crew, possible provision for 200 troops (usually less) |

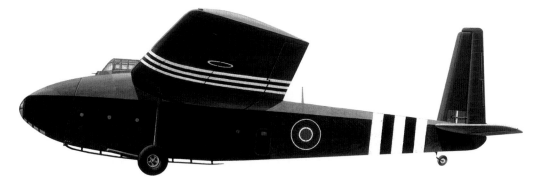

*The General Aircraft Hamilcar was a large British transport glider, capable of carrying a small tank. The first example flew in 1942, and the type was ready to be used in the Allied D-Day Invasion of June 1944. Usually a four-engined bomber such as a Handley Page Halifax was needed to tow one of these large gliders into the air. As with the Messerschmitt Me 321/323, a powered version of the Hamilcar was tried out, propelled by two radial engines.*

wood or the simplest metal structures – gliders were expendable, and were not really made to be used over and over again. The DFS 230 in effect proved the concept of glider-borne assault. On 10 May 1940, German forces invaded France and the Low Countries. On that day, DFS 230s were used to transport fully-armed German troops onto the site of the vitally-important Fort Eben-Emael in Belgium – and capture it in a brief but decisive battle. This was the first use of gliders in a major war, and it caught the attention of the world – and military planners everywhere. Towed by transport aircraft (which themselves could bring in further troops), combat gliders had the great advantage of depositing their troops right into the scene of the attack, silently, without the need for the troops wasting time to link up (paratroops dropped by transport aircraft, on the other hand, can be scattered over a wide area and so are less effective until they have all successfully linked-up).

The success of German airborne troops in the 'Blitzkrieg' launched against the Low Countries and France encouraged British Prime Minister Winston Churchill to seek the establishment of similar forces in Britain, and soon the United States was following suit. In fact, the Americans had already toyed with the concept for several years and had experimented some time before with paratroops. Events during the early stages of the war were watched closely by planners in America and lessons were learned about the effective German use of airborne forces. This Allied interest was further extended following the successful use of airborne troops by the Germans for the invasion of the strategic island of Crete in the Mediterranean during 1941.

The use of gliders was central to this rapid and decisive movement of men, but gliders also started to be used specifically for carrying cargo. Development of the huge Messerschmitt Me 321 showed how important the glider became. Indeed, the Me 321 was the greatest example of the cargo-carrying glider, but in the Allied forces too the glider was being developed for cargo and equipment-carrying in addition to transporting troops into battle.

The greatest employment of gliders was in the Allied invasion of mainland Europe (Operation Overlord), which began in the early hours of 6 June 1944, with a glider-borne assault by British

# Military Gliders *continued*

The Airspeed Horsa was Britain's principal troop and general purpose glider in World War Two. Able to carry up to 15 fully-armed troops or cargo, it took part in several Allied' airborne operations.

**Specifications – Airspeed Horsa Mk.I**

| | |
|---|---|
| Wingspan | 88 ft |
| Length | 67 ft |
| Maximum gliding speed | 110 mph |
| Maximum take-off weight | 15,500 lb |
| Accommodation | Two crew, up to 25 troops (often less) |

COMMONWEALTH OF DOMINICA $2

'D' Day 6th JUNE 1944 - BRITISH HORSA GLIDERS LAND MORE TROOPS.

COMMONWEALTH OF DOMINICA 65c

'D' Day 6th JUNE 1944 - U.S. WACO GLIDER BRINGS REINFORCEMENTS.

Created by Waco, an American company well-known during the 1930's for its light aircraft, the CG-4A Hadrian was the only American glider to see major combat service in World War Two. It was a significant asset to the Allies, able to carry up to 15 fully-armed troops or cargo and it took part in several of the Allies' airborne operations. Used for the D-Day operations and the Rhine Crossing, many examples were ready for use in the Far East should it necessary for the Americans to launch an attack on Japan. As things transpired this was not needed, the dropping of the atomic bombs on Japan in August 1945 ended the need for an airborne assault on Japan itself.

It was not just the Germans and Allies who developed military gliders. In Italy, the use of transport gliders was also recognized, although there was never the same level of development or deployment. Shown in the photograph is an Aeronautica Lombarda (SAI/Ambrosini) training glider, intended for the Italian glider training school of Orio al Serio (Photo: via Hans Meier).

forces to seize a strategic bridge (known forever after as 'Pegasus Bridge') in northern France. Gliders played a vital role in the Allied operations during the D-Day period, the efforts of the gallant glider crews and the troops they carried as well as the aircraft that towed them into battle were an important element of the D-Day operations. Gliders were similarly used in September 1944 for the massive Allied landings and in the Netherlands for the famous Arnhem operations (Operation 'Market Garden'). Unfortunately, on this occasion, the main bulk of the Allied ground forces were too far away to link up with the airborne troops and the operation was a failure. In March 1945, during Operation 'Varsity' or the Rhine Crossing, Allied forces again went into battle in gliders and as paratroops, this successful operation helping to lead to Allied victory in Europe two months later.

The glider had thus become an important weapon of warfare. However, the increasing sophistication of air defences, and the development of different tactics and operational requirements, has subsequently rendered the assault glider obsolete. Today gliders remain in military service, but they are mainly sailplanes or motorized gliders (with a small engine attached) which give air experience to trainees and perform some training aspects. The concept of a troop-carrying glider going into battle has disappeared.

# Ryan Trainers

On 8 June 1934, the prototype Ryan ST (Sport Trainer) made its first flight from Lindbergh Field, California. Built mainly of metal but with some wood construction, the low-wing tandem two-seater was the first of a line of trainers to find widespread service with the U.S. and other military forces. The prototype suffered from being underpowered, so the 95 hp Menasco B-4 was replaced by a 125 hp Menasco C-4 and then a 150 hp C-4S as the ST-A then ST-A Special. In September 1937, the Mexican air force ordered six as STMs (Sport Trainer Military), followed in 1938 by orders from Ecuador, Guatemala and Honduras, the last two countries including examples armed with 0.3 in (7.62 mm) machine guns. China received a batch as STM-2E/Ps, while a large batch was ordered for the Dutch East Indies as STM-2 landplanes and STM-S2 seaplanes. Some 37 of these escaped to Australia when the Japanese invaded, joining the Royal Australian Air Force. An ST-A.1 acquired as the XPT-16 for evaluation at Wright Field, Ohio, was the U.S. Army Air Corps' first monoplane primary trainer. A mid-1939 order followed for 15 STM.1s as YPT-16s, of which approximate-

ly 13 were re-engined with 125–132 hp Kinner R-440-1 radial engines (in place of the 125 hp Menasco L-365-1 inline) as YPT-16As. These initial 16 aircraft were the vanguard of around 1,193 that joined the Army Air Force as PT-20s, PT-21s, PT-22s and PT-25s. The first were 30 (or possibly 40) PT-20s with a stronger airframe and wider cockpits than the PT-16s. Powered by L-365-1s, most if not all survivors were later re-engined with the R-440-1 (PT-20A) or 125 hp Menasco D-4 (PT-20B). 100 PT-21s, powered by the 132 hp R-440-3, were acquired for use by civil contract flying schools. The most numerous variant was the PT-22 Recruit, a version of the ST.3KR powered by the Kinner R-540-1. 1,023 PT-22s were ordered in 1941, including three completed as ST-3Ss for the Ecuadorian air force. In addition, 25 ST-3S twin-float seaplanes originally ordered for the Dutch navy were completed for the U.S. Army as PT-22As. A total of 250 PT-22s were re-engined with the R-540-3 as PT-22Cs. The final version acquired by the Army comprised five ST.4s for evaluation as YPT-25s, built of plastic-

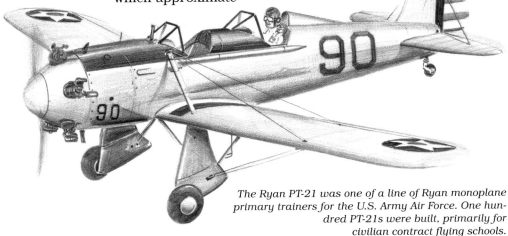

*The Ryan PT-21 was one of a line of Ryan monoplane primary trainers for the U.S. Army Air Force. One hundred PT-21s were built, primarily for civilian contract flying schools.*

Two views of a preserved Ryan PT-22 in the United States. The PT-22 can be recognized by the prominent loop on the aileron near to the wingtip. The undercarriage view shows the main legs unusually uncovered (Photos: John Batchelor).

bonded wood construction and powered by a 185 hp Lycoming O-435-1. The U.S. Navy also used a PT-21 variant, the NR-1 with a 130 hp Ranger L-440-3 powerplant and a lockable tailwheel. 100 were acquired, the majority being flown until mid-1944 at Naval Air Station Jacksonville, Florida. In U.S. service, the Ryan series were the first production monoplane primary trainers for the U.S. Army, and they complemented the Boeing Stearman biplane (see pages 74 to 75) rather than replacing it – indeed, their service lives in many cases did not extend to the end of the war.

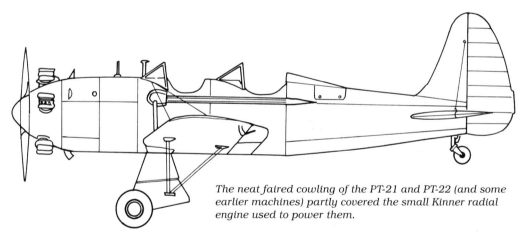

The neat faired cowling of the PT-21 and PT-22 (and some earlier machines) partly covered the small Kinner radial engine used to power them.

**Specifications – Ryan PT-22 Recruit**

| | |
|---|---|
| Wingspan | 30 ft 1 in |
| Length | 22 ft 5 in |
| Maximum speed | 131 mph at sea level |
| Maximum take-off weight | 1,860 lb |
| Range | 352 miles |
| Service ceiling | 15,500 ft |
| Engine | One Kinner R-540-1 radial piston engine, of 160 hp |
| Crew | Two |

# Junkers Ju 188

The highly-successful Junkers Ju 88 medium bomber (see pages 72 to 73) gave significant service to the Luftwaffe for a number of years in a variety of distinct roles. Plans to eventually replace it with a more advanced and capable successor under the so-called 'Bomber B' program (as shown on pages 296 to 297) were not successful. Nevertheless, intended improvements were partly included in the Ju 88B project, with a new forward fuselage and cockpit arrangement compared to the standard Ju 88A layout. By a long development process, this work led to the interim Ju 188, which became an important if less well-known type in its own right.

Between 1941 and 1942, several development aircraft flew with major aspects of the intended Ju 188 layout, including extended and pointed wingtips for higher altitude work, a redesigned forward fuselage, and a more square-shaped vertical tail (as also used on the Ju 88G). Due to this continuing work, it is difficult to pin down the initial flight date for the first real Ju 188, but it was possibly in June 1941. An intended powerplant for the Ju 188A-series was the Junkers Jumo 213 inline engine, but development problems with this engine delayed the Ju 188A and resulted in the BMW 801G radial-powered Ju 188E being the first main production version. This model entered service trials during 1943, and it commenced major combat action in October 1943. Some operations were flown over England. The Ju 188E was a fast medium bomber and pathfinder version, and it was followed by the BMW-engined Ju 188D-series of reconnaissance aircraft. Other developments led to the Ju 188R night fighter, several examples of which appear to have been made, the Ju 188F reconnaissance aircraft, and high-altitude pressurized Ju 188S and Ju 188T versions, which again only

*With its pointed wingtips, new vertical tail shape and new forward fuselage and cockpit, the Junkers Ju 188 was markedly different in appearance to the Junkers Ju 88 from which it was developed. It was produced in a number of versions, the most important being the Ju 188E bomber and Ju 188D reconnaissance aircraft.*

appeared in small numbers, plus a low-altitude attack derivative of the Ju 188S. There was also a planned Ju 188G-series, with a two-gun rear fuselage mounting for fending off attacks from behind. Other high-altitude versions, the Ju 188J, 'K' and 'L,' were continued under the Ju 388 program covered on pages 296 to 297. Total production of the Ju 188 is claimed to have been just short of 1,100. In combat, the Ju 188 is probably best remembered for taking part in the socalled 'Baby Blitz' (Operation 'Stein-bock') on Britain in early 1944. Pathfinder Ju 188s also sometimes accompanied 'Mistel' composite aircraft on their operations during early 1945 (see pages 304 to 305). Post-war, the Ju 188 was used by France's Aéronavale naval air arm. Some of these were captured examples, but twelve are believed to have been built from stocks of spare parts at Toulouse in south-western France. The type served with the French as a medium bomber and test aircraft.

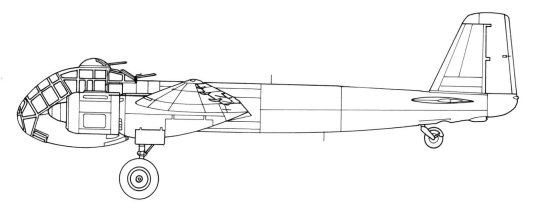

*Most versions of the Junkers Ju 188 were powered by the BMW 801 radial engine as shown here on a Ju 188F reconnaissance aircraft.*

## Specifications – Junkers Ju 188E-1

| | |
|---|---|
| Wingspan | 72 ft 2 in |
| Length | 49 ft 1 in |
| Maximum speed | 310.5 mph at 19,685 ft |
| Maximum take-off weight | 30,864 lb |
| Range | approximately 1,209 miles |
| Service ceiling | 30,512 ft |
| Armament | One 20 mm cannon in forward fuselage, two 13 mm (0.51 in) machine guns in dorsal positions (one in turret), one or two 7.92 mm (0.312 in) machine guns in ventral position rearwards-firing, up to 6,614 lb of bombs |
| Engine | Two BMW 801G-2 radial piston engines, of 1,740 hp each |
| Crew | Four |

# North American P-51 Mustang

A number of aircraft types are justifiably referred to as legends from the Second World War period, and one of these is the North American P-51 Mustang. Indeed, there are many who consider this superb fighter to be the best combat aircraft of the war years, even better than such famous and well-loved types as the Supermarine Spitfire. Without doubt the Mustang was virtually flawless in the various roles it undertook, and was rarely bettered by any other fightter. It was capable of taking on – and usually beating – any piston-engined fighter that the Germans, Japanese and Italians could field against it, and if it started with an advantage it could often take on and shoot down the Germans' faster jet-powered aircraft as well. As an escort fighter for American bombers over northern Europe, the Mediterranean and southern Europe, and in the Pacific, it was supreme, and is without doubt the best-ever piston-engined fighter to fulfil that role. The eventual defeat of the Luftwaffe, and of the Imperial Japanese army and naval aviation elements, was as much due to the destruction wrought on them by Mustangs as to any other means. The Mustang was the principal member of the trio of American fighters of the later war period – the Republic P-47 Thunderbolt and the Lockheed P-38 Lightning were the other two. Both those fighters were highly competent and have their passionate adherents, but the Mustang tends to stand above the undoubted achievements of those other two types.

The Mustang, somewhat ironically, was not designed to meet an official U.S. military specification, but came about in response to a 1940 British

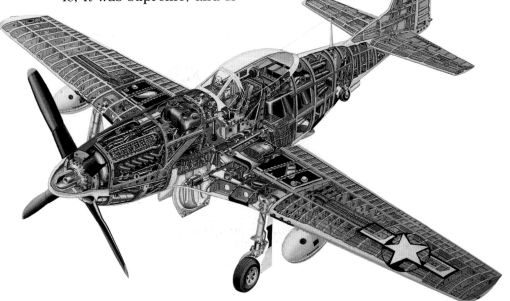

*The P-51 Mustang was a beautifully streamlined creation with an all-metal structure and the ability to fly long distances aided by its underwing jettisonable fuel tanks. It had an efficient laminar flow wing and the version shown, the P-51D, had a 'teardrop' cockpit canopy for increased pilot vision.*

request for a fast, heavily-armed fighter able to operate effectively at high altitudes. This was something of a tall order, but North American Aviation designed and built the prototype in approximately 122 days. Designated NA-73X, the first example flew on 26 October 1940. It was clear from the start that this beautifully streamlined, powerful aircraft was a winner. The first of 620 production Mustang Mk.Is for the RAF flew in April 1941, powered by a 1,150 hp Allison V-1710-39 engine. Many of these aircraft were initially used for low-level operations and army co-operation work. The first Mustang air-to-air victory ever was appropriately scored by an American pilot flying with the RAF during the failed Dieppe landings by Canadian forces in August 1942. It was the first of many. The U.S. Army recognized the fighter's potential – especially after the Pearl Harbor attack – and following evaluation of early production Mustang Is, began to order the type. The first two U.S. Mustang variants, both optimized for ground attack and designated A-36A Apache and P-51A, were Allison-powered. The Allison V-1710 was a good engine for lower altitude work, but was not so good at higher altitudes, where it needed a bulky turbo-supercharger to give it a lift in performance. Trials with Mustangs fitted with Rolls-Royce Merlin engines, and license-built Packard Merlins showed a dramatic improvement in performance. Development work was carried out simultaneously in Britain and America, improving both the maximum speed, and more importantly, the aircraft's high-altitude capabilities. Manufacture of the Merlin-powered P-51B commenced in earnest in 1943. North American's Inglewood, California, factory duly built 1,988 P-51Bs. A new factory at Dallas, Texas, built 1,750 more with the designation P-51C.

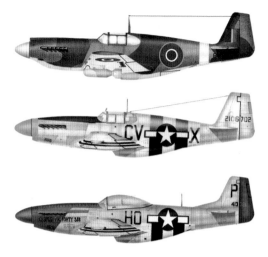

*1) 10657 – An Allison-engined RAF-operated Mustang Mk.I, with underwing bomb.*

*2) 10658 – A P-51B Mustang of the Eighth Army Air Force's 359th Fighter Group wearing full black and white 'Invasion Stripes' for D-Day operations in June 1944.*

*3) 10659 – A victim of what we now know as 'friendly fire' was the Eighth Army Air Force's leading Mustang ace, George E. Preddy, Jr. of the 352nd Fighter Group shot down by American ground fire on Christmas Day, 1944. This was one of his aircraft.*

P-51Bs of the 354th Fighter Group flew their first operational escort mission from England, escorting B-17s to Kiel and back, a round trip of some 1,000 miles in December 1943. Hitherto the American bombers had been unprotected on some of their longer missions because other American fighters did not have the range to escort them all the way and back. The advent of the Mustang changed all that because, with jettisonable long-range fuel tanks beneath their wings, the Mustangs had the ability to stay with the bombers all the way and back, even to distant targets. Britain ordered almost 1,000 P 51B/Cs under Lend-Lease, designated Mustang Mk III. Early Merlin-powered Mustangs had a heavily-framed cockpit canopy like their Allison-

# North American P-51 Mustang *continued*

engined predecessors that reduced pilot visibility and some were fitted with a rearwards-sliding Malcolm Hood, a kind of fishbowl-shaped, clear molding. For a more permanent solution, North American tested two P-51Bs with a one-piece 'teardrop' sliding canopy and cut-down rear fuselage. The new layout was designated XP-51D, and also pioneered for the planned P-51D production model was the installation of three 0.5 in (12.7 mm) caliber machine guns in each wing instead of the P-51B/C's two. Service entry for the P-51D was the spring of 1944, and this version was the superlative Mustang model. P-51Ds rapidly became the standard equipment of the England-based Eighth Fighter Command, and they served just as effectively in other theaters of the war as well, including the Pacific. Production totalled 8,102 P-51Ds and 1,337 P-51Ks (which had Aeroproducts propellers instead of the Hamilton Standard propellers of other Mustang versions). Some 865 became Mustang IVs with the RAF, and 309 were finished as armed and equally deadly reconnaissance F-6Ds or F-6Ks,

mainly for the Army Air Force. Continuing development resulted in the lean-looking P-51H, too late for service at the end of World War Two. This was the fastest Mustang of all, with a top speed of some 487 mph. Production was also carried out in Australia, where the Commonwealth Aircraft Corporation built 200 generally similar to the P-51D. In addition to service with American, British and Commonwealth forces during the war, Mustangs (particularly reconnaissance models) were flown by French forces on the Allied side. Two American Mustang pilots were awarded the Medal of Honor and some of the Allies' top aces flew Mustangs, including George Preddy (see color sideviews).

To meet a 1943/1944 specification for a very long-range bomber escort, North American carried out a further re-design to mating two modified Mustang fuselages to a central, armed wing central section to produce the F-82 Twin Mustang. Equipped with radar, it was also a useful if interim night fighter. However, this unusual

The Confederate Air Force (now the Commemorative Air Force) is one of many preservation groups that keeps historic aircraft flying, including this P-51D Mustang during the 1970's. The Mustang has been converted into a two-seater to give a ride to a passenger in a very cramped rear seat *(Photo: John Batchelor).*

*Representative of the Eighth Army Air Force's highly successful bomber escort P-51D Mustangs is this colorful example from the 361st Fighter Group. Total Mustang manufacture was around 15,686 examples.*

aircraft was too late for World War Two service, although it was involved in the air war during the Korean War right from the start in the summer of 1950. By then, the P-51 Mustang itself had ceased to be of vital importance to the U.S. as a fighter, but flew many combat missions in Korea as a fighter-bomber. Mustangs were exported widely after the war to a multitude of operators – and in the Dominican Republic, the type remained in front-line service into the 1980's! There was also a number of special post-war conversions and upgrades, including the Cavalier Mustang, and the turboprop-powered Piper Enforcer.

## Specifications – North American P-51D Mustang

| | |
|---|---|
| Wingspan | 37 ft |
| Length | 32 ft 3 in |
| Maximum speed | 437 mph at 25,000 ft |
| Maximum take-off weight | 12,100 lb |
| Range | 1,650 miles with drop tanks |
| Service ceiling | 41,900 ft |
| Armament | Six 0.5 in (12.7 mm) wing-mounted fixed forward-firing machine guns, up to 2,000 lb of bombs beneath the wings, or unguided rockets |
| Engine | One Packard V-1650-7 Merlin inline piston engine, of 1,720 hp (maximum setting) |
| Crew | One |

# Martin Baltimore

The Martin Model 167 Maryland proved to be a successful light bomber and attack aircraft. It served principally with British and Commonwealth forces, and was originally created to meet a design competition of the U.S. Army Air Corps for a light bomber and attack aircraft. Further development of the Maryland design led directly to the Martin Model 187 Baltimore light bomber, which first flew on 14 June 1941. Created specifically to British requirements for an improved and more capable Maryland, the Baltimore featured a refined airframe comprising in particular a deepened (but still narrow) fuselage and a crew of four compared to the three-man Maryland. It included a four-gun forward-firing armament in the wings, an increased bomb-carrying capacity, and defensive armament that included (when fitted) a battery of rearwards-firing machine guns in the

lower fuselage and a dorsal gun position. The latter was found to be inadequate on the first main combat model, the Mk.II, comprising just two flexible-mounted machine guns. This led to the adoption of a four-gun turret in the Mk.III, and a two-gun turret in the later production versions. Initial deliveries were made to Nos.55 and 223 Squadrons, RAF, in the spring and early summer of 1942. The type went on to serve widely with British and Commonwealth units in the North African and Mediterranean theater. Following Allied victory in North Africa, Baltimores were in the thick of the action over Italy and others served over the Balkans.

Although some units converted onto other types, several continued to use the Baltimore until the end of the war. Like the Maryland, no Baltimores served with American forces, despite the Baltimore's all-American manu-

*The Martin Baltimore was a successful, if not particularly widely-known, light bomber that served virtually exclusively in North Africa, the Mediterranean and over southern Europe. Shown is a Mk.I or Mk.II with the twin flexible-mounted dorsal machine guns of the early-model Baltimores.*

facture. Unusually, historians agree over production totals for the Baltimore – 50 Mk.I, 100 Mk.II, 250 Mk.III, 281 Mk.IIIA (A-30), 294 Mk.IV (A-30A), and 600 Mk.V (A-30A) – with a grand total of 1,575. Production ended in 1944, the latter batches with an 'A' prefix being supplied under Lend-Lease arrangements. In addition to light bombing, some Baltimores served (like the Maryland) as long-range reconnaissance aircraft. Baltimores were additionally employed by a Greek unit fighting alongside the Allies for the liberation of Greece from the Germans and by pro-Allied Italian forces. Some found their way to Turkey. A small number served with Britain's Royal Navy but on shore-based second-line duties, and the Free French similarly used a number – the final Baltimores in service continuing in French operation several years after the war ended.

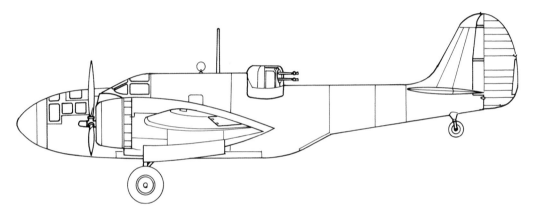

*The Martin Baltimore Mk.III introduced much heavier rearward-firing capability in its dorsal position with a four-gun Boulton Paul turret. Later versions had a two-gun American Martin turret. Baltimores were effective light bombers, usually operating by day but sometimes at night also.*

### Specifications – Martin Baltimore Mk.IV

| | |
|---|---|
| Wingspan | 61 ft 4 in |
| Length | 48 ft 6 in |
| Maximum speed | 305 mph at 11,500 ft |
| Maximum take-off weight | 22,600 lb |
| Range | 1,082 miles |
| Service ceiling | 23,300 ft |
| Armament | Four 0.303 in (7.7 mm) fixed forward-firing wing-mounted machine guns, two 0.5 in (12.7 mm) machine guns in dorsal turret, provision on some aircraft for rearward-firing ventral machine guns, 2,000 lb of bombs |
| Engine | Two Wright R-2600-19 Cyclone radial piston engines, of 1,600–1,660 hp each |
| Crew | Four |

# Martin B-26 Marauder

The use of tactical air power was a significant asset that the Allies employed to the full in all theaters of war of World War Two. Tactical aircraft struck at comparatively short-range military targets on the battlefield, behind the lines, at air fields and other targets such as shipping in coastal waters directly linked to the enemy's war machine and its supply. Tactical aircraft ranged from fighter-bombers such as the Hawker Typhoon and Republic P-47 Thunderbolt, to medium bombers such as the North American B-25 Mitchell. This was different to the doctrine of strategic bombing, which eventually used much larger heavy bombers to strike much longer-range targets, such as factories in the rear. One of the tactical medium bombers that was much used by the Allies during the war was a high-performance aircraft originally

developed at the Glenn L. Martin Company of Baltimore, Maryland, in the United States. This organization already had some pedigree in creating aircraft according to this general classification with the design of the Maryland light bomber (pages 134 to 135), a successful type that led to the Baltimore light bomber. These tactical aircraft were designed according to a U.S. Army Air Corps requirement of 1938 for a light bomber and attack aircraft. Martin now turned its attention to a larger and higher-capability aircraft, and the result was the B-26 Marauder. Intended to meet a demanding 1939 U.S. Army Air Corps request for a high-speed medium bomber, Martin's Model 179 proposal was a completely different aircraft to the Maryland and was considered to be so far in advance of competing submissions that the company was awarded an immediate contract for 201 of these

*The Martin B-26 Marauder was of basically all-metal construction, with some fabric-covered control surfaces. Shown is a B-26C, which illustrates the conventional horizontal carriage of the bombs within the fuselage.*

aircraft in September 1939. This 'off the drawing board' decision required no prototype or pre-production aircraft to be built, and the first production B-26, which was in effect the prototype, was flown on 25 November 1940. Provisionally named the Marauder, the B-26 had a crew of five (this was increased to seven on later models), and was powered by two 1,850-hp Pratt & Whitney R-2800-5 Double Wasp radial engines. The first B-26s easily met the officially required performance figures during their service testing, but this good performance was achieved at the expense of poor low-speed handling characteristics.

The first main production model was the B-26A (139 built), and this introduced improvements considered to be necessary from early service experience including more power and heavier armament. However, the resulting increases in weight only aggravated the low-speed handling difficulties. Training accidents became a

major problem, and an official board of investigation was created to decide whether to end production. Fortunately it instead recommended modifications to try to improve low-speed performance, and to revise handling techniques and procedures. The first truly mass-produced model was the B-26B (1,883 built), with 2,000 hp R-2800-41 engines, armament revisions and increased armor protection. This version introduced, from the 642nd example onwards, a 6 ft increase in wing span, a taller vertical tail and increased armament. 208 B-26Bs were later converted as the AT-23A for use as target-towers and gunnery trainers. Some B-26Bs became CB-26Bs following conversion as simple transports. Illustrating the increased tempo of production, a second production line was opened for the B-26 series at Omaha, Nebraska, to augment Martin's manufacture at Baltimore. This new line built 1,210 B-26C, similar to the B-26B. Some of these later became AT-23B trainers, others went to the U.S. Navy as the JM-1 (J = General Utility) including a small number of JM-1P reconnaissance aircraft. The next major production model was the B-26F,

*The 'YA' fuselage codes and yellow tail stripe identify this B-26C Marauder as belonging to the 555th Bomb Squadron, 386th Bomb Group, U.S. Ninth Army Air Force based at Great Dunmow, East Anglia, England. This was during the D-Day period (note the black and white 'D-Day' stripes painted on the aircraft during that momentous time).*

# Martin B-26 Marauder *continued*

300 of which were built. This version introduced an increase in wing incidence, aimed at improving the B-26's protracted problem with take-off performance. The fix worked, veterans subsequently recalling how much better the later Marauders flew. The final production version was the B-26G, of which 893 were built plus 57 TB-26G unarmed crew trainers and target-towers – some of the latter became the U.S. Navy's JM-2. Under Lend-Lease arrangements, the Marauder was supplied in some numbers for British use, over five hundred duly being operated by RAF and South African Air Force squadrons in several main versions – the Mk.I (B-26A), Mk.IA (B-26B), Mk.II (B-26C), and Mk.III (B-26F and B-26G).

In combat the B-26 did not have a particularly happy start, especially in Europe where early low-level operations with the Eighth Army Air Force were disastrous. In the Pacific, where the type initially entered combat with the 22nd Bomb Group (eventually of the Fifth Army Air Force), there was more success, although the Marauders were in short supply for some time. From late 1942, B-26B and B-26Cs began to appear in North Africa, equipping units of the U.S. Twelfth Army Air Force. They provided useful support to Allied ground forces in the subsequent campaigns in Sicily, Italy, and southern France. In northern Europe, after a poor start with the Eighth Air Force, the B-26 found its true role as a medium bomber at medium altitude with units of the tactical U.S. Ninth Army Air Force. The Marauder went on to record the lowest attrition rate of any American aircraft operated by the U.S. Ninth Air Force in Europe and the type was particularly in demand during the run-up to D-Day and in the fierce fighting in Normandy following the Allied landings. In common with other tactical assets of the U.S. forces, as soon as it was safe, the Ninth's Marauder units moved from their bases in England to the continent after D-Day. They then continued to follow the advancing Allied armies across Europe, operating from air bases vacated by the retreating Germans (or sometimes from specially-constructed landing grounds). British and Commonwealth Marauders also had a generally successful combat history, particularly alongside American units in operations in the Mediterranean area, and Marauders were also put to good use by Free French forces.

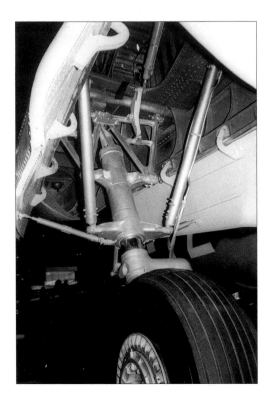

*The B-26 Marauder's front undercarriage leg consisted of this rather complicated arrangement (Photo: John Batchelor).*

The Marauder did not have a long career after the end of World War Two, and soon disappeared into the pages of history.

*A contemporary photograph of the tail gun position of an early B-26 Marauder. The aircraft is painted in the classic color scheme of U.S. Army Air Force aircraft of the early and mid-war period, olive drab upper surfaces and neutral gray undersides*
*(Photo: The Glenn L. Martin Company).*

**Specifications – Martin B-26G Marauder**

| | |
|---|---|
| Wingspan | 71 ft |
| Length | 56 ft 1 in |
| Maximum speed | 283 mph at 5,000 ft |
| Maximum take-off weight | 38,200 lb |
| Range | 1,100 miles |
| Service ceiling | 19,800 ft |
| Armament | Nine to eleven 0.5 in (12.7 mm) machine guns in dorsal and tail turrets, attached to front fuselage, and flexible-mounted in nose or elsewhere, up to 4,000 lb of bombs |
| Engine | Two Pratt & Whitney R-2800-43 Double Wasp radial piston engines, of 2,000 hp each |
| Crew | Seven |

# Boeing B-17 Flying Fortress

The effectiveness of air power was amply demonstrated during the First World War – the first major conflict in which military aircraft played a part. Nevertheless, there were still many in the post-war military establishments around the world who remained unconvinced of the military effectiveness of aircraft. In the United States during the 1920's, a considerable conflict developed between those who advocated an expanded air force, and the many more who were against the arguments for air power. A famous supporter of aviation was William 'Billy' Mitchell (the B-25 Mitchell medium bomber was named after him – see pages 152 to 155). Mitchell was eventually court-martialled for daring to speak out and act for air power, but his ideas took hold. Some advocates of air power thought that heavily-defended bombers would always be able to successfully fight their way through to their targets, even in daylight in the face of fighter opposition. The result was the doctrine of unescorted daylight bombing, which the Americans championed in World War Two. This idea led to the creation of bombers bristling with defensive machine guns, of which the ultimate example was the B-17 Flying Fortress. The B-17 was designed to meet a 1934 U.S. Army Air Corps requirement for a long-range, high-altitude daylight bomber. The prototype Boeing Model 299, powered by four 750 hp Pratt & Whitney Hornet engines,

LE16   B.17 F. U.S.A.F.

SIERRA LEONE

*The Boeing B-17 Flying Fortress was certainly aptly named – well-armed and intended to defend itself against fighter attack.*
*The B-17 also carried what in its day was a useful bomb load. Nevertheless, several of the other heavy bombers of World War Two could carry more, and were potentially more versatile.*
*Shown in this cutaway illustration is a B-17F, which lacked the chin turret of the B-17G, but did carry the ventral retractable ball turret shown. Note the fuel cells within the wings.*

*An in-flight photograph of a preserved Boeing B-17 in the United States during the 1970's. Today there are several B-17s still airworthy, very rare relics of these powerful and at one time very numerous bombers (Photo: John Batchelor).*

first flew on 28 July 1935. Boeing already had experience in streamlined high-performance aircraft with such designs as the Monomail civil mail carrier and the B-9 bomber, and the B-17 was the finest example yet of the then-developing all-metal fast monoplane bomber concept. Unfortunately, the first B-17 was later destroyed in an accident, but thirteen YlB-17s and one Y1B-17A were ordered for service testing, powered by four Wright R-1820 Cyclone radial engines as the standard for all later B-17s. These led to the first production batch of 39 B-17Bs, featuring a modified nose, enlarged rudder and various other modifications. After them came 38 B-17Cs with some minor changes. Twenty were supplied to Britain's RAF as the Fortress Mk.I in 1941, and they were tried out as high-altitude bombers – without much success. At the time of America's entry into World War Two, the B-17D (42 built) was in service. This was generally similar to the B-17C, but these early Fortresses suffered badly in the initial stages of the Pacific war. A completely revised tail design of far greater area was introduced on the B-17E, which also had improved armament – including a very necessary tail gun position in a re-designed rear fuselage. The B-17E was the first version of the Flying Fortress to see combat with American forces in the European theater, operating initially with the 97th Bomb Group in August 1942. The Flying Fortress continued to give service in the Pacific, but its numbers there were never very large and that theater was almost exclusively the preserve of the B-17's stablemate, the B-24 Liberator. The RAF received over forty B-17Es under the designation Fortress IIA. 512 B-17Es were manufactured, this variant being followed into serv-

*A close-up photograph of the engine front and cowling of a preserved Boeing B-17. The Flying Fortress was powered by four turbocharged Wright R-1820 Cyclone radial engines. It was not just aircraft that American industry mass-produced during World War Two, but aero engines and all the other equipment required by these high-performance warplanes. (Photo: John Batchelor).*

225

# Boeing B-17 Flying Fortress *continued*

*The nose of 'Sentimental Journey,' a gleaming air-worthy Boeing B-17 preserved in the United States. American aircraft during World War Two – particularly the bombers – were renowned for their 'pin-up' artwork (Photo: John Batchelor).*

ice by the further refined B-17F, which entered production in 1942. Total production of this highly important version was 3,405 by several factories, including some 40 examples converted to the long-range reconnaissance role as the F-9/F-9A. Another 19 were delivered, mostly to RAF Coastal Command, as the Fortress II. Some of the final B-17Fs were fitted with a chin-mounted remote-controlled turret containing a pair of heavy machine guns to guard against increasingly successful frontal attacks by German fighters.

The B-17F bore the brunt of the early daylight bombing missions by the Eighth Army Air Force over Occupied Europe. Often these raids were unescorted (particularly those of longer distances, beyond the range of early American escorts), leading to significant losses to German fighters. Only later in the war, after it was realized that full fighter escort all the way to the target was an absolute necessity for the bombers, were the B-17s able to sustain the type of continuous bombing against industrial targets that was so instrumental in winning the war in Europe. This bombing campaign was carried out alongside the RAF, whose Avro Lancasters and other bombers operated predominantly by night.

Increasing armament and a host of other minor revisions, plus the introduction of the chin turret, led to the B-17G, the most significant production model. 8,680 were built. 98 B-17Gs were also supplied to the RAF, where several were used for electronic countermeasures as a part of the secret No.100 Group – even as long ago as 1944, warfare was starting to include 'black boxes.' Flying Fortresses subsequently played a major part in the air war over Europe, operating alongside B-24 Liberators from England (and in southern Europe with the Fifteenth Army Air Force). As air superiority was increasingly won by the Allies, some B-17Gs dispensed with the chin turret. Nevertheless, this was an often brutal conflict – a number of Flying Fortress crew members, some posthumously, were awarded the Medal of Honor, America's highest military decoration for bravery.

Several B-17Gs were converted for reconnaissance as the F-9C, while the U.S. Navy and U.S. Coast Guard employed approximately 47 PB-1W and PB-1G for maritime surveillance and aerial survey. Some B-17s of various types were modified for air-sea rescue work as the B-17H, with an air-droppable lifeboat carried beneath the fuselage.

Total B-17 production was around thirteen thousand. After the war ended, the B-17 was rapidly withdrawn from front-line service and its place was completely taken by the much more powerful Boeing B-29 Superfortress. Some B-17s were later used in test programs or as fire-bombers, while others flew overseas including French examples on aerial cartography work. A handful operated for Zionist forces in the creation of the state of Israel later in the 1940's.

*Shown under German fighter attack, a Boeing B-17G takes evasive action during a bombing raid. The aircraft wears the colorful late-war markings of the 447th Bomb Group, U.S. Eighth Army Air Force, based at Rattlesden, Suffolk, England. Later in the war, American combat aircraft such as this one started to do away with camouflage paint, air superiority increasingly being gained against the Luftwaffe over Germany.*
Reproduced by Courtesy
of Murray Codman.

**Specifications – Boeing B-17G Flying Fortress**

| | |
|---|---|
| Wingspan | 103 ft 9.5 in |
| Length | 74 ft 4 in (depending on tail turret fitted) |
| Maximum speed | 287 mph at 25,000 ft |
| Maximum take-off weight | 65,500 lb |
| Range | 2,000 miles |
| Service ceiling | 35,600 ft |
| Armament | Thirteen (usual) 0.5 in (12.7 mm) machine guns, in various turrets or flexible-mounted, up to 4,000 lb of bombs (more on shorter missions) |
| Engine | Four Wright R-1820-97 Cyclone radial piston engines, of 1,200 hp each |
| Crew | Ten |

# Consolidated B-24 Liberator

Almost always overshadowed by the Boeing B-17 Flying Fortress, the Consolidated B-24 Liberator was one of the two main heavy bombers employed by the Americans during World War Two, the other being the B-17. However, by the end of the war a new type of heavy bomber, the much larger and more capable B-29 Superfortress, had come into service. The Liberator could carry more bombs than the B-17 and was generally faster, but it never received the publicity or the limelight always given to the B-17 and, later, to the B-29. It has since been argued that the B-24 was a more difficult aircraft to fly than the B-17, could take much less battle damage and was rather more prone to take-off accidents. However, to those who flew in the B-24, it was by far the better of the two and was certainly made in greater numbers, in more variants and flew longer in a much wider variety of roles. The actual number of B-24s built

is controversial, but the most reliable total – 18,482 – makes the Liberator the most widely produced American warplane of the Second World War period.

The B-24 originated as the Consolidated Model 32, a major feature of which was its exceptionally high aspect ratio Davis wing. This helped to give the Liberator its excellent long-distance range and load-carrying capability – although it was not a wing design that received wide acceptance at the time. Another B-24 feature was its deep, roomy fuselage that enabled the aircraft to carry a large bomb load – and also made it suitable for conversion as a transport. The sole XB-24 prototype flew on 29 December 1939, followed by seven YB-24 service trials aircraft and 38 initial production B-24As (few were delivered as such). Some 175 were ordered by the French, but France was defeated before they could be delivered

*Of all-metal construction, the Consolidated B-24 Liberator's structure was of unusual configuration for its time, although it was ultimately a great success. All major production versions were powered by the R-1830 Twin Wasp radial engine.*

*One of the principal users of the B-24 Liberator during World War Two was the U.S. Eighth Army Air Force, on its long and difficult bombing campaign over occupied Europe and Germany from bases in England. This drawing shows an Eighth Air Force B-24H, serial number 42-50397, wearing the markings of the 392nd Bomb Group.*

and many were sent instead to Britain, together with important additional orders from Britain (some under Lend-Lease) in the ensuing years. Here the initial arrivals were designated LB-30 or LB-30A (LB = Land Bomber, a Consolidated designation), some being used by the British airline B.O.A.C. for transatlantic ferry flights using the Liberator's excellent long range capability. Some went to the RAF's Coastal Command as the Liberator Mk.I, equipped with an early form of ASV search radar.

The first B-24A deliveries to the U.S. Army were made in the summer of 1941, but continuing revisions were constantly being made to the Liberator layout, including a fuselage stretch and the introduction of turbo-supercharged engines and revised armament. This use of exhaust-driven turbochargers was crucial to the success of many American combat aircraft of World War Two, and was a technology in which the Americans led the world. The first U.S. version actually to serve long-term in the bomber role (most of

the previous aircraft were non-operational) was the B-24D, which was essentially similar to the B-24C except for its higher rated engines and increased maximum take-off weight. Production of the B-24D by Consolidated, including ten by Douglas, totalled 2,728. Some were supplied to Britain as the Liberator III and IIIA, a number with British Boulton Paul gun turrets. In 1943, many U.S. Army B-24Ds engaged in maritime reconnaissance and anti-submarine patrol were withdrawn, this role transferring to the U.S. Navy and its PB4Y-1 (a B-24D equivalent). Some B-24Ds had an Erco ball turret in their noses. 801 B-24Es were built by Convair (as Consolidated was known from 1943), Douglas and Ford, distinguishable from the B-24D chiefly by their different propellers. North American Aviation manufactured 430 B-24Gs, some of them with a powered gun turret installed in the nose. An Emerson nose turret and R-1830-65 engines characterized the B-24H, 3,100 of which were completed by Convair, Douglas and Ford. Like

229

# Consolidated B-24 Liberator *continued*

the B-17, the B-24 started out with inadequate frontal armament to ward off head-on fighter attacks, hence the addition of a turret to the nose of the aircraft to replace the original 'greenhouse' of the B-24D and earlier models with its flexible-mounted machine guns. In addition, these three companies, plus North American, manufactured 6,678 B-24Js, with a Consolidated or Motor Products nose turret as standard and a ventral Briggs ball turret. Many were used by the RAF in addition to the Americans, Coastal Command Liberators being particularly important in helping to close the 'Atlantic Gap' and taking the war to German U-Boats. Other armament variations characterized the B-24L built by Convair and Ford and the B-24M from the same suppliers. Further contracts were curtailed in 1945 – the increasingly-successful B-29 having an effect

on production of the conventional heavy bombers that went before it. A major re-design, however, had by then led to the PB4Y-2 Privateer for the U.S. Navy. Featuring a single vertical tail, a greatly stretched fuselage and many other changes, this long-range bomber and patrol aircraft was probably the greatest development of the B-24 line. The prototype first flew on 20 September 1943 and some 739 were built by Consolidated/Convair at San Diego. A cargo/transport version of the Privateer, the RY-3, was also manufactured in much smaller numbers.

B-24 Liberators were a significant part of the U.S. Eighth and Fifteenth Army Air Forces' daylight bombing campaign of Occupied Europe and Germany alongside the B-17 Flying Fortress. They exclusively took part in the famed low level raid against Axis oil targets at Ploesti, Romania, on 1 August 1943 –

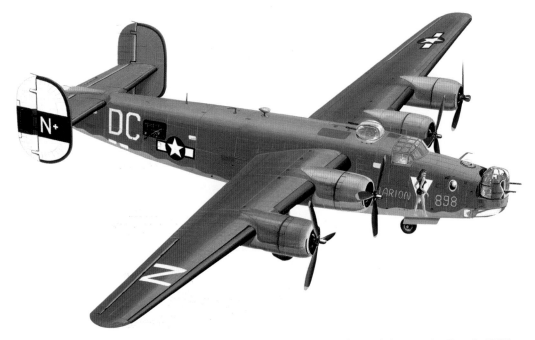

*The 'DC' fuselage code identifies this Liberator as belonging to the Eighth Army Air Force's 577th Bomb Squadron, 392nd Bomb Group, based at Wendling, Norfolk, in England's East Anglia.*

one of the war's most famous operations. However, the type was especially important in the Pacific theater, where its excellent range was particularly valuable and where the B-17 was used in much fewer numbers.

Several Liberator crew members were awarded the Medal of Honor, America's top military gallantry award. One posthumously received the Victoria Cross, Britain's highest gallantry medal. The B-24 also gave important service as a transport aircraft, the B-24D-related C-87 being used for this role. Britain's Prime Minister Winston Churchill employed a specially converted early-mark Liberator as his personal transport, named 'Commando.' Another important adaptation of the Liberator was the F-7 photo-reconnaissance aircraft. Others were utilized as cargo transports and C-109 fuel tanker aircraft, and for weather reconnaissance. In addition to those serving with the U.S. forces and the RAF, considerable numbers also operated with other Allied units. The end of the war saw the rapid demise of the Liberator bomber fleets, the B-29 Superfortress being the Army Air Force's new strategic bomber. However, the Privateer continued in service for some time after the war, rare U.S.-operated examples flying as electronic intelligence gathering (Elint) aircraft during the Cold War while more normal Privateers served with several countries including France.

**Specifications – Consolidated B-24J Liberator**

| | |
|---|---|
| Wingspan | 110 ft |
| Length | 67 ft 2 in |
| Maximum speed | 290 mph at 25,000 ft |
| Maximum take-off weight | 65,000 lb |
| Range | 2,100 miles |
| Service ceiling | 28,000 ft |
| Armament | Ten 0.5 in (12.7 mm) machine guns (in front, mid-upper, ball, and tail turrets, and one at each waist window), up to 12,800 lb of bombs |
| Engine | Four Pratt & Whitney R-1830-65 Twin Wasp radial piston engines, of 1,200 hp each |
| Crew | Ten |

# Consolidated PBY Catalina

The Consolidated Model 28 Catalina holds the distinction of being the world's most widely produced flying-boat. The prototype Model 28 was built for the U.S. Navy as the XP3Y-1, making its first flight in March 1935. Sixty initial production examples were built as PBY-1s, followed by 50 PBY-2s, 66 -3s and 33 -4s. They equipped some 15 squadrons within the U.S. Navy by the end of 1939, the first being VP-11F in October 1936. Engine power had increased from 900 hp on the PBY-1 to 1,050 hp on the PBY-4. The next variant, the PBY-5 featured R-1830 radials of 1,200 hp and extra fuel tanks. It was also built by the Naval Air Factory as the PBN-1 and by Boeing Canada as the PB2B-1 and – with taller tail surfaces – as the PB2B-2. An amphibious version, the PBY-5A was also produced, with licence production being undertaken as the PBV-1A

by Vickers of Canada. 130 PBV-1As went to the Royal Canadian Air Force as Canso As, while another 230 were delivered to the U.S. Army Air Force as OA-10A-VIs for the air-sea rescue role. The Air Force also used ex-Navy PBY-5As (as OA-10s), PBY-6As (OA-10Bs) and some PB2B-2s. The final American production version was the amphibious, tall-tailed PBY-6A, of which 175 were built.

During the war U.S. Catalinas were used for anti-submarine patrols, claiming the sinking of 20 U-Boats, while others were flown on night attacks against Japanese warships. Britain purchased just over 100 Catalina Mk.Is and Mk.IIs, both similar to the PBY-5, after having acquired a single Model 28-5 for

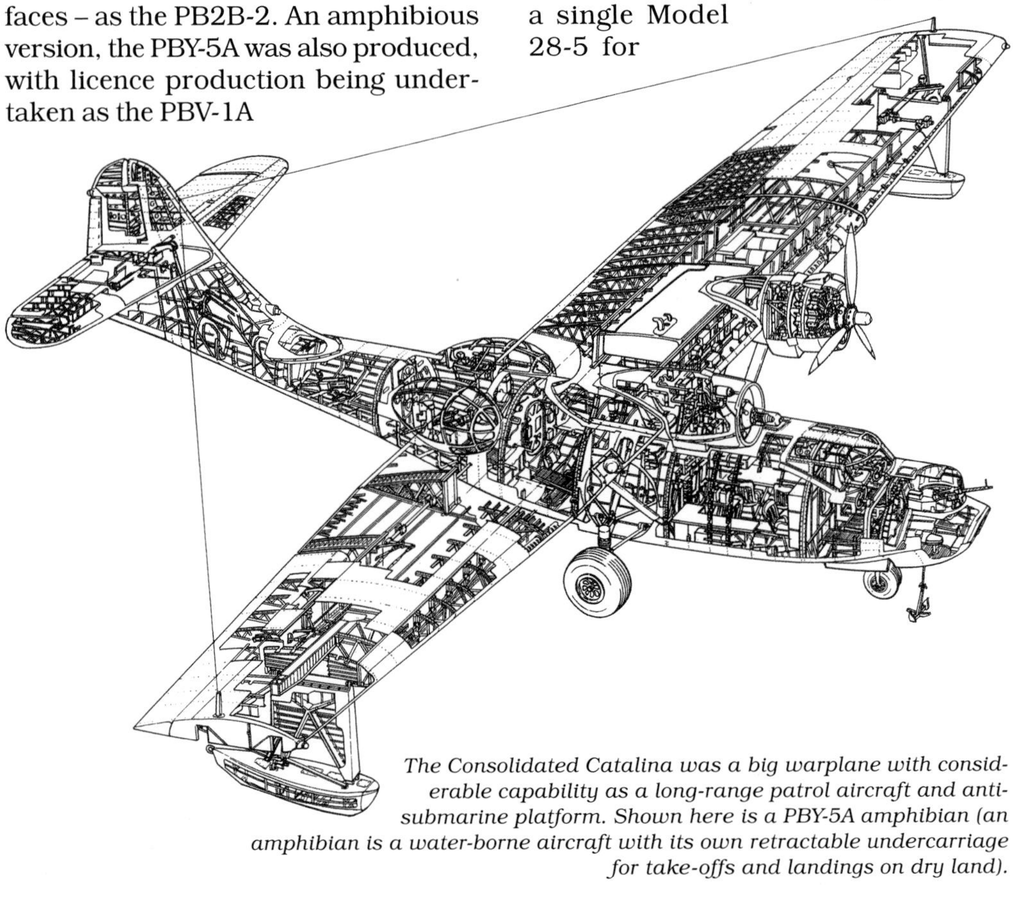

*The Consolidated Catalina was a big warplane with considerable capability as a long-range patrol aircraft and anti-submarine platform. Shown here is a PBY-5A amphibian (an amphibian is a water-borne aircraft with its own retractable undercarriage for take-offs and landings on dry land).*

hydrodynamic hull trials. A single Model 28-3 was also purchased in 1940, becoming the first to enter operational RAF service with No. 209 Squadron. Canadian Vickers supplied 36 PBY-5s as Mk.IIAs. The Mk.III was a PBY-5A version used as a northern Atlantic ferry. More Catalinas were transferred under Lend-Lease to the RAF as Mk.IBs (PBY-5B), Mk.IVAs (PBY-5), Mk.IVBs (PB2B-1) and Mk.VIs (PB2B-2). RAF. Catalinas were involved in the sinking of the Bismar-ck, as well as hunting submarines across the globe and rescuing personnel from the sea. Some were transferred to Commonwealth air forces, while B.O.A.C. used several for passenger and mail services. Catalinas also served with – amongst others – the air arms of Brazil, Chile, Denmark, France, the Netherlands, Norway, the Soviet Union (where the type was produced primarily as the GST), and Sweden.

*The Catalina's big wing featured wingtip stabilizing floats that retracted in flight to form the wing's wingtips.*

**Specifications – Consolidated PBY-5A Catalina**

| | |
|---|---|
| Wingspan | 104 ft |
| Length | 63 ft 10.5 in |
| Maximum speed | 179 mph at 7,000 ft |
| Maximum take-off weight | 35,420 lb |
| Range | 2,350 miles |
| Service ceiling | 13,000 ft |
| Armament | One or two 0.3 in (7.62 mm) machine guns in bow, one in ventral position firing aft, two 0.5 in (12.7 mm) machine guns in the beam blisters, plus up to 4,000 lb of bombs or depth charges |
| Engine | Two Pratt & Whitney R-1830-92 Twin Wasp radial piston engines, of 1,200 hp each |
| Crew | Eight or nine |

# Naval Aircraft Factory N3N

The Naval Aircraft Factory was established in 1918 in the United States Navy Yard, Philadelphia, Pennsylvania. It was created to give the United States naval aviation organization, then in its relative infancy, its own test and manufacturing facilities. In its early days this involved the construction of complete aircraft, and led to the factory creating several of its own designs. The most impressive of these was the Felixstowe-based PN series of twin-engined patrol flying-boats.

By the early-1930's the Factory's aircraft manufacturing role had virtually disappeared, and it was mainly involved in the testing of materials, structures, engines, catapults and other equipment destined for naval aviation use, as well as in the development of specifications and standards for naval aircraft. In 1935, a Bill passed through the U.S. Congress which required that at least ten per cent of the aircraft and engines bought by the U.S. naval aviation should be of Government manufacture. At that time, the U.S. Navy was developing a neat, biplane primary trainer for U.S. Navy use. This duly entered production as the Naval Aircraft Factory N3N. When the XN3N-1 prototype first flew in August 1935, the design was intended to replace Consolidated NY-2 and NY-3 biplane trainers then in use. Provision was made for conventional wheeled or floatplane

undercarriage layouts. After some refinement, the type entered production by the Naval Aircraft Factory. The N3N-1 first production version was powered by the 220–240 hp Wright J-5 (R-790) Whirlwind radial engine of which the U.S. Navy already held stocks. Some later N3N-1 instead had a more modern Wright R-760 Whirlwind, and later many existing N3N-1 were re-engined with the R-760. Some 180 N3N-1 were built before production switched to the N3N-3 with modified tail surfaces, of which 816 were constructed. These had the R-760 engine as standard, and they became a standard primary trainer for U.S. Navy airmen during World War Two. They could be configured with either wheeled or float undercarriage. Due to the distinctive yellow paint scheme of these well-liked trainers, they were nicknamed the 'Yellow Peril.' Pupil pilots from Britain were also trained on the type in the United States, and it served alongside the naval versions of the Boeing Stearman (see pages 74 to 75). Four examples also operated with the U.S. Coast Guard. A small

*A preserved Naval Aircraft Factory N3N-3 floatplane in the United States. Surviving examples are now rare and much sought-after by collectors.*
*(Photo: John Batchelor).*

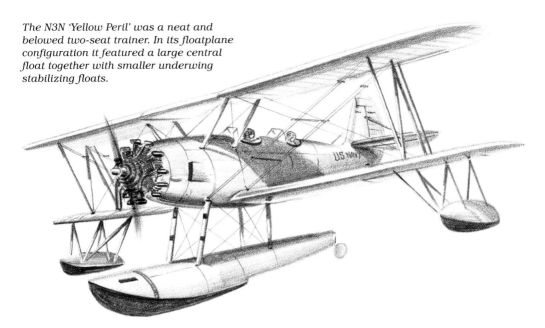

*The N3N 'Yellow Peril' was a neat and beloved two-seat trainer. In its floatplane configuration it featured a large central float together with smaller underwing stabilizing floats.*

number of seaplane examples were retained by the U.S. Navy after the war, and the survivors of these continued in service until 1961 – the last biplanes in U.S. military service.

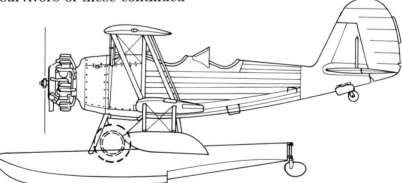

*The N3N was mainly of metal construction with mostly fabric covering. The dotted lines here indicate the position of the main wheels when the conventional wheeled undercarriage was fitted.*

## Specifications – Naval Aircraft Factory N3N-3

| | |
|---|---|
| Wingspan | 34 ft |
| Length | 25 ft 6 in |
| Maximum speed | 126 mph at 5,000 ft |
| Maximum take-off weight | 2,792 lb |
| Range | approximately 470 miles |
| Service ceiling | 15,200 ft |
| Engine | One Wright R-760-2 (or similar model) Whirlwind radial piston engine, of 235 hp |
| Crew | Two |

# Messerschmitt Bf 109 Late Series

The successful early to mid-World War Two versions of the famous Messerschmitt Bf 109 are covered on pages 64 to 67. Continuing development led to the later Bf 109G and Bf 109K models, and these two persisted in Luftwaffe service through to the end of the Second World War, with production and recycling of earlier airframes continuing at the end. This was achieved despite the widespread service of Germany's other main World War Two single-engined fighter, the Focke-Wulf Fw 190 (see pages 274 to 277). The Bf 109G was a developed version of the Bf 109F, powered by the Daimler Benz DB 605 inline engine with some versions featuring a crude form of 'pressurization.' The Bf 109G also, however, included considerable weight escalation due to the need to equip these aircraft with an increasing array of weapons to counter Allied fighters and heavy bombers. The first production sub-types, the Bf 109G-1 and G-2, entered service in 1942. More Bf 109G were built than any other mark of Bf 109, and there was a wealth of different versions and sub-types, including some fitted with wooden tails to ease manufacturing considerations. The Bf 109G served on all the war fronts where the Luftwaffe was active, and was increasingly involved in trying (unsuccessfully) to counter the daylight bombing raids on Germany and occupied Europe by American heavy bombers with their deadly escort fighters. A two-seat trainer version of the G-series, the Bf 109G-12, was also built. Continuing development led to the Bf 109K, the final major production version which was starting to serve in numbers at the end of the war. Amongst the many famous German pilots who flew the Bf 109 in combat was Erich Hartmann, who is the highest-scoring ace of all time, with 352 victories. Many of Germany's allies also flew the Bf 109, notably including Hungary (who also produced it under license), Italy and Finland. The type's combat career did not end with World

*The Messerschmitt Bf 109 was a compact fighter of all-metal construction, with fabric-covered control surfaces. This drawing shows one of the later war layouts of the type – note also the neat installation of the fuel tank behind the pilot's seat.*

War Two. Originally combat-tested in the Spanish Civil War, the Bf 109 was appreciated by the Spanish who built it as the Hispano Buchon in a variety of different versions, many being powered by the Rolls-Royce Merlin engine which normally powered the Bf 109's great rival, the Supermarine Spitfire! Spanish Buchons served into the 1960's. In post-war Czechoslovakia, the type was built as the Avia S-199 (and CS-199 two-seater), some of these flying for Israel in that country's fight for freedom in the later 1940's. A large number of Bf 109s of all types were built by several other companies in addition to Messerschmitt, to the overall total of some 35,000 examples (exact figures are impossible to verify).

This beautifully-preserved Messerschmitt Bf 109G-6 belongs to the National Air and Space Museum in Washington, D.C., in the United States (Photo: NASM).

**Specifications – Messerschmitt Bf 109G-6/U4**

| | |
|---|---|
| Wingspan | 32 ft 6.7 in |
| Length | 29 ft 4 in |
| Maximum speed | 386 mph at 22,638 ft |
| Maximum take-off weight | 6,944 lb |
| Range | approximately 621 miles (with drop tank) |
| Service Ceiling | 37,894 ft |
| Armament | One 30 mm or 20 mm (0.787 in) cannon engine-mounted, two 13 mm (0.51 in) machine guns fixed forward-firing in upper forward fuselage |
| Engine | One Daimler Benz DB 605A inline piston engine, of 1,685–1,475 hp |
| Crew | One |

# Supermarine Spitfire Later Series

The superlative Supermarine Spitfire was one of the classic warplanes of all time. The Spitfire created a legend for itself with its success in the Battle of Britain in 1940. However, even the best combat aircraft need continuing development to keep up with improvements in opposing warplanes and to include the latest advances in power and armament. The Spitfire was no exception and was in continuous production throughout World War Two, during which time it went through many developments and was produced in a multitude of different versions and sub-types. One of the greatest spurs to the continued development of the Spitfire was the operational debut and front-line service of the German Focke-Wulf Fw 190 fighter (see pages 274 to 277). For a time this excellent aircraft gained ascendancy over the Spitfire above Western Europe, and the Spitfire was rapidly given a more powerful version of the Merlin engine and other improvements to create the Mk.IX. This model was built in large

numbers (some 5,665) and was the equal of the Fw 190A in most respects. The first air-to-air victory of a Mk.IX was against an Fw 190 in July 1942, and the type went on to be one of the principal marks of Spitfire operated in the mid to later-war period. There were also some two-seat trainers.

Continuing work along different lines of development saw the famous Rolls-Royce Merlin inline engine that powered all these earlier Spitfire versions replaced by a newer and more powerful Rolls-Royce engine, the Griffon. This power plant was first tried out in a Spitfire Mk.IV, and became an important engine type for many later-war Spitfires and post-war marks. Amongst the first production Spitfires with this new powerplant was the Mk.XII, which excelled at lower levels and was one of several Spitfire marks that became involved with further air defense above Britain, the countering of German V1 'flying bombs' in 1944. Further developments led on to several more important Griffon-engined Spitfire marks,

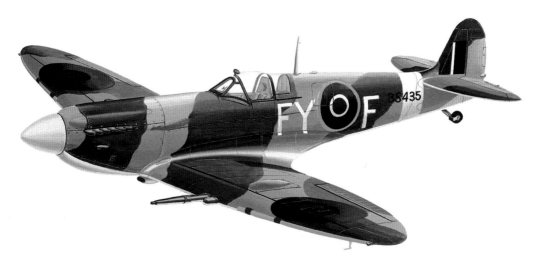

*Continuing development of the Supermarine Spitfire led to the Mk.IX, derived from the Mk.V, which was an increasingly effective counter to the Luftwaffe's Focke-Wulf Fw 190 fighter. The Mk.IX shown here, serial number BS435, belonged to the RAF's No.611 Squadron ('FY' code letters).*

*Only 100 examples of the Spitfire MK.XII were built, but they were early users of the Rolls-Royce Griffon inline engine, which gave them a good turn of speed. In this painting, Mk.XII EB-B of No.41 Squadron, RAF, is being flown by Jack Bradshaw of Dallas, Texas. He flew as a volunteer with the RAF from 1941, and is seen here taking on a V1 'flying bomb.' He later flew P-47 Thunderbolts with his fellow Americans (see pages 194 to 197).*

including the Mk.XIV and the fast photo-reconnaissance Mk.XIX. Spitfires fought on all the battle fronts where the RAF and Commonwealth forces were involved, not just as fighters but with a useful air-to-ground capacity and usually with a bomb carried beneath the fuselage. A variety of wing types and armaments were used, and further design work led to a revised vertical tail shape on some aircraft. The Spitfire was one of the aircraft types that helped the Allies to victory in 1945, and its service continued post-war overseas as well as in Britain.

Many foreign pilots fighting with the RAF flew Spitfires after their homelands had been occupied by the Germans and the Spitfire was an important part of several major air forces after the war as an export aircraft, including notably France, Israel, the Netherlands and Czechoslovakia. The final Spitfires in RAF service (three Mk.XIX) were retired in the late 1950's. The total number of all Spitfires built was just over 20,300, plus several late mark navalized Seafires which are similarly Griffon-powered.

### Specifications – Supermarine Spitfire F.Mk.XII

| | |
|---|---|
| Wingspan | 32 ft 7 in |
| Length | 32 ft 8 in |
| Maximum speed | 392 mph at 24,000 ft |
| Maximum take-off weight | 7,400 lb |
| Range | 493 miles |
| Service ceiling | 37,350 ft |
| Armament | Two 20 mm cannons and four 0.303 in (7.7 mm) machine guns wing-mounted forward-firing, up to 500 lb bomb beneath fuselage |
| Engine | One Rolls-Royce Griffon IV inline piston engine, of 1,720–1,735 hp |
| Crew | One |

# Heinkel He 177 Greif

It is perhaps a good thing for the Allies that the German aircraft industry was never able to produce a successful long-range heavy bomber for service in World War Two. True, the Focke-Wulf Fw 200 (see pages 122 to 123) saw comparatively widespread service, but that design was not a dedicated bomber and was anyway an adaptation of a civil transport. However, various attempts were made by the Germans to produce a viable long-range 'heavy,' and the most notable was the Heinkel He 177 Greif (Griffon/Griffin). Designed to a 1936/1937 requirement from Nazi Germany's Air Ministry that became known as 'Bomber A,' the He 177 first flew on 19 November 1939.

From the first, Heinkel tried out radical solutions to try to meet the desired performance capabilities. Designed under Heinkel's project number P.1041, the He 177 was large and needed engines of greater power than those then available. Engine maker Daimler Benz's solution was to couple two existing DB 601 inline engines to drive a single propeller shaft, calling the resulting design the DB 606. Later, paired DB 605 engines called DB 610 were substituted. This plan never

worked satisfactorily, mainly due to the problems of integrating such a radical engine arrangement into the bomber's airframe. Overheating and frequent engine fires resulted. The main undercarriage was also unusual, comprising twin main legs under each engine nacelle which retracted sideways into the lower wing, inboard and outboard of the engine nacelles. This formidable undercarriage was needed to support the weight of the aircraft, which grew and grew as it was developed. The He 177's test program was punctuated by serious crashes, including some caused by engine fires. A pre-production batch of He 177A-0 examples was followed by the He 177A-1, the initial production version. This was succeeded by several later A-series He 177s, divided into a number of sub-types due to armament changes and other alterations. Some 1,200 of all versions were eventually built. The type began to serve in numbers in late 1942/early 1943, and operated on anti-shipping, conventional bombing and makeshift transport tasks (it was completely unsuited for the latter). The He 177 is best known for being the carrier aircraft for the Henschel

*Although it looked like a twin-engined aircraft, the Heinkel He 177 in effect had four engines, two in each nacelle. The type was not successful in its major intended role, and by late 1944 a growing number of these large aircraft lay redundant on German airfields.*

*The He 177V2 second prototype/development aircraft. This was one of several early He 177s that was lost in a fatal crash due to shortcomings in the He 177 design (Photo: Deutsches Museum, Munich).*

Hs 293 missile, the first guided missile ever to be used in any quantity in warfare. It was also planned that the He 177 would carry Germany's atomic bomb, which was fortunately never built.

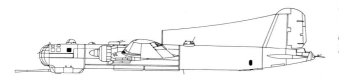

*The He 177A-3/R5 featured a 75 mm cannon for ground attack duties, but only a handful are believed to have been built.*

*The He 177A-6/R2 was a planned He 177 upgrade with better armament and a re-designed nose, but was not proceeded with.*

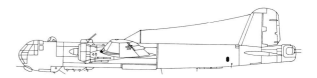

**Specifications – Heinkel He 177A-5/R2**

| | |
|---|---|
| Wingspan | 103 ft 1.75 in |
| Length | 72 ft 2 in |
| Maximum speed | 304.5 mph at 19,685 ft |
| Maximum take-off weight | 68,343 lb |
| Range | 3,418 miles |
| Service ceiling | 26,247 ft |
| Armament | Three 7.92 mm (0.312 in) machine guns, three 13 mm (0.51 in) machine guns (turret-mounted), two 20 mm cannons, up to 2,205 lb of bombs and/or two Hs 293 guided missiles mounted beneath the wings |
| Engine | Two Daimler Benz DB 610A/B (two coupled DB 605 inline piston engines), of 2,950–3,100 hp each |
| Crew | Six |

# Bachem Ba 349 Natter

The Bachem Ba 349 Natter was designed as a semi-expendable, rocket-propelled, point defence interceptor in an attempt to counter the ever-increasing American daylight bombing raids that were crippling German industry and infrastructure towards the end of the Second World War. The aircraft was to be constructed from as many non-strategic materials as possible, while take-off and landing procedures were to be kept as simple as possible to minimize the time taken to train new pilots on the type. The Natter (Viper) was intended to be of all-wooden construction. Power was supplied by a Walter HWK 109-509A or later mark rocket motor, fuelled by T-Stoff (hydrogen peroxide) and C-Stoff (a methanol and hydrazine hydrate solution). Additionally, four solid fuel booster rockets were attached externally to the rear fuselage. The Natter was intended to be armed with twenty-four R4M

or Föhn 73 mm (2.87 in) unguided rockets housed behind a plastic jettisonable nose cap. The aircraft was launched from an 80 ft high almost vertical launching tower, and had an armored cockpit. Approaching his target, the pilot would jettison the nose cap and fire off his rockets in a single salvo. He would then initiate a separation sequence which saw the rear fuselage detach from the cockpit and parachute to the ground for further use. Simultaneously the pilot would abandon the aircraft and parachute to safety.

The brainchild of Erich Bachem, the Natter first flew as a towed glider in November 1944, making its first unmanned vertical powered flight in December 1944. On 1 March (some sources say 28 February) 1945 the first manned, powered flight of a Natter took place. For reasons unknown, the test pilot became unconscious during the flight and was killed when the aircraft crashed to the ground. Developed with the initial backing of the S.S. and its leader Heinrich Himmler, the program was later given a low priority although Bachem eventually developed a more potent Ba 349B series with a revised air-

The Bachem Ba 349 Natter was made from wood and featured a battery of unguided rockets in its nose. The design was simplicity itself, but was never used in combat.

frame. Production of the type continued until the Natter factory was captured, but no further manned firings are believed to have been made. Natter manufacture was intended (or expected) to comprise 50 A-series airframes, followed by Ba 349B production. Only three B-series examples might have been built, although this is in doubt. A selection of the early Natters was found near the end of the war by the Allies apparently combat ready, but the type never became fully operational.

*Right:*
*A very fine replica Bachem Ba 349 Natter. Note the external rockets for additional power during take-off attached to the rear fuselage (Photo: John Batchelor).*

*Below:*
*The Ba 349 Natter took the idea of an austere fighter to the extreme. It was one of several desperate late-war programs instigated while Germany was losing the war.*

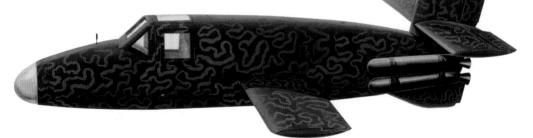

**Specifications (some estimated) – Bachem Ba 349B Natter**

| | |
|---|---|
| Wingspan | 13 ft 1.5 in |
| Length | 19 ft 9 in (possibly less) |
| Maximum speed | 620 mph at 16,405 ft |
| Maximum take-off weight | 4,920 lb |
| Endurance | approximately 4 minutes, possibly more |
| Service ceiling | approximately 45,930 ft |
| Armament | unguided rocket batteries, or (proposed) two 30 mm fixed forward-firing cannons |
| Engine | One Walter HWK 509C-1 liquid-fuel rocket motor, of 4,410 lb st, plus four Schmidding solid-fuel rocket boosters of up to 2,205 lb thrust each |
| Crew | One |

# Henschel Hs 129

Reflecting the huge diversity of aircraft types that fought in the Second World War, the Henschel Hs 129 was a dedicated ground attack aircraft that packed a massive punch in some of its versions. The type was designed in response to a 1937 call for a small twin-engined ground attack aircraft by Nazi Germany's air ministry. The initial Hs 129V1 first flew in the spring of 1939 and was followed by two more prototypes. They had cramped cockpits, an armament of two 20 mm cannons and two 7.92 mm (0.312 in) machine guns, but proved difficult to control with insufficient power from their two 465 hp Argus As 410A inline engines. However, eight pre-production Hs 129A-0s were ordered, with some going to the Luftwaffe's 5.(Schlacht)/LG 2 in late autumn 1940 for an operational evaluation. The shortcomings of these aircraft proved bad enough for the Luftwaffe to refuse to accept the type into full operational service. Thus, in early 1941, two Hs 129A-0s were re-engined with French Gnome-Rhone 14M4/5 radial engines and modified with a revised cockpit, as development aircraft for the Hs 129B-0 pre-production series, ten of which were delivered from late 1941. These proved to be far more satisfactory, and the B-model entered production in 1942.

Eventually some 879 Hs 129s including prototype/development aircraft were built up to September 1944. The Hs 129B-1's basic armament was two 20 mm cannons and two 7.92 mm (0.312 in) machine guns, but several armament variations were introduced. A 30 mm cannon was fitted under the fuselage of the Hs 129B-1/R2, while the B-1/R3 had four additional 7.92 mm (0.312 in) machine guns and the B-1/R4 could carry various bomb combinations including 96 SD-2 anti-personnel bombs. The B-1/R5 was a camera-equipped reconnaissance version. The 'R' part of these designations stood for Rüstsatz, meaning a conversion set that could be added onto the basic aircraft in the field rather than being built in at the factory during manufacture. The first Hs 129B-1s were delivered during the spring of 1942, the type becoming operational on the Eastern Front in May. This was the theater of operations where the majority of Hs 129s fought, but some also flew in com-

*Hardly an elegant aircraft, the Henschel Hs 129 was a functional design that gained considerable success in its specialist ground attack roles. The type served mainly on the Eastern Front against Soviet forces, but some were based in North Africa and the Mediterranean.*

bat in the Mediterranean and North Africa. By mid-1943, the type was in significant use on the Eastern Front, and was proving highly capable in the anti-tank and general attack roles. Nevertheless, the thick armor of Soviet KV-1 and T-34 tanks resulted in further armament development being required, the resultant Hs 129B-2 series seeing a general up-gunning of the Hs 129, with heavier weapons carried in a gun pod beneath the fuselage. However, the need for even larger caliber anti-tank weapons resulted in the fielding in mid-1944 of the Hs 129B-3, mounting a large 75 mm anti-tank

gun with twelve 26.5 lb (12 kg) rounds. Only some 25 B-3s were built, but they were amongst the most heavily-armed aircraft of the Second World War – other warplanes of the period that similarly carried very heavy armament including two attack versions of the North American B-25 Mitchell (see pages 152 to 155). Although the Hs 129 was undoubtedly an effective specialized attack aircraft, and was responsible for the destruction of a great many Soviet tanks, the overall war situation for German forces on the Eastern Front nevertheless resulted in eventual Russian victory.

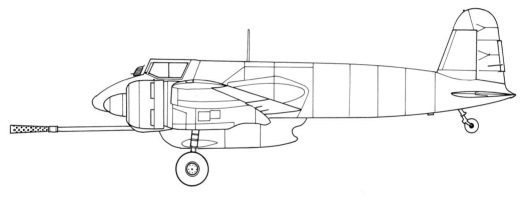

*One of the most heavily-armed aircraft of the Second World War was the Henschel Hs 129B-3, which carried a 75 mm anti-tank gun in a large pod beneath its fuselage. All production Hs 129 aircraft, including this version, were powered by French Gnome-Rhone radial engines.*

## Specifications – Henschel Hs 129B-1/R1

| | |
|---|---|
| Wingspan | 46 ft 7 in |
| Length | 31 ft 11.75 in |
| Maximum speed | 253 mph at 12,566 ft |
| Maximum take-off weight | 11,266 lb |
| Range | 348 miles |
| Service ceiling | 29,528 ft |
| Armament | Two 20 mm (0.787 in) cannons and two 7.92 mm (0.312 in) machines guns, two 110 lb bombs or two packs each containing 48 anti-personnel bombs |
| Engine | Two Gnome-Rhone 14M4/5 radial piston engines, of 700 hp each |
| Crew | One |

# Messerschmitt Me 210 and Me 410

Initial success with the Messerschmitt Bf 110 design (see pages 140 to 141), and confidence within Germany's air ministry in the twin-engined heavy fighter 'destroyer' concept led to a successor design with wider capabilities being sought for future operations. Responding to these 1938 requirements, Messerschmitt came up with the Me 210 design, again a two-seat, twin-engined heavy fighter with twin fins and rudders. The prototype flew in September 1939, but problems at once arose, the aircraft having major instability problems. Re-designed with a conventional single vertical tail and a deepened rear fuselage partly redressed the situation, but already a production order 'off the drawing board' for Me 210A series aircraft had been made starting in 1940. Initial deliveries were made in 1940 of the first Daimler Benz

DB 601 inline engined aircraft, and production series of heavy fighter, fighter-bomber and reconnaissance versions were envisaged and commenced. Eventually the problems with the type were so grave that production was suspended in the first half of 1942 and although it briefly resumed the type never fulfilled its operational requirements. Although some examples did see Luftwaffe service, it was one of Germany's allies, Hungary, that made a success of the type. Production under license of the slightly improved, DB 605-engined Me 210C created an aircraft that performed effectively in combat with the Hungarian air force alongside the Germans, particularly on the Eastern Front. As many as 267 examples might have been manufactured in Hungary, with locally-built engines produced under license. Mean-

*The Messerschmitt Me 410 was a multi-role fighter and fighter-bomber that gained some success, even in the interception of American heavy bombers over Germany. It was intended as a replacement for the Messerschmitt Bf 110.*

while, a major re-working of the Me 210 in Germany led to the much more successful Me 410 series. These were powered by DB 603 engines in a refined and partly reworked wing and fuselage design, and although problems still existed, this derivative was much more combat-capable. Sometimes called the Hornisse (Hornet), the Me 410 flew in development form in 1942. The initial Me 410A-1 was a light bomber, but there were many subsequent derivatives, including reconnaissance, heavy fighter and even a night fighter development. The type entered front-line service in the spring of 1943, and operated in the Mediterranean and particularly over Germany – over the latter, some heavily-armed Me 410 were operated as bomber-destroyers against American heavy bomber formations. Sometimes they achieved success, but if they came upon American fighter escorts the result was usually disastrous for them. Some Me 410 were used as fast intruders in the so-called 'Baby Blitz' on Britain during early 1944. Total production of the Me 410 series is believed to have run to some 1,160 examples.

*A unique feature of the Me 210/410 series was the installation in the fuselage amidships of remotely-controlled aft-firing machine guns on moveable and trainable mountings. Photo shows the trunnions within the fuselage for their operation (Photo: John Batchelor).*

**Specifications – Messerschmitt Me 410A-1/U2**

| | |
|---|---|
| Wingspan | 53 ft 7.75 in |
| Length | 40 ft 11.5 in |
| Maximum speed | 388 mph at 21,980 ft |
| Maximum take-off weight | 21,276 lb |
| Range | 1,050 miles |
| Service ceiling | 32,808 ft |
| Armament | Two 20 mm cannons and four 7.92 mm (0.312 in) machine guns fixed forward-firing in nose, two 13 mm (0.51 in) machine guns in rearwards-firing remote-controlled fuselage fittings |
| Engine | Two Daimler Benz DB 603A inline piston engines, of 1,750–1,850 hp each |
| Crew | Two |

# Curtiss SB2C Helldiver

Known as the 'the beast' to its pilots, the Curtiss SB2C Helldiver was a large aircraft that was designed as a replacement for the Douglas SBD Dauntless in the scout/dive-bomber role from U.S. aircraft carriers. The XSB2C-1 prototype made its first flight on 18 December 1940, but was only followed by the first SB2C-1 production aircraft in mid-1942 following a rather problematic development. Alongside Curtiss-built Helldivers, Fairchild in Canada and the Canadian Car and Foundry produced the aircraft as the SBF and SBW. Deliveries to the U.S. Navy started to scouting squadron VS-9 in December 1942, but the type was not deployed operationally until late in 1943. Its first action was an 11 November 1943 raid by VB-17 on Japanese-held Rabaul, New Britain. Helldivers also served with land-based U.S. Marine

Corps units. The SB2C-1C had four 20 mm cannons in its wings in place of the SB2C-1's four 0.5 in (12.7 mm) machine guns. Progressive improvement then took place resulting in a variety of production models in the SB2C-3, SB2C-4, and SB2C-5 series, with their equivalent Canadian-built versions. Over seven thousand one hundred Helldivers were produced in total. The U.S. Army Air Corps' own interest in dive-bombers, increased by the success of the Junkers Ju 87 'Stuka' in Europe, resulted in an order for the Helldiver as the A-25A Shrike in 1941, 900 being allocated. In any event, little use was made of them by the Army Air Force, with some being converted for target-towing duties while the majority went to the U.S. Marine Corps as SB2C-1As. A number were passed to the Royal Australian Air Force.

*The Curtiss SB2C Helldiver was a big, all-metal construction warplane, with folding wings in its nautical versions – although those destined for the Army Air Force did not have this feature.*

An SB2C Helldiver shows its enormous, perforated flaps during its landing approach to an aircraft carrier. This does not appear to be a very successful landing attempt – the aircraft is too high to catch the arrester wires on the deck, and probably had to go around again (Photo: U.S. Navy).

Twenty six SBW-1Bs were delivered to Britain's Royal Navy as Helldiver Mk.Is, but they were not used operationally. At the end of World War Two, Helldivers disappeared fairly quickly from the active U.S. Navy roster, but the type duly served with the armed forces of Greece, Thailand, France, Italy and Portugal.

This SB2C-3 Helldiver belonged to the U.S. Navy bombing squadron VB-7 while aboard the aircraft carrier U.S.S. Hancock in October 1944. The Greek letter Omega on the vertical tail identified this unit at that time.

**Specifications – Curtiss SB2C-1 Helldiver**

| | |
|---|---|
| Wingspan | 49 ft 9 in |
| Length | 36 ft 8 in |
| Maximum speed | 281 mph at 12,400 ft |
| Maximum take-off weight | 14,760 lb |
| Range | 1,110 miles |
| Service ceiling | 24,700 ft |
| Armament | Four 0.5 in (12.7 mm) machine guns forward-firing in the wings and two 0.3 in (7.62 mm) or one 0.5 in (12.7 mm) flexible-mounted in the rear cockpit, provision for 1,000 lb bomb load internally or other combinations including small underwing loads |
| Engine | One Wright R-2600-8 Cyclone radial piston engine, of 1,700 hp |
| Crew | Two |

# Mitsubishi G3M and G4M

Famous for its design of the ubiquitous A6M fighter (see pages 174 to 175), and many other warplanes that played a large part in Japan's war effort during World War Two, Mitsubishi also created a series of bombers for the Imperial Japanese Navy's air arm that were notable for their excellent range capabilities. In the early 1930's, Mitsubishi instigated a number of design studies for long-range twin-engined aircraft, of which the Ka-9 reconnaissance machine offered most potential. Further design work led to a bomber/transport layout initially called the Ka-15. First flown in July 1935, this design showed much promise and was produced from mid-1936 as a naval aviation land-based bomber designated G3M1, with the initial service designation Type 96 Attack Bomber Model 11. 34 of these original aircraft were built before further development led to the more powerful G3M2 series, which had increased fuel capacity for long-range operations. In August 1937, several of these aircraft based on Taipei (Taiwan) flew a bombing raid to targets in China 1,250 miles away, at that time one of the longest such raids ever accomplished. Continuing development led to a string of production versions with increased armament and parallel development created a line of transport derivatives and conversions under the designation L3Y1 and L3Y2. Some of these transports were used by Japan's small paratroop forces. Most famously, G3M bombers were in action on 10 December 1941 (three days after the Pearl Harbor attack) when they were part of a force located off the coast of Malaya. The bombers targeted the British capital ships H.M.S. Prince of Wales and H.M.S. Repulse, sinking both of these major warships in an attack that re-wrote the text books on naval warfare.

Production of the G3M line totalled 1,048, 636 by Mitsubishi and 412 by Nakajima. The G3M was known to the Allies for identification purposes as 'Nell,' the L3Y transports being known as 'Tina.' Mitsubishi's design team next turned their attention to bettering the G3M's exceptional performance to meet a naval specification of 1937/1938. The result was the famous G4M series, which was

Grenada
Grenadines    $2

MITSUBISHI G3M1

*The Mitsubishi G3M series proved highly successful early in World War Two.*

one of Japan's principal bomber types of World War Two. Known to the Allies for identification purposes as 'Betty,' over two thousand four hundred of these were built in several distinct versions.

*In addition to military transport derivatives of the G3M bomber, there were several civil conversions for Japanese operators as shown here.*

*The Mitsubishi G3M series gave a potent long reach to Japan's bomber force. This proved valuable on a number of occasions, most notably on 10 December 1941 when a force that included G3M bombers successfully attacked two British capital ships at long range and sank them.*

**Specifications – Mitsubishi G3M3 Model 23**

| | |
|---|---|
| Wingspan | 82 ft 0.25 in |
| Length | 53 ft 11.75 in |
| Maximum speed | 258 mph at 19,357 ft |
| Maximum take-off weight | 17,637 lb |
| Range | 3,871 miles |
| Service ceiling | 33,727 ft |
| Armament | One 20 mm cannon in dorsal turret, three or four 7.7 mm (0.303 in) machine guns in other turret or flexible locations, up to 1,764 lb of bombs or torpedo |
| Engine | Two Mitsubishi Kinsei 51 radial piston engines, of 1,300 hp each |
| Crew | Seven |

# Kawasaki Ki-61 Hien

Although the Japanese aircraft industry had been unfairly denigrated in the 'West' for years prior to the Second World War, in reality the Japanese proved themselves highly capable of designing and building a number of world-class military aircraft with which they went to war in the late 1930's and early 1940's. The Mitsubishi A6M Zero (see pages 174 to 175) was the equal of anything that the Allies had in service in the Far East at the start of the Pacific war. Continuing work by a number of manufacturers led to several other very capable fighters such as the Nakajima Ki-43 Hayabusa and Nakajima Ki-44 Shoki. However, as was the case with Italy's aircraft industry, the emphasis in Japan was on the use of air-cooled radial engines. It was only with German help that potentially more powerful and aerodynamically more efficient, liquid-cooled inline engines became available to Japanese manufacturers – a similar situation was also the case with the Italians.

The only major Japanese fighter of World War Two powered by an inline engine was the Kawasaki Ki-61 Hien (Swallow). The Ki-61 came about from a Japanese re-evalution of maneu-verability coupled with the use of radial engines. The Kawasaki company had obtained a manufacturing license in the late 1930's to build the German Daimler Benz DB 601 inline engine in Japan, and this helped Kawasaki to design and build two complementary inline-engined fighter designs. The ensuing interceptor Ki-60 design did not progress very far, but the Ki-61 general-purpose fighter went on to great success in the mid-war years. The first flight was in December 1941, and a long series of prototype/development and pre-production aircraft (typical for Japanese manufacturers) was followed by a progression of production models. The initial series version, the Army Type 3 Fighter Model 1, was itself built in various distinct models.

The Hien entered service with the Imperial Japanese Army air arm in 1943, flying its first major combat over New Guinea in June 1943. It was immediately a great success, catching Allied pilots unawares with its excellent climb and dive performance, although lacking the high degree of maneuverability normally associated with Japanese fighters. Progressive

*The Kawasaki Ki-61 Hien bore a resemblance to the German Messerschmitt Bf 109, for which it was sometimes mistaken. It was more than a match for early-war American fighters like the Curtiss P-40 and Bell P-39 Airacobra, but was out-fought by later and better American fighters. Poor quality control and a shortage of its Japanese-built German engine also caused problems.*

improvements included upgraded armament, but the decrease in manufacturing quality in Japan under relentless American bombing and the appearance of better Allied fighter aircraft led to the Hien losing its ascendancy. Production ended in early 1945, after over 2,600 had been built. Some 275 unfinished Ki-61 airframes were later fitted with 1,500 hp Mitsubishi Ha-112 radial engines as the Ki-100, plus a batch of 99 new-built examples. The Ki-100 proved to be a very capable fighter, but its small production numbers negated its potential effectiveness. The Ki-61 Hien was known to the Allies for identification purposes as 'Tony.'

*The Kawasaki Ki-61 Hiens attempted to defend Japan against increasing American advances. Pictured is Ki-61-I model of the 23rd Independent Chutai, Imperial Japanese Army Air Force, at Yontan, Okinawa, in April 1945.*

**Specifications – Kawasaki Ki-61-I-KAI-hei Hien**

| | |
|---|---|
| Wingspan | 39 ft 4.5 in |
| Length | 29 ft 4 in |
| Maximum speed | 360 mph at 16,405 ft |
| Maximum take-off weight | 7,650 lb |
| Range | 360 miles plus |
| Service ceiling | 32,808 ft |
| Armament | Two 20 mm cannons fixed forward-firing in upper forward fuselage, two wing-mounted 12.7 mm (0.5 in) machine guns |
| Engine | One Kawasaki Ha-40 (licence-built Daimler Benz DB 601A) inline piston engine, of 1,175 hp |
| Crew | One |

# Vought F4U Corsair

One of the most important American naval fighters of World War Two was the Vought F4U Corsair. Operating principally in the Pacific theater, the Corsair proved to be a match for most Japanese fighters, alongside the Grumman F6F Hellcat (see pages 266 to 267). The type also gave very important service to Britain's Fleet Air Arm. The Corsair was a product of the Vought-Sikorsky division of United Aircraft Corporation, but was later manufactured by more than one company – as was also the case with other principal warplanes of the Second World War. The original Vought V-166B prototype of the Corsair, designated XF4U-1, first flew on 29 May 1940. Designed in response to a 1938 U.S. Navy fighter demand, it had been mated from the start with a new and powerful engine, the Pratt & Whitney R-2800. This highly-successful radial engine also powered other American warplanes of

World War Two, and its 2,000 hp made it one of the most powerful engines of its day. Initial testing went well – several months later the Corsair became the first American warplane to fly faster than 400 mph. This was a huge leap forward in the performance of naval fighters, American naval aviation until recently having used much slower biplanes. The initial production Corsair was the F4U-1, the first of which flew in June 1942. F4U-1s started to reach the U.S. Navy in the summer and autumn of 1942, but the type was at first a disappointment to the Navy – having several shortcomings as an aircraft carrier-based fighter, including a hard undercarriage and poor pilot visibility. The U.S. Marine Corps had no such misgivings and readily accepted the Corsairs for land-based Pacific operations. This represented the start of a production life of over ten years, during which some 12,571 Corsairs were built up to late 1952. The first Corsair opera-

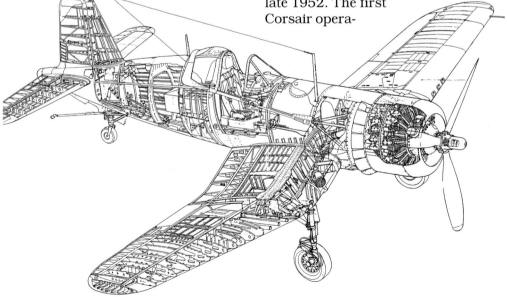

*The unusual wing arrangement of the F4U Corsair is illustrated here. The wings actually folded upwards from the lowest point to allow for stowage within an aircraft carrier's below decks hangar. Note also the arrester hook beneath the tail.*

tional missions were flown by U.S. Marine Corps squadron VMF-124 (VMF = Marine Fighter Squadron) in February 1943. The Corsair's distinctive, inverted gull-wing configuration avoided the excessively long undercarriage legs that would otherwise have been necessary to provide clearance for the powerful engine's large-diameter propeller. However, the far-aft positioning of the cockpit allowed pilots a comparatively poor view forward when landing and taxiing. Hence during the F4U-1 production run, a new, raised cockpit canopy was introduced. This basically created the F4U-1A variant, and finally did away with the original framed 'birdcage' type canopy of the initial production Corsairs. Two outside suppliers, Brewster (with the F3A Corsair) and Goodyear (with the FG Corsair), were introduced into the Corsair production program. Goodyear-built Corsairs were excellent, but the Brewster-built machines were full of faults. Eventually the Brewster company was removed from the Corsair program, and it was not long before that company disappeared altogether. The next version was the Vought F4U-1C, armed with four 20 mm wing cannon instead of the former six machine guns. The F4U-1D (Goodyear's equivalent being the FG-1D) had an R-2800-8W water-injection engine and provision for

A beautiful in-flight view of four privately-owned Corsairs in flight. The photograph was taken over the United States in the 1970's or 1980's, and is one of those pictures that would be hard to recreate nowadays. Corsairs are now very prized 'Warbirds' and worth a lot of money. (Photo: John Batchelor).

# Vought F4U Corsair *continued*

eight underwing rocket projectiles or two 1,000 lb bombs beneath the inner wing panels. Goodyear eventually built over four thousand FG-1s and FG-1Ds (although these figures are now the subject of considerable debate) and Vought well over four thousand F4U-1 series of all versions.

A considerable number (possibly as many as 1,977, but again this is now open to revision) were supplied to the Fleet Air Arm as Corsair Mks.I to IV, and a smaller number to the Royal New Zealand Air Force. The British Corsair Mks.II to IV had each wingtip 'clipped' by 8 in to allow for stowage aboard the cramped confines of smaller Royal Navy aircraft carriers. The Fleet Air Arm first successfully operated Corsairs from aircraft carriers, in the first half of 1944. Initial operations included attacks in April 1944 against the German battleship Tirpitz in Norwegian waters. A Canadian naval reserve Corsair pilot was posthumously awarded

the Victoria Cross for his actions flying a Fleet Air Arm Corsair just before the war ended.

Over the course of 1943, twelve F4U-1s were modified by the Naval Aircraft Factory to F4U-2 standard with four wing guns and airborne interception radar in a fairing on the right-hand wing, these being amongst the first single-seat radar-equipped night fighters to see service. Some others were modified to F4U-1P photo-reconnaissance standard. The next production model was the F4U-4, with six 0.5 in (12.7 mm) machine guns in the wings and a 2,100–2,450 hp R-2800-18W radial engine. Deliveries began later in 1944, and included batches of radar-equipped F4U-4E and F4U-4N Corsair night fighters and F4U-4P camera-equipped reconnaissance aircraft. Goodyear also built five F2G-1 and five F2G-2, these low-altitude and redesigned ultimate Corsairs being powered by the 3,000 hp R-4360-4 Wasp Major radial engine. Further deliveries were stopped by the end of the war, but the

*American-operated Corsairs gained a very good kill ratio against Japanese aircraft during air-to-air combat in the Pacific during World War Two. Late in the war American and British-operated Corsairs were usually (but not always) painted overall 'Glossy Sea Blue', this being the correct name for a shade that is often erroneously called "midnight blue."*

*The very far aft position of the Corsair's cockpit in relation to the wing is shown in this view. This made landings onto aircraft carriers potentially difficult, but the British Fleet Air Arm had no problem flying Corsairs from carriers and showed the U.S. Navy how to do it right.*

F2G was one of the most powerful piston-engined fighters ever produced. During World War Two, American-operated Corsairs operated principally from land bases in the Pacific theater. They were deadly opponents for the Japanese, and achieved a kill ratio (victories compared to aircraft lost) in air-to-air combat of some eleven-to-one. Showing the importance of the type, production continued in the United States after the war. This included the F4U-5, capable of reaching 470 mph; the AU-1 (originally F4U-6); and the F4U-7. Some of these later marks also saw considerable combat, with U.S. forces during the Korean War of 1950 to 1953, and with French forces in the bitter fighting in French Indochina and during the Suez operations in 1956. Other export operators included Latin and South American countries such as Argentina, Honduras and El Salvador. The latter two countries fought each other during 1969 in the 'Football War,' Corsairs flying on both sides during that conflict.

**Specifications – Vought F4U-1A Corsair**

| | |
|---|---|
| Wingspan | 40 ft 11.75 in |
| Length | 33 ft 4.5 in |
| Maximum speed | 395 mph at 24,000 ft |
| Maximum take-off weight | 11,093 lb |
| Range | 1,015 miles |
| Service ceiling | 37,000 ft |
| Armament | Six 0.5 in (12.7 mm) machine guns wing-mounted fixed forward-firing |
| Engine | One Pratt & Whitney R-2800-8 Double Wasp radial piston engine, of 2,000 hp |
| Crew | One |

# Douglas SBD Dauntless

The Douglas SBD Dauntless was the only U.S. aircraft to participate in every Pacific naval battle, where reportedly no other weapon sunk more Japanese shipping. It continued to fight long after its intended successor, the Curtiss SB2C Helldiver (see pages 248 to 249), had entered service. The Dauntless was a development of the Northrop XBT-2. Northrop became closely affiliated with Douglas, and a re-design of the XBT-2 led to the XSBD-1 Dauntless prototype. Contracts were issued for 57 SBD-1s and 87 SBD-2s in April 1939, with production starting in 1940. SBD-1s were first delivered to VMB-2 of the U.S. Marine Corps in late 1940. The SBD-2 added armor and an increased fuel capacity, early deliveries being made to the U.S.S. Enterprise's bombing squadron VB-6. The SBD-3 began entering service in March 1941, featuring self-sealing fuel tanks and more armor. The SBD-4, built by Douglas at El Segundo, California, featured a 24 volt electrical system while

the similar SBD-5 was produced at Douglas' new factory at Tulsa, Oklahoma. The final production version of the Dauntless was the SBD-6, with the more powerful R-1820-66 Cyclone radial engine. The last of 5,936 Dauntlesses built was completed in the summer of 1944, but the type continued to serve with the U.S. Navy and Marines until just after World War Two.

The first major success for Navy SBD squadrons was the Battle of Coral Sea. In May 1942, the Japanese light aircraft carrier Shoho was sunk after being attacked by SBD-2/3s and Douglas TBD-1 Devastators. The next major battle was near the atoll of Midway, where 54 SBD-3s from the U.S.S. Enterprise (VB-6 and VS-6) and Yorktown (VB-5) helped to sink three of Admiral Yamamoto's large aircraft carriers and damaged a fourth on 4 June 1942. From August 1942, Guadalcanal in the Solomon Islands became the focus of fighting. Wherever the Navy or Marines fought, SBDs provid-

*Of all-metal construction, the compact SBD Dauntless was a sturdy aircraft with a good safety record. Particularly evident in this drawing are the perforated wing flaps and dive brakes.*

ed air support. This included combat in the Solomons and in the advance towards Rabaul, New Britain, or in attacks on isolated Japanese island garrisons in the Central Pacific. The U.S. Army Air Force acquired 168 A-24s (ex SBD-3A), 170 A-24As (SBD-4 equivalents) and 615 A-24Bs (SBD-5 equivalents) at times called Banshees, using some in limited combat operations. A number survived in U.S. Air Force service until 1950, but not in front-line service. Other operators included Free French forces, Mexico and New Zealand, while a small number were evaluated by Britain's Royal Navy. Mexico retired the last operational examples in the late 1950's.

*On the deck of a U.S. Navy aircraft carrier in the Pacific, an SBD Dauntless gets the go-ahead for take-off from the launch officer with his chequered flag (Photo: U.S. Navy).*

**Specifications – Douglas SBD-5 Dauntless**

| | |
|---|---|
| Wingspan | 41 ft 6 in |
| Length | 33 ft |
| Maximum speed | 252 mph at 13,800 ft |
| Maximum take-off weight | 10,882 lb |
| Range | 773 miles |
| Service ceiling | 24,300 ft |
| Armament | Two 0.5 in (12.7 mm) machine guns in the nose and two 0.3 in (7.62 mm) machine guns flexible-mounted in the rear cockpit, up to 2,250 lb of bombs |
| Engine | One Wright R-1820-60 Cyclone radial piston engine, of 1,200 hp |
| Crew | Two |

# Vought OS2U Kingfisher

Conceived as a replacement for the earlier Vought O3U Corsair biplane, the Kingfisher was an all-metal construction seaplane built for the U.S. Navy and intended as a scouting aircraft operating from that service's battleships and cruisers. With the exception of the fabric-covered control surfaces and the trailing edge of the wings, the entire airframe featured metal skin, which was spot-welded – one of the first, if not the first, American aircraft to be so built. The Kingfisher could be flown either as a landplane with a conventional wheeled undercarriage or, with a single central Edo float and two underwing stabilising floats, as a seaplane.

Powered by a Pratt & Whitney R-985-4 Wasp Junior radial engine of 450 hp, the prototype XOS2U-1 Kingfisher first flew as a landplane on 1 March 1938 and later as a seaplane on 19 May the year. The Kingfisher was produced in three principal variants, the OS2U-1, the OS2U-2 and the OS2U-3. Offensive armament consisted of two 325 lb bombs or depth charges on racks under the wings. Throughout its career, although designed as a scout, the Kingfisher

also found use as an anti-submarine aircraft as well as in the search and rescue, observer training and photographic survey roles. Some of the notable events in the Kingfisher's operational career included an attack on 15 July 1942, when two aircraft from U.S. Navy scouting squadron VS-9 operating out of Cherry Point assisted in the sinking of U-Boat U-576 off North Carolina. A similar incident occurred on 15 May 1943 when a Kingfisher from Key West helped sink U-176 off the Bahamas. Perhaps the most famous incident concerning the Kingfisher occurred on 11 and 12 November 1942 with the rescue of the crew of a B-17 Flying Fortress that had ditched in the Pacific. The crew of the B-17 included Captain Eddie Rickenbacker, the famous American World War One fighter ace, and was rescued in two attempts. Unable to take off, and the Kingfisher taxied over 40 miles to reach landfall. During its career, the Kingfisher was widely exported with examples being operated by Britain's Royal Navy, the Royal Australian Air Force, the Dutch East Indies, the Dominican

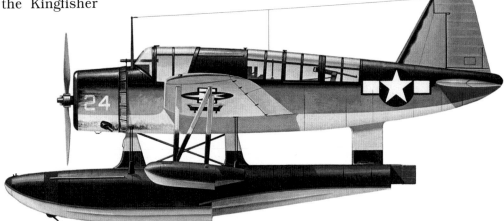

*A Vought OS2U in U.S. Navy colors, showing off the prominent central float of the seaplane version of this versatile and successful aircraft.*

*Several OS2U Kingfishers fly in a neat echelon formation. This is the seaplane version of the Kingfisher, capable of catapult launch from U.S. warships. The type was in service throughout America's involvement in World War Two (Photo: U.S. Navy).*

Republic, Argentina, Chile and Mexico. A total of 1,519 Kingfishers of all marks were produced, with the final 300 examples being constructed by the Philadelphia Navy Yard (Naval Aircraft Factory) in order to free up Vought's production facilities for manufacture of the F4U Corsair fighter.

**Specifications – Vought OS2U-3 Kingfisher (seaplane)**

| | |
|---|---|
| Wingspan | 35 ft 11 in |
| Length | 33 ft 7 in |
| Maximum speed | 170 mph at 5,500 ft |
| Maximum take-off weight | 6,000 lb |
| Range | 805 miles |
| Service ceiling | 16,000 ft |
| Armament | One 0.3 in (7.62 mm) machine gun fixed forward-firing in upper forward fuselage, one similar caliber machine gun flexible-mounted in rear cockpit, two 100 lb (45 kg) or 325 lb (147 kg) bombs beneath the wings |
| Engine | One Pratt & Whitney R-985-AN-2 Wasp Junior radial piston engine, of 450 hp |
| Crew | Two |

# Nakajima Ki-84 Hayate

One of the best fighters available to Japanese forces during World War Two was the Nakajima Ki-84 Hayate (Gale). It was one of the few Axis fighters, German or Japanese, in the latter stages of the war that could hold its own against the best Allied fighters, such as the P-51 Mustang and F6F Hellcat. Like many of the late-war Axis warplanes, however, it came too late and was not available in sufficient numbers to affect the course of the air war. This was as true for the Japanese in the Pacific as it was in Europe for the Germans with their own late-war fighter designs. The Japanese Ki-84 additionally suffered from other late-war difficulties including a lack of skilled workers to build production aircraft to a high standard, a lack of good pilots due to combat attrition and eventually a lack of fuel.

Design of the Ki-84 started several years earlier when Japan's fortunes were much better. In the early stages of the Pacific war, the Imperial Japanese Army air service had a number of operational fighters including the Nakajima Ki-43 Hayabusa ('Oscar'), Nakajima Ki-44 Shoki ('Tojo'), and Kawasaki Ki-61 Hien. These were very capable opposition to Allied aircraft of the early to mid-war period, but were generally outclassed by later, better Allied types. Development of the Ki-84 began in late 1941/early 1942, to find a successor to types such as the Ki-43 and to keep up with Allied fighter advances. The first of two prototypes flew in April 1943, and a very large batch of 83 service test/trials aircraft followed them. A second trials batch of 42 examples was also built in the first half of 1944. Manufacture commenced of production-standard aircraft in April 1944 as the Army Type 4 Fighter, the Hayate being built in four main versions depending on the armament fitted, with the Ki-84-II having a part wooden fuselage rather than the

*A Nakajima Ki-84-Ia wearing the tail markings of the 52nd Sentai. The Ki-84 was fast, agile, and had armor protection for its pilot, but its capabilities were adversely affected by indifferent performance from poorly-constructed and unreliable engines.*

predominantly metal construction of the other production aircraft. The first production model was the Ki-84-Ia. Three production plants were involved in the manufacturing program, two in Japan and one in Manchuria. Several experimental models were also envisaged, including an attempt to build a fully wooden version – reflecting the raw material shortages that were increasingly facing Japanese industry. Production of the Ki-84 eventually totalled some 3,577 examples accepted by the Imperial Japanese Army air service. The Ki-84 first went into action over Japanese-occupied China against U.S. bombers in a service trial in the summer of 1944. It was not until late 1944 that the type entered comparatively widespread service, initially in the bitter air fighting over the Philippines from October 1944. As the Japanese were pushed back across the Pacific, the Ki-84 eventually ended up defending the Japanese home islands, its role in this capacity ceasing with Japan's defeat in August 1945. The Ki-84 was known to the Allies for identification purposes as 'Frank.'

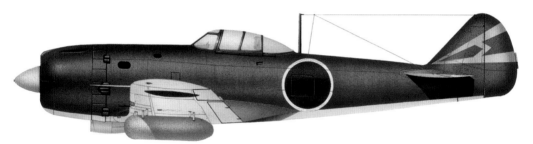

*A Nakajima Ki-84-Ia Hayate carrying underwing fuel tanks. The Hayate was treated with respect by the Americans, but all too often these excellent warplanes were flown by inexperienced pilots who were unable to make the best of the type's capabilities.*

**Specifications – Nakajima Ki-84-Ia Hayate**

| | |
|---|---|
| Wingspan | 37 ft 1 in (or slightly less) |
| Length | 32 ft 6.5 in |
| Maximum speed | 427 mph at 19,685 ft |
| Maximum take-off weight | 8,576 lb |
| Range | 780 miles |
| Service ceiling | 36,090 ft |
| Armament | Two fixed forward-firing 12.7 mm (0.5 in) machine guns in upper forward fuselage, two 20 mm wing-mounted cannons |
| Engine | One Nakajima Ha-45 21 radial piston engine, of 1,990 hp |
| Crew | One |

# Dornier Do 335

Potentially one of the most powerful single-seat piston engined fighters ever built, the Dornier Do 335 was a unique aircraft that illustrated the type of forward-thinking and radical innovation that characterized some parts of the German aircraft industry before and during World War Two. The unconventional layout of the Do 335 comprised two inline engines within the fuselage, one conventionally situated in the fuselage nose driving a tractor propeller, the other buried within the fuselage behind the cockpit driving a pusher propeller at the tail with an extension shaft. In fact, the pusher propeller layout was not unknown by any means, pusher configuration aircraft having a long history in the development of aviation. Some Dornier flying boats (and a variety of other aircraft) had already featured propellers at each end of their individual engine nacelles driven by tandem engines within the nacelles. The use of this layout for a high-performance combat aircraft was new, however, and the Do 335 offered high performance from the two engines coupled with a streamlined and efficient design.

In 1937, Claudius Dornier suc-cessfully patented a powerplant layout based on these basic principles, and to prove the feasibility of the rear-mounted propeller and extension shaft concept a small demonstrator aircraft was built. This was the Göppingen Gö 9, a neat little pusher monoplane that successfully demonstrated that the principle worked.

In 1942, the German air ministry issued a specification for a high-speed intruder aircraft, and Dornier submitted designs to this specification based on the propeller at each end concept. Eventually the officially-required specification was amended to a multi-role fighter, and Dornier thus altered the fore-and-aft design to become a family of fighter and reconnaissance aircraft layouts. The new type was designated Do 335 and often called Pfeil (Arrow). The prototype first flew in the autumn of 1943. It was certainly a radical design and in the ensuing months a number of specific versions were developed by Dornier which eventually encompassed both single and two-seat versions, plus a radar-equipped night fighter layout and many day fighter and reconnaissance developments. The first pre-production Do 335A-0 aircraft flew in

*The very first Dornier Do 335 to fly was the V1 prototype/development aircraft coded 'CP+UA', which first flew in the autumn of 1943. Note the rear pusher propeller so distinctive of the Do 335.*

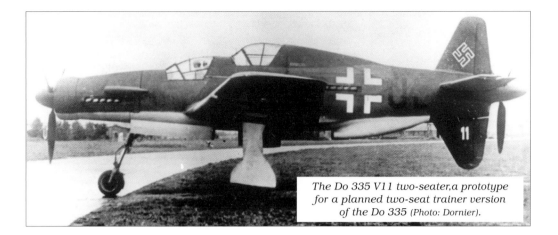

*The Do 335 V11 two-seater, a prototype for a planned two-seat trainer version of the Do 335 (Photo: Dornier).*

the summer of 1944 and followed a number of prototype/development aircraft. Later that year a Luftwaffe evaluation unit began preparing for full service entry. The initial production version was the Do 335A-1, whose manufacture apparently began later in 1944 and which appears to have been in production near to the war's end – but seemingly never reached front-line combat units. Late in the war a number of Do 335s were captured by the Allies and evaluated for their secrets, including the primitive ejection seat provided for the pilot.

*The Do 335 V4 was intended as a development aircraft of the planned Do 435 derivative of the Do 335, but time ran out and the Do 435 was never built.*

**Specifications – Dornier Do 335A-1**

| | |
|---|---|
| Wingspan | 45 ft 3.25 in |
| Length | 45 ft 5.25 in |
| Maximum speed | c. 478 mph at 21,000 ft |
| Maximum take-off weight | 21,164 lb |
| Range | 867 miles |
| Service ceiling | 37,400 ft |
| Armament | One 30 mm forward engine-mounted cannon, two 15 mm cannons in upper forward fuselage, up to 2,205 lb of bombs internally and externally |
| Engine | Two Daimler Benz DB 603A or E-series inline piston engines, of 1,750 hp each |
| Crew | One |

265

# Grumman F6F Hellcat

The Grumman F6F Hellcat was designed as a successor to the F4F Wildcat (see pages 182 to 183). The XF6F-1 made its maiden flight on 26 June 1942 powered by a Wright R-2600-10 Cyclone, but within a month this powerplant was replaced by the more powerful Pratt & Whitney R-2800-10 Double Wasp, producing the XF6F-3. Production F6F-3s abandoned the spinner used by the XF6F-3, added six 0.5 in (12.7 mm) machine guns in the wings and the provision for a ventral jettisonable fuel tank.

The first of over 4,400 F6F-3s was rolled out to make its first flight on 4 October 1942, deliveries to the U.S. Navy commencing in January 1943. Versions of the F6F-3 were the FGF-3E and FGF-3N night fighters equipped with wing pods containing APS-4 or APS-6 radars. The F6F-3N also featured an R-2800-10W boosted to 2,200 hp, which was additionally fitted to late production F6F-3 and the

F6F-5, the second major production variant. The F6F-5 also had a strengthened airframe and redesigned engine cowling. Over 8,000 were built, along with some 1,529 F6F-5N night fighter versions. A few were converted for photo-reconnaissance as F6F-5Ps.

While the type's short development and production period highlighted the great rush to produce the new fighter, the Hellcat proved to be exactly what the U.S. Navy required to defeat Japanese fighters. It went on to become a war-winning weapon, destroying 4,947 (possibly more) hostile aircraft. The first F6F-3s assigned to fleet units were received by VF-9 onboard the aircraft carrier U.S.S. Essex in January 1943, although it was VF-5 that first took Hellcats into combat in late August 1943. Many aces were created flying the Hellcat. The top scorer with 34 kills – and a Medal of Honor award – was Commander David McCampbell of VF-15/CVG-15.

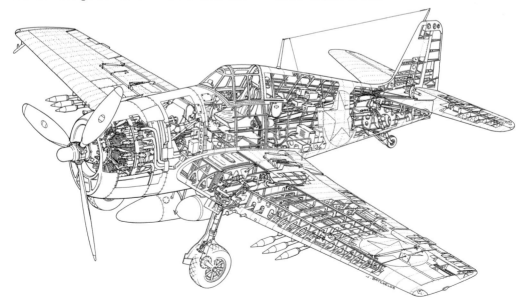

*The Grumman F6F Hellcat was of basically all-metal construction and had folding wings for stowage aboard aircraft carriers. Its bomb load (when used) consisted of two bombs carried beneath the inner wings.*

Maldives
RF6.50+50

GRUMMAN F6F-3 HELLCAT

*With its tailhook down for catching the arrester wires on the aircraft carrier's deck, an F6F Hellcat comes in to land. Together with the Vought F4U Corsair, the Hellcat was the principal U.S. Navy fighter of World War Two, and was highly successful.*

Hellcats were also used by the U.S. Marine Corps and the Royal Navy, which originally elected to use the name Gannet before adopting Hellcat. British versions were the Mk.I (ex F6F-3) and Mk.II (ex F6F-5, including some night fighters). No.800 Squadron was the first operational unit to fly the type in the Royal Navy, starting in the summer of 1943. British Hellcats were used primarily in the Pacific but also in European waters, such as in the attacks on the German capital ship Tirpitz in April 1944. As Lend-Lease aircraft they were retired soon after the end of the war. During the post-war period, the U.S. Navy used F6F-5K target drones, even flying them unmanned on one way missions against targets in Korea in the early 1950s. The French naval air arm was an important post-war user, employing Hellcats in combat in French Indochina. F6F-5s were also operated by the Uruguayan naval air arm.

**Specifications – Grumman Hellcat Mk.II**

| | |
|---|---|
| Wingspan | 42 ft 10 in |
| Length | 33 ft 7 in |
| Maximum speed | 371 mph at 17,200 ft |
| Maximum take-off weight | 13,753 lb |
| Range | 1,040 miles |
| Service ceiling | 36,700 ft |
| Armament | Six fixed forward-firing wing-mounted 0.5in (12.7mm) machine guns, plus six 60 lb unguided rocket projectiles or two 1,000 lb bombs |
| Engine | One Pratt & Whitney R-2800-10W Double Wasp radial piston engine, of 2,000–2,200 hp (with water injection) |
| Crew | One |

# Northrop P-61 Black Widow

It was Britain and Germany who perfected the art of night fighting during the early stages of World War Two, Britain having been the world-leader in radar development during the 1930's. From the early part of the war onwards, the need for night fighters grew to counter the increasing use of bomber aircraft by night. In both Britain and Germany, the miniaturization of radar equipment allowed aircraft to carry radar aloft to aid in finding enemy bombers in the darkness, allied to ground-based radar stations. In view of post-war developments, it is surprising that the United States was somewhat behind with this technology, and only came up to Britain's standards when the British gave radar technology to the Americans – as also happened after World War Two with some of the ingredients for the design of supersonic aircraft.

In the United States, the first operational night fighter was the Douglas P-70, a makeshift type, and the Americans also used some British Bristol Beaufighter night fighters. Like the Germans, the Americans attempted to create their own night fighter, the Northrop P-61 Black Widow. Designed to meet a 1940 Army Air Corps requirement for a radar-carrying night fighter, the P-61 was a large aircraft about the size of a medium bomber. The prototype XP-61 officially flew first on 26 May 1942, and after some design alterations and a series of YP-61 development/test aircraft, it entered production as the P-61A in 1943. There were, however, delays in the whole program associated with the eventually commendable Western Electric SCR-720 AI (airborne interception) radar as fitted in the P-61. Originally armed with a formidable array of guns, the P-61 experienced problems with its remotely-controlled dorsal turret, which was deleted from the 38th P-61A and later reinstated, some turrets featuring two rather than four machine guns. For long-distance ferry flights this dorsal position was sometimes fitted with an auxiliary fuel tank.

P-61s started entering Army Air Force service in late 1943 for U.S.-based

*A Northrop P-61B Black Widow of the 550th Night Fighter Squadron, Thirteenth Army Air Force. This squadron operated in the Dutch East Indies in the early part of 1945 as the Japanese were gradually driven back from their early conquests.*

training. In about April 1944, the first operational aircraft were delivered to the 6th Night Fighter Squadron in the Pacific, which scored the first kill on the night of 30 June 1944. In Europe, the 422nd and 425th NFSs began flying the P-61 in May 1944, starting by shooting down a V1 'flying bomb' in mid-July 1944. From then onwards, increasing numbers of P-61s came into service and the type operated well in Europe, the Mediterranean and the Far East. Some night fighter units employed their Black Widows as night intruders carrying bombs on special shackles. Continuing development led to the P-61B (with later SCR-720 radar) and P-61C models, but production ended after World War Two with 706 (including prototypes) built. A specially-streamlined derivative with a fighter-like 'teardrop' cockpit canopy was manufactured (36 examples) as the F-15A Reporter photo-reconnaissance version. The U.S. Navy/Marine Corps also used the P-61B in small numbers as the F2T-1 for night fighter crew training in anticipation of post-war jet-powered night fighters.

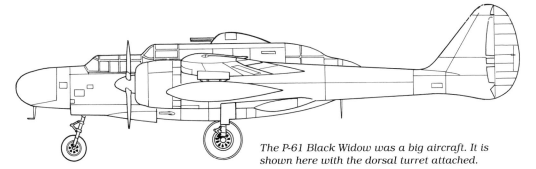

The P-61 Black Widow was a big aircraft. It is shown here with the dorsal turret attached.

**Specifications – Northrop P-61A Black Widow**

| | |
|---|---|
| Wingspan | 66 ft |
| Length | 48 ft 11.2 in |
| Maximum speed | 369 mph at 20,000 ft |
| Maximum take-off weight | 32,400 lb |
| Range | approximately 1,000 miles |
| Service ceiling | 33,100 ft |
| Armament | Four 20 mm cannons in lower forward fuselage and (some aircraft) four 0.5 in (12.7 mm) machine guns in dorsal turret |
| Engine | Two Pratt & Whitney R-2800-10 or –65 Double Wasp radial piston engines, of 2,000–2,040 hp each |
| Crew | Three |

# Arado Ar 234 Blitz

Although both Britain and Germany achieved the great success of bringing jet-powered fighter aircraft into operational service prior to the end of World War Two, only Germany achieved the double distinction of also commencing the front-line use of a jet-powered bomber. This was the Arado Ar 234, which actually entered service initially on fast reconnaissance missions. The Ar 234 derived from requirements outlined by Germany's air ministry for a reconnaissance aircraft able to fly at greater speeds and at higher altitudes than those attainable by existing Allied fighters which would be expected to intercept it. The then on-going developments in jet propulsion promised to help meet the demanding specification and in 1940 Arado began design work, the project being known as E.370. The original requirement called for long range capabilities, and to allow sufficient room within the aircraft for fuel tanks (bearing in mind the high fuel consumption of early jet engines) the design dispensed with a conventional undercarriage. Instead it was intended to take off from a jettisonable wheeled trolley and land with a retractable set of skids. This was completely unsatisfactory, and most later development aircraft and production Ar 234s featured a conventional retractable undercarriage in a widened and revised fuselage with altered fuel tankage.

The first Ar 234 flew on 30 July 1943, delayed by the late arrival of flight-cleared engines. There followed several further prototype/development aircraft. Most of these were twin-engined but two were four-engined – the V6 with four BMW 003 turbojets in separate nacelles, and the V8 with two paired BMW 003s under each wing. The retractable undercarriage layout was tried out on the V9, which first flew in March 1944 and which was effectively the prototype for the production B-series Ar 234 –

*Bearing the 'F1' fuselage code of Luftwaffe bomber wing KG 76, the world's first-ever jet bomber unit, this Arado Ar 234B-2 has a bomb mounted below its engine cowling; a bomb could also be mounted beneath the fuselage additional to the lower cowlings.*

the Ar 234B-1 reconnaissance aircraft; and the B-2 reconnaissance-bomber, often called Blitz (Lightning). To enable take-offs at high weights or from short runways two Walter rocket booster packs could be installed beneath the wings.

The Ar 234B-2 entered service with the Luftwaffe's KG 76 in the later months of 1944, flying its first major operations on 24 December 1944 during the failed German Ardennes offensive. These were the world's first true jet-bomber operations. Prior to this, starting on 2 August 1944, two of the A-series prototypes had flown special reconnaissance missions from a base in France over the post-D-Day battle-fields in Normandy – again a first in aviation history. Overall, 210 B-series Ar 234s were delivered to the Luftwaffe, plus around 20 Ar 234C – a more powerful four-engined development also with reconnaissance and bomber applications. Several Ar 234B are believed to have flown as improvised night fighters. The Ar 234 was a great success in combat, its speed and high altitude flight giving Allied fighters little chance to catch it. Eventually, a lack of fuel ended Ar 234 operations, and post-war the victorious Allies took great interest in this excellent aircraft and its intended (but never built) successors, which were even more advanced.

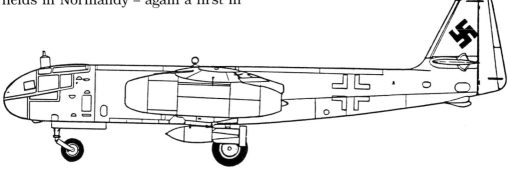

*The Arado Ar 234 was of all-metal construction, and was surprisingly conventional in layout considering the type's advanced nature. The Ar 234B-1 was a reconnaissance aircraft, the Ar 234B-2 was a bomber-reconnaissance model.*

**Specifications – Arado Ar 234B-2**

| | |
|---|---|
| Wingspan | 47 ft 3.25 in |
| Length | 41 ft 5.5 in |
| Maximum speed | 460 mph at 19,685 ft |
| Maximum take-off weight | 22,046 lb |
| Range | 969 miles |
| Service ceiling | 32,808 ft |
| Armament | 1,102 lb of bombs externally mounted, possibly more (some aircraft: two fixed fuselage-mounted rearwards-firing 20 mm cannons) |
| Engine | Two Junkers Jumo 004B turbojet engines, of 1,980 lb st each (some aircraft: two additional 1,100 lb st Walter 109–500 liquid-fuel rockets) |
| Crew | One |

# Fieseler Fi 156

Although high speed is often a necessity for front-line warplanes, other performance considerations are of higher importance for military aircraft engaged in tasks other than aerial combat or bombing. For observation and army co-operation, the ability to fly in a slow, stable manner with excellent visibility for the crew and to land and take off from unprepared surfaces in the shortest of distances were of the greatest importance. In Britain, the Westland company created the Lysander army co-operation aircraft with just these characteristics (see pages 32 to 33). In Germany, an aircraft with similar capabilities was also produced, but according to a completely different design layout. This was the Fieseler Fi 156 Storch (Stork), and like the Lysander, it was a great success in its intended roles and many others as its military service widened.

The Fi 156 grew from studies carried out by the Fieseler company into short take-off and landing capabilities. Essentially starting out as a private venture, the type attracted the interest of the German military even though Fieseler had intended to aim at the civilian market. The first of three prototype-development aircraft flew in 1936. These aircraft proved the design's excellent low-speed and short take-off and landing qualities, and the type entered production for the Luftwaffe for short-range army co-operation and observation roles – although in practice the Storch performed many other tasks including staff transport and casualty evacuation. Ten pre-production aircraft followed, one appearing in 1937 at a major aviation meeting at Zurich, Switzerland, where it created great interest. With high-lift devices on its wings, including leading edge slats, the Storch could fly as slow as

*The Fieseler Fi 156 Storch was an ungainly-looking aircraft with its stalky main undercarriage and high-lift wings. The type's most famous exploit was the rescue of the Italian dictator, Benito Mussolini, by German forces from imprisonment on the Gran Sasso in September 1943, using the smallest of landing areas.*

32 mph under full control and could almost hover in a headwind. Deliveries of the initial Fi 156A-1 production model began in late 1937/early 1938. Several of these aircraft went to Spain as transport and utility aircraft for the German Condor Legion. Further development led to the Fi 156C, which introduced a flexible-mounted machine gun in the rear of the cabin in the Fi 156C-2 version. Production examples were assigned as liaison aircraft to many front-line operational units and others were delegated to short-range reconnaissance/observation tasks. The Fi 156C-series went on to see extensive service with the Luftwaffe on all its operational fronts and was followed by the Fi 156D, which was essentially a casualty evacuation model with large fuselage doors to allow for the internal stowage of a stretcher. Production of the Storch increasingly moved from overworked German factories to occupied France and the former Czechoslovakia. Post-war production and service continued in both of the latter two countries. Approximately 2,549 (possibly more) Fi 156 were built up to the end of World War Two. In addition to Luftwaffe service, the Storch also flew with various other countries including Switzerland, Italy, Croatia, Bulgaria, Hungary, Sweden, and Romania.

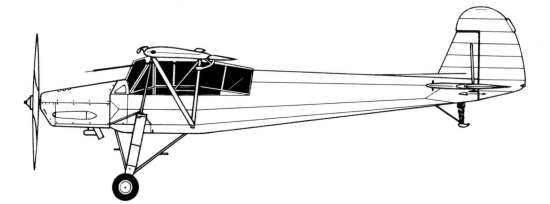

*The Fieseler Fi 156's tall undercarriage was capable of absorbing the considerable loads imposed by high descent landings, a vital part of the type's short landing capability.*

**Specifications – Fieseler Fi 156C-2**

| | |
|---|---|
| Wingspan | 46 ft 9 in |
| Length | 32 ft 5.75 in |
| Maximum speed | 108.75 mph at sea level |
| Maximum take-off weight | 2,921 lb |
| Range | 239 miles |
| Service ceiling | 15,092 ft |
| Armament | One 7.92 mm (0.312 in) machine gun on flexible mount in rear of cockpit |
| Engine | One Argus As 10C inline piston engine, of 240 hp |
| Accommodation | Two crew, one passenger could also be carried |

# Focke-Wulf Fw 190A Series

One of the outstanding fighter aircraft of World War Two was Germany's Focke-Wulf Fw 190. Developed before the war and entering service in 1941, the Fw 190 was a versatile fighter, fighter-bomber and ground attack aircraft for the Luftwaffe and was built in large numbers. It was a worthy opponent for Allied fighters, particularly early in the war. Its high-altitude performance was enhanced, leading to a developed model, the Fw 190D-series (see pages 292 to 293).

In 1935 the Messerschmitt Bf 109 was chosen as Germany's main modern fighter and gave outstanding service to Germany's Luftwaffe. However, there were those in Germany's military leadership who were not satisfied with Germany having just one main fighter type (most other major countries were developing more than one major advanced fighter program), and a new requirement was drawn up in 1937 for a fighter that would fill the gap if any problems developed with the Bf 109 series. Under the design leadership of

the talented Kurt Tank, Focke-Wulf created the Fw 190. Although there was already a tradition of liquid-cooled inline engines for German fighters, such as the Daimler Benz DB 601 inline engine of the Bf 109, Focke-Wulf chose the new BMW 139 radial, which was still being developed.

The initial Fw 190, the Fw 190V1, first flew on 1 June 1939. A major early problem was engine overheating, partly due to the aircraft's tight cowling arrangement. Otherwise testing went well and construction proceeded of further prototypes. Due to continuing problems with the BMW 139, the fifth Fw 190 (the third to be completed) was re-engined with the new BMW 801C 14-cylinder radial engine and this powerplant was subsequently fitted to all the production A-series aircraft plus their attack counterparts. Following a batch of pre-production Fw 190A-0, during which a slightly longer span wing and other improvements were standardized, the first production model was the Fw 190A-1.

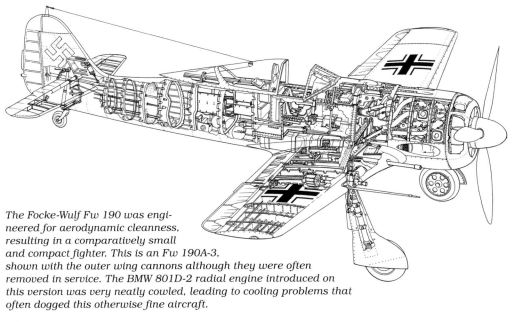

*The Focke-Wulf Fw 190 was engineered for aerodynamic cleanness, resulting in a comparatively small and compact fighter. This is an Fw 190A-3, shown with the outer wing cannons although they were often removed in service. The BMW 801D-2 radial engine introduced on this version was very neatly cowled, leading to cooling problems that often dogged this otherwise fine aircraft.*

*The Focke-Wulf Fw 190's cockpit was very well laid out, in a modern and logical way. The use of side consoles to neatly arrange their various dials and pieces of equipment was a new concept in the 1940's. At that time most aircraft simply had all this equipment bolted untidily to the fuselage framing and structure.*

This entered service in 1941, the first unit being the Luftwaffe fighter wing JG 26 in occupied France, which received its first aircraft in late July/early August 1941. These initial examples caused a major surprise to the RAF, which by then had some useful knowledge of the Messerschmitt Bf 109. It was not until the advent of the Supermarine Spitfire Mk.IX with its two-stage supercharged Merlin engine that the balance in the air war over northern Europe again swung to the Allies.

The Fw 190A-1 was followed by a succession of A-series fighter versions, all of which introduced progressive improvements to armament and capability. Early on in its operational life, the Fw 190 was recognized as having good capabilities for ground attack, and a succession of conversion sets or Rüstsätze was made available to allow bombs or other stores to be carried. Several important changes were also made to the design itself. The Fw 190A-3, for example, introduced the BMW 801D-2 radial engine to the Fw 190 series, this version of the engine powering many of the subsequent A-series Fw 190s. Slots in the fuselage side behind the engine bay were also added to allow hot air to escape from

the engine area, the BMW 801 itself being prone to overheating in its Fw 190 application. The Fw 190A-5 introduced an altered forward fuselage with the engine relocated slightly further forward. Some A-5s were modified as two-seat Fw 190A-5/U1 trainers. The Fw 190A-6 introduced a slightly lightened wing structure. The Fw 190A-7, which entered production in late 1943, had a revised armament of four 20 mm cannons in the wings and two 13 mm (0.51 in) machine guns in the upper forward fuselage. Only 80 aircraft of this series were built before it was supplanted by the Fw 190A-8, which was the definitive A-series Fw 190 in many ways, and a formidable combat aircraft. Amongst other improvements the A-8 was fitted with a nitrous oxide or methanol-water power boost system, which wrung some extra power from the BMW 801D-2 engine. Some Fw 190A-8s

# Focke-Wulf Fw 190A Series *continued*

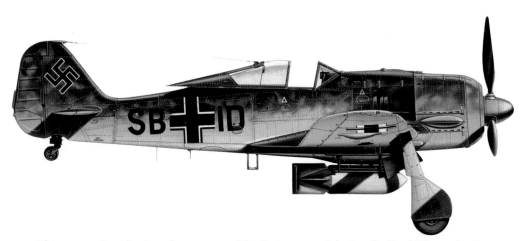

The Focke-Wulf Fw 190 was
arguably Germany's best fighter
of the Second World War. It was
sometimes called Würger (Shrike), but
nowadays the popular and much over-used nickname
'Butcher Bird' is often used instead.

were also converted into two-seat
trainers as the Fw 190A-8/U1 (sometimes called Fw 190S-8). The final
A-series Fw 190 was the higher-pow-
ered Fw 190A-9. Other A-series versions were planned but not built.
Although designed as a fighter, the Fw
190 proved readily adaptable to the
attack role, and two dedicated attack

series were developed, the short-range
battlefield support ground attack Fw
190F-series and the longer-range fighter-bomber Fw 190G-series. Early
examples of these two models were
closely based on or converted from
A-series Fw 190s, but both grew into
highly important production series in
their own right. Some replaced the

*This composite side-view shows some of the features used during the Fw 190's production
run. Important points are the neat and compact structure, the tightly-cowled radial engine,
the excellent weapon-carrying capability and other features such as the rearwards-sliding
cockpit cover.*

famous Junkers Ju 87 (see pages 50 to 51) in the close support role. Both series could be fitted with a large array of different weapon options hung on a variety of different external stores carriers. In addition to these versions, a large number of special Fw 190 models were adapted to specific tasks. These included an interim night fighter and a specially armed and armored version for close attacks against formations of B-24 Liberator and B-17 Flying Fortress American daylight bombers.

Production of the Fw 190 was carried out by Focke-Wulf and several other companies. This was often the case in many countries with major production series of important combat aircraft. However, in Germany it was necessitated due to the heavy bombing by the Allies of aircraft production facilities. Later in the war some of the German aircraft factories were literally forced underground or shifted to remote locations in order to escape the bombing. Due to such factors, it is absolutely impossible to say how many Fw 190s were built. It is possible that the figure was somewhere over twenty thousand, but many production records were lost in the bombing. In addition, several manufacturers recycled damaged or out-of-service airframes and used them to built new Fw 190s, thus complicating the picture even further.

In addition to the widespread and successful service for Germany's Luftwaffe, the Fw 190 also operated with a number of other countries. One of Germany's allies, Hungary, employed the Fw 190 on the Eastern Front alongside the Germans in their struggle against the Soviet Union. Neutral Turkey also operated the Fw 190. After the war, the newly reformed French air force also used the type. Examples of the Fw 190 had already been manufactured or recycled in France. Surplus airframes were put together after the war at the French manufacturing center and 64 were assigned to the French air force.

**Specifications – Focke-Wulf Fw 190A-8**

| | |
|---|---|
| Wingspan | 34 ft 5.5 in |
| Length | 29 ft 4.25 in |
| Maximum speed | 402 mph at 18,045 ft |
| Maximum take-off weight | 9,788 lb |
| Range | 495 miles plus |
| Service ceiling | 33,793 ft |
| Armament | Two 13 mm (0.51 in) machine guns fixed forward-firing in upper forward fuselage, up to four 20 mm cannons forward-firing in the wings, provision for considerable under fuselage or underwing stores depending on specific equipment fits |
| Engine | One BMW 801D-2 radial piston engine, of 1,700 hp |
| Crew | One |

# Heinkel He 162

In the final stages of World War Two, the German aircraft industry was beginning to produce a number of innovative and forward-looking designs that could have made a considerable impact on the direction of the war if it had continued after May 1945. The Messerschmitt Me 262 jet fighter (see pages 298 to 299) was one of these, but it was not the only jet fighter that was in production in Germany late in the war. Also being produced, and ready to join combat, was the Heinkel He 162 Salamander, sometimes known as the 'Volksjäger' (Peoples' Fighter). Perhaps the most remarkable facet of this aircraft's existence was the short space of time taken to design it. Stemming from a German Air Ministry requirement issued on 8 September 1944, the order specificed that the resulting aircraft be ready for mass-production by 1 January 1945! Several

aircraft manufacturers vied for this program, but Heinkel was the winner and design work proceeded quickly from mid-September under Heinkel project number P.1073. Heinkel was actually a good choice for this work. On 27 August 1939, the world's first-ever jet-powered aircraft had made its first official flight. This was the Heinkel He 178, and at that time Heinkel had been a pioneer in jet aircraft design, despite the company's normal work on bomber aircraft. The He 162 was designed from the start to be an austere fighter, capable of being constructed by a semi-skilled labor force and made from non-essential materials due to increasing shortages in Germany. The idea was to quickly and easily manufacture a capable fighter that could counter the air superiority of the Allies and successfully take on the American fighters and bombers which

*At the end of World War Two the Allies captured a number of complete and flyable Heinkel He 162 fighters. Some of these were taken away for evaluation, German technology being of great interest at that time. One of the survivors is the He 162A shown here, preserved in Britain (Photo: John Batchelor).*

increasingly dominated the airspace over Germany. Development work was completed by the end of October 1944, and manufacture began of the first aircraft. Although metal was used for construction of most of the fuselage, wood was employed where possible. The He 162V1 was first flown on 6 December 1944, but crashed four days later, killing its pilot. Part of the aircraft's wooden wing came apart when one of the glued joints failed. The aircraft's light structure was found to be unable to take the two planned 30 mm cannons, and so two cannons of lighter caliber were fitted in production examples. After a batch of pre-production test aircraft the initial production He 162s were delivered to the Luftwaffe in early 1945. They differed from the first aircraft in several respects including the addition of turned-down wingtips. The only Luftwaffe unit to convert into the type was JG 1, elements of this fighter wing becoming operational in April 1945. Due to a lack of fuel, the unit never appears to have operated against the Allies and so this highly rushed fighter project was never able to prove itself in combat.

*Of unconventional layout and developed very quickly, the Heinkel He 162A was never able to prove itself in combat. It was, however, one of the first jet-powered aircraft ever to reach a front-line operational unit. Approximately 116 were completed, with construction taking place increasingly in underground production centers to avoid Allied bombing.*

## Specifications – Heinkel He 162A-2

| | |
|---|---|
| Wingspan | 23 ft 7.5 in |
| Length | 29 ft 8.33 in |
| Maximum speed | 522 mphat 19,685 ft |
| Maximum take-off weight | 5,941 lb |
| Range | 385 miles |
| Service ceiling | 39,500 ft |
| Armament | Two 20 mm cannons fixed forward-firing in the lower forward fuselage |
| Engine | One BMW 003E-1 or –2 turbojet engine, of 1,764 lb st |
| Crew | One |

# Messerschmitt Me 163 Komet

The development of rocket propulsion was pioneered in several countries well before the start of World War Two. It was a technology that was known and understood in the previous century, but pioneers in several countries including Germany, Russia and the United States gradually applied its potential to aviation during the inter-war period. In Germany, Fritz von Opel and others successfully flew rocket-powered gliders in the late 1920's, and the military potential of this form of propulsion became increasingly obvious. During the 1930's Alexander Lippisch in Germany carried out important research into tailless gliders and this aerodynamic development work was considered the preparatory work for a rocket-powered fighter. Lippisch and several colleagues joined the Messerschmitt company in 1939, taking with them the DFS 194 tail-less glider design. This was successfully married to a Walter liquid-fuel rocket motor that gave the glider amazing performance when it

was flown in 1940. Development of a fighter based on this research was duly given the go-ahead and the new type was designated Me 163 as a security cover (the previous Bf 163 was a light aircraft program). The initial prototype was flown as a glider first, before attempts were made to fly early prototype aircraft under power in 1941. These tests went well, the first apparently being made in August 1941. In October that year a prototype was towed to some 13,123 ft where the rocket motor was started. The resulting speed attained exceeded 623 mph in level flight, thus surpassing the then-recognized world speed record. The initial batch of non-operational Me 163A series prototype/development aircraft was followed by the main production model, the Me 163B. Pre-series Me 163B-0 and production Me 163B-1 were built, some by light aircraft manufacturer Klemm as a major sub-contractor. Approximately 360, possibly more, were eventually made. Initial deliveries to the Luft-waffe were achieved in

*The Messerschmitt Me 163's design owed much to the research into tailless gliders by Alexander Lippisch. It had a jettisonable main undercarriage, bumpy landings being made on the lower fuselage skid to avoid the weight and complexity of fitting a retractable undercarriage. A two-seat trainer, the Me 163S, also existed.*

early 1944 to an evaluation and trials unit, which flew the first sorties in May 1944 against American daylight heavy bombers.

The Me 163, however, was not an easy aircraft to operate. Its volatile T-Stoff (hydrogen peroxide) and C-Stoff (a methanol and hydrazine hydrate solution) rocket fuel was dangerous and operational endurance lasted only several minutes before the fuel ran out and the aircraft reverted to being a vulnerable glider. The only fighter wing to operationally fly the Me 163 was the specially-formed JG 400, with many of its operations being made from Brandis near Leipzig. Various combat operations were flown from July 1944, gaining a number of successes against American heavy bombers. Lack of fuel and the deteriorating war situation eventually stopped Me 163 operations, and similarly concluded work on its successor, the Ju 248/Me 263, which had a conventional tricycle undercarriage. (See pages 288 to 289.)

*The Messerschmitt Me 163B was the world's first operational rocket-powered fighter. It was fully operational in 1944 and is credited with shooting down several American heavy bombers. Another German rocket-powered point defence fighter, the Bachem Ba 349 Natter (see pages 242 to 243) was also developed.*

### Specifications – Messerschmitt Me 163B-1

| | |
|---|---|
| Wingspan | 30 ft 7.33 in |
| Length | 19 ft 2.33 in |
| Maximum speed | 597 mph at 29,528 ft |
| Maximum take-off weight | 9,502 lb |
| Endurance | approximately 8 minutes of rocket burn |
| Service ceiling | 39,698 ft |
| Armament | Two 20 mm or two 30 mm cannons forward-firing in wing roots |
| Engine | One Walter HWK 509A-2 liquid-fuel rocket motor, of approximately 3,750 lb st |
| Crew | One |

# Fairey Barracuda

Greatly delayed by official prevarication and indecision, the Fairey Barracuda was designed according to Specification S.24/37 for a torpedo-bomber to replace the Fairey Albacore (see pages 100 to 101) in Britain's Royal Navy. Originally designed as a low wing two-seat monoplane around the 24 cylinder Rolls-Royce Exe engine, the cancellation of this engine, together with the Admiralty's insistence on the inclusion of a third crew member, signaled the start of the Barracuda's problems. The inevitable transition from the low to a high wing configuration, necessitating a much longer and complex undercarriage, together with the increase in size and weight occasioned by the third crew member, meant that the 1,300 hp Merlin 30 engine fitted to the Mk.I version left the Barracuda very underpowered. Although this was somewhat addressed by fitting the Merlin 32 of 1,640 hp in the later Mk.II and Mk.III versions, along with the fitting of a four-bladed propeller in place of the original

three-bladed unit, lack of power dogged the Barracuda until the introduction of the Mk.V version. The Barracuda Mk.III was basically a Mk.II fitted with ASV Mk.10 radar in a lower fuselage radome. The prototype Barracuda first flew on 7 December 1940 and featured an Albacore style fin and rudder. This was later changed to a higher strut-braced tailplane when it was discovered that the large Fairey-Youngman flaps fitted under the wings interfered with the airflow over the tail. Production of Merlin-powered Barracudas totaled some 2,570. The first flight of the Barracuda Mk.V was in November 1944. This version was powered by a Rolls-Royce Griffon 37 engine of 2,030 hp and featured increased fuel

The Gambia    D5

FAIREY BARRACUDA II

*In appearance an unconventional aircraft that looked as if it had been designed by a committee, the Fairey Barracuda was not well liked. At the end of the war, many were simply dumped into the sea off the decks of aircraft carriers, especially in the Pacific.*

capacity together with an enlarged fin and rudder, essentially the aeroplane the Barracuda should have been from the start. Although 140 examples were ordered, the war's end ensured that only about 30 Barracuda Mk.Vs were delivered. Operationally the Barracuda is best remembered for the attack in April 1944, when aircraft operating from the aircraft carrier H.M.S. Victorious inflicted heavy damage on the German battleship Tirpitz in Norwegian waters. Other famous operations by Barracudas were their participation in raids on Japanese-held oil refineries in Sumatra, which helped to cut oil production by one third. By the end of the war, Japanese oil production had still not fully recovered from these raids.

*The Barracuda achieved some successes during its operational life and was one of the chief aircraft carrier-borne Fleet Air Arm aircraft in the latter stages of World War Two. It featured folding wings for its life aboard the confines of aircraft carriers.*

**Specifications – Fairey Barracuda Mk.II**

| | |
|---|---|
| Wingspan | 49 ft 2 in |
| Length | 39 ft 9 in |
| Maximum speed | 228 mph at 1,750 ft |
| Maximum take-off weight | 14,100 lb |
| Range | 684 miles |
| Service ceiling | 16,600 ft |
| Armament | Two flexible rearward-firing 0.303 in (7.7 mm) machine guns in rear cockpit, one 1,610 lb torpedo or similar beneath the fuselage or up to 1,600 lb of bombs, mines or depth charges |
| Engine | One Rolls-Royce Merlin 32 inline piston engine, of 1,600–1,640 hp |
| Crew | Three |

# Hawker Tempest

Although the Hawker Typhoon eventually matured into an excellent ground attack aircraft, it was originally intended instead as an interceptor fighter at all altitudes. During the protracted development phase of the aircraft, it became clear to Hawker that a number of major alterations to the Typhoon design would be necessary for the type to fulfil its primary role. This potentially meant a significant redesign of the wing to give better performance at higher altitudes, and the provision for more fuel to allow the aircraft a longer endurance. A modified design layout was subsequently submitted to Air Ministry Specification F.10/41. Hawker's approach successfully gained an order for two prototypes, tentatively known as the Typhoon Mk.II. However, there were so many important differences between the Typhoon and the new design that, before the prototype had flown, the type was renamed Tempest.

The prototype Tempest Mk.I flew in February 1943 and an initial production contract was allowed for 400 Tempest Mk.Is. They were intended to be powered by the Napier Sabre IV engine, but this was later cancelled and the contract amended in favor of the Bristol Centaurus-powered Tempest Mk II. However, delays with this engine, and the cancellation of the planned Tempest Mks.III and IV, resulted in the first Tempest to enter production being the Tempest Mk.V, powered by the Napier Sabre II as used by the Typhoon. The Tempest Mk.V entered RAF service in the spring of 1944, at which time it could claim to be the fastest and most powerful fighter in service anywhere in the world. Following initial fighter bomber missions over Occupied Europe, the newly-formed Tempest squadrons were assigned to the air defence of Great Britain, operating against the Vl flying bombs (see pages 302 to 303) being launched against Britain at the time. The Tempest's high speed allowed it to become one of the main defences against the V1, shooting down an impressive proportion of more than 1,800 flying-bombs brought down by fighters. Later the Tempest Mk.V squadrons flew alongside other Allied 2nd Tactical Air Force units on the Continent. There they joined Typhoon squadrons, often flying 'Cab Rank' standing patrols, ready to be called in at short notice to the attack by ground controllers against German forces on the battlefield. In the meantime, the Centaurus-powered Tempest Mk.II had moved forward, having first flown in June 1943. Production examples only reached the RAF after the war ended, however, and the type was lat-

The Hawker Tempest Mk.II was powered by a mighty Bristol Centaurus radial engine of 2,520 hp, but was too late to see service in World War Two

er flown by India and Pakistan. There was additionally a Tempest Mk.VI, which first flew in May 1944, but similarly only entered front-line service after the war. Total Tempest V production was some 805 aircraft, plus 142 Mk.VI and 450 Mk.II. Further development of the basic Typhoon/Tempest layout led to the excellent Fury and Sea Fury of the post-Second World War years.

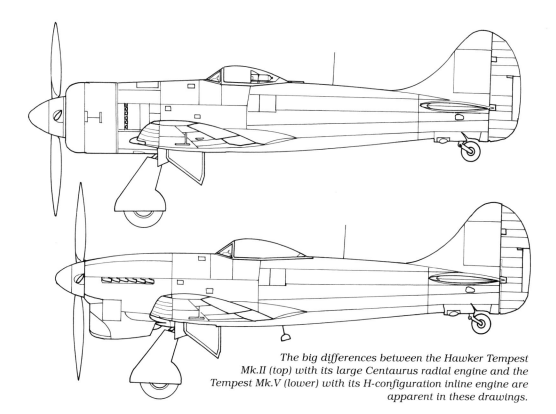

*The big differences between the Hawker Tempest Mk.II (top) with its large Centaurus radial engine and the Tempest Mk.V (lower) with its H-configuration inline engine are apparent in these drawings.*

**Specifications – Hawker Tempest Mk.V**

| | |
|---|---|
| Wingspan | 41 ft |
| Length | 33 ft 8 in |
| Maximum speed | 426 mph at 18,500 ft |
| Maximum take-off weight | 13,540 lb |
| Range | 740 miles |
| Service ceiling | 36,500 ft |
| Armament | Four fixed forward-firing wing-mounted 20 mm cannons, various underwing armament options including two 500 lb bombs, eight 60 lb unguided rocket projectiles |
| Engine | One Napier Sabre IIA inline piston engine, of 2,180 hp (other marks of this engine also available) |
| Crew | One |

# Kamikaze

As the general war situation worsened for the Japanese, more and more desperate measures were envisaged in order to prevent the increasingly overwhelming tide of American military power in the Pacific from finally defeating Japan. Drawing from Japanese warrior traditions, the concept of Kamikaze (Divine Wind) suicide attacks gradually became more and more prominent as the war progressed. These started to be made by Japanese pilots in increasing numbers during 1944 and the battles for control of the strategically-vital Philippines saw especially widespread use of Kamikaze attacks that employed existing aircraft, sometimes bombers but often comparatively high performance attack aircraft or fighter–bombers. At first these were ad hoc missions, but as Japan's situation worsened the whole concept took on an ominously more organized form when it started to become obvious to Japanese planners that the Japanese home islands themselves would eventually be subject to American invasion. Conventional defence was becoming less possible – a significant part of Japan's fleet had been sunk and the Americans enjoyed an increasing level of air superiority over the Japanese homeland. In response, plans were drawn up for the production of specially-designed suicide aircraft as a potentially successful means of fighting back. Two types in particular were manufactured. The first was the Yokosuka MXY7 Ohka (Cherry Blossom). Design work commenced in summer 1944 and the first example flew later that year. The Ohka was a crude, piloted flying-bomb with a warhead of 2,645 lb and was powered by a solid-fuel rocket – although developed versions (which were not flown) would have had turbojet power. The Ohka was carried aloft beneath a Mitsubishi G4M 'Betty' bomber specially-converted into a 'mother' plane. The Ohka was an Imperial Japanese Navy program, and 755 are believed to have been built by March 1945. At least one U.S. warship is thought to have been sunk by an Ohka, but the 'motherships' were very

*The Yokosuka MXY7 Ohka had a maximum speed of at least 404 mph, although it would go faster as it dived onto its target. The type had to be air-launched from a 'mothership,' the pilot sealed within his cockpit.*

286

*The Yokosuka MXY7 Ohka was the crudest of weapons, a manned suicide flying-bomb, powered by a solid-fuel rocket. These machines actually became operational, but suicide missions tended to be more successful using conventional operational aircraft.*

vulnerable to fighter attack and the Ohka did not have the intended impact.

Also developed for suicide missions was a conventional aircraft, the Nakajima Ki-115 Tsurugi (Sabre). Built from non-strategic materials such as steel and wood, the Ki-115 was a simple design with a fixed undercarriage that was supposed to be jettisoned after take-off. It could be built by semi-skilled labor, and a recess below the fuselage could be fitted with a bomb of up to 1,764 lb. Design work was completed in early 1945, and flight trials appear to have commenced soon after. These revealed very unpleasant handling characteristics and although some 104 examples were built they were not used operationally.

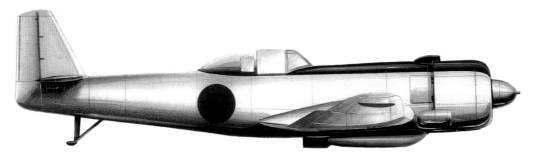

*The Nakajima Ki-115 Tsurugi was a quickly-designed, manned flying-bomb aircraft which had poor flying qualities. Over one hundred were made, but none appear to have flown operationally.*

**Specifications – Nakajima Ki-115 Tsurugi**

| | |
|---|---|
| Wingspan | 28 ft 2.5 in |
| Length | 28 ft 0.66 in |
| Maximum speed | 342 mph at 9,185 ft |
| Maximum take-off weight | 6,349 lb |
| Range | 746 miles |
| Armament | One bomb of up to 1,764 lb |
| Engine | One Nakajima Ha-35 radial piston engine, of 1,130 hp (other options available) |
| Crew | One |

# Japanese and German Experimentals

There is little doubt that the Second World War was the catalyst for the development of many aspects of aviation technology. The continuing development and practical employment of jet engines is the most conspicuous example of this, as was the continuing development of rocket propulsion. Rocket technology had its own major influences in the post-war years with the 'Space Race' between the Soviet Union and the United States. Nazi Germany in particular moved the boundaries forward in a number of key areas of aeronautics and propulsion in the later war years. These advances were stopped by the end of the Second World War and Germany's defeat, but if the war had continued after 1945, it is possible that the Luftwaffe would have had a number of interesting new aircraft types to put into service. Most of these would have been advanced jet-powered fighters and bombers. A large amount of mythology has developed in recent years over what the 'Luftwaffe 1946' would have looked like, with

several advanced combat aircraft in service if the war had continued after 1945. However, it is equally doubtful that the Germans would have been able to bring many of these programs to fruition, given the massive disruption of the German aircraft industry and infrastructure due to Allied bombing and losses of experienced pilots in combat.

In Japan too, some advanced designs were on the drawing boards, although some of these had strong German influences. Both the jet-powered Messerschmitt Me 262 and the rocket-powered Messerschmitt Me 163 described earlier made a great impression on the Japanese. In the case of the Me 163, a major program was initiated in Japan during late 1943 to recreate this rocket fighter for Japanese manufacture and operations. Supply of complete aircraft from Germany at that stage in the war was inconceivable due to the deteriorating war situations in both countries. Technical information on the Me 163 and its Walter rocket motor

*The Mitsubishi J8M1 Shusui was a remarkable joint Imperial Japanese Army-Navy project.*
*A fatal crash, and the end of World War Two, terminated the program.*

were therefore transported to Japan by submarine and flown the rest of the way. The Japanese copy of the Me 163 was designated J8M1 Shusui (Sword Stroke). In a prodigious feat of engineering the Japanese aircraft industry was able to produce initially unpowered glider copies of the Me 163, and eventually a fully-working rocket-powered copy. The first wooden glider (designated MXY8 Akikusa [Autumn Grass]) flew in December 1944, and

an unpowered prototype Shusui was towed into the air in January 1945. The Japanese suffered the same problems with volatile liquid rocket fuel as the Germans did, and many other difficulties had to be overcome before the first powered flight could be attempted on 7 July 1945. Unfortunately, the rocket motor malfunctioned and the aircraft crashed, killing its test pilot. Within weeks Japan surrendered, thus ending the whole project.

*An advanced fighter that was being developed in Japan during the late war period was the canard ('tail'-first) Kyushu J7W1 Shinden (Magnificent Lightning). It first flew in August 1945, several days before the war ended, and could have been an effective interceptor against American bombers with its nose-mounted cannons. A turbojet-powered J7W2 was in the planning stage.*

**Specifications (some estimated) – Mitsubishi J8M1 Shusui**

| | |
|---|---|
| Wingspan | 31 ft 2 in |
| Length | 19 ft 10 in |
| Maximum speed | 559 mph at 32,808 ft |
| Maximum take-off weight | 8,565 lb |
| Service ceiling | 39,370 ft |
| Armament | Two 30 mm cannons, one in each wing root |
| Engine | One Mitsubishi-consortium Ro.2 (KR-20) rocket motor, of 3,307 lb st |
| Crew | One |

# Commonwealth Aircraft

The spread of aviation around the world in the early years of the twentieth century saw many countries, large and small, develop their own indigenous aviation industries. In Australia, this came about due to military expediency during the 1930's, when rearmament in the face of the growing threat from Germany and Japan made the expansion of aviation forces a necessity. Hitherto Australia – formerly a part of the British Empire and by then of the British Commonwealth – had had its military aircraft supplied by Britain. In 1936, however, the Commonwealth Aircraft Corporation was established in Australia to create and build aircraft specially for the Australian armed forces. Initial plans were not ambitious and it was decided to base the first indigenous Australian type on an established and successful design. After some deliberation, the Australians obtained a license to build and develop a North American Aviation design, the NA-16, which was the first of the line of the soon-to-be-famous Texan/Harvard advanced trainer (described on pages 96 to 97). Two

pattern aircraft were duly supplied to Australia from America and the resulting Australian design, called the Commonwealth Wirraway, resembled the second of these, the rather more advanced NA-33. The first Wirraway flew on 27 March 1939 and eventually 755 of these two-seat single-engine aircraft were built. A general purpose aircraft type, Wirraways served as trainers in the Australian contribution to the large Empire Air Training Scheme, but many operated in more warlike roles as stop-gap fighters and light attack aircraft. Some served successfully as army co-operation aircraft especially during the bitter fighting against the invading Japanese in New Guinea. On 26 December 1942, a Wirraway shot down a Japanese Mitsubishi A6M fighter, a unique and unexpected air combat success.

The likelihood of very few supplies of modern warplanes being made available from hard-pressed Britain in the early war years forced the Australians into considerable improvisation. In addition to the production under license in Australia of some established

*The plucky little Commonwealth Boomerang was a successful Australian fighter and ground attack aircraft whose creation took only a matter of months from initial design to the completion of the first prototype. Sturdy and maneuverable, it was known as the 'Boomer' to the Australians.*

warplanes, such as the Bristol Beaufort, further Australian development of the Wirraway resulted in the creation of a neat single-seat fighter and attack aircraft, the Commonwealth Boomerang. The prototype of this Wirraway derivative first flew on 29 May 1942. Using as many Wirraway components as possible, but smaller overall than the Wirraway and designed for only one occupant, a total of 250 Boomerangs were built, production ceasing in early 1945. The Boomerang entered Royal Australian Air Force service in the latter half of 1942, entering combat in the spring and summer of 1943 and serving well into 1945.

The Commonwealth company also worked on a rather more ambitious warplane project during the war, the twin-engined Woomera light bomber and attack aircraft. The first example flew in September 1941 but extensive re-design led to a developed version which did not fly until July 1944 – by which time sufficient aircraft from the United States were available to make the project not worth contunuing.

*The twin-engined Commonwealth Woomera was an ambitious light bomber, ground attack and reconnaissance warplane project that was never produced.*

**Specifications – Commonwealth CA-12 Boomerang**

| | |
|---|---|
| Wingspan | 36 ft |
| Length | 25 ft 6 in |
| Maximum speed | 305 mph at 15,500 ft |
| Maximum take-off weight | 8,032 lb |
| Range | 930 miles |
| Service ceiling | 34,000 ft |
| Armament | Two 20 mm cannons, four 0.303 in (7.7 mm) machine guns, all wing-mounted |
| Engine | One Australian-built Pratt & Whitney R-1830-S3C4G Twin Wasp radial piston engine, of 1,200 hp |
| Crew | One |

# Focke-Wulf Fw 190D and Ta 152

The outstanding Focke-Wulf Fw 190 (see pages 274 to 277) was one of Germany's best combat aircraft throughout the Second World War. However, one of its shortcomings was a lack of real engine power at high altitudes, although the type's BMW 801 was a good performer lower down. A number of attempts were made to remedy this situation. One of these was to fit development examples of a turbo-charged BMW 801 into the Fw 190 airframe under the Fw 190C program, a project aircraft (the Fw 190V18) being used for this purpose. However, the science of turbo-charging engines was not so advanced in Germany and this plan failed.

With the demise of this and other projects, Focke-Wulf turned to a completely different engine type instead. This was the comparatively new Junkers Jumo 213 inline, which was really developed as a high-perform-

ance engine for bombers, but which turned out to be a suitable engine for fighter applications as well. Development Fw 190s with longer fuselages were flown with the Junkers Jumo 213 from 1943, and this work led to a new Fw 190 series, the Fw 190D. This version was planned in a number of specific models for various tasks, but the first to enter production, during 1944, was the Fw 190D-9. Although Luftwaffe pilots were at first sceptical of this new fighter with its bomber engine, in fact the 'Dora-9' turned out to be an exceptional combat aircraft – probably the only German piston-engined fighter to give Luftwaffe pilots a sporting chance at altitude against American fighters like the P-51 Mustang. The Fw 190D-9 entered service in the autumn of 1944 and was an immediate success. Approximately 700 were made in several different manufacturing locations by Germany's

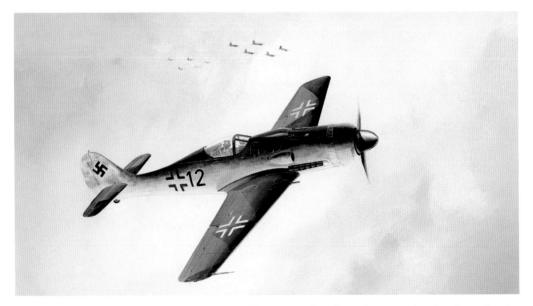

*A rather evocative painting of a lone Focke-Wulf Fw 190D-9 with an American bomber formation in the background. When it entered service in the autumn of 1944, the Fw 190D-9 was Germany's best front-line piston-engined fighter, but it was 'too little, too late' to turn the tide for the Germans – and too many good pilots had already been lost in combat by then.*

increasingly fragmented aircraft industry before the war ended (some of these might have been 'recycled' earlier Fw 190s, rebuilt). Some were used as protection fighters for the Messerschmitt Me 262 jet fighter during take-off and landing when the jets were particularly vulnerable to being shot down. Several other D-series versions were also built, including the Fw 190D-11 and Fw 190D-13 fighters. Continuing development work led to a related but in effect new fighter, the Ta 152 (Ta = Kurt Tank, its chief designer and inspira-

tion). Powered by a Jumo 213E-series engine, the Ta 152 was a stretched, cleaned-up, long-wingspan derivative of the Fw 190. Ambitious plans existed at the end of the war for several production series, but only a small number of Ta 152H were built before the war ended. Little more than a handful of these excellent high-altitude fighters flew operationally.

*The Fw 190D-9 was Germany's best single-engine fighter of the late war period and it was a match for the best of the Allied fighters then available. Despite its round cowling, it was powered by an inline engine.*

**Specifications – Focke-Wulf Fw 190D-9**

| | |
|---|---|
| Wingspan | 34 ft 5.5 in |
| Length | 33 ft 5.25 in |
| Maximum speed | 426 mph at 21,653 ft |
| Maximum take-off weight | 10,670 lb |
| Range | 519 miles |
| Service ceiling | 43,307 ft |
| Armament | Two 13 mm (0.51 in) forward-firing machine guns in upper forward fuselage, two 20 mm cannons in wing roots |
| Engine | One Junkers Jumo 213A-1 inline piston engine, of 1,770 hp |
| Crew | One |

# Fiat G.55 Centauro

Often regarded as Italy's finest combat aircraft of the World War Two period, the Fiat G.55 Centauro (Centaur) was the result of an evolutionary process in Italian fighter design. For years, Italy's fighter pilots preferred the open cockpit, biplane fighter layout as epitomised by the Fiat C.R.42 (see pages 94 to 95).

By the start of Italy's involvement in World War Two during June 1940, a more up-to-date generation of fighters such as the Fiat G.50 and Macchi C.200, were coming into prominence. These represented the first generation of Italian fighter design of the late 1930's and Second World War period. A second generation followed, exemplified by such types as the Macchi C.202 Folgore, which were interim types based on existing designs whose performance was improved by the addition of German DB 601 inline engines. By 1941, the Italian air ministry was looking to create a new generation of high performance fighters, based on the most

advanced Italian design layouts but with the best-available German inline engines. The Fiat G.55, Reggiane Re.2005 Sagittario and Macchi C.205 Veltro, were the resulting members of this third generation of wartime Italian fighters. In fact, Fiat had been starting to examine modern layouts from around 1939, and had initially intended to place a DB 601 inline engine into the G.50 airframe, but soon realized that a much more modern aerodynamically refined airframe was needed. This led to the G.55, the prototype of which first flew on 30 April 1942. At once, the new design showed promise and large production orders followed for the G.55, powered by a Fiat licence-built copy of the German DB 605 engine. A pre-production batch of 12 examples was to have been followed by substantial production, but by the time of the Italian armistice in September 1943, only 12 (possibly several more) production aircraft had reached the

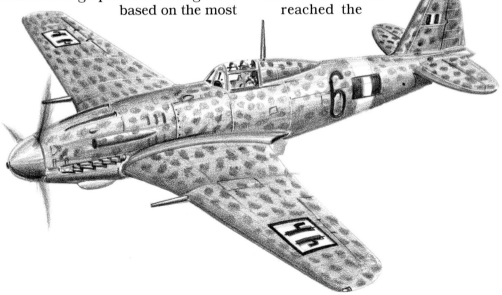

*A Fiat G.55 I Series in A.N.R. markings. The G.55 was a worthy opponent of Allied fighters and was even admired by the Germans – beating German fighters in a fly-off on one occasion.*

Regia Aeronautica. Following Italy's capitulation the northern Italian forces remained loyal to the Germans and Fiat's factories in the north continued to produce the G.55 for the pro-German A.N.R. (Aeronautica Nazionale Repubblicana). Some 274 were built in this second stage, and the Germans were highly complimentary of the type, although eventually forcing the Italians to begin standardization on the Messerschmitt Bf 109. However, Fiat clandestinely continued manufacture, re-establishing itself in the world of post-war production. The Italian aircraft industry picked up after the war ended, and the G.55 (now called G.55A) was used as an advanced trainer for the new Italian air force (A.M.I.). A two-seat version (G.55B) was also developed and export sales were made – particularly to Argentina. Some ex-Argentine aircraft were later flown by Egypt against Israeli-operated Spitfires. A further development was the Rolls-Royce Merlin-powered Fiat G.59 single and two-seater of the later 1940's.

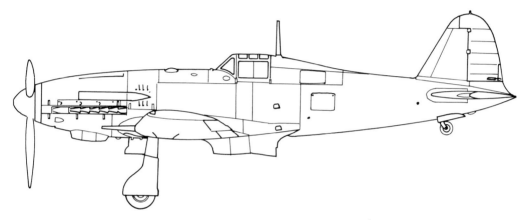

*The Fiat G.55 featured all-metal construction and fabric-covered control surfaces. Early aircraft had four machine guns mounted in the forward fuselage, but production examples had two, plus one engine-mounted and two wing-mounted cannons. A DB 603A-engined prototype was flown as the Fiat G.56*

**Specifications – Fiat G.55 (I Series)**

| | |
|---|---|
| Wingspan | 38 ft 10.5 in |
| Length | 30 ft 8.75 in |
| Maximum speed | 385 mph at 26,247 ft |
| Maximum take-off weight | 8,201 lb |
| Range | 652 miles |
| Service ceiling | 42,651 ft |
| Armament | One engine-mounted 20 mm cannon, two wing-mounted 20 mm cannons, two 12.7 mm (0.5 in) machine guns in upper forward fuselage, all fixed forward-firing, plus provision for a small bomb beneath each wing |
| Engine | One Fiat RA.1050 RC.58 Tifone (licence-built Daimler Benz DB 605A) inline piston engine, of 1,475 hp |
| Crew | One |

# Junkers Ju 288 and Ju 388

The so-called 'Bomber B' development program was initiated in 1939 to give the Luftwaffe a worthy successor to the Junkers Ju 88 and Heinkel He 111 medium bombers (even though the Ju 88 had barely had time to prove its worth). It would also provide an advanced and highly capable tactical aircraft to complement the Heinkel He 177 'Bomber A' heavy bomber. Five different manufacturers were contenders in the 'Bomber B' program. One of these was Junkers with the Ju 288, which was an advanced high-altitude derivative of the Junkers Ju 88. In any event, none of these five designs eventually reached operational status. There were various technical reasons for this, together with the development problems that plagued the engines intended for the aircraft of this project. However, as a parallel program Junkers had been working on its own less ambitious potential successor to the Ju 88, and this eventually became the Ju 188 (see pages 212 to 213).

The first prototype aircraft of the Junkers Ju 288 flew on 29 November 1940, and a long series of prototypes was planned, reflecting a number of intended specific production layouts and roles. The bomber would have been pressurized for high-altitude flight, but Junkers' work was dogged with problems and the whole 'Bomber B' program was abandoned in mid-1943. Twenty-two prototype/development Ju 288 were built. Although the Ju 288 did not succeed, further work by Junkers on the Ju 188 as a high altitude aircraft led to the Ju 388. Under the so-called 'Hubertus Program,' development of this high altitude aircraft pressed onwards in three main versions – the Ju 388J heavy fighter and night fighter (to combat possible raids on Germany by Boeing B-29 Superfortress bombers, which never took place); the Ju 388K bomber; and the Ju 388L reconnaissance aircraft.

Although it generally resembled the Ju 88, the Ju 388 was an advanced aircraft with two important features – a pressurized cabin for high altitude flight, and turbo-supercharged engines for good performance even at high altitude. It was the only German aircraft of the war to see actual service that had this turbo-supercharging. The Ju 388L was the most advanced of the three versions, when the decision to concentrate on jets and single-engine fighters late in 1944 ended the project. Approximately 47 Ju 388L were made as well as a small number of prototype/development aircraft of the other two, and possibly some pre-pro-

*The Junkers Ju 288 was an ambitious project that never came to fruition.*
*In production form the type would have eventually replaced the Ju 88 and other medium bombers.*

duction and early production examples. Several Ju 388L were flown by experimental/evaluation Luftwaffe organizations, this being the closest that any came to front-line operational units. Further development could have led to the magnificent Junkers Ju 488 four-engined strategic bomber, but this project too was halted.

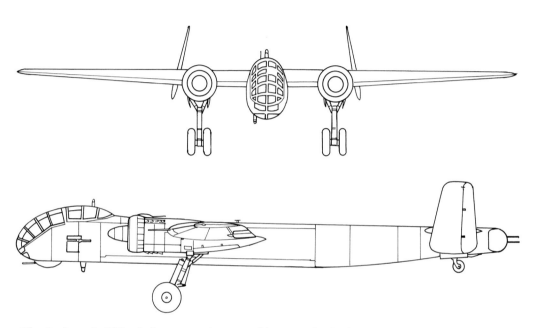

*The Junkers Ju 288 only bore a passing resemblance to the Junkers Ju 88. The forward fuselage contained a pressurized cabin and twin tail units were introduced together with other features like a remotely-controlled tail gun position on some of the planned versions.*

**Specifications (projected) – Junkers Ju 288A**

| | |
|---|---|
| Wingspan | 72 ft 2 in |
| Length | 54 ft 5.5 in |
| Maximum speed | 401 mph at 19,685 ft |
| Maximum take-off weight | 38,140 lb |
| Range | 2,392 miles |
| Service ceiling | 33,793 ft |
| Armament | Two 13 mm (0.51 in) machine guns in remotely-controlled turrets, plus other possible weapon locations, up to 6,614 lb of bombs |
| Engine | Two Junkers Jumo 222A/B inline piston engines, of 2,000 hp each |
| Crew | Three |

# Messerschmitt Me 262

Of all the technological advances that came to the fore during World War Two, one of the most important without doubt, was the employment of jet propulsion in front-line combat aircraft. Both Germany and Britain were at the forefront of this significant line of development. Both countries were able to design and build viable jet-powered fighter aircraft that were in service by the end of the war.

Germany's direct contemporary of Britain's Gloster Meteor (see pages 322 to 323) was the Messerschmitt Me 262, arguably a more advanced design with its swept-back wings and axial-flow turbojet engines – both forerunners of post-war developments. The Me 262 also had a rival in Germany, the Heinkel He 280 twin-jet fighter, but this less advanced type was officially cancelled in 1943. The Me 262 grew out of Messerschmitt's own design studies of the late 1930's and subsequent official requirements, but was chronically delayed by technological considerations and engine development problems. The first aircraft

did not feature the production Me 262's tricycle undercarriage, instead having a tailwheel undercarriage layout. Due to delays with its intended jet engines, the first Me 262V1 aircraft initially flew with a Junkers Jumo 210 piston engine in its nose during April 1941. The first flight with Junkers Jumo 004 axial-flow turbojets was made by the third aircraft (the Me 262V3) on 18 July 1942 – much earlier than the first Gloster Meteor flight. A large amount of testing and development work was duly carried out by a series of prototype and trial aircraft, during which the tricycle undercarriage layout was adopted. Production Me 262s started to be built in quantity during 1944. Although the aircraft was originally intended as a fighter, the Nazi leader Adolf Hitler insisted on it being developed as a fast bomber, resulting in many further delays. Nevertheless, initial deliveries of fighter Me 262s were made to an evaluation and trials unit and this took the Me 262 into

*This is what an operational Messerschmitt Me 262A-1a fighter would have looked like. The type was the first jet fighter ever to fire its guns in combat, and was principally involved in defending German airspace against American bombers.*

combat in July 1944 – the first jet fighter ever to fly in combat, although the Meteor became operational in a regular unit sooner than the Me 262 (at roughly that time). The basic fighter Me 262 was the Me 262A-1a, built in several versions including a fighter-bomber. Hitler's much-loved fast bomber was the Me 262A-2a, and the A-5a was a reconnaissance version. The two-seat Me 262B-1a was a trainer, later developed into the B-2a radar-equipped night fighter. Some of these versions saw combat, and revealed how significant a warplane the Me 262 really was. However, despite its speed and advanced design the Me 262 was vulnerable at take-off and landing, and to defend it local airfield defence was handled by Focke-Wulf Fw 190D fighters. It is sometimes claimed that 1,433 Me 262s of all types were built, but this is hard to verify. Post-war, captured Me 262s were of great interest to the Allies for evaluation. In post-war Czechoslovakia, the type underwent limited production from stocks of parts by Avia, as the S-92 single-seater and CS-92 two seater.

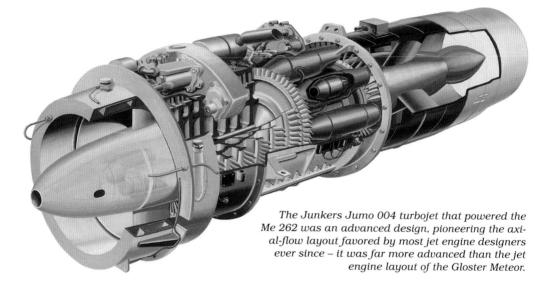

*The Junkers Jumo 004 turbojet that powered the Me 262 was an advanced design, pioneering the axial-flow layout favored by most jet engine designers ever since – it was far more advanced than the jet engine layout of the Gloster Meteor.*

**Specifications – Messerschmitt Me 262A-1a**

| | |
|---|---|
| Wingspan | 41 ft 2.5 in |
| Length | 34 ft 9.25 in |
| Maximum speed | 540.6 mph at 19,685 ft |
| Maximum take-off weight | 14,052 lb |
| Range | 441 miles plus |
| Service ceiling | 38,714 ft |
| Armament | Four 30 mm cannons fixed forward-firing in the forward fuselage |
| Engine | Two Junkers Jumo 004B-1 or -2 turbojet engines, of 1,984 lb st each |
| Crew | One |

# Consolidated Coronado

From an age when maritime patrol was performed by large, long-range flying-boats, one of the most impressive of its type was the Consolidated Coronado. Derived from a 1935 U.S. Navy requirement for a long-range ocean reconnaissance flying-boat, the prototype XPB2Y-1 first flew on 17 December 1937. It was produced by Consolidated, a company that was already conversant with maritime aircraft designs and whose PBY Catalina (see pages 232 to 233) won great fame in World War Two. The Coronado was designed to complement the Catalina by providing a longer range and a larger offensive payload compared to the smaller Catalina, but the design ran into problems. These mainly concerned lateral stability in flight, together with the design of the lower hull (fuselage), and a result of this was a complete tailplane redesign plus fuselage revisions. The resulting vertical tails eventually resembled those of Consolidated's famous bomber design, the B-24 Liberator (see pages 228 to 231). These redesigns did not adversely affect the timing of the Coronado program as the U.S. Navy was short of funds at that time and procurement of the type was slow. Eventually in March 1939, six of the first production model (the PB2Y-2) were ordered and delivered in late 1940. The major production version was the PB2Y-3; 210 of these were ordered. The Coronado was equivalent to the Royal Air Force's

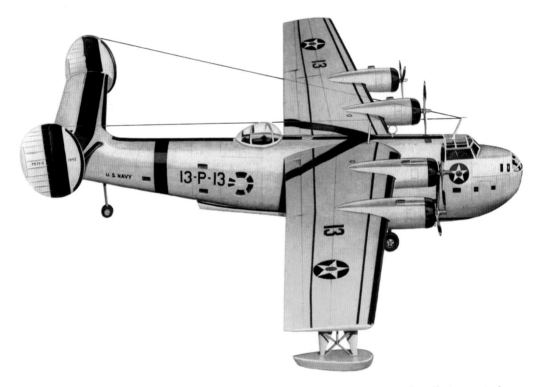

*This colorful Consolidated PB2Y-2 Coronado is from the U.S. Navy squadron that operated this initial mark of Coronado, VP-13. The PB2Y-2 in effect served as a service-test version for the main production Coronado, the PB2Y-3. It is shown here in the colorful period of U.S. Navy markings just prior to American entry into World War Two.*

Short Sunderland (see pages 76 to 77), and it featured wing-tip stabilizing floats that retracted upwards in flight to make wingtips – exactly as on the Catalina. Unlike both the Catalina and Sunderland, however, the Coronado was not used widely for maritime patrol, although some were fitted with air-to-surface vessel (ASV) radar. Later in the war, many were employed as long-range transports primarily for cargo. Ten were supplied to Britain, most later serving with the RAF's Transport Command on freight services. Eventually several of the U.S. Navy's Coronados were specially-converted for casualty evacuation, while others served as dedicated transports. This was something of a waste for an aircraft with such excellent range potential, but the Coronado's long-range maritime patrol role was increasingly taken over by shore-based U.S. Navy PB4Y Liberators and Privateers. Production ceased in 1943.

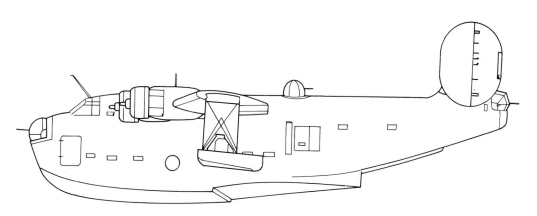

*The PB2Y-3 illustrated here was of all-metal structure with fabric covering the control surfaces. The Coronado was a big flying-boat that never fully fulfilled its primary role of long-range maritime patrol.*

## Specifications – Consolidated PB2Y-3 Coronado

| | |
|---|---|
| Wingspan | 115 ft |
| Length | 79 ft 3 in |
| Maximum speed | 223 mph at 20,000 ft |
| Maximum take-off weight | 68,000 lb |
| Range | approximately 2,370 miles |
| Service ceiling | 20,500 ft |
| Armament | Eight 0.5 in (12.7 mm) machine guns in various turrets and flexible mounts, up to 12,000 lb of bombs or depth charges (rarely carried) |
| Engine | Four Pratt & Whitney R-1830-88 Twin Wasp radial piston engines, of 1,200 hp each |
| Crew | Nine or ten |

# V1 and V2

On 13 June 1944, London was hit by the first of over 2,400 V1 flying bombs, which were small cruise missiles powered by a simple pulse jet. While the destruction created heralded a new phase of aerial warfare, for the Germans it was only the first of a range of intended Vergeltungswaffe (Revenge or Reprisal Weapons). Since mid-1942, the German company Fieseler had been working on the Fi 103 pilotless aircraft program. The first unpowered test example was dropped from a Focke-Wulf Fw 200 in December 1942, with a powered launch accomplished at the Peenemünde-West experimental establishment from a launch ramp. In July 1943, a special unit was set up to train firing crews and to work out operational usage of the Luftwaffe's new weapon. Approximately 29,000 examples were to be built by Fieseler, Volkswagen at Fallersleben and in the mines at Mittelwerke near Nordhausen by slave labor. Officially called the Fieseler Fi 103, the title V1 was also used for the weapon. The operational intention was to saturate the

Allies' air defences with multiple launches of V1s, but in the event the number of launches did not meet requirements. Once they were identified by aerial reconnaissance, the Allies bombed the launch ramps at every opportunity and of the over 8,000 V1s launched at London, just under 70% were destroyed or crashed before reaching their target. Some 1,200 were air-launched from Heinkel He 111H-22s, but these carrier aircraft proved to be vulnerable to Allied fighters. As well as London, many were launched at the port of Antwerp in Belgium.

The second Vergeltungswaffe weapon was the German army's A-4 (V2) surface-to-surface ballistic missile, the culmination of years of research into rocket flight by Werner von Braun and other German pioneers. The first test flight in mid-1942 was unsuccessful, but in late 1942, a completely successful demonstration of the missile took place. Hitler ordered the A-4 into production, the plan being to produce a mobile firing unit able to launch mis-

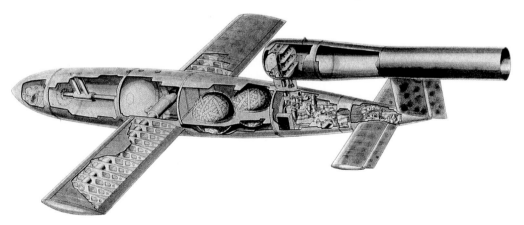

*Simplicity itself, the Fieseler Fi 103 (V1) was designed to be mass-produced and was intended to be made of mixed metal and wood. After its launch from a catapult-equipped ramp, the V1's on-board gyroscope fed signals to the craft's elevators and rudder to control attitude and direction, and when a pre-set distance had been flown the power plant was cut out, creating a terminal dive.*

siles and then move on before being attacked. Production started at a new plant south of Peenemünde in late 1943, but was eventually dwarfed by the output of the Mittelwerke mines. Several thousand A-4s were built. The first two operational A-4s were launched in Paris on 6 September 1944 (although unsuccessfully), before England was targeted with the first of over one thousand three hundred missiles two days later. Antwerp was another A-4 target, with around 1,600 fired at it by 27 March 1945. Unlike the noisy Fi 103, there was no warning of the A-4 because it was supersonic – its sound arrived after it had hit. Operationally the A-4 had little effect on the conduct of the war, but it could have proved far more potent if the ground war had not continued to be successfully pursued by the Allies. The rocket technology of the V2 provided the post-war basis for all subsequent ballistic missiles developed for both military and space exploration tasks.

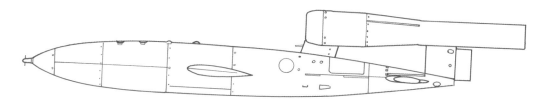

*A weapon with many names. The Fieseler Fi 103 'flying bomb' was also called the V1, FZG 76, and was nicknamed 'Doodlebug' and 'Buzz Bomb.' Whatever you wanted to call it, the unwelcome arrival of one of these weapons brought great destruction and loss of civilian life.*

**Specifications – Fieseler Fi 103 (V1)**

| | |
|---|---|
| Wingspan | 17 ft 4.75 in |
| Length | 25 ft 11 in |
| Maximum speed | 401 mph at sea level |
| Maximum take-off weight | 4,806 lb |
| Range | approximately 149 miles depending on cut-out system |
| Armament | 1,874 lb of various explosives in the fuselage |
| Engine | One Argus As 109-014 pulse jet, of 600 lb st |
| Crew | None; one in Reichenberg IV manned version |

# 'Mistel' Composite Aircraft

The German series of 'Mistel' (Mistletoe) composite aircraft was conceived to provide a means of aiming a large warhead at a specific target, achieving this by the odd combination of two aircraft joined together. The concept involved the two taking off together, the upper (manned) element guiding the combination towards the target and then detaching and flying away having aimed the lower (unmanned) part at the target.

The idea of a two-aircraft combination was not new, and had been tried out long before the war started. The main application during the 1930's was the Short-Mayo Composite commercial aircraft (covered in Volume 1 of *The Complete Encyclopedia of Flight*). In that case, a large flying-boat (the 'Maia') was the lower component, and the seaplane 'Mercury' was mounted on top. The 'Maia' contributed the power to get the two combined aircraft into the air and start the journey, with the upper 'Mercury' eventually taking off from atop the lower so that it could continue the journey using its own hitherto untouched fuel supply. This combination worked well, and considerably extended the range of the 'Mercury,' but such experiments were ended with the start of World War Two

In Germany the concept had also been tried out by the glider and sailplane specialists D.F.S., using light aircraft above a D.F.S. 230 glider. This led to having a Messerschmitt Bf 109 attached above a similar glider (see pages 204 to 209). Official interest led to experiments employing a Bf 109F mounted above a Junkers Ju 88A-4 bomber, and this led to a series of 'Mistel' combinations initially called 'Beethoven.' At first the Ju 88 retained the normal manned nose/cockpit while the concept was tested and for training, but for operations the Ju 88's normal nose was removed and replaced by a large warhead, with a long detonation fuse projecting from the new nose. The bomber would then of course be unmanned, all control for take-off and targeting coming from the pilot of the fighter attached above. Initial operational 'Mistel' combinations were the Mistel 1 with a Bf 109F-4 above a Ju 88A, but later combinations used Ju 88 night fighters, similarly unmanned and warhead-equipped. To this was

*Later operational 'Mistel' combinations invariably featured a Focke-Wulf Fw 190 as the upper part of the combination, and an unmanned explosive-equipped Junkers Ju 88 as the lower component. Illustrated is a typical Mistel 2, with an Fw 190A-8 above and a warhead-armed Ju 88G below.*

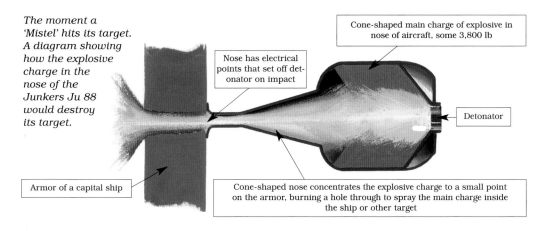

*The moment a 'Mistel' hits its target. A diagram showing how the explosive charge in the nose of the Junkers Ju 88 would destroy its target.*

Cone-shaped main charge of explosive in nose of aircraft, some 3,800 lb

Nose has electrical points that set off detonator on impact

Detonator

Armor of a capital ship

Cone-shaped nose concentrates the explosive charge to a small point on the armor, burning a hole through to spray the main charge inside the ship or other target

added the Focke-Wulf Fw 190 as the upper component, which came into the program later in 1944. This created the Mistel 2 series of combinations. At one stage, the idea was to use the Heinkel He 177 as the lower component, as there were many redundant He 177 on German airfields by late 1944 as the German bomber force became increasingly superfluous. The lumbering and heavy 'Mistel', with a top speed of only some 236 mph, first went into action just after D-Day in June 1944, when Mistel 1 combinations were used against Allied shipping off the French coast. Results were indifferent and flights had to be increasingly made at night due to overwhelming daytime Allied air superiority. There was a plan to attack the British naval base at Scapa Flow in early 1945 from Denmark, but this plan was abandoned, as was a long-range strike on Russian power plants. The final weeks of the war saw 'Mistel' combinations in action against road and river bridges to stop Russian advances on the Eastern Front. In the 'Witches' Dance' operations in April 1945, several road bridges were attacked by Fw 190/Ju 88 combinations with a fighter escort and guided by Junkers Ju 188 pathfinders. Overall, however, the 'Mistel' did not deliver the spectacular results expected of it, and further advanced plans for using jet-powered aircraft did not materialise – the concept has never been used in warfare since.

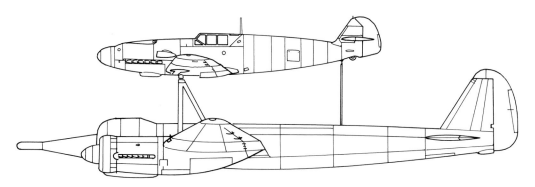

*A Mistel 1 combination, with a warhead-armed Junkers Ju 88A-4 as the lower part, and a Messerschmitt Bf 109F as the upper component of the composite.*

# Boeing B-29 Superfortress

The Second World War was ended by a single weapon delivered by a single aircraft type. On 6 August and 9 August, 1945, two atomic bombs were dropped on Japan, leading directly to the Japanese surrender several days later and the final end to the world's greatest and most devastating conflict. The means of delivery of the two atomic bombs was a large bomber aircraft that had a profound effect on the course of world history – the Boeing B-29 Superfortress. This larger-than-life bomber was every bit a record-breaker at the time of its operational debut in 1944. During just over a year of operational deployment, the B-29 re-wrote the manual on aerial bombing. Hitherto the heavy bomber had been of the same class and size of bombers as Britain's Avro Lancaster or the American B-17 Flying Fortress and B-24 Liberator. The B-29 tore up that set of accepted specifications, which had only existed for several, years – with the operational debut of such types as the B-24 and Lancaster – and brought the heavy bomber classification up several notches in terms of standard bomb-carrying capability

and performance. Yet the B-29 was developed near the end of the era of piston-engined bomber aircraft and several years after World War Two ended, even the ground-breaking B-29 was replaced by jet-powered bombers of considerably higher capability.

The B-29 was the outcome of design studies that commenced in the later 1930's to find a very long range bomber to augment the shorter range heavy bombers such as the B-17 Flying Fortress then being developed. Three prototypes of Boeing's design proposals were ordered and the first of these flew on 21 September 1942. By then substantial orders had already been placed, the United States having joined the war the previous December and having recognized the necessity for a very long-range bomber. Initial deliveries began in 1943 and B-29 production took place at five factories by three companies – Boeing, Martin and Bell. There were differences in detail between production aircraft from these companies. The Bell-built B-29B had reduced armament and was the fastest of the various production marks. A reconnaissance version

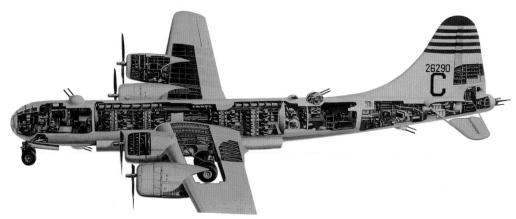

*The all-metal Boeing B-29 was aptly named Superfortress. All production B-29s were basically the same except for detail differences. The Boeing Renton plant's B-29A had slightly increased wing span.*

*Arguably the most famous single aircraft in history is the 'Enola Gay,' the B-29 that dropped the atomic bomb on Hiroshima on 6 August 1945.*

was designated F-13 (later RB-29). A variety of other specialist versions included a weather reconnaissance WB-29 derivative, and the air-drop lifeboat-carrying SB-29 rescue aircraft. The B-29 championed several technical steps forward in warplane design and technology. These included cabin pressurization, and the use of remote-controlled gun turrets, periscopically sighted by gunners seated within the fuselage away from the turrets themselves.

In late 1943, the decision was taken to use the B-29 exclusively against the Japanese. The first units of the new U.S. Twentieth Army Air Force to be equipped with the B-29 were deployed to bases in India and China in the spring of 1944. They included the 444th and 468th Bomb Groups. A major air supply bridge over the Himalayas (the 'Hump') needed to be maintained to keep these aircraft in the air from Chinese bases. The first combat mission was flown on 5 June

1944 against Bangkok in Japanese-held Thailand. Attacks on the Japanese home islands began on 15 June, the India-based bombers staging to a Chinese airfield to make the raid. The establishment of operational bases in the newly-captured Marianas islands in the Pacific Ocean in 1944 brought the B-29s much closer to Japan, and a general redeployment began from bases in India and China. New B-29 units also moved in directly to the Pacific from the U.S. This development

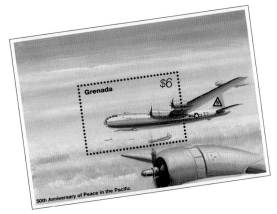

307

# Boeing B-29 Superfortress *continued*

*The co-pilot's position in the cockpit of the preserved B-29 named 'Fifi.' The normal B-29 crew complement was ten, but the B-29A could carry eleven (Photo: John Batchelor).*

was soon followed by a complete revision of tactics. Previously, the B-29s had usually been directed onto specific industrial targets. This policy was advocated by Army Air Force General Haywood S. Hansell. However, accuracy was difficult to achieve in some cases, and with Hansell's removal and replacement by General Curtis LeMay, the B-29s were subsequently sent out principally on devastating large-scale low altitude night incendiary area attacks on civilian areas in Japan's principal cities and some smaller ones. This alone, however, was

apparently not enough to break the will or the fighting spirit of the Japanese. The B-29s that dropped the atomic bombs on the Japanese cities of Hiroshima and Nagasaki on 6 and 9 August 1945, 'Enola Gay' and 'Bockscar' respectively, were specially-configured, prepared and assigned to the 509th Composite Group. Under the code-name of the 'Manhattan Project,' the development of atomic weapons had been given top priority by the Americans. After much experimentation, the first-ever atomic test blast took place in the New Mexico desert in July 1945. The only Allied aircraft capable of carrying the resulting atomic bomb over the distances required was the B-29. In dropping the two atomic bombs in August 1945, the B-29 was prominently and permanently written into the pages of history.

The B-29 continued to be the strategic bomber mainstay of the U.S. Army Air Force after the war, and production continued into 1946. B-29 production reached 3,960

*Currently the only flyable B-29 in the world is 'Fifi' of the Commemorative Air Force in the United States. This aircraft is one of the few survivors of the B-29 line and is a favorite at air shows. (Photo: John Batchelor).*

*Preserved after World War Two, the famous atomic bomber 'Enola Gay' remained in this dismantled condition for many years. It was recently restored and reassembled and is now on display at a new facility of the National Air and Space Museum in the United States at a Washington, D.C. airport.*
*(Photo: John Batchelor).*

including the prototypes – 2,756 by Boeing, 536 by Martin, and 668 by Bell. The independent U.S. Air Force was created in 1947 and the B-29 was its first strategic bomber. The B-29 was soon at war again, seeing almost continual action during the three years of the Korean War from 1950 to 1953. Here it came up against jet fighters (Chinese and North Korean-operated MiG-15s), and suffered significant losses on a number of occasions, but it also became an important asset in the United Nations forces deployed to the defence of what became South Korea. Further development led to the B-50, in essence a B-29 with its piston engines augmented by jet engines. The B-29 was also operated in important numbers by Britain, whose RAF flew over eighty of the type from 1950 under the name Washington.

**Specifications – Boeing B-29A Superfortress**

| | |
|---|---|
| Wingspan | 142 ft 3 in |
| Length | 99 ft |
| Maximum speed | 357 mph at 25,000 ft |
| Maximum take-off weight | 135,000 lb |
| Range | up to 4,000 miles |
| Service ceiling | 33,000 ft |
| Armament | Twelve 0.5 in (12.7 mm) machine guns in remote-control turrets, one 20 mm cannon in tail, up to 20,000 lb of bombs |
| Engine | Four Wright R-3350-23A Cyclone radial piston engines, of 2,200 hp each |
| Crew | Ten or eleven |

# Sikorsky Helicopters

The evolution of the helicopter was a long and rather painful process that took much longer than the measures necessary to create viable man-carrying aircraft. The pioneering rotary-wing efforts of a number of individuals in several countries are covered in Volume 1 of *The Complete Encyclopedia of Flight*. Suffice to say that what is often regarded as the first technically successful helicopter (although it looked very different to today's sleek and refined helicopters) was the German Focke-Achgelis Fa 61 of 1936. Focke-Achgelis and Flettner in Germany continued this pioneering work. However, in the United States, significant development work was also taking place. A number of companies were involved in this process, but by far the most important was the progress made by Igor Sikorsky.

Born in Russia, Sikorsky emigrated to the United States in 1917. His pre – World War One helicopters were failures, so he moved on to achieve a fair amount of success in aircraft design, before returning to helicopter work in the 1930's. It was Sikorsky as much as anyone who finally

solved several of the continuing problems associated with vertical take-off and landing, coupled with successful rotor-borne flight. As a part of United Aircraft Corporation, Sikorsky designed and built the very important experimental VS-300 – often seen as the father of all modern helicopters. It first flew untethered in May 1940, and was used to solve several of the difficulties of helicopter flight, including the problem of torque from the main rotor, by the eventual use of a single vertically-mounted tail rotor. This at last allowed practical helicopters to be built and official interest led to the development of the VS-316, which in military prototype form was known as the XR-4. It first flew on 14 January 1942, and successful development led to its production as the world's first mass-produced military helicopter, the R-4 series. Built for the U.S. Army Air Force, the U.S. Navy and Coast Guard (as the HNS-1), and for Britain as the Hoverfly Mk.I (52 examples), the R-4 entered operational service in early 1944 during a combat evaluation in Burma with British and American forces fighting the Japanese. Used mainly for liaison and casu-

*Sikorsky continually refined his helicopter experiments in the late 1930's and early 1940's, the VS-300 providing the basis for the R-4 series.*

*The pontoon-equipped Sikorsky XR-4 seen making a landing aboard a specially-built landing pad mounted on the tanker S.S. Bunker Hill in May 1943. Early German Flettner helicopters also flew from ships (Photo: U.S. Army Air Force).*

alty evacuation, the type nonetheless carried out the first-ever combat rescue behind enemy lines in April 1944. The R-4 also pioneered operations from the decks of ships and further development led to the R-6 series (Hoverfly Mk.II), which used the moving parts of the R-4 but in a more streamlined fuselage. Together the R-4 and R-6 marked the start of modern helicopter operations.

*This Sikorsky YR-4B shows the distinguishing features of the type, including its steel tube fabric-covered fuselage and mixed-construction main rotors with fabric-covering.*

### Specifications – Sikorsky R-4B

| | |
|---|---|
| Main Rotor Diameter | 38 ft |
| Fuselage Length | 35 ft 5 in |
| Maximum speed | 81 mph at sea level |
| Maximum take-off weight | 2,535 lb |
| Range | 230 miles |
| Service ceiling | 8,000 ft |
| Armament | Provision on some aircraft for small bomb load or depth charge |
| Engine | One Warner R-550-3 radial piston engine, of 200 hp |
| Crew | Two |

# Douglas DC-4 and C-54

During the 1930's, the Douglas Aircraft Company of Santa Monica, California, came to the fore as one of the world's premier producers of commercial passenger aircraft. This reputation was sealed for all time with the Douglas DC-3 (DC = Douglas Commercial), which gained great fame in the military transport role as the C-47. The DC-3 was a twin-engined transport, and Douglas next looked to create a larger, four-engined passenger aircraft with greater capacity and range. The result was the DC-4, which first flew in June 1938 as the DC-4E, powered by four recently-developed Pratt & Whitney R-2180 Twin Hornet radial engines.

At first this design was not a success, despite having such advanced (for its day) features as passenger cabin pressurization, and despite the consider-

able interest shown in the design by major airlines such as United Air Lines. Re-design led to a slightly smaller DC-4A configuration, with problems like the cabin pressurization solved, and the type was at once ordered in quantity by several commercial airlines in 1940.

The DC-4 also had obvious potential as a military transport. With the American entry into World War Two following the Japanese attack on Pearl Harbor in December 1941, the whole DC-4 program was taken over by the military and henceforth the DC-4 was produced for the U.S. Army Air Force as the C-54, and U.S. Navy as the R5D. The first C-54 production aircraft started to enter service from May and July 1942 at the start of a considerable line of military transport versions. The civil airliner was planned to accommodate 42 passengers but the military models were designed for 26 passengers, or later 49 troops in the longer-range C-54B. A special VC-54C was made as a V.I.P. Presidential transport, and similarly a special 'one-off' was fitted out for V.I.P. use by Britain's Prime Minister Winston Churchill. The C-54 and R5D in various versions

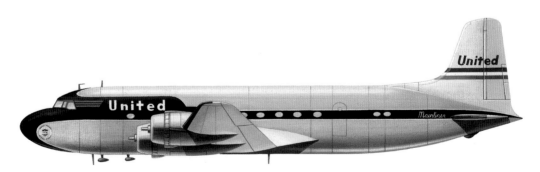

*The Douglas DC-4/C-54 line of civil and military transports represented a further stage in the development of long-range passenger services around the world.*

went on to serve worldwide during the war, with over one thousand military examples built – some 839 were still in service at the end of the war. Operations included the hazardous airlift from Indian airfields over the Himalayas (the famous transport route over the 'Hump') to U.S. bases in China fighting against the Japanese. The final production model was the C-54G of 1945 and the type continued in military service in various roles after the war ended. Post-war service included participation in the Berlin Air Lift of 1949 to 1950. Production of civil DC-4s resumed after the war (as the DC-4-1009) and 79 of these were made – augmented by the release to the civil market of many former mili-

tary C-54s. Further development led to the DC-6 post-war line of transports, while conversion by Aviation Traders in Britain created the Carvair transport, of which 21 were built.

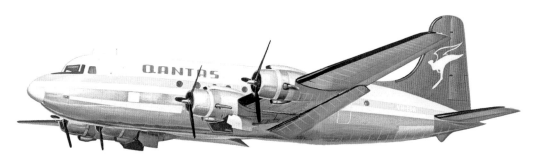

*Bridging the gap between military transport operations in World War Two and civil flying post-war was the Douglas DC-4/C-54 line. This particular aircraft, registration VH-EDA, flew with the Australian airline Qantas post-war, being a DC-4-1009 originally delivered in March 1946 and joining Qantas in February 1949.*

**Specifications – Douglas C-54B Skymaster**

| | |
|---|---|
| Wingspan | 117 ft 6 in |
| Length | 93 ft 11 in |
| Maximum speed | 274 mph at 14,000 ft |
| Maximum take-off weight | 73,000 lb |
| Range | 3,900 miles |
| Service ceiling | 22,000 ft |
| Engine | Four Pratt & Whitney R-2000-7 Twin Wasp radial piston engines, of 1,350 hp each |
| Accommodation | Three crew, up to 49 troops |

# Focke-Wulf Ta 154

Even before the start of World War Two it had become clear to planners in some countries that aerial warfare in the future would not take place exclusively during the day. Nowadays, the concept of a front-line combat aircraft being able to operate at night and in bad weather is commonplace, indeed an absolute necessity for all operational military aircraft, but in the 1930's this was a comparatively novel concept. In Britain, developments in radar technology not only allowed for early warning of incoming attacks by bomber formations by ground-based radar. With continuing developments, radar equipment eventually became miniaturized enough to be taken aloft by a completely new breed of aircraft, the dedicated radar-equipped night fighter. Most early night fighters of the Second World War era were not radar-equipped, instead relying on crude aids

such as searchlights or the pilot's own flying abilities. Soon, however, radar was being fitted in aircraft, usually twin-engined types powerful enough to lift the radar equipment and still carry a useful armament, and roomy enough to carry the radar equipment and its operator. Even so, most night fighters that evolved during the war were existing types converted for the purpose. Only one aircraft, the Northrop P-61 Black Widow (see pages 268 to 269) was designed from the first for this purpose.

In Germany, the development of a night fighter arm to combat increasing nocturnal raids by RAF bombers over Germany started late. A rudimentary system existed from 1940 and eventually several existing aircraft types were successfully converted into night fighters – along with major developments in ground-based early-warning radars. It was, however, seen by the Nazi

The Focke-Wulf Ta 154 was a mainly wood night fighter, although shown in this view without radar. It has recently been claimed that up to fifty production examples of the Ta 154A-1 and A-4 series might have been completed.

regime as defeatist to think in such defensive terms. Thus the development of Germany's one purpose-built night fighter, the Focke-Wulf Ta 154, started late. The first prototype flew on 1 July 1943, and the type was unique for a German aircraft of its day by being of mainly wood construction and covering – similar, in fact, to Britain's de Havilland Mosquito (see pages 106 to 109). Appropriately, the name Moskito is often used for the Ta 154. It exhibited good performance in its prototype form. The first production examples flew in mid-1944, but two crashed soon after – revealing serious manufacturing problems: the glue used to join the production air-craft together had rotted the wood. Other problems resulted in the program being cancelled later in 1944. Several of the initial aircraft were fitted with FuG 212 or FuG 220 'Lichtenstein' radar and it is claimed that they saw some operational use. Several developments were intended, including an improved Ta 154C series and the Ta 254, but none progressed very far. Plans were developed to employ unfinished production airframes as 'Formation Destroyers,' packed with explosives and flown as a detachable 'Mistel' type combination into American bomber formations. This idea did not become operational.

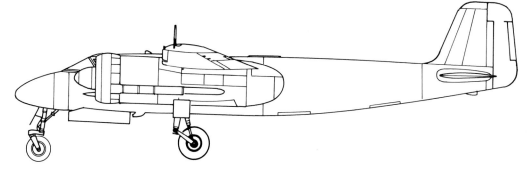

*The Focke-Wulf Ta 154 was designated in this way (instead of having an Fw prefix) for its designer, Kurt Tank. This drawing shows a pre-production or early production layout without radar.*

## Specifications – Focke-Wulf Ta 154A-1 (some data provisional)

| | |
|---|---|
| Wingspan | 52 ft 6 in |
| Length | 41 ft 2.75 in (with radar installed) |
| Maximum speed | 404 mph at 23,250 ft |
| Maximum take-off weight | 19,687 lb |
| Range | 848 miles |
| Service ceiling | 35,760 ft |
| Armament | Two 20 mm and two 30 mm cannons, fixed forward-firing in fuselage sides |
| Engine | Two Junkers Jumo 213E inline piston engines, of 1,750 hp each (it has also been claimed that Jumo 211-series engines powered Ta 154A-1 aircraft) |
| Crew | Two |

# Heinkel He 219

This advanced, powerful and potentially highly effective night fighter began life somewhat ironically as a fighter-bomber proposal in the early war period. Initial studies gained little official interest, especially as Heinkel was supposed to concentrate mainly on bomber designs, but as the need for night fighters to combat RAF night raids over Occupied Europe and Germany became more pressing, the Heinkel design studies were resurrected as a potential night fighter. Even then the He 219, as it was eventually designated, suffered from considerable opposition by some high-ranking Nazi leaders. Despite this, the He 219 was developed into an excellent night fighter, which also introduced a new development into the world of combat aircraft that has become in more recent times an indispensable piece of equipment – an ejection seat for each of its crew members.

The first He 219, the He 219 V1, flew on 15 November 1942. The fourth prototype/development aircraft, the He 219V4, was fitted with airborne interception radar, marking the start of a major development program that led to a large variety of different marks, sub-types and armament/equipment options. Many of these were not built and development was repeatedly compromised by official indifference or even opposition, together with Allied bombing of the Heinkel facilities, particularly at Rostock in northern Germany. A pre-production batch of He 219A-0 machines was produced in early 1943, by which time the He 219 had been flown at least once against other German night fighters – including the improvised Junkers Ju 88S and Dornier Do 217N – and its capability had surpassed all. The He 219A-0 made its combat debut in June 1943, when a single aircraft shot down five RAF Lancasters in the same sortie. Several more operations were flown during which a number of de Havilland Mosquitos were brought down – making the He 219 the only night fighter in the German inventory to challenge the outstanding Mosquito. Nevertheless, despite all this, the project was curtailed in May 1944. Nonetheless, Heinkel was somehow able to continue production and eventually some 288 He 219 of all types were produced. Principal production marks included the He 219A-2, A-5 and A-7, all upgraded by various Rüstsatz sets to improve their armament options. They were, however, too few to affect the air war, which was increasingly turning against the Germans, but the He 219 certainly proved its worth

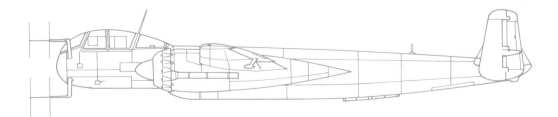

*Sleek and purposeful, the Heinkel He 219A-series were fitted with Lichtenstein radar equipment (hence the antennae fitted to the nose). Most were two-seaters like that illustrated, although some had a third crew member in a revised cockpit.*

in the limited service that it managed to perform. Finally the ending in later 1944 of virtually all aircraft programs in Germany except for jet aircraft and single-engine fighters saw the permanent cessation of the He 219 as a production type.

*The 'G9' codes on this Heinkel He 219A show that it belonged to NJG 1, the first (and only) Luftwaffe night fighter wing (NJG) to fly the type in combat. The name Uhu (Eagle Owl) is sometimes associated with the He 219.*

### Specifications – Heinkel He 219A-7/R2

| | |
|---|---|
| Wingspan | 60 ft 8.3 in |
| Length | 53 ft 7.25 in (including radar antennae) |
| Maximum speed | 363.5 mph at 19,685 ft |
| Maximum take-off weight | 33,289 lb |
| Range | 1,150 miles |
| Service ceiling | 32,152 ft |
| Armament | Two 20 mm cannons in wing roots, two similar in ventral fuselage pannier, two 30 mm cannons in fuselage firing obliquely upwards (when fitted) |
| Engine | Two Daimler Benz DB 603E or G-series inline piston engines, of 1,800–1,900 hp each |
| Crew | Two |

# Grumman F8F Bearcat

The pace of fighter design accelerated rapidly in the 1930's and during World War Two. By the end of the conflict, the ultimate piston-engined all-metal cantilever monoplanes were either just in service or about to enter service. These aircraft were a massive step forward from the biplanes that were in front-line service just ten or so years before. Yet the time of these high-performance warplanes was already limited. The advent of jet propulsion was on the verge of rendering the superb propeller-driven fighters of the latter half of World War Two obsolete as front-line combat aircraft.

One of the ultimate piston-engined fighters of the late war period was the Grumman F8F Bearcat, a fighter intended for U.S. Navy service against the Japanese in the Pacific but produced just too late to serve operationally in the con-

flict. It was, in fact, the last in a line of piston-engined, carrier-based Grumman fighters that dated back to the Grumman FF biplane of 1931 – again reflecting how quickly fighter design had moved forward in that short space of time. The Bearcat was designed to meet U.S. Navy requirements for a carrier-based fighter able to operate on all sizes of U.S. aircraft carriers – some of which were smaller escort-type craft. It was required to have good low-level performance and maneuverability, and a high rate of climb for interception duties. In effect, Grumman fed all the lessons learned from the superb monoplane fighters, including the F4F Wildcat and F6F Hellcat, into its design. Fitted with one of the most powerful engines available, plus an airframe that was amazingly

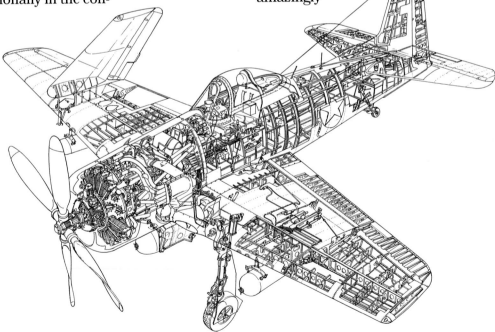

*The Grumman Bearcat was of all-metal construction. Its wings could be folded (as shown here) for storage within the confines of aircraft carrier hangars – although it was a comparatively small aircraft by naval standards.*

small compared to many carrier-based fighters, the Bearcat exhibited excellent all-round performance. The prototype XF8F-1 flew in August 1944, and an opening order for 2,023 was placed in October that year. The first U.S. Navy unit to work on the F8F-1 initial production version, VF-19, was doing so in May 1945. This squadron was still preparing for combat in August 1945 when the Second World War ended. There were several specific models in the F8F-1 and F8F-2 main production versions, including day fighters, radar-equipped night fighters, and reconnaissance platforms. The end of the war resulted in production contracts being severely cut and eventually 1,266 Bearcats (some sources claim 1,191) were built, up until the spring of 1949. Post-war service included operations with the U.S. Navy prior to the widespread introduction of jet-powered fighters, and also service with Thailand and South Vietnam. The Bearcat's most significant military duty was in French combat operations in Indochina during that period.

*An F8F Bearcat, bearing post-World War Two markings, shown with its wings folded. In civilian hands, several specially converted Bearcats have become famous in more recent times for air racing and as record-breakers, establishing the Bearcat as one of the fastest piston-engined aircraft ever built.*

**Specifications – Grumman F8F-2 Bearcat**

| | |
|---|---|
| Wingspan | 35 ft 10 in |
| Length | 27 ft 10 in |
| Maximum speed | 447 mph at 20,000 ft |
| Maximum take-off weight | 13,500 lb |
| Range | approximately 1,105 miles |
| Service ceiling | 42,000 ft |
| Armament | Four fixed forward-firing wing-mounted 20 mm cannons, underwing rockets or bombs up to some 2,000 lb |
| Engine | One Pratt & Whitney R-2800-30W Double Wasp radial piston engine, of 2,250 hp |
| Crew | One |

# Focke-Achgelis and Flettner Helicopters

A considerable amount of development work was needed to perfect the helicopter as a viable flying machine. The glory of creating arguably the world's first technically successful helicopter went to the German Focke-Achgelis company, with the Fa 61 (originally called the Fw 61), which first flew in June 1936. The story of this innovative helicopter is told in Volume 1 of *The Complete Encyclopedia of Flight*. Also actively developing rotary-wing flight in Germany at that time was the Anton Flettner Flugzeugbau, and this company also invented helicopter types, one of which entered operational service. At Focke-Achgelis, development work on the Fa 61 layout of large twin main rotors led to the Fa 226 Hornisse (Hornet), a projected civil transport helicopter for the airline Deutsche Lufthansa. This design had obvious military potential, and was developed as the Fa 223 Drache (Kite or Dragon). The initial example, the Fa 223V1, accomplished its first untethered flight on 3 August 1940. The type's development program included the breaking of several world records in the class relevant to the Fa 223 and several distinct production versions were envisaged in addition to transport tasks. These included rescue (with one of the first examples of an airborne rescue winch), casualty evacuation, reconnaissance and light bombing, with even an anti-submarine role envisaged (although the slow and lumbering approach of an Fa 223 would not have had much of an element of surprise to it!). Further development work in fact concentrated these different roles into one planned production model, the Fa 223E. A number of prototype/development examples were built, and the type entered limited production in a factory at Berlin-Tempelhof. However, the end of World War Two came before the Fa 223 could be developed or built to its full potential. The type nevertheless was of interest to the Allies after the war ended, and a small number were additionally built in post-war Czechoslovakia from German-manufactured components. Some development work was also continued in France after the war. The Flettner company, in contrast, approached

*The Flettner Fl 282 Kolibri was one of three helicopter types that can claim to have seen front-line service during World War Two (the others being the Sikorsky R-4 series and the Focke-Achgelis Fa 223).*

helicopter design differently, concentrating on a single main rotor mounted on top of the fuselage of the helicopter (the layout favored nowadays). The first successful design was the Fl 265, with two counter-rotating main rotors to counteract torque. Although this model aroused interest for possible production, further development led to the Fl 282 Kolibri (Hummingbird). A wide variety of prototype/ development examples were built, some flying from German ships in 1943 on trials and eventually operationally on patrol and escort duties. Series production never really commenced due to American bombing of potential production centers, and so development of helicopters in general after World War Two took place mainly in the United States.

*The ungainly but airworthy Focke-Achgelis Fa 223 was entering production in the later stages of World War Two, and several reached Luftwaffe service although the Fa 223's layout was something of a development dead end.*

**Specifications – Focke-Achgelis Fa 223E**

| | |
|---|---|
| Rotor Diameter | 39 ft 4.5 in (each) |
| Fuselage Length | 40 ft 2.25 in |
| Maximum speed | 109.5 mph at 6,562 ft |
| Maximum take-off weight | 9,513 lb |
| Range | 435 miles |
| Service ceiling | 15,994 ft |
| Armament | One flexible nose-mounted 7.92 mm (0.312 in) machine gun, two 551 lb bombs or depth charges |
| Engine | One Bramo Fafnir 323D-2 or Q-3 radial piston engine, of 1,000 hp |
| Crew | One or more (depending on role) |

# Gloster Meteor

The development of jet engine technology and improvements in aerodynamics, taking into account the new power and speeds involved in jet-powered flight, moved forward at a remarkable rate during World War Two. Both Britain and Germany were eventually able to field fully-operational jet-propelled warplanes prior to the end of the conflict. Germany had already put into service several jet-powered aircraft, such as the Messerschmitt Me 262 and Arado Ar 234. In Britain, jet engine technology had similarly moved on from the pioneering work of Frank Whittle. Britain's first jet design, the Gloster E.28/39, was basically a test aircraft and had flown in May 1941. The Gloster company and Frank Whittle were colleagues and it appeared logical that Gloster should take their own pioneering work forward to design a viable jet-powered fighter for front-line service. This led to the creation of the Gloster G.41 Meteor.

The Meteor became highly significant as the only British (and the only Allied) jet fighter to achieve operational status during World War Two. The low thrust output of the jet engines then available dictated the adoption of a twin-engined configuration, but apart from its radical engines the Meteor was of completely conventional design – even lacking the advanced swept wings of the Messerschmitt Me 262. Eight prototypes were eventually completed, and it was the fifth of these that made the Meteor's first flight on 5 March 1943. It was powered by two de Havilland Halford H.I turbojets of approximately 1,500 Ib st. Production began with twenty Meteor Mk.Is powered by 1,700 Ib st Rolls-Royce Welland turbojet engines. One of these was exchanged in 1944 for an American Bell YP-59A Airacomet (the first real American jet aircraft, which did not become operational during the war). Some sixteen of the Meteor Mk.I were delivered, from July 1944, to the RAF's No.616 Squadron. This unit therefore became the first-ever regular operational unit to operate jet-powered aircraft. Its Meteors were soon in action against German V1 weapons – two were brought down over southern England on 4 August 1944. The first model to be produced in quantity was the Meteor Mk.III, of which Gloster built 210. The first fifteen

*The Gloster Meteor was a foretaste of the future of air warfare. Interestingly, the type was to have been called Thunderbolt until that name was adopted for the Republic P-47. The Meteor had growth potential in addition to being radical – there were many post-war versions.*

of these had Welland engines, the remainder Derwents, and the final fifteen featured modified engine nacelles of improved design. Two RAF Meteor-equipped squadrons duly served with the Allied 2nd Tactical Air Force on mainland Europe during the final weeks of the war. However, there do not appear to have been any engagements between these Meteors and the type's German counterpart, the Me 262, in aerial combat. The world therefore had to wait until the Korean War of 1950 to see the first jet vs. jet combats in a major war.

One Meteor Mk.III was re-engined with two 3,500 lb st Derwent Mk.V turbojets, and was flown in mid-1945 as a prototype for the post-war Meteor Mk.IV version. All subsequent Meteor development and production took place after the war had ended. The Meteor was thus a major step towards the future of warplane development – the world of military aviation had certainly changed a great deal in just a few short years of warfare.

*The 'YQ' fuselage code on this Gloster Meteor F.Mk.III belongs to No.616 Squadron, RAF, the world's first regular operational unit to fly jet-powered aircraft. It operated from continental Europe in the final weeks of the war. The Mk.III amongst other improvements featured a sliding cockpit cover compared to the Mk.I's upwards-opening unit.*

**Specifications – Gloster Meteor F.Mk.III**

| | |
|---|---|
| Wingspan | 43 ft |
| Length | 41 ft 3 in |
| Maximum speed | 493 mph at 30,000 ft |
| Maximum take-off weight | 13,300 lb |
| Range | 1,340 miles – but much less on combat missions |
| Service ceiling | 44,000 ft |
| Armament | Four fixed forward-firing nose-mounted 20 mm cannons in fuselage nose |
| Engine | Two Rolls-Royce Derwent I turbojet engines, of 2,000 lb st each |
| Crew | One |

# Index

# Index

# Index